Birds of Fire

Refiguring American Music

A series edited by Ronald Radano and Josh Kun

Charles McGovern, contributing editor

Birds of Fire

Jazz, Rock, Funk, and the Creation of Fusion

Kevin Fellezs

DUKE UNIVERSITY PRESS   Durham and London   2011

© 2011 Duke University Press
All rights reserved
Printed in the United States
of America on acid-free paper ∞
Designed by Amy Ruth Buchanan
Typeset in Quadraat by
Tseng Information Systems, Inc.
Library of Congress Cataloging-
in-Publication Data appear on
the last printed page of this book.

For Kazuma and Hatsune Kido

Rasta was a funny language, [because Jamaican Rastafarians] borrowed from a text—the Bible—that did not belong to them; they had to turn the text upside-down, to get a meaning which fit their experience. But in turning the text upside-down they remade themselves. . . . And in so doing, they did not assume that their only cultural resources lay in the past. They did not go back and try to recover some absolutely pure "folk culture," untouched by history. . . . [They said,] "Don't tell us about tom-toms in the forest. We want to use the new means of articulation and production to make a new music, with a new message." This is a cultural transformation. It is not something totally new. It is not something which has a straight, unbroken line of continuity from the past. It is transformation through a reorganization of the elements of a cultural practice, elements which do not in themselves have any necessary political connotations. It is not the individual elements of a discourse that have political or ideological connotations, it is the ways those elements are organized together in a new discursive formation.

—**Stuart Hall** (emphasis added)

contents

acknowledgments

This book is the result of a long and arduous journey I might never have completed except for the many midwives, partners, and helpmates I found among family members, friends, and colleagues. First among these have been the members of my dissertation committee. My adviser, Angela Davis, pushed me to clarify points and reconsider underlying assumptions in my arguments, and her insights and intellectual rigor have proven essential to my growth as a scholar. James Clifford remains a profound influence, and his painstaking probing of categories and perspectives informs my work. Herman Gray continues to provide a foundational compass for my theoretical framings, shaping the scope and the stakes at play in my endeavors. Eric Porter provided more than a model for my own work—his insightful readings and warm collegiality remain sources of inspiration. I am deeply grateful for the generous guidance and support of each of these people.

My University of California President's Postdoctoral Fellowship at the University of California, Berkeley, under the benevolent mentorship of Jocelyne Guilbault has continued to prove invaluable. My two years there were further rewarded by time spent with Bonnie Wade and Ben Brinner. I was also fortunate to meet a number of engaged, and engaging, graduate students who were in residence at the time and would like to single out some of them in particular: Marie Abé, Duncan Allard, Eliot Bates, Rebecca Bodenheimer, Charles Ferris, Jeff Packman, John-Carlos Perea, Matthew Rahaim, and Francesca Rivera.

I would be extremely remiss if I did not mention the profound inspiration and guidance that I received from Mary Scott, without whom I would have never embarked on the academic travels that have led me to this book. I was also deeply influenced by Cristina Ruotolo, my master's thesis adviser, whose thoughtful guidance motivated my initial investigation of fusion music. I remain indebted to both of them in ways that I can never fully repay.

My qualifying exam writing partners—Karen DeVries, Michelle Erai, and

Krista Lynes—each of whom certainly gave more than they received in our group meetings, read early drafts of this work, prodding me to be clearer and better reasoned about my arguments and assertions. Scholars who generously shared their time and insights include Paul Anderson, Tamar Barzel, Harris Berger, David Borgo, Scott DeVeaux, Bernard Gendron, John Howland, Rhoshanak Kheshti, George Lipsitz, Steven Pond, Ronald Radano, Tricia Rose, Barry Shank, Andy Sutton, Jeffrey Taylor, Gary Tomlinson, Sherrie Tucker, Grace Wang, Christopher Washburne, Steve Waksman, and Deborah Wong. I have benefited from the supportive camaraderie of a number of colleagues at the University of California, Merced—especially Susan Amussen, Robin DeLugan, Jan Goggans, Kathleen Hull, Sholeh Quinn, and Cristián Ricci. I want to single out fellow "SSHA-mates" Ignacio Lopez-Calvo, Sean Malloy, and ShiPu Wang for providing much-needed critique, advice, and encouragement throughout this entire process.

My initial research depended on recordings that had not yet been digitized and on archival materials that fly below the radar of institutional archives, and I want to thank Richard Freeman, Michael Kenny, and Nicholas Rubtzoff for their generosity in giving me access to their vast recording and music magazine collections.

I would never have been able to complete this manuscript without the patience and enthusiasm of my editor, Ken Wissoker, whose guiding hand kept this project moving despite unforeseen setbacks. I also want to thank the three anonymous reviewers whose insightful readings and commentaries made this work stronger and more nuanced. I am also deeply appreciative of the work of my copy editors, Joe Abbott and Neal McTighe, who gave my work a much-needed final polish. Any faults in the text remain my own.

Finally, I want to thank my parents, Andrew and Bessie, for sacrificing so much to give me the opportunities they never enjoyed. And because you make it all worthwhile, Laurie, I humbly offer my deepest love and affection.

I am grateful to John Howland and Lewis Porter, the coeditors of the journal *Jazz Perspectives* (Routledge), for their permission to publish the chapter "Emergency! / *Tony Williams*," which first appeared in a modified form in the January 2008 issue.

introduction

Contemporary music has absorbed the whole thing called rock or rock and roll and what's coming out right now is a wide variety of creative efforts by people with both jazz and rock backgrounds. It's not classifiable as either jazz or rock, it's just music that is as good as the people doing it. — **Larry Coryell**

For Christ's sake, I wish somebody would make up a name for this kind of music, 'cause it ain't jazz and it ain't rock. It's got overtones of both, but it's really got no name of its own. — **Jeff Beck**

In 1969 the jazz impresario George Wein decided to book rock acts for the first time at the Newport Jazz Festival as a way to attract young people and, more important, to reap greater ticket sales. He would not be entirely disappointed. Large crowds of young rock fans converged on the small Connecticut town that gave the festival its name to hear Jeff Beck, Jethro Tull, Sly and the Family Stone, and Led Zeppelin. Unfortunately, the inadequate facilities and security forces were overwhelmed by the thousands of fans, many of whom expressed their disappointment in the lack of tickets by simply forcing their way into the festival during Sly and the Family Stone's set. *Rolling Stone* described the scenario:

> Everything went off. The rain. The crowds. Firecrackers. And, above all, establishment paranoia. . . . To prevent more damage to the fence, the gates were opened and bands of wild hippies, LSD on their breath, swarmed through, pushing the bleacher audience forward, vaulting over the VIP box seats, shoving into the press section, slamming the customers into the stage, all the while Sly, monarch of his own fascist jungle, urging everyone higher! Higher! Higher! . . . [Wein] stalked the stage, crying, "Alright you kids, be cool, be cool, we don't want any riots," as

firecrackers shot into the crowd, fist fights erupted between what one observer described as gas station attendants and boogalooers, and hippies leaped over the bodies—flashing the victory sign furiously—and one acid tripping lady went into her own gymnastic reverie. Sly played on, digging it, and the audience still with seats stood on them. To the encore applause for Sly, Wein replied: "that's all—Sly isn't playing anymore."[1]

Dan Morgenstern opined in the pages of *Down Beat*, "What, then, caused the Newport debacle? Specifically, I think (aside from the crucial lack of suitable facilities to accommodate the crowds) *a clash between two kinds of fans and two kinds of music.* The jazz fans had come mainly to listen, while the rock fans were mainly there to create—and be part of—a 'scene.'"[2]

Despite Wein's assessment in his recent memoirs that "by almost any standard, [the 1969 Newport Jazz Festival] had been a huge [economic] success," he also lamented, "I still consider it the nadir of my career," agreeing with Morgenstern, who wrote in his review that "the rock experiment was a resounding [artistic] failure."[3] Two years later, however, when Wein decided to book another rock band for his festival, he hedged his bets with a relatively unknown act, hoping that the large unruly crowds of rock fans who had descended on the festival in 1969 would stay away—along with the municipal fines for property damage, fees for an increased police presence, and any lingering ill feelings among Newport's civic officials. Booking the relatively unknown Allman Brothers Band in January, he could not have foreseen their popularity exploding before the festival's summer opening, and, once again, an unexpected turnout of rock fans appeared in the sleepy resort village. It was no small irony that Wein's worst fears were realized when, as Dionne Warwick sang Burt Bacharach's hit song "What the World Needs Now Is Love," those fans broke onto the concert stage, destroying the piano and ending their rioting only after police arrived with tear gas. The city fathers, fed up with troubles of crowd control, shut the 1971 festival down.[4]

Forced to relocate for the next year's event, Wein moved his festival to New York City, continuing to book jazz acts such as Duke Ellington, Dave Brubeck, and Dizzy Gillespie. He also booked a new act that had begun merging jazz and rock: the Mahavishnu Orchestra. The band's explosive popularity after less than a year's existence was underscored by its headlining engagement at Carnegie Hall while established jazz acts—the alto saxophonist Julian "Cannonball" Adderley's quintet and Oscar Peterson in a solo piano set—appeared as openers. That the band's music was distinct from "real jazz" was aptly captured by Morgenstern in his review: "In more than one way, Mahavishnu's music was a tremendous contrast [with Peterson's preceding set]—the most obvious being one man on stage with an acoustic instrument as compared to five men surrounded by all kinds of electronics, including those giant Leslies."[5] As we will see, their use of electronic equipment signaled their allegiance to rock rather than jazz aesthetics for many jazz observers.

While there were no reports of rock fans rioting at the new venue for the 1972 festival, the Mahavishnu Orchestra's subversion of jazz aesthetics would prove to have a longer-lasting effect on jazz critics and musicians. For many fans of straight-ahead jazz the situation was made worse by being an "inside" job executed by bona fide jazz musicians rather than an assault by callow rock fans. While jazz observers may have found it easy to dismiss Jethro Tull and its fans, they found it far more difficult to disregard John McLaughlin, the guitarist who was currently recording with Miles Davis; Jan Hammer, a former pianist for Sarah Vaughn; or the bassist Rick Laird, who quit Buddy Rich's big band just prior to joining the Mahavishnu Orchestra.[6]

The Newport Festival "debacles" of the era capture the broad outlines of fusion's eventual position vis-à-vis jazz: fusion was too loud, too raw, and too aggressively "uncool," as Wein's admonition to Sly Stone's audience implied, to live comfortably alongside the many other styles of jazz and would eventually be exiled from "real jazz" as an aberrant hybrid, neither jazz nor rock. Yet why would Wein continue to book nonjazz acts despite his feeling that his "rock experiment was a resounding [artistic] failure"? As Mahavishnu Orchestra's headlining above the more established mainstream jazz of Adderley and Peterson suggests, fusion's popularity—and commercial appeal to booking agents and festival organizers—signaled rock's eclipsing of jazz in popular culture and, of greater concern for jazz critics and musicians, among artistic circles, as well, at precisely the time when jazz was fervently establishing its tentative foothold in "legitimate" culture.

At the time, the question about whether fusion was an ill-advised clash between, or a creative merging of, jazz and rock or funk shaped the debates about their definitions, including whether jazz and rock were "merely" popular music genres or art (funk was decidedly not a part of this discussion) and whether or not the incompatibilities between the musical demands jazz placed on musicians and audiences and the more plebeian pleasures of rock and funk were insurmountable. Indeed, because their music was often challenging and explicitly virtuosic, fusion musicians raised questions about whether it was safe to assume that rock and funk were inferior to jazz on a musical level at all. Consequently, many of the debates within jazz swirled between, on one hand, arguments by some jazz musicians and critics that jazz was irrevocably harmed by any association with rock or funk and, on the other hand, the counterarguments forwarded by other jazz musicians and critics that jazz needed an electric jolt to wake it out of its increasingly moribund state.

By 1977, when Jeff Beck's plea to name "this kind of music" was published, it had been a little over a decade since the "ain't jazz, ain't rock" music's first raucous echoes began resonating beyond the jam sessions of young musicians blending jazz, rock, and funk. This book focuses on four of those young musicians — Tony Williams, John McLaughlin, Joni Mitchell, and Herbie Hancock — who created an explicitly transgeneric form of music, sounding out the gaps between musical difference as spaces where individuals might reshape musical traditions, conventions, and assumptions. This does not make their music entirely unique — musicians have often borrowed from, been taught by, or collaborated with musicians across limits of various kinds. I also do not wish to elide the very real differences between various musical traditions or historical contexts, but I want to recognize the *continual* process of transformation musical practices undergo regardless of the geographical location of the musicians or the ideologies that construct "musician" and "music" in a specific geographical and historical context. Moreover, this process of interaction and exchange between tradition and innovation redraws musical borderlines, creating a "new tradition" that rests atop the sedimented interchanges of the past, awaiting its own transformation.

The "ain't jazz, ain't rock" music of these young birds of fire flew between these layers of musical traditions, reshaping the rigid forms through which they coursed while simultaneously exposing the gaps *and* connecting the diverse strata between which their music swooped and rose.[7] We should ask, however, what is unique and worth considering about the particular fusing activities of these particular musicians (Williams, McLaughlin, Mitchell and Hancock) within these particular music genres and traditions (jazz, rock, funk) at this particular time (1970s)?

As I have noted, musical mixture is not in itself news. This is especially true in traditions such as jazz or rock, in which musicians and critics have long recognized the inclusive nature of the music. However, these young musicians' musical mixtures generated critical heat in the 1970s because of the disparate, even diametrical, ways in which jazz, rock, and funk were positioned *as genres* at the time. The implications of this particular generic conjuncture answers to the second, more salient, question of significance — a reply that will be taken up throughout the rest of this book.

Briefly, these "ain't jazz, ain't rock" musicians troubled genres by *staying between them*, creating an informal, even feral, set of musical practices and aesthetics. By doing so, they articulated a way of being both inside and out-side of genre categories, disturbing assumptions about musical traditions, including the ways in which membership (legitimacy), mastery (authority), and musical value are ordered. Most important, they transformed the re-lationship of individual musicians to musical traditions. The point I would like to draw is this: the "ain't jazz, ain't rock" music of these young musi-cians was not so much a hybrid as an "in-between" categorization that could conceivably be an "is jazz, is rock" as much as an "ain't jazz, ain't rock" set of musical practices and aesthetics. Importantly, their music *remained be-tween* genres—indeed, the kind of music they created has yet to coalesce into a genre of its own. As the title of Jazziz magazine's March 2003 issue, *The F Word: Between Rock and a Hard Place*, demonstrates, fusion's liminality remains contentious—especially when one considers what the "f word" usually connotes. Why the Jazziz editors would choose such a title is a riddle I will attempt to unravel in the following pages.

In fact, I mean to argue against the reductive attitude of "f word" shame and disregard that this "ain't jazz, ain't rock" music usually summons in conversations among jazz and rock scholars by foregrounding the musi-cians' own reasons for creating this music. The title of this book, *Birds of Fire*, speaks to the airy yet luminous freedom these young musicians actively sought, soaring between the categories on which musical practices and dis-course rested and that they believed all too often constrained their artistic efforts. In taking my cue from the title of the second Mahavishnu Orchestra recording, I hope to indicate the bright flames these early fusion musicians ignited and, like the crackling embers of a bonfire escaping into the night air, while quickly dissipating, left a smoky trail behind them. The pungent aroma of their presence lingers in the currents of contemporary music, an influence still felt in the cooling drafts around those warming themselves in the glowing fires of today's generic mixings and in which discussions of topics such as musical authenticity and artistic legitimacy continue to forge listeners' perceptions and evaluations.

By the early 1970s, jazz, rock, and funk were positioned in diametrically op-posed ways, and by mixing them together, fusion musicians participated in a larger shift, not simply in the categories but in the categorization process itself. In moves similar to Rastafarians turning the Christian Bible "upside-down" in order to "remake themselves," these young musicians were creating "a new music with a new message" from practices that were neither entirely new nor mere pastiches of older conventions. Most significantly, they were motivated by the idea of innovative mixture rather than adhering to a modernist compulsion to produce sui generis originality. Thus, the attention their music received was often occupied with the ways in which their musical blendings troubled ideas about the continuity of musical traditions, ethnic or nationalist pride in relation to a particular set of musical practices and aesthetics, and the divide between art and commerce.

The "new messages" I want to explore are manifest in the particular ways that Williams, McLaughlin, Mitchell, and Hancock tried in their music to elude restrictive generic conventions by questioning the connections genre categories forged between musical sounds and social categories such as race. They proceeded by sounding out their "in-between-ness" as a strategy to foreground individual agency in the face of histories of generic separation that remained deeply rooted in the cultural inertia of popular music understandings. Barry Shank, in his trenchant analysis of race in popular music, argues convincingly that critical evaluations are never concerned exclusively with aesthetic or formal analytics but are judgment calls on the part of listeners, "who, in the process of discrimination, are always responding to extra-musical social and political considerations as well as the music 'itself.'"[8] Indeed, as I will show, discussions regarding the incompatibility between jazz, rock, and funk were partially shaped by received ideas regarding the defining of insiders and outsiders for each genre, often by emphasizing the racial makeup of musicians and audiences.

Even listeners reticent to address extramusical topics such as race have rarely depended solely on the sounds of the music to support their views on genre classifications or musical value. As the chapter "Where Have I Known You Before?" will show, musical debates were often more concerned with social or emotional affect than, say, the preponderance of antiphony or the presence of a particular harmonic progression or rhythmic pattern, with the notable exception of the rhetorical emphasis on swing rhythms within jazz discourse. Moreover, as Theodore Gracyk argues in his study of rock aesthetics, demarcating musical genres by musicological analyses may not yield the precise boundaries of a set of musical practices, nor may performance style clearly map an idiom's boundaries, because musical practices overlap genres in many cases.[9] All three genres (funk, rock, jazz) under primary consideration here, for example, can boast a riff-oriented repertoire that draws on the blues pentatonic scale, as well as compositions that are based primarily on a groove-oriented bass line. Indeed, there are many paths out of a genre but few barriers to keep us in (which may contribute to the impassioned debates surrounding legitimacy within a given genre).

In maintaining that so-called extramusical concerns are fundamental to teasing out meaning from sounding, I want to build on the idea of genre as culture by pointing to the mixing of genres as a performance of transculturality. Musicians and listeners use genre rules to construct, patrol, and maintain the boundaries between insider and outsider. Accordingly, I agree with Fabian Holt, who understands genre formation as "always collective, musically and socially (a person can have his or her own style, but not a genre). Conventions and expectations are established through acts of repetition performed by a group of people, and the process of genre formation is in turn often accompanied by the formation of *new social collectivities.*"[10]

With this understanding we should not find it mere coincidence that the transgeneric music of Williams, McLaughlin, Mitchell, and Hancock—music that articulated a multiple sense of belonging *and* nonbelonging—emerged in the wake of the identity politics of the period. While challenging both essentialist and identitarian justifications for adhering to sanctioned practices by invoking individual agency against the limits set by historical legacies, institutional interests, and cultural chauvinisms, the music of Williams, McLaughlin, Mitchell, and Hancock in the 1970s pointed to the agentive empowerment that being "between genres" offered them, as a space where a "new social collective" based on *balancing between* those limits that would otherwise inhibit them could emerge. Fusion articulates the ill-fitting intercultural mergings occurring at the breaches of cultures, mergings that have become increasingly central to individuals' mobile sense of belonging among competing sets of loyalties. For example, as I will explore more deeply later, Hancock's use of technology extended relations between incongruently positioned black communities when he justified his use of Pygmy music based on a long Afrodiasporic history of transcultural citational practices as a "brothers kind of thing," transforming the shared music between them in a contested dance between "history" as represented by the music of the Pygmies and "the future" as represented by the electronic technologies used both to access and to transpose their music.

This is not a dialectical process. The "new music" produced by Williams, McLaughlin, Mitchell, and Hancock was not born of a neat synthesis of, for instance, jazz and rock. Rather, their music was a complex meeting of antagonistic aesthetics, divergent histories, and incongruent practices. Indeed, the debates about whether they initiated "transformations of older structures" to create "novel hybrid forms" or to reinvigorate jazz enflamed the jazz world in the early 1970s. While the verdict landed mostly on the "novel hybrid form" side of the debate, discussions dealt almost exclusively with the transformation of the older structure, if you will, of jazz practice and sense of historical development. Williams, McLaughlin, Hancock, and, in particular, Mitchell (as she has never been considered a jazz musician) did not help matters by mixing things up in widely idiosyncratic ways. Theirs was not a program of synthesis but an aesthetic of mixture, a construction in the liminal spaces between genres.

As detailed throughout this book, the blended music of these four young professional musicians formed a "broken middle," flowing across, between, and through geographic, temporal, cultural, national, ethnic, and generic limits. These young musicians transformed the ways in which music marked those exchanges by questioning conventional mappings of identity as articulated through musical genre formation, performance practices, and the bodies who perform them. I borrow the idea of a "broken middle" from Isobel Armstrong, who uses the phrase to think through the problem of simultaneously occupying the terms of the dialectic in order to replace the "triumphalist dialectic of resolution [with] *a new synthesis, with a logic of breakdown. It is at the point of contradiction, where opposites fail to transform one another,* that intellectual struggle is at its most perilous and stressful, and where a painful restructuring of relationships comes about at the site of the middle, the third term. *The broken middle is . . . always the most significant point of the triune relationship in dialectical thought.*"[11]

I will be using Armstrong's idea to position the music considered in this book as a set of musical and discursive practices situated within a "broken middle," an overlapping yet liminal space of contested, and never settled, priorities between two or more musical traditions. Her idea of the broken middle occupying a state of permanent instability—a logic of breakdown, a point of contradiction—speaks to the way in which the music of Williams, McLaughlin, Mitchell, and Hancock oscillated between "jazz," "rock," "funk," and "classical" music, epitomizing none but incapable of breaking away completely into its own space. In fact, I want to emphasize the brokenness of Armstrong's articulative notion. This is not a comfortable or smoothly articulated space. It is a complex space, full of incongruities. Armstrong continues, measuring temporality into the dialectical equation, which, like trying to freeze the constantly changing hues of fluttering leaves in one's gaze, only affirms that "the middle is *always shifting, since we live in time:* the third term might become the moment of a postulated starting point for another middle," potentially metastasizing, continually interconnecting and complicating dialectical relations.[12]

Armstrong's notion that the broken middle is the point "where a painful restructuring of relationships comes about" speaks to the creative tension found in the broken middle, a space of possibilities, of in-between-ness, of restructuring. But—and this is a crucial point—a space of "painful restructuring" is also a space with the potential to liberate one from dogma and convention. As Armstrong notes, it is not a process without some cost, but there are rewards, as well. As we will see, Joni Mitchell speaks eloquently about the price as well as the rewards of "not belonging to anything."[13] As both agents and reactants to the particular historical context in which their music was initially heard, and because they were operating within the broken middle, a space pregnant with the possibilities for change, Williams, McLaughlin, Mitchell, and Hancock joined and severed generic differences, revealing links as well as gaps between musical idioms—sutures shown to be dynamic and mutable, ever open to new orders of (dis)placement.

The broken middle, a space of shifting thought, arrives, then, in the efforts to occupy multiple, sometimes contradictory, positions—the logic of breakdown through time. These young musicians created recordings and performances shaped by altering generic codes and mixing stylistic gestures from different traditions, including those they could not claim to master. This "painful restructuring" suggested new relations between mastery and virtuosity, legitimation and technique, authority and authenticity. Moreover, they merged musical elements from disparate musical traditions in different ways at different times rather than concentrating on a single transformative set of musical practices—thus performing a number of different "fusions." Tony Williams, John McLaughlin, Joni Mitchell, and Herbie Hancock exemplify the manifold sounding out of the broken middle in fusion music throughout the 1970s.

A main thread shared by them, then, is not that they each mixed jazz with other nonjazz music but that their music sounded out—represented, articulated, and performed—the broken middle between genres and music cultures writ large, highlighting the agency of given individuals in facing the social norms that seek to limit and define them. This is a particularly salient point in considering fusion as a space in which musicians pushed back against the conventions of the music industry, the desires of listeners, and the requirements of genre. Or, as Josef Zawinul, cofounder of the fusion group Weather Report, expressed it: "That was one thing about this album [Mr. Gone, Columbia 1978] which I think is good, which I really love us for—

Herbie Hancock and the Headhunters' *Head Hunters* front cover.

that we did not try to jump on the bandwagon of a 'Birdland' [a hit from the previous album, *Heavy Weather*, Columbia 1977]. Because that was suggested to us. 'Hey, man, write another 'Birdland' and you'll sell a million fuckin' records.' Fuck you, man—we're gonna do what we're gonna do."[14]

No less confrontationally, the album cover of Herbie Hancock's *Head Hunters* (1973) recording echoed the sonic recontextualizations contained in the music by representing the broken middle as an imaginary mixture of "timeless" African headgear and modern recording technology. As Steven Pond observes, "Hancock playfully portrays a trickster god; even the mask is a trick."[15] The trickster god is a liminal deity, as Samuel Floyd notes in *The Power of Black Music*, situated both inside and outside space and time, living in the "nooks and crannies and at crossroads," ready to enter a "situation in order to upset its normal harmony and create dramatic contrast."[16] Sitting at an electronic keyboard, Hancock wears a large African-style mask with red potentiometers for eyes and a voltage meter for a mouth. This imaginative mixture of the primitive and the modern underscores the collision and cohesion—rather than the dialectical play of opposites—fusion music enacted on genre expectations. Today's samplers, DJs, and mixmasters create sonic fusions as increasingly commonplace enactments of no-longer-imaginary soundscapes, articulating the ironic, fluid nature of postmodern identity by routinely manipulating everything from advertising jingles to traditional Balkan folk music in remixes, mashups, and sampled loops. This brave new audio world has been shaped, in part, by the creative work of Williams, McLaughlin, Mitchell, Hancock, and their cohorts in bands such as Return to Forever, Weather Report, and Nucleus—not to mention more obscure groups such as Fourth Way and Catalyst—each of whom sounded out the creative possibilities of being in multiple spaces at once, in the broken middle between genres, traditions, and cultures.

Themes and Variations

I want to pause momentarily for a word about my research methodology before outlining the structure of the book. While I am not primarily interested in pursuing fusion's inclusion into an official jazz history, the empirical data, if you will, have been culled from historical sources that are largely jazz-oriented: publications such as *Down Beat*, *Metronome*, and *Jazz and Pop*. I also consulted more mainstream material such as the *New York Times* and rock-oriented literature such as *Crawdaddy!*, *Rolling Stone*, and *Creem*. Finally, there are the recordings, memoirs, biographies, liner notes, critical reviews, letters to the editors, and advertisements of these artists—in sum, the archival documents of conventional music history research. Additionally, I was uninterested in interviewing fusion musicians, especially Williams, McLaughlin, Mitchell, and Hancock. First, and unfortunately, Williams was no longer alive when I began this project. More important, I did not want retrospective recollections spanning thirty-plus years. There was ample material in the music journals, trade publications, recordings, and other accessible items from the 1970s to aid me in my attempt to capture the musicians and listeners, particularly critics, in the heat of the moment.

As I detail later, there is already a rehearsed fusion narrative that has begun to serve as a whispered addition to the "official narrative" that Scott DeVeaux skillfully delineates in his essay "Constructing the Jazz Tradition."[17] My larger point is not to dismantle jazz's—or, for that matter, rock's—"official" narrative but to describe how fusion musicians traversed the broken middle between genres (including their "official" narratives), forcing the recognition of a space that functions more than as a merely liminal "third space," to borrow Homi Bhabha's term, of between-ness but more fully a fluid "space of its own" in which recognized generic landmarks might be thought of as the "middle spaces" constructed out of and between the currents of mixings, blendings, and mergings that define the broken middle.

The first three chapters sketch the discursive backdrop provided by jazz, rock, and funk musicians, critics, and audiences, which animated the broader discussions within which Williams, McLaughlin, Mitchell, and Hancock produced their creative work. The first chapter, "Bitches Brew," is an investigation into the question of genre, which lies at the heart of this study. As the chapter title implies, the concoction of musical sounds, performance aesthetics, and critical and fan discourse subsumed beneath a genre name can be more productively thought of as a fluid distillation of those elements than as a concrete formation or, worse, as merely a marketing term.

The second chapter, "Where Have I Known You Before?," is a tripartite narrative that traces a short history of jazz, rock, and funk discourse as developed primarily through discussions among musicians and critics. I want to provide the larger context through which I mean to apprehend more fully Williams's, McLaughlin's, Mitchell's, and Hancock's liminal music, which dominates the latter part of the book. The chapter concludes with an overview of the bands and musicians who were considered fusion during the 1970s. Since this chapter delineates the separate worlds of jazz, rock, and funk, I thought each genre necessitated the sharper distinctions. Therefore, each genre has its own section, marked by titles and epigraphs along with internal nontitled section markers without epigraphs. I apologize for any confusion this may cause readers.

The third chapter, "Vital Transformation," is concerned directly with the motivating ideas young jazz musicians held when they began to merge jazz with contemporaneous popular music styles in the late 1960s. The focus on the early years prior to fusion's explosion on the national and international scenes provides the immediate milieu against which the remainder of the book is situated.

Subsequent chapters focus on one of four particular musicians—Tony Williams, John McLaughlin, Joni Mitchell, and Herbie Hancock—to explore more deeply the implications that arose from the practices of these young "birds of fire." Williams, McLaughlin, Mitchell, and Hancock each responded differently to the question of how musicians can be simultaneously inside and outside a given musical tradition, implicitly challenging cultural authenticity, legitimacy, and authority; and each gave, in return, prompts of his or her own. The dilemma shifts, then, from whether fusing certain musical idioms did or did not constitute jazz (or any other established genre) to a question of whether a musician can ever find legitimacy across divergent traditions, particularly when she or he attempts to share membership in musical cultures often viewed as antagonistic and to which the musician may not, at least initially, "legitimately" belong.

"Emergency!" focuses on the drummer Tony Williams's early fusion of hard rock and jazz, which, through a series of recordings under the Lifetime moniker, embodied the racialized tensions circling beneath the surface of genre. Williams's appreciation for rock musicians such as Jimi Hendrix and bands such as the Beatles not only challenged the particular racialization of rock but also questioned his fellow jazz musicians' view of rock as a benighted idiom unworthy of serious consideration.

The following chapter, "Meeting of the Spirits," focuses on John McLaughlin and the ways in which his economic success complicates any innocent notion of merging musical traditions by highlighting the complex relationship between transcultural music production and whiteness, even as he explicitly dedicated his music to spiritual ideals throughout the decade. McLaughlin's own wary cognizance of the racialized implications for intercultural exchange highlights how music critics often cast this "ain't jazz, ain't rock" music within miscegenational terms.

The next chapter, "Don Juan's Reckless Daughter," centers on a participant, Joni Mitchell, whose inclusion might at first appear overly idio-syncratic. However, I mean to position her music of the 1970s against a backdrop of musical migrations. As she began using jazz musicians in her recordings of this period, her generic border crossing from pop-folk music into music with jazz affiliations was construed as trespassing by jazz critics and aimless wandering by rock critics, placing her creative work in an ille-gitimate and liminal space—a broken middle between pop and jazz. I also mean to juxtapose her generic travels to her binational living arrangement, in which Canada is a refuge, a "solitary station," a place she finds as neces-sary to her as her "need [for] the stimulation of the scene in Los Angeles."[18]

The following chapter, "Chameleon," focuses on Herbie Hancock and his strategies for aligning an aesthetic informed by various experimental tradi-tions (computer- and synthesizer-assisted composition, free jazz), as well as popular music (funk, rock, disco), into a viable and sustainable career. Hancock's particular brand of music complicated conventional conceptions of blackness—in terms of creativity, commercial viability, and technologi-cal acuity—by performatively linking jazz and funk music, electronic tech-nology, and his personal political ideas. Furthermore, the implications of his decision to weld these specific musical practices together highlight how economics and race worked together in marking genre parameters, prac-tices, and participants at the time.

The final chapter offers a brief survey of the current activities of Hancock, McLaughlin, and Mitchell, as well as the final recordings of Williams, and a consideration of the legacy of their 1970s work on contemporary popular music. I ask the reader to remain mindful of how each of the main themes of this book—the racialized and gendered implications of genre formation; intercultural exchange as a means for questioning and complicating nor-mative cultural hierarchies; negotiating difference, not with the intent of capturing holistic integration nor celebratory authenticity but by embody-ing and performing the complicated (mis)understandings and incomplete, fissured formations between cultural groups; and, finally, the ways in which they manifested an emerging global consciousness and translocal cultural expression in non-elite spaces and bodies—interconnect, interact, and interpenetrate each other. Ultimately, it is this multiple, simultaneous, and contradictory positioning that most characterizes fusion music, transform-ing the musicians, their audiences, and the music—sound, practice, and discourse—they share.

one

I don't like labels too much but they're a necessary convenience. I use [jazz/funk], or jazz/rock or fusion. I use all those labels. —**Herbie Hancock**

Jazz fusion is another idiom. It uses elements of jazz and elements of popular forms, but it established its own idiom. —**Herbie Hancock**

Since flying between and among genres is a central motif of this work, it is necessary to establish my conception of genre. One of my central assumptions is that genres represent more than the aesthetic tastes of collective groups of listeners and musicians or the interests of the music industry. As Fabian Holt demonstrates throughout *Genre in Popular Music*, a *"genre can be viewed as a culture* with the characteristics of a system or systemic functions," and "genres are identified not only with music, but also *with certain cultural values, rituals, practices, territories, traditions, and groups of people.*"[1] I also understand genre as a logic through which ideas about race, gender, and social class are created, debated, and performed through musical sound and discourse. Genre is the index against which musical value is determined by critics, musicians, and fans alike, despite almost universal disavowal for drawing rigid lines around musical practices. Indeed, like the category of race, genre continues to hold discursive sway despite widespread acknowledgment of its limits, elisions, and errors.

Herbie Hancock's comment about the creation of an entirely new idiom may point us in the right direction for naming Beck's "ain't jazz, ain't rock" music, but *fusion*, as a distinct term for a particular set of musical practices, has not gained much traction within musical discourse except as part of the conceptual mélange of words such as *translocal, diasporic,* and *hybridized,* which are used to describe contemporary musical mergings across cultures and idioms. Steven Pond begins his insightful analysis of *Head Hunters* by introducing the term *fusion jazz* to keep from "restricting research to a genre [in order] to concentrate on the . . . various kinds of fusing activity" Hancock and his band enacted.[2] Pond skillfully delineates an array of fusing activities located in the recording, detailing the intricate interweaving of sounds, discourse, and the music industry with a careful ear, lucidly grounding his analyses in the sonic text. I am likewise more interested in thinking through the possible meanings the "fusing activities" of these young musicians might have produced than in gainsaying debates regarding genre formation.

Following David Brackett, I view *genre* as the "point of articulation between music analysis—the formal or technical description of music—and the social meanings and functions of music" and thus a keyword in my exploration of fusion's musical meaning.[3] In fact, Pond also spends some time grappling with the problem of genre and genre naming. The difficulty of slotting the "ain't jazz, ain't rock" music into its "correct" genre becomes apparent as soon as the attempts to define jazz, rock, or funk begin—a discursus appearing prior to any discussion of reasonably defining the "ain't jazz, ain't rock" music itself. Indeed, jazz, rock, and funk inhabit sets of "already impure" musical practices caught within fuzzy, contentious borders. However, it is not only that musicians and listeners recognize that genres sound out a putatively common set of central characteristics—enabling the distinguishing of a jazz from a rock composition, for instance—but that genres have also managed to instantiate a number of institutional, commercial, and discursive formations that inculcate a sense of "jazzness" or "funkness" in listeners and musicians that has been denied the "ain't jazz, ain't rock" music under study here. In fact, many genre names have become identified with radio formats as both have become inextricably linked in their use as vernacular shorthand among musicians, fans, and critics. It is important, however, to keep in mind at least one distinction: radio format names are usually more narrowly defined by market demographics (i.e., audience constitution), whereas genre names refer more often to musical practices, though both genre and radio format names tend to obscure the racialized and gendered underpinnings of their categories. Still, as Holt astutely notes, "Naming a music is a way of recognizing its existence and distinguishing it from other musics. The name becomes a point of reference and enables certain forms of communication, control, and specialization into markets, canons, and discourses."[4] Although there are inevitable exclusions in any categorization, a term eventually emerges that typically attempts to capture a central salient characteristic of a given set of musical sounds and practices.

Therefore, while recognizing its ambiguity, I will use the simple term *fusion*, not only because it was used throughout the 1970s to differentiate the music discussed within these pages from other kinds of music but because it succinctly captures the eclectic aesthetic the young "ain't jazz, ain't rock" musicians enacted.[5] For my purposes *fusion* will refer to a merging of jazz, rock, and funk music aesthetics and practices and the subsequent (or, better, the further) blurring of these large-scale genre boundaries in articulation with other musical traditions that each musician engaged in a more limited fashion. Fusion musicians articulated uneven and variable musical mergings that did not wholly displace the given genre terms (*jazz, rock, funk*) but allowed another term (*fusion*) to continually trouble, perplex, and contest those given categories—a broken middle through which the correspondences between musical genre and identity were transformed. Fusion, as a "not-quite-genre," points out the instability of all genre designations and highlights the fluidity of musical practices that genre names attempt to freeze in order to give discussions about music a meaningful starting point. In fact, while Holt frequently refers to the music as jazz-rock fusion in order to distinguish it from other styles of jazz, he states, "In retrospect, the term fusion more adequately represents the plurality and hybridity of the phenomenon," adding elsewhere that *fusion* "is not a hyphenated term and does more justice to the somewhat hybrid character of this field of jazz, which draws heavily not only on rock but also on soul and funk."[6] As Holt suggests, whether jazz-rock, jazz-funk, or jazz-xyz, strings of hyphenated terms are often clumsy and fail to provide sufficient definitional clarity.

Genre, as Keith Negus rightly insists, translates dynamic musical practices into "codified rules, conventions and expectations, not only as melodies, timbres and rhythms but also in terms of audience expectations, market categories and habits of consumption."[7] More to the point, genre discourses and constraints are not only concerns for musicians. A genre's culture, if you will, is not only exhibited through the creation and performance of music but is just as conspicuous through its consumption. Genre as a distillation of musical meaning can be seen in the clothing and heard in the language of its musicians, critics, and fans quite apart from the "music itself."[8] Fans pay close attention to the way they dress, speak, even move, ordering their life around their consumption of a musical genre or tradition—in effect, performing culture and identity through music. Fans' decisions about clothes fashions, hair design, and bodily adornments, or lack thereof, the employment they seek, and the social networks they participate in can be affected by the music culture with which they identify.[9]

For instance, consider the sartorial transformation of Miles Davis, who dressed in tailored Brooks Brothers suits throughout most of the 1960s, to become one of the era's representative icons of jazz as serious music. His cool, distanced onstage demeanor underscored the gravitas he believed that he and his music deserved. But his 1970 appearance at the Isle of Wight Festival found him in a bright orange leather jacket, bellbottom jeans customized with rhinestones, and a pair of gold platform shoes, all of which signaled his "electric turn" toward rock and funk. Davis was candid about the correlation: "[In the late 1960s] I was changing my attitude about a lot of things. . . . Everybody was into blackness, you know, the black consciousness movement, and so a lot of African and Indian fabrics were being worn. . . . I had moved away from the cool Brooks Brothers look and into this other thing, which for me was more happening with the times."[10] Many of Davis's peers, however, remained committed to promoting mainstream jazz as a crucial accomplishment for black musicians and black culture writ large. Understandably, the more formal presentation he had partially defined remained a vital jazz practice for those musicians.

Davis further unsettled jazz practices by reversing the conventional master-apprentice relationship. He not only dressed like the younger musicians in his bands, but he also gleaned new musical ideas and approaches from them, creating an incredibly dense library of collaborative music with younger musicians throughout the early 1970s. Yet even with a musician of Davis's stature, the mixing of jazz, rock, and funk was not universally admired.

I am less inclined to view fusion as a style of jazz than to heed Hancock's description of fusion as a "new idiom." Whether one views fusion as a "new idiom" or merely another style of jazz is particularly significant given that, as Simon Frith admonishes, genre "labeling lies, in practice, at the heart of pop value judgments."[11] As an example of how genre naming matters for the music at hand, let us consider Stuart Nicholson's argument for the term *jazz-rock*.[12] Nicholson makes "a distinction between it and fusion (and its latter-day equivalents, variously described as smooth jazz, quiet storm, lite-jazz, hot tub jazz, or yuppie jazz)."[13] Indeed, *jazz-rock* was as common a term for the music as *fusion* was at the time. Yet the implied privileging of jazz above rock is problematic given that musicians from either side of Beck's "ain't jazz, ain't rock" divide helped create the music.[14]

The overreliance on rock to describe all nonjazz popular music is fundamentally troubling. More important, *jazz-rock* completely elides fusion musicians' artistic claims to other musical practices and aesthetics beyond jazz and rock, oversimplifying their eclecticism. The term *jazz-rock* implicitly ignores such creative efforts as the funk-based experimentalism of the Herbie Hancock "Mwandishi" Sextet, the bluegrass-inflected compositions and performance style of the Dixie Dregs, and the transcultural mergings of Shakti—all viewed as fusion bands by critics and audiences, even while they acknowledged the vast differences in approaches and repertoire among the bands.

Mark Gridley argues that much of the music that has been called jazz-rock fusion is better named jazz-funk.[15] John Covach complicates matters further by noting the overlapping aesthetics of progressive rock and fusion, though he is careful to keep the distinctions between the two styles in mind. Covach's assertion that the overlap "balances between [the] two styles, refusing to be forced into a single category," is especially relevant here.[16] The term *jazz-rock* also obscures the fusion music created during the 1970s by bands such as Soft Machine, Bruford, and Brand X formed by rock musicians with decidedly heterodox tastes and abilities, further problematizing any privileging of jazz over rock. Finally, a demotic example: Michael J. West cogently sums up the problem of genre naming in the case of fusion, writing, "One of the most confusing aspects of the fusion universe is that, although the whole point of the music was to break down the barriers between rock and jazz, the very act of fusing the two genres seems to have created new boundaries between them. As a case in point, ever notice how, if the music was made by people inside the jazz sphere, it's called fusion—but if it was made by people in the rock sphere, it's jazz-rock?"[17] Writing in 2007, West's observation that fusion erected, rather than bridged, differences between the two idioms indicates how this particular mix of genres remains contentious and unsettled.

A fundamental problem with defining fusion is the large variety of soundings that can be understood as part of this particular set of musical "fusing activities." Negus neatly captures the situation fusion musicians confronted: "The desire for free combination and a fluid crossing of boundaries confronts the very way in which such genre practices are constrained and how 'musicians, producers, and consumers are already ensnared in a web of genre expectations.'"[18] Accordingly, the musical blends of Williams, McLaughlin, Mitchell, and Hancock reshaped the dialectical tensions within jazz, rock, and funk between such perpetually unresolved antagonisms as those found between innovation and tradition or commercial success and aesthetic value. These tensions initiated often thorny discussions between these musicians and their audiences, including critics and other music industry professionals, and the exchanges among them reveal much. As their interviews at the time made abundantly clear, these musicians were keenly aware of the ways in which external relationships among various musical genres were articulated through hegemonic cultural hierarchies. Moreover, they recognized that these hierarchies reflected elite cultural values that simultaneously helped to create broader cultural meanings while effectively extending the particularist claims of elite culture into universal and transcendent "truths" that spoke to everyone, regardless of social positioning or cultural orientation. This, in turn, affected the way musical acts were evaluated and categorized.

Pierre Bourdieu described this cultural dilemma: "the paradox of the imposition of legitimacy is that it makes it impossible ever to determine whether the dominant feature appears as distinguished or noble because it is dominant . . . or whether it is only because it is dominant that it appears as endowed with these qualities and [as] uniquely entitled to define them."[19] In musical terms, if concert music audiences were not educated to believe Wagnerian opera being performed uptown was inherently superior culturally, spiritually, or intellectually to the evening of punk music offered downtown, the vast network of foundational subsidies, governmental aid, and public interest that support Wagnerian opera might take their financial, as well as other, less material, support elsewhere. The corporate and elite patrons who invest their capital and efforts into sustaining high culture may be doing so in some measure for the social capital that accrues—a social value that manifests itself materially in the high salaries of symphonic and other arts workers; the subsidization of the complex of buildings that house the ballet, opera, and symphony companies; and the satellite facilities of nearby conservatories and private teachers. Those cultural forms that invigorate the broader culture but lack this institutional patronage must make it on their own, that is, in the marketplace or through private subsidizing efforts. Symphonies, for all their social cachet, could not survive on ticket sales alone.[20]

But neither could jazz, particularly if one looks at jazz after 1945. Paul Lopes begins his incisive study of the ways in which jazz music troubled the high/low cultural divide by highlighting the racialized dynamics caught within the marking of the two cultural spheres in a chapter titled "The Quest for Cultural Legitimacy": "The greatest challenge in the evolution of jazz music in the twentieth century was in disturbing the racial hierarchy in

American culture. From the beginning, the defining of American high art and American popular art always included the question of race with institutions carefully policing the segregation of African American culture."[21] Bebop and free jazz have been accused of intellectualization, but, by and large, the move to authorize them as legitimate jazz styles has been sanctioned by jazz critics and musicians because of the historical situation Lopes describes. As jazz was transformed into a recognizably high art form by these two styles in particular, it not only attenuated racialized condescension and denigration, but it also vindicated jazz critics and musicians who had been arguing for jazz's "proper" place in the cultural hierarchy.[22]

Yet even when genre categories are mobilized with an awareness of their textual or factual shortcomings, they guide musicians' and audiences' participation in the precise rituals that the "proper" consumption of a particular musical act demands, as well as the terms through which the rules for participation are often inscribed. As we will see, the music industry's initial bewilderment with fusion recordings would chafe against these musicians' desires to build new audiences for their music rather than relying on already-formed demographic groups or markets. Indeed, genre formation is a dynamic process as fans' and the music industry's ever-shifting interests perform substantial roles in shaping genre categories—that, in other words, the categories are not "natural" or static. Yet, for example, an unreflexive racialized logic maintained its hold in popular music discourse, helping to restrict certain genres to primary if not exclusive participation by particular racialized groups.

The racialized logic supporting generic categories held up, despite open acknowledgment by musicians for their frequent collaborations with musicians across racial lines, musical cultures, traditions, and genres. Additionally, listeners, particularly youth, were expanding their listening repertoire to include a diverse array of musical genres during the 1970s, as evidenced by the rise of underground FM stations, such as San Francisco's KSAN, in which open-ended playlists became the norm.[23] Yet it was also true that practice reinforced rhetoric as, in the main, for example, white audiences and musicians produced and consumed rock, while black audiences and musicians produced and consumed funk, and rural white audiences and musicians produced and consumed country music. This reflects the self-reinforcing logic of genre, wherein, for example, the relationship between racialized groups and musical sounds becomes naturalized through the processes that, to quote Holt again, "identify not only with music, but also with certain cultural values, rituals, practices, territories, traditions, and groups of people."[24] Eventually, those relationships become subsumed within the generic categories themselves, reappearing as a natural correspondence between sound, musician, and listener. However, the relationship between genre and identity is more clearly seen as "unnatural" and constructed when musicians such as Williams, McLaughlin, Mitchell, and Hancock rub against the grain of generic conventions, unmasking genre's veiled racialized or gendered assumptions.

In considering a transcultural musical idiom such as fusion, in which the racial implications of genre are heightened, I heed Ronald Radano's cautionary observation that while "to talk about race and music means crossing boundaries, embracing the mixture of genre and repertory, and accepting that race is everywhere in music . . . world music and postmodern hybridities have yet to eliminate racial barriers, and they show no signs of masking the conditions that give rise to racial differences."[25] Indeed, when the African American drummer Tony Williams led the mixed-race fusion ensemble Lifetime, he faced sharp criticism from a number of different groups, including black nationalists and white jazz critics. Lifetime's reaction, in part, was to turn up the volume and kick out the jams, burying racialist critique under a sonic brew of hard rock and soul jazz mixed with a healthy dose of elements borrowed from psychedelia and the experimental art music of the time, highlighting the band's commitment to the fusing of multiple difference(s). The racialization of musical genres certainly continued, but Lifetime—and fusion writ large—emphatically sounded out the possibilities for a cultural politics of mixture and diversity.

Still, as Radano's warning suggests, in the cut-'n'-mix, sampled mashup, and shuffle-mode soundscape of postmodernity, in which listeners as well as musicians alter musical histories, contexts, and trajectories, the relations and patterns of power that affect musical reception and appreciation can appear immutable by remaining obscured or by simply "disappearing." In light of these pointed concerns, what did these musicians' fusing of musical genres and traditions signal? Was fusion musicians' willingness to challenge established hierarchies and orthodox judgments of value a reasoned questioning of the fundamental assumptions about musical authority and legitimation in (popular) music culture? Or was it, as some would accuse, merely a rationale for dilettantism by incompetent young rock musicians aspiring to perform jazz or, worse, a cynical ploy by jazz musicians seeking popular appeal and economic gain?

There are certainly other catalysts for change, including developments in communication technologies. Twentieth-century musicians accessed increasing amounts of their musical inspiration from recorded music—a situation Murray Schafer identified as "schizophonia, the split between an original sound and its electroacoustical transmission or reproduction."[26] Audiences, including musicians, were hearing music more frequently as recordings rather than as live performances in an increasingly sound-saturated world.[27] The separation of an "original sound" and its reproduction and consumption had significantly altered the relationship between music and musician. Since their appearance, sound recordings have ignited aesthetic, cultural, economic, and legal debates among musicians, fans, and critics concerning ideas about, for instance, the impact of technology on musical creativity.

Recording technologies also placed technical demands on the performers that transformed the music itself. For instance, to produce better audio fidelity, compositions and arrangements were shortened to accommodate the technical shortcomings of early recording technology. Another example can be heard in the developments in microphone technology, which played a part in transforming popular vocal styles from the brassy vocals of Sophie Tucker, whose vocal power could overcome the limits of early recording technologies, to the close-miked crooning of Bing Crosby. Further, recordings made musical performances permanent and repeatable, which was, as we will see, crucial to both jazz and rock in a number of distinct ways.

While there is much to be celebrated in these gains, there were cultural losses, as well. In terms of jazz, beyond attenuating the improvisational aspect of the music, recordings helped weaken an oral tradition as increasing numbers of fledgling jazz musicians began learning their music from recordings rather than directly from a live mentor. Although the "university of the road" maintained many aspects of an oral tradition, by the end of the 1970s, many jazz musicians gleaned their knowledge from recordings, which had become important sources of jazz performance practices as many of the first- and second-generation jazz musicians were beginning to expire or withdraw from active professional music careers.

This transformation fueled an increasing sense in the jazz world that some of jazz's core aesthetics were being eroded by a fastidious reliance on records rather than "on the bandstand" training, contributing to a loss of creative vitality in the music.[28] In a 1959 *Down Beat* interview, the pianist Teddy Wilson noted, "When I came up, there was a good deal of local influence. We would travel 30 miles or so to hear another musician who had his own way of playing. Musicians developed different approaches to music in different cities. But today the same jazz records are available and popular all over. They influence young musicians in New York, Atlanta, Paris, or Tuskegee, at the same time. *All this tends for conformity*."[29] In fact, a major impetus for these young fusion musicians was the desire to break out of the conformity Wilson is referring to by using, ironically, the very products he found problematic — recordings available across the globe — to fine-tune individualistic approaches to composition and performance. In other words, fusion musicians used recordings to "relocalize" musical approaches in order to achieve uniquely individual voices.

Rock, too, felt the effects of improved recording and broadcast communications technologies throughout the 1960s and 1970s. The rise of multitrack recordings allowed creations of sound worlds that were truly otherworldly. Famously, for example, the Beatles retired from live performances after a 1966 U.S. tour to concentrate on recordings. One of the results of their decision was that their recordings became increasingly difficult, if not impossible given the technological restraints of the time, to render live. Slightly earlier, the Beach Boys' Brian Wilson was producing recordings with vocal and instrumental arrangements that required multitrack recording technology. The Beach Boys' 1966 recording *Pet Sounds* (Capitol) remains a stunning example of Wilson's capabilities — with the assistance of modern recording technology — to render a musical act that was impossible to achieve otherwise.

The aesthetic changes tracked by the development of technology included a dramatic reversal. Throughout the 1960s and 1970s, popular musicians and recording engineers — with the noticeable exception of jazz musicians and producers, in rhetoric if not practice — were increasingly disinterested in capturing live performances in as transparent a manner as possible. Rather, innovations such as multitracking recording technologies allowed musicians the ability to build "inauthentic" experiences — a single vocalist could sound like a choir, complete with harmonic and contrapuntal distinctions between "voices," or musicians could seem to be performing on multiple instruments at once as, for example, Stevie Wonder's "one man band" recordings of the 1970s affirmed.[30]

The contentious debates surrounding the "ain't jazz, ain't rock" music pitched technology, musical creativity, and artistic innovation, on one hand,

and authenticity, musical knowledge, and musical traditions, on the other. These were never mutually exclusive positions, nor do I intend to posit a crude binary or dialectic—most musicians and listeners were spread along a wide horizon of possibilities between the two poles and could hold varying, even contradictory, views depending on what kind of music they might be asked about. On one hand, for example, a listener might find that a folk music recording was harmed by the injection of multitracked vocal choruses, sound effects such as musique concrète–like snippets of dialogue, or reverse-tracked guitar leads. On the other hand, that same listener could conceivably enjoy, even celebrate, those same elements in a psychedelic rock recording—whether or not both recordings were produced contemporaneously. However, the debates were often caged within the polarities cited above.

I will detail these developments later but will precede that discussion by touching on the historical development of the schizophonic cultural moment in which fusion musicians found themselves. Jazz is arguably a child of recording technology. As Jed Rasula points out, the rise of jazz at the time of early recording technology had profound effects on the music itself, as well as its meanings.[31] The good news was that recordings disseminated the music widely across the globe because musicians no longer had to travel to a location for audiences to hear and enjoy their music. For the first time in history musicians might have fans that never saw them perform live. Recordings assisted in breaking the color line in the United States by allowing the access of black music by white listeners in a time of legal segregation. Along with recording technologies and their networks, as broadcast communications improved and slowly moved toward national coverage, radio ensured the increased availability of music from outside local and regional areas to listeners anywhere a radio or gramophone could be found.[32]

A listener can hear the effect of schizophonia on fusion in the introductory section of the Herbie Hancock composition "Watermelon Man." The percussionist Bill Summers arranged an introduction based on the music used by BaBenzélé Pygmy hunters to celebrate a successful hunting expedition. Significantly, Summers did not have firsthand contact with the BaBenzélé but accessed these sounds through the commercial recording *The Music of the Ba-Benzélé Pygmies* (Nonesuch 1966), from field recordings originally produced by the ethnomusicologists Simha Arom and Geneviéve Taurelle.[33] To recreate the sound of BaBenzélé Pygmy *hindewhu* (single-note stem whistles), Summers blew into beer bottles. The hocketting between BaBenzélé Pygmy voices and the whistles is evoked by Summers and the electric keyboards of Hancock. Coupled with the funk rhythmic accompaniment, the introduction reconfigured the relationship of an imaginary primitivist Africa to electronic technology through its representation of modern black diasporic musical culture in the image and sound of the electronic headhunter, the cultural cannibal. The resonance of the title and the music marked the arrival of a distinct idiom emerging from Hancock and the Headhunters' journeys across temporal, aesthetic, and cultural borders.

As the "Watermelon Man" example also indicates, while often respectful of musical traditions, Williams, McLaughlin, Mitchell, and Hancock felt no compulsion to render a set of musical practices in conventional ways; rather, they felt free to manipulate musical elements in any way they believed was true to their own aesthetic goals while drawing freely from any musical tradition with which they might come into contact. Their sense of artistic autonomy from tradition can be seen as an outgrowth of the attitude of "nonrepresentationality" that recording technology and distribution networks allowed. No longer restricted by time or space, musicians were less hampered by technology but increasingly restrained by audience expectations and music industry interests. Williams's, McLaughlin's, Mitchell's, and Hancock's freedom from convention and tradition marked their music as profoundly unsettling for the type of listeners—fans as well as critics— who thought that music which undermined rather than extended generic expectations moved uncomfortably beyond innovation.

These four musicians questioned such idiomatic sanctimony by creatively welding together a set of musical practices that were labeled, for the most part, "jazz" or "rock" or "funk." Yet by the middle of the decade they were creating a diverse yet coherent set of recordings and live performances from their mixed-genre music, fundamentally challenging generic assumptions. As I will detail throughout the text, however, these musicians' blendings of jazz, rock, funk, and other musical traditions had so undermined conventional notions of what it meant to perform popular music, particularly within jazz circles, that musicians, critics, and fans are still dealing with the reverberations of those disputes. Ironically, fusion never ably coalesced into a genre of its own partly because it continued to be heard as a substyle of jazz.

Before tracing the discursive histories on which fusion musicians created their music, I offer a brief listing of bands in order to note, in extremely broad strokes, the variety of musical activities in which artists who may be reasonably defined as "fusion musicians" engaged during this period. This list will also provide the reader with an idea of the range of bands and musicians considered "fusion," especially since the text is primarily concerned with four artists. It will also indicate how various fusion musicians often used musical mixtures for radically different musical ends. Additionally, since the tensions between musicians' practices and genre expectations will remain an operative idea throughout this study, I also mean to draw a loose constellation of musicians and bands as a broad artistic backdrop for the more particularized discussions of Williams, McLaughlin, Mitchell, and Hancock. They may have been singular participants in the creation of this "ain't jazz, ain't rock" music, but they were certainly not the only musicians engaged in blending jazz, rock, and funk.

While the distinctions between various bands or sets of bands are highlighted in the following descriptions in order to showcase the rich variety of fusing activities that occurred under the sign "fusion," it is important to remember the commonalities fusion musicians shared, including, as DeVeaux notes, "the use of electric instruments, modern production techniques, and a rock- or funk-oriented rhythmic feeling."[34] While his short list is composed from a jazz perspective, from a rock critic's viewpoint, fusion was notable for its extended solo improvisations, complex nonstrophic forms, and emphasis on technical, rather than merely expressive, performance styles. Finally, I provide this list of fusion bands not to form a canon or "center" but to articulate fusion's very anticanonical formation. As I have mentioned, the "many fusions" I enumerate below failed to coalesce into a coherent genre, a failure that speaks to the broken middle enunciated by fusion musicians.

Some of the first commercial successes by a fusion group were the so-called big band rock of Blood, Sweat & Tears. Blood, Sweat & Tears led a subset of fusion that blended the sophisticated horn arrangements and jazz harmonies of the big band ensemble with the energy and volume of rock music, typified by big band–like ensemble writing for a horn section, electric guitars soloing above the riffing of the horns, and the "square" rhythms of rock.[35] Blood, Sweat & Tears was a favorite with *Down Beat* readers in 1969, who voted the group Number One in the Rock/Pop/Blues Group category by an overwhelming majority and placed its album second only to Miles Davis's *Filles de Kilimanjaro*.[36] Other big band rock groups such as Chicago (Transit Authority), the Don Ellis Orchestra, Chase, and the Brecker Brothers were also successful in welding big band instrumentation (multiple brass and woodwind instruments) to electric instrumentation (electric bass, guitar, and keyboards). There were also rock bands with horn sections such as the Flock, from which violinist Jerry Goodman would emerge as a founding member of the Mahavishnu Orchestra, and Matrix.[37]

Bands such as Lifetime, Mahavishnu Orchestra, Gateway, and Eleventh House appeared more like rock bands, fronted as they were by an electric guitarist, who was often complemented by electronic keyboardists. These bands' sounds shared jazz's reliance on virtuosic improvisations coupled with volume levels and instrumentation more in keeping with contemporaneous rock bands such as Cream, the Jimi Hendrix Experience, and Led Zeppelin. As with any generalization, there are numerous qualifications to this description once one begins citing specific bands: for instance, in Mahavishnu's case there was the addition of Jerry Goodman's violin; Gateway was a guitar-driven "power trio" yet incorporated acoustic pieces in its repertoire; and Eleventh House leaned toward funk as much as rock for its rhythmic and timbral elements.

Other bands such as Steps Ahead boasted a front line of Michael Brecker's tenor saxophone and Mike Mainieri's electric vibes; Weather Report featured Wayne Shorter's saxophones, Joe Zawinul's keyboards, and, during one incarnation of the band, Jaco Pastorius, whose fretless bass pyrotechnics helped position the electric bass as a "legitimate" instrument in jazz;[38] and the "electric" version of Return to Forever, which, in addition to Chick Corea's keyboards and initially Bill Connor's and then Al DiMeola's guitar, also featured a bass virtuoso in Stanley Clarke.

Bands led by virtuoso soloists such as the violinist Jean-Luc Ponty adhered to the "hard rock meets jazz" models provided by Lifetime and Mahavishnu Orchestra. However, rather than rely too heavily on this reductive description, readers should note that these bands used musical elements borrowed from jazz, including unison lines from big band swing, the antiphonic "trading fours" of bebop, and the use of scales and thematic materials from non-Western musical traditions. However, it was the merging of hard rock rhythms and loud volume, in addition to the virtuosic display by its soloists and the complex harmonies and polymeters borrowed from jazz and non-Western musical traditions, which contributed to their attraction to rock fans. Additionally, this rock-oriented fusion appeared to obscure its debt to African American music, deepening the schism between it and "real jazz" for some jazz listeners.

Blurring the hard rock and jazz connection further were bands such as

Traffic, which featured flutist Jim Capaldi, as well as multi-instrumental prodigy, Stevie Winwood, in extended improvisational sections within compositions that were more complex than conventional strophic pop song forms. The template for the jam bands of the current era can be traced to bands such as the Allman Brothers, which featured extensive improvisational "jams" led by the virtuosic guitarists Duane Allman and Dickey Betts. Blurring these loose distinctions even further are the "postrock" instrumental groups of the 1970s such as U.K., Gong, Soft Machine, Colosseum, Brand X, Magma, Univers Zero, and Present. Many of these bands can be noted for positioning their music as art, often reiterating high cultural arguments and concerns as justification. Finally, the influence of fusion bands on the broader popular music sphere was evidenced by popular acts of the era such as Steely Dan, Al Jarreau, and Michael Franks.

Another strand of fusion merged jazz and funk and is exemplified by the music of Herbie Hancock's bands, both the avant-garde "funkisms" of Mwandishi and the more mainstream funk stylings of the Headhunters. Beyond funk's musical elements, groups such as the Crusaders, Donald Byrd and the Blackbyrds, and Osibisa also engaged black political and social interests through an active engagement with Afrodiasporic musical practices. The connections between their music and those broader Afrodiasporic cultural practices are not necessarily innocent—witness Steven Feld's suggestive critique of Hancock's use of BaBenzélé Pygmy music as cultural appropriation masking as ethnic affinity.[39]

A number of other solo artists also produced funk-influenced fusion albums during the 1970s, such as Stanley Turrentine, Hubert Laws, and George Benson. Along with many of their peers on the Creed Taylor International (CTI) label and its subsidiary, Kudu Records, these musicians created a rhythm-and-blues, funk-inflected fusion that, despite funk's strong identification with urban African American lived experiences, became the prototype for what is now called "smooth jazz." A primary CTI in-house arranger was Bob James, whose early work as a free jazz pianist has been overshadowed by his association with the record label, leading to his subsequent dismissal as a "fuzak" keyboardist.[40] The genre has become so synonymous with commercial interests and a musically conservative, even naive, aesthetic that Stuart Nicholson uses the term to disparage fusion music as "yuppie/smooth/hot tub" jazz.

While smooth jazz may have followed mainstream jazz into the elite hotels and shopping malls of the bourgeoisie—the drummer Steve Smith calls it simply "easy listening," a designation that is ripe for Adorno's critique of mass (production) culture—its audience has drawn consistently from communities of color.[41] In truth, contrary to Nicholson's implication of "yuppie jazz" as a genre created for white suburban consumption, smooth jazz has a significantly large middle-class black, Asian American, and Latina/o following. As Christopher Washburne notes in relation to Kenny G, "smooth jazz is not a blip in jazz history, a mistake fueled by consumerism and mass market appeal that will be corrected any time soon. Rather, it is firmly rooted within a long-standing tradition located within the jazz tradition itself."[42] Yet, undoubtedly, smooth jazz as a commercial genre grew in part out of corporate desires to appropriate fusion's more pop-friendly elements.

To return to the 1970s: rhythm-and-blues and funk groups of the period that shared some correspondences with the funk-influenced fusion groups mentioned above include Tower of Power, Cold Blood, and Stuff. Today, acid jazz can be seen within the lineage of jazz-funk fusion. Acid jazz's recuperation of earlier "soul jazz" or hard bop through the use of sampling older hits links it directly to jazz. A well-known example is the British group Us3's sampling of Herbie Hancock's "Cantaloupe Island" for its hit "Cantaloop (Flip Fantasia)" in 1992.

Another group of fusion bands embraced free jazz aesthetics rather than the more bebop-oriented harmonic complexities of the "hard rock" fusion groups mentioned above. Miles Davis's groups throughout the early 1970s merged free jazz, funk, rock, and bebop elements, exemplifying this approach to weld seemingly incongruent musical idioms. Artists such as the guitarists Sonny Sharrock and James "Blood" Ulmer merged the post-tonality of free jazz with the volume of hard rock, borrowing rhythmically from rock, free jazz, and funk. This particular stream of fusion music has reemerged as an important, if generally unacknowledged, influence in some of the work of experimental musicians such as John Zorn, Marc Ribot, and Henry Kaiser. The first Weather Report album fits into this category though subsequent albums showcased increasingly through-composed tracks, as well as early cross-cultural blendings of traditional non-Western musics that would eventually become known as "world music."[43] Other bands such as Oregon and Ornette Coleman's Prime Time integrated jazz and rock aesthetics with non-Western music.

Finally, one type of fusion focused on blending country-and-western and bluegrass music with jazz and rock aesthetics. The Dixie Dregs were arguably the most well-known of these groups, and their legacy can be heard in the contemporary music of artists such as the banjoist Bela Fleck and his band, the Flecktones. This blend can also be heard in the early country gospel–tinged music of Keith Jarrett and Gary Burton, two artists not often associated with early fusion. Yet Burton's *Tennessee Firebird* (RCA 1966) was one of the first fusion recordings, and, as the name implies, he covered country classics such as "I Can't Help It (If I'm Still in Love with You)" and "Born to Lose," as well as Bob Dylan's "Just like a Woman" and "I Want You."

This country-influenced fusion in jazz has precedents in an earlier era. Western swing big bands such as Bob Wills's Texas Playboys and Milton Brown and the Musical Brownies popularized a blend of country-and-western music and jazz in the 1930s and 1940s. It should be noted that Bob Wills and other western-swing bands are rarely mentioned in jazz histories or in critical jazz writings. However, their legacy continues and can be heard in contemporary western-swing bands such as Asleep at the Wheel and Norton Buffalo's Stampede. In fact, there is a long tradition of "crossing" between country music and blues, as well as between white hymnody and black spirituals—a cross-cultural flow that prefigures the fusion movement.

I will not make the arbitrary distinction pace Nicholson and Gridley between fusion music as represented by bands such as Mahavishnu Orchestra, Return to Forever, Eleventh House, Lifetime, Weather Report, the Brecker Brothers, the Jazz Crusaders, the Headhunters, and Mwandishi, and latter-day smooth jazz bands and artists such as Spyro Gyra, Kenny G, David Benoit, Bob James, Earl Klugh, Boney James, and Eric Marienthal. As Christopher Washburne argues, Kenny G is "with us whether we like it or not." Washburne points out that "the conceptual language employed within jazz discourses" is "insufficient for the challenge of understanding smooth jazz, its historical baggage, and stylistic affiliations. What I am suggesting is that instead of marginalizing, yet again, a major popular influence on current jazz styles, we should aspire to refine and adapt our historical conceptual lens through which we deal with these phenomena and in the process align jazz scholarship with more cutting-edge popular music/culture studies."[44] One can easily substitute *fusion* for *smooth jazz* here. Again, Washburne's concerns are not as consequential if one thinks of fusion less as a jazz substyle than as a distinct idiom moving between jazz and other genres, which is my central assertion (and is one reason I shy away from using the term *fusion jazz*). As Burton and other young fusion musicians would discover, in addition to open-eared jazz fans, fusion audiences would consist of listeners whose tastes ran toward the progressive end of rock, including bands such as Henry Cow, Pink Floyd, and Soft Machine.

While early fusion bands performed at jazz clubs such as the Village Vanguard, the Blue Note, and Lennie's-on-the-Turnpike, they also performed at more rock-oriented venues such as the Both/And, the Scene, and both Fillmores, East and West. Audiences for the more experimental rock bands and nascent fusion groups overlapped, despite generic separation by the recording industry, evidenced, for example, by Miles Davis or the Mahavishnu Orchestra as opening acts for rock groups such as the Grateful Dead and the "prog rock" band Emerson, Lake and Palmer.[45] Yet these early fusion bands continued to maintain a sizable jazz audience, and, as I have noted, most of the written interest for their work came largely from jazz critics. As their music and the variety of venues in which they performed attests, however, their work shifted uneasily among genres, particularly in relation to critical legacies that necessarily insisted on creating and maintaining distinctions. It is to these divergent histories that we now turn.

two   Where Have I Known You Before? / *fusion's foundations*

This music is new. This music is new music and it hits me like an electric shock and the word "electric" is interesting because the music is to some degree electric music. . . . Electric music is the music of this culture and in the breaking away (not the breaking down) from previously assumed forms a new kind of music is emerging.
—Ralph J. Gleason

If music has something to say to you—whether it's jazz, country blues, Western or hillbilly, Arabian, Indian, or any other Asian, African, South American folk music— take it. Never restrict yourself. —**Larry Coryell**

In tracing the discursive histories of jazz, rock, and funk, I focus on the ways that racialized ideologies support generic categorizations because race was a fundamental fulcrum on which fusion troubled established relationships between music and meaning. Accordingly, a central problem for many listeners was that, independent of the genre they claimed as "their own," the aesthetics of jazz, rock, and funk were simply too disparate, primarily because of the ways in which genres had been racialized. This idea of incommensurable mixture goes to the heart of the debates surrounding the "ain't jazz, ain't rock" music of these young musicians.

By the mid-1970s, jazz, rock, and funk were widely recognized as musical genres with distinctive aesthetics and histories, including a defining core of musicians and recordings. These distinctions would necessarily emphasize the differences among the three genres. To cite an easy contrast that reflected the general sense at the time: where jazz was seen as sophisticated, intellectual, even abstract, rock and funk were in essence primal and visceral, less able to shake off their orientation to the sensual in the way jazz had slowly done as a corollary to its move from a popular form to an art music.[1] Rock and funk, meanwhile, enjoyed their own distinctions in terms of representation and performance—differences that were often openly discussed in racial terms. Rock and funk's connection to particular bodies (white for rock, black for funk) enabled or constrained musicians' attempts to mix the two, as the racially integrated rock band Mother's Finest attested to in its 1976 song "Niggizz Can't Sang Rock & Roll." As we will see, in combining these traditions, Williams, McLaughlin, Mitchell, and Hancock were accused by some listeners of creating a sonic Frankenstein's monster, depleting jazz's cerebral delights while divesting rock and funk of their celebrated physicality.

Nor did they limit their blendings to rock and jazz. A wide variety of music attracted the attention of Williams, McLaughlin, Mitchell, and Hancock, who collectively cited Karlheinz Stockhausen, John Cage, Ravi Shankar, and Allah Rakha, as well as Jimi Hendrix, Sly Stone, the MC5, Charlie Parker, and John Coltrane, as influential—not to mention McLaughlin's study of South Asian music or Mitchell's affinity for the music of folk musicians such as Tom Rush.

As their cited influences attest, however, these musicians consciously avoided an "anything goes" attitude in their musical hybridizations. They were highly selective about the composition and balance of their mixtures, neither arbitrary nor naive in their borrowings of elements from various musical traditions. They did not simply cart over everything from a given genre or tradition and match it up to their counterparts in other genres or traditions. However—and this is the cause for much of the concern from critics—they could be unapologetically idiosyncratic in their choices for combining various genres and traditions. Following their own tastes, they selected specific elements within a chosen genre or tradition, sometimes disregarding the uses any element may have fulfilled in its original context and reengineering them to suit their own eclectic aesthetic.

Yet for the most part, after the heated debates of the late 1960s and 1970s, jazz critics seemed to settle the question of whether fusion music was jazz by simply ignoring it. Part of the reason fusion created such strong divisions within the jazz community was due to the sense by mainstream jazz musicians and listeners that fusion's aesthetic compromises hastened the "death of jazz"—a trope that has haunted jazz periodically since the moldy figs and their swing adversaries contested the definition of "real jazz" in the 1930s. Indeed, until recently, trade and scholarly publications that focused on jazz were uniformly circumspect about fusion. Jazz critics applauded Tony Williams for his postfusion acoustic jazz recordings, for instance, while remaining virtually silent about Lifetime, his seminal fusion trio. Likewise,

Williams's final recordings with Bill Laswell, which returned him to the decidedly avant rock direction Lifetime first explored nearly three decades before, have been largely ignored by jazz critics.

Still, we should hear the genre mixtures of Williams, McLaughlin, Mitchell, and Hancock as sounding out the contingencies of transcultural exchanges rather than as the polished efforts of finished cultural projects. Therefore, to understand what motivated fusion musicians to make the sort of musical mixtures they did and why it proved controversial, we need to step back for a brief moment to consider the path these musicians and their predecessors took to arrive at the "ain't jazz, ain't rock, (ain't funk)" music of the 1970s.

Ain't Rock

> I could put together the greatest rock 'n' roll band you ever heard. —Miles Davis

> We're not a rock band. —Miles Davis

In the period between the Second World War and the rise of fusion in the late 1960s, various subgenres of jazz—bebop, jump blues, third stream, soul jazz, cool, and free jazz—were the shifting sands on which the roles that race, gender, and social class played in jazz were debated. For critics reticent to engage the links between race and genre head-on, appeals to jazz as a mark of U.S. national identity helped negotiate around the role social identity played in the relationship between jazz and elite art culture. In 1938 Winthrop Sargeant, while arguing against the idea that jazz was an art music, suggested that "while [jazz's] ancestry may be African and European, it is none the less a peculiarly American form of musical expression. The spontaneous, improvisatory aspect of jazz is remarkably adapted to the musical needs of a pragmatic, pioneering people. Like the typical American, the jazz musician goes his own syncopated way, making instantaneous and novel adjustments to problems as they present themselves."[2] Sargeant's vision of the jazz musician's individualistic "syncopated way" as the solution to "problems" projects a remarkably autonomous world of individuals free to make "instantaneous and novel adjustments" as their response. His description merges a thoughtful pragmatism—a down-to-earth, do-it-yourself work ethos—to an adventurous pioneering spirit—a willingness to break free of precedent and follow one's muse. Sargeant heard the resolution, the synthesis, if you will, between the two ideals in a jazz music appreciated by a racially unmarked American subject.

Race was implicit, however, in the arguments between jazz critics and musicians over whether jazz was art music or a popular, even populist, music. In attempting to displace the social and political articulations of jazz artists by inadvertent or intentional inattentiveness to the underlying discourse of race, jazz critics often aestheticized a politically charged cultural practice and attenuated the oppositional strain in the music.[3] As jazz became increasingly recognized as art music—rather than as mere entertainment or as part of an ephemeral popular culture—black jazz musicians, in particular, were both wary and inviting of their rising cultural capital. As early as 1925, Joel Rogers, writing in Alain Locke's anthology The New Negro, recognized that in "white society's interest in [jazz there was] both a means for jazz to fulfill America's democratic potential and the risk that black contributions might be erased."[4]

For their part black jazz musicians often linked jazz to ideas about American individualism and exceptionalism as a way to alleviate racial condescension. Yet working in a social milieu that celebrated their music but continued to bar them from political and social opportunities left many black jazz musicians ambivalent about their position as artists and entertainers. The marked difference between jazz as art and jazz as the "people's music," as Sidney Finkelstein called it,[5] has been negotiated in various ways: from Jelly Roll Morton's insistence on the importance of jazz as "pure music" to Duke Ellington's engagements with long forms; from big band swing's mass popularity to bebop's bohemian exclusivity; from the New Orleans and blues primitivist mythologies to the urbane intellectualism of third stream and bebop; and from the emotional distance of cool to the sweat-invoking dance rhythms of soul jazz. Caught in the bind of American racial politics, Ellington recognized the deep irony at the heart of jazz discourse, writing, "I contend that the Negro is the creative voice of America, is creative America, and it was a happy day in America when the first unhappy slave was landed on its shores. . . . Its guarded leisure and its music, were all our creations."[6] Marking American-ness in an explicitly racialized way, Ellington voiced the racial contradiction that jazz music articulated: a "free" music created by "unfree" musicians was American, not simply because the "typical American goes his own syncopated way" through the workings of an innate democratic impulse but, rather, because of institutionalized racism and its effects on black and white Americans.

Indeed, how could one speak of black and white cultural interaction in the United States without addressing the long history of unequal relations of power between the two groups, inflected through race? One way was to focus on the class cleavages art discourse engendered and downplay the racial dynamics. In the mid-1950s the jazz critic Marshall Stearns argued against the growing perception of jazz as an art music because it militated against jazz's ability to sound out American democracy. "In our time," wrote Stearns, "jazz is debunking the myths of 'fine art' and the social pretensions of the concert hall. To allow that jazz should be granted a role in the world of art, for example, leads to disconcerting questions about who is really cultured in our society."[7] Yet while Stearns discussed jazz's development in black American culture, he argued that jazz's growth was an example—a praxis, in a way—of the triumph of "All-American" democratic ideals. Implying that jazz's conquest of the rest of the world mirrored the benefits of U.S. global hegemony, Stearns quoted a European jazz fan, Olaf Hudt-walker, who declared, "A jam session is a miniature democracy. Every instrument is on its own and equal. The binding element is toleration and consideration for the other players."[8]

Stearns developed his argument more clearly along nationalist lines when he compared jazz's "free-swinging stride" to "the Prussian 'goose-step'": "A dramatic illustration of the healthy, realistic qualities of jazz is furnished by a comparison of the Prussian 'goose-step' and the free-swinging stride of the New Orleans march. Both are responses to military music but the difference is immense. Contrary to the robot-like motions of the goose-step, the New Orleans marcher enjoys a freedom of movement that mirrors the spirit of the music. *The New Orleans marchers may appear relatively unorganized, but their motions permit greater individual expression and symbolize a truer community of interests.*"[9]

Stearns's comparisons between the mechanical and the human, the Prussian and the American, linked political ideologies to musical styles, emphasized by his marking of jazz as an American expression of individualism. Moreover, when Stearns offered his argument for jazz as the sounding out of an American democratic ideal, he quickly moved past his guarded nods toward race (particularly if we acknowledge the "New Orleans marchers" as black Americans): "On a more abstract level, jazz offers a common ground upon which the conflicting claims of the individual and the group may be resolved—a problem that has vexed our times. For the jazzman, the dancer, and even the sympathetic listener can express himself individually and, at the same time, participate freely in a creative whole. In other words, he can 'belong' by participating in collective improvisation, and simultaneously let off his own brand of steam, solo."[10]

Jazz's resolution for the "conflicting claims of the individual and the group" can be found in its performative and aesthetic dimensions—dimensions Stearns noticeably removed from *specific* group experiences. Stearns goes further, citing the "religious fervor . . . typical of the response that jazz evokes in many people" because of jazz's ability to invoke "direct and immediate contact between human beings," for though "jazz expresses the enforced and compassionate attitudes of a minority group . . . in a fundamental sense, none of us is wholly free."[11] Linking the black American experience to the wider public, Stearns, however unwittingly, erased the particular histories of black American lives.

In 1961 the critic Martin Williams opened his *Where's the Melody? A Listener's Introduction to Jazz* with an introductory chapter entitled "An American Art." Williams began, "If we know anything about jazz at all, we have probably heard that it is supposed to be an art—our only art according to some; 'America's contribution to the arts,' according to certain European commentators. It has also the kind of prestige that goes with praise from the 'classical' side of the fence."[12] By the early 1960s, jazz had become a deracinated art form by many mainstream jazz critics—even if acknowledging its roots in African American culture—that was exported to the rest of the world in order to show the openness and inclusiveness of U.S. democracy. As Williams also noted, "[The U.S.] State Department is willing to export jazz to answer for our cultural prestige abroad."[13] In fact, Stearns and Williams both argued that jazz was superior to European art music for its improvisational freedom, expressive élan, and universal appeal.

By the 1960s, black writers such as Amiri Baraka, writing as LeRoi Jones, and A. B. Spellman were far less positive about the erasure of the blackness of jazz culture than Stearns and Williams, hearing in jazz the sounds of black resistance to cultural dilution and appropriation by nonblack musicians and critics.[14] In a polemical essay, "Jazz and the White Critic," Baraka answered writers such as Stearns by noting, "Usually the critic's commitment was first to his *appreciation* of the music rather than to his understanding of the attitude which produced it. . . . The major flaw in this approach to Negro music is that it strips the music too ingenuously of its social and cultural intent."[15] Many jazz musicians even questioned using the term *jazz* to describe their music because of its association with sexual licentiousness, vice, and criminality rather than a phrase such as "America's classical music," which implies another, sanctioned set of associations.

Baraka argued pointedly in *Blues People* that white bebop musicians and fans were drawn to the music because they recognized the outsider status of black Americans and hoped to acquire, through their involvement with jazz, distance from bourgeois culture: "The white beboppers of the forties were as removed from the society as Negroes, *but as a matter of choice.* The important idea here is that the white musicians and other young whites who associated themselves with this Negro music identified the Negro with this separation, this nonconformity, though, of course, the Negro himself had no choice."[16] The dialectical relationship between primitive blackness, on one hand, and modernity, on the other, produced a "black modernity," represented by the figure of the black bebop musician and out of which displays of white transgression were performed and articulated. As Ingrid Monson points out, "Whether conceived as an absence of morality or of bourgeois pretensions, this view of blackness, paradoxically, buys into the historical legacy of primitivism and its concomitant exoticism of the 'Other.'"[17]

A key difference between white and black bebop musicians and audiences, as Baraka adroitly pointed out, was an individual's agentive power as determined by race. White musicians and listeners can opt in and out of their outsider status, but blacks, with their visible epidermal uniform, possessed fewer options for transcending their otherness. But Baraka also lambasted middle-class blacks whose rejection of jazz and the blues signaled their "desire to become vague, featureless, Americans."[18] Baraka was disheartened by "Negroes, jazz musicians and otherwise, who have moved successfully into the featureless syndrome of [mainstream American] culture, who can no longer realize the basic social and emotional philosophy that has traditionally informed Afro-American music."[19] He warned them that though they entered the broader social world equipped with college degrees and other "fundamental prerequisites of worth in society [they will soon realize it] becomes meaningless once those prerequisites are understood and desired, then possessed, and still the term of separation exists."[20] As might be indicated by these statements, Baraka was fiercely polemical throughout *Blues People*, reacting strongly against the idea that bebop and the blues represented a broadly American, rather than a specifically black American, cultural perspective.

Although some jazz musicians spoke to social issues directly in their creative work—famously with Billie Holiday's version of "Strange Fruit" (1939) and Max Roach's "We Insist! Freedom Now!" suite (1960)—many mainstream jazz critics remained concerned with artistic issues such as modes of self-expression and formal musical issues. Ironically, as Eric Porter argues, the "debates about bebop . . . played a crucial role 'in preparing the way for the emergence and acceptance of an avant-garde jazz' by making it 'possible' and 'very natural' to refer to jazz as 'an art music.'"[21] Jazz musicians' rise in cultural capital mitigated much of the progressive political edge some of them honed even while helping "to generate a subsequent understanding of black avant-garde music as an articulation of political assertiveness and cultural resistance."[22] A paradox arose in the late 1950s and early 1960s as the mainstreaming of jazz was accomplished through an increased use in Hollywood soundtracks, use of jazz musicians and arrangers in adult-oriented "easy listening" orchestras who referenced jazz in their performances and recordings, and the hard bop and cool jazz chart successes that obscured, for all but the most adventurous listeners, the more explicitly politicized music of composers such as Charles Mingus, Max Roach, and Rahsaan Roland Kirk or the challenging music of free jazz artists such as Cecil Taylor or Albert Ayler. While jazz aficionados searched out Mingus or Kirk, many listeners heard jazz through the compositions of Henry Mancini or Stan Kenton, echoing the dominance of the "sweet" dance bands during the 1930s.

There were white critics of the 1960s such as Ralph J. Gleason and Nat Hentoff, who were less willing to limit their comments to the aesthetic qualities of jazz musicians' creative work. Explicitly leftist writers such as Sidney Finkelstein and Frank Kofsky, while little noted today, raised important questions regarding the position of black working musicians in larger contexts than mainstream jazz criticism or the purportedly objective stance of professional historians normally allowed at the time.[23] While Kofsky's overzealous political stance may have caused him to overstate certain ideas, he captured cogently the political awareness of black jazz musicians in the 1960s when he proposed that although the "appeal of black nationalism . . . has fluctuated greatly [throughout jazz's history, black] jazz musicians have ample cause for being particularly susceptible to the seductive strains of black nationalism."[24] Indeed, Kofsky and other left-leaning critics supported Baraka's clear-eyed assertion that "Negro music is always radical in the context of formal American culture."[25]

Aesthetic arguments continued to dominate critical debate. In 1960, when the free jazz alto saxophonist Ornette Coleman released *The Shape of Jazz to Come*, he initiated vehement arguments within the jazz world regarding the role of Western tonality and swing rhythms in jazz music. As Charles Mingus stated in a *Down Beat* interview in May 1960, "Now, aside from the fact that I doubt [Ornette Coleman] can even play a C scale in tune, the fact remains that his notes and lines are so fresh. . . . I'm not saying everybody's going to have to play like Coleman. But they're going to have to stop playing [like] Bird [Charlie Parker]."[26]

That same year, John Coltrane released *My Favorite Things*, which became a popular hit for him and "reintroduced" the soprano saxophone back into jazz music. More important, the recording showcased Coltrane's interest in the musical traditions of India through his use of modal, rather than tonal, harmonic frameworks. Also significant was Coltrane's announcement of his attraction to free jazz aesthetics with another 1960 recording entitled *The Avant-Garde*. Coltrane's involvement with free jazz did much to legitimize the style for jazz critics owing to his proven stature within jazz's mainstream, having performed and recorded with Miles Davis and Thelonious Monk, among others.[27]

Ted Gioia posits that by the late 1960s, free jazz and fusion were "mirror images" of each other.[28] As I have been suggesting, while free jazz helped move jazz even closer to artistic respectability than bebop before it, fusion was seen as moving jazz toward popular accessibility, a space devoid of high cultural legitimacy. Gioia asserts that this opposition was little noted at the time by jazz critics because of an increasingly fragmenting jazz world. While Gioia's view of the joined polemics of free jazz and fusion vis-à-vis mainstream jazz is apt, I want to suggest that the jazz world has *always* been fragmented, and it has been the glossing by historians after the fact that has given jazz history the seamless lineage it enjoys—at least until one begins to look at the 1960s. Different generations of jazz musicians had always crisscrossed stylistic borders as, most famously, when the vocalist Billy Eckstine's big band ensemble in the 1940s included Dizzy Gillespie on trumpet, Charlie Parker on alto saxophone, and a number of other young musicians associated with bebop, a then-new controversial style of jazz. Yet as Ken Burns's *Jazz* documentary series indicated, jazz histories are often at a loss to explain the apparent dismantling of a central jazz narrative in the 1960s.

Although the 1960s are often described as a time of a fragmented jazzscape, however, it may be more productive to think of the period as one in which heightened accumulations of jazz styles were plied across an ever widening set of practices and critical views. Hard bop recordings sat beside free jazz albums in record store bins while mainstream jazz recordings maintained a bebop-inflected core. So-called Dixieland or traditional jazz experienced a revival, especially in Britain and the West Coast of the United States, where bandleaders such as San Francisco's Lu Watters and Turk Murphy began recording albums that revisited New Orleans repertoire and performance styles.

But even as the 1960s jazz world struggled to accommodate free jazz, by the end of the decade jazz was being challenged in another direction by fusion. Significantly, the rhetorical positioning, by musicians and critics alike, of free jazz and fusion as oppositional to "straight-ahead" or mainstream jazz signaled a collective movement by jazz musicians away from a central idea of jazz into a multiplying array of "jazzes." Early fusion musicians' efforts exemplified the tensions this growing inclusivity brought to bear by matching posttonality to funk rhythms while claiming that they were fundamentally jazz musicians. While fusion artists shared free jazz artists' aesthetic struggles, because of fusion musicians' simultaneous engagements with popular music, their aesthetic and political challenges have been overlooked. Pressing this further, I would also suggest that the link between black nationalist politics and free jazz is a construction and is not the result of a "natural" fit between a political ideology and a musical aesthetic. Free jazz artists were a heterogeneous group with a wide spectrum of political views, as interviews with various free jazz artists reveal. In other words, the links between fusion and an apolitical stance are no more "natural" than the connections between free jazz and particular political ideologies.

For example, the critical perspective that aligned free jazz primarily, if not exclusively, with 1960s-era black nationalist separatists obscured other perspectives. One of free jazz's leading lights, Albert Ayler, stated in a 1963 interview that free jazz "is based on an integrated theory, white people can play it too." Ayler suggested that "it is undeniably time for a change, but you have to be ready for it. Everybody's not. Some people don't want to be free."[29] The range of opinions about free jazz found in Arthur Taylor's Notes and Tones further illustrated the diversity of jazz's black artistic community regarding politicized music, free jazz, and the historical moment in which free jazz was taking shape (although the book first appeared in 1977, the majority of the interviews were conducted between 1968 and 1972). Yet a majority of the written material on free jazz is devoted to the links between it and the black political struggles of the period.[30] As Iain Anderson notes, free jazz was increasingly visible as a jazz idiom, though "on the edges of the tradition."[31]

Still, there is a reason free jazz was once called "freedom jazz" by many of its adherents. Many free jazz players looked to liberate themselves not only from conventional Western musical norms and concerns (thematic development, harmonic progressions, rhythmic propulsion) but also from political oppression and cultural exploitation. In this milieu free jazz *as avant-garde black music* was viewed as political in contradistinction to other jazz styles such as hard bop. Fusion musicians, though less explicitly political, were actively involved with alternative spiritual beliefs and other socially transformative praxis — actions and beliefs that did not register as viable substitutes for direct political action or revolutionary rhetoric during the late 1960s. For example, when the free jazz saxophonist Archie Shepp compared his saxophone to a machine gun in the hands of a Viet Cong soldier, stating, "We are only an extension of that entire civil rights–black Muslims-black nationalist movement that is taking place in America," his politicized rhetoric afforded a certain legitimacy that was denied to fusion musicians such as John McLaughlin or Chick Corea, both of whom advocated religious or spiritual solutions to social and political crises at the time.[32]

Critics may simply have missed, or dismissed, the message. Fusion artists appealed to a variety of nonpolitical changes for their audiences, speaking of spiritual transformation, often in the earnest voice of the newly converted. Chick Corea, the pianist/keyboardist for Miles Davis's electric groups, as well as leader of his own fusion group, Return to Forever, wrote a column in the October 28, 1971, issue of *Down Beat*, entitled, "The Function of an Artist." He argued for an artist's role in creating, "even if only in our imaginations, ideal scenes of what we would like the world to be like in some not too distant future."[33] Corea's view that an artist's "good intentions" served as a code of ethics was shared by other fusion artists, including his fellow pianists Mike Nock and Herbie Hancock. Corea stated elsewhere:

> The true leaders of opinion on this planet are celebrities and artists: people who do something aesthetic for others. People look up to these leaders for evaluation and opinions. . . . So artists can create a future for this planet by what they think and what they do, which makes the role of the artist one of great responsibility. This is something inherent in the artist, something most artists do without being aware of how they do it. But to be aware of how you do it is even more effective, because you begin to feel the responsibility to continually put out the truth and it kind of puts you on your guard to learn, to be honest, and to improve.[34]

As I will detail in "Meeting of the Spirits," the idea of enlightening audiences was important for many fusion musicians. However, I want to highlight two things at this point. First, fusion musicians' interest in various spiritual traditions had more in common with the social transformations advocated by free jazz artists than was noted at the time. This had an impact on my second point, namely, that the focus on spirituality placed many fusion artists in the countercultural rather than the politically radical currents of the era.

Yet, ironically, given the widespread representation of free jazz as the sounding out of radical black nationalism, by the late 1960s, many jazz musicians associated with the free jazz movement found increasing patronage from elite institutions in the form of grants, commissions, prizes, and academic positions. As Iain Anderson points out, "paradoxically, both [free jazz's] growing association with cultural nationalism, and parallels between free jazz and Euro-American concert tradition, opened doors in the nonprofit sector."[35] The contradiction between free jazz musicians' radical political rhetoric and the fact that they were seeking public and private institutional funding would not blemish free jazz artists' legitimacy in the same way that commercial success would later stain fusion musicians' creative efforts (in fact, it worked to legitimize free jazz artists as "high culture" artists). Anderson notes the price of this upward mobility for free jazz musicians:

> In 1965 Archie Shepp sounded a note of desperation when he told a reporter: "We can't let the [black] audience escape. We must bring into our music every stench of the streets, every tragedy, don't let them rest." By 1968 he admitted to having lost almost all contact with black listeners. Record sales, availability of work, and the reluctant testimony of sympathetic musicians and critics indicate a small, predominantly white, middle-class, and often intellectual or artistic audience. Support in black neighborhoods remained tenuous throughout the decade [1960s], undermining [black] nationalist authority and enabling the trade press to frame free jazz on the edges of the tradition.[36]

Shepp's eventual turn to an R&B orientation compromised his work for some critics—yet he continued to be heard as a jazz musician. Similarly, though jump blues, hard bop, and soul jazz did not fit into a narrative of jazz music's increasing complexity and refinement, failing to excite much interest in critical circles, the styles were often heard as part of an expansive definition of the jazz tradition.[37] Jazz critics often dismissed hybrid efforts such as third stream and cool jazz as effete yet still considered them part of a jazz tradition. Like bebop and big band swing before it, free jazz eventually managed to become part of an ever-widening definition of jazz, though arguably remaining marginalized.

By the mid-1960s, however, many jazz musicians recognized their increasing displacement from the popular music mainstream and attempted to regain some ground lost to rock by covering a particular range of rock songs. Beatles tunes, in particular, became commonplace on recordings though these recordings were often seen as calculated strategies to garner larger record sales. In 1966 Duke Ellington recorded his arrangements of the Beatles' "All My Loving" and "I Want to Hold Your Hand" on *Ellington '66* (Reprise), while Count Basie also gave a nod to rock's growing popularity, recording *Basie's Beatle Bag* (Verve). Still, the title of Gerry Mulligan's recording consisting largely of popular music covers, *If You Can't Beat 'Em, Join 'Em* (Limelight 1965), expressed many older jazz musicians' attitudes about rock music at the time.

In other ways, however, mainstream jazz continued to affect, and to be affected by, nonrock popular music throughout the 1960s. Stan Getz led a small movement of jazz musicians who embraced bossa nova, a musical style imported from Brazil; the tenor saxophonist enjoyed a hit with his rendition of Antonio Carlos Jobim's "Girl from Ipanema" in 1962. The soul jazz pianist Ramsey Lewis became part of "The In Crowd" with his hit instrumental single of that title in 1965. Jazz's mainstream appeal was apparent as Broadway and Hollywood composers increasingly used elements of jazz music in their soundtracks. Successful film composers such as Henry Mancini, who placed second behind Duke Ellington in the 1967 Annual *Down Beat* Reader's Poll, had started out as jazz musicians, bringing their jazz skills and tastes to bear on their vocational creations. Hollywood also used long-established jazz tropes for its narratives in films such as *Paris Blues* (1961), including the idea of the jazz musician as an outsider to "straight" society, including the concert music tradition, as well as popular music's commercial concerns.

It was widely acknowledged in jazz circles that fusion musicians were not the first to merge jazz with other musical idioms, nor were they the first to introduce innovations that would incite a redefinition of jazz. Dizzy Gillespie's meetings with Mario Bauza and Chano Pozo merged Afro-Cuban musical sensibilities with bebop aesthetics, for instance, and represent a prior moment of mixing that John Storm Roberts calls "the first of the fusions."[38] Many jazz musicians, including some of the most creative innovators, are part of a long history of cross-cultural music. Ferdinand "Jelly Roll" Morton insisted that authentic jazz required a "Spanish tinge," and his works often drew on European concert music. His use of Chopin's "Funeral March" on his own "Dead Man Blues," for instance, is a sly comment on the differences between European and African American sensibilities toward death and death rites and rituals. Ellington's continual effort to extend jazz forms into larger compositions that did not follow Eurocentric forms or structures is another case in point.[39]

Paul Lopes argues, "The jazz art world . . . ultimately staked claim to a unique tradition in American music that bridged various cultural distinctions active in both high and popular art in the United States. This art world was a unique combination of both populism and elitism—a celebration of the artistry of popular culture and a striving of many for high art status."[40] Yet young jazz musicians who were beginning to fuse rock with jazz at the time read the cultural landscape in ways that contrasted sharply with jazz musicians and critics, of either mainstream or experimental bent, who appeared increasingly uninterested in music deemed "popular."

Ain't Jazz

> A lot of jazz players make the mistake of aiming just for the listener's head and don't try to get to their body. Rock gets to people's bodies and people have to be moved. —Larry Coryell

> [The Beatles] have such a freshness. They approach their thing with just as much finesse and enthusiasm as does John Coltrane. They are "now" and are the greatest. —Larry Coryell

As noted by Bernard Gendron and Theodore Gracyk, a number of constituencies began to take popular music seriously during the 1960s.[41] Not just fans but writers and social critics heard a growing sophistication in rock. As Gendron observes, rock displaced jazz in the dominant cultural hierarchy not by "rising 'higher' than high-cultural music—it is still ranked lower—but by making the latter less culturally relevant where it matters," in the myriad venues where fans, critics, and musicians debated rock aesthetics and otherwise "made [rock music] meaningful."[42] While lyrical content received most of the attention, observers such as Chester Anderson, who noted the correlations between rock and baroque music in a 1967 *San Francisco Oracle* article, were also acknowledging the increasing musical refinement of rock musicians.[43] The Beatles' 1967 release *Sgt. Pepper's Lonely Hearts Club Band* signaled the arrival of the rock concept album—a recording with related compositions, not simply a compilation of hit tunes or a hit tune coupled to filler material. *Sgt. Pepper's* indicated, in fact, the change in rock audiences' tastes from 45 rpm singles to the 33⅓ rpm "long player" or LP. As rock audiences matured, so did the format for production and consumption, which granted musicians the ability to produce more complex works by providing the time for them to develop musical and lyrical themes.

As a corollary, in the same year as *Sgt. Pepper's*, The Pretty Things released a rock opera, *S.F. Sorrow*, predating The Who's more celebrated *Tommy* by a year. These were the activities of serious musicians, unfazed by conventions and music industry dictates for musicians working in the popular music arena. As Paul Williams noted in *Crawdaddy!* as early as 1966, "But one thing has changed over the years, one minor detail: the music has gotten better. So much better, in fact, that there are even people who are beginning to take rock 'n' roll very seriously indeed."[44]

The seriousness with which critics began analyzing rock music can be read in the pages of collections such as the 1969 anthology *The Age of Rock*, which included articles by the classical composer Ned Rorem on the Beatles, H. F. Mooney's *American Quarterly* essay on the shift in popular music tastes from the 1920s to the 1960s, and Ralph Gleason's "Like a Rolling Stone" article for the *American Scholar*. The collection's subtitle, "Sounds of the American Cultural Revolution," indicates the paradigm-shifting possibilities that rock held out for its serious listeners at the time.

In fact, early black rockers such as Ike Turner, Little Richard, Chuck Berry, and a host of New Orleans–style boogie-woogie players such as Fats Domino and Robert "Professor Longhair" Byrd gave early rock 'n' roll its musical language, as well as its sociopolitical temperament, that is, the voicing of black, later teen, rebellion, including the articulation of anti-bourgeois ideas; the complication of black/white binarisms and polarities through an aesthetic of mixing; an enthusiastic, even confrontational, use of volume, rhythmic velocity, and sense of timbral experimentation; and the celebration of the physical and, as it was increasingly marketed and heard as a white genre, the reengagement of the body in white, middle-class social spheres. The acknowledgment by early white rockers such as Elvis Presley, Jerry Lee Lewis, and Carl Perkins of the influence of black musicians or the impact of Hank Williams, Jimmie Rodgers, and country-and-western music on Chuck Berry, Little Richard, and Ellas "Bo Diddley" McDaniel indicate the cross-cultural roots of the music.[45]

Initially, rock 'n' roll had performed a genre-blending aesthetic of its own, appropriating elements from the blues, rhythm and blues, gospel, and country and western before its recognition as a distinctive music idiom enabled rock musicians to begin border crossings of their own (again, these generic designations are used here as shorthand signifiers for broad spectrums of musical creation and consumption). The first rock 'n' roll record is widely credited to a 1951 recording by Jackie Brenston, an African American saxophonist, whose backup band was led by Ike Turner, of a song titled "Rocket 88" at Sam Phillips's Sun Studios.[46] However, rock 'n' roll and rhythm and blues served as audio signs marked "Whites Only" and "Coloreds Only," respectively, in the segregated record shops, radio markets, and corporate divisions throughout the U.S. music industry and the broader American landscape in which it operated. In time the racialized separation of musical genres assumed an authoritative backdrop in musical discussions, affecting the ways audiences and artists perceived particular artists and genres. As *de jure* market segregation transformed into de facto market stratification, the so-called race market morphed into the "rhythm-and-blues" market.

In another sense, however, rock 'n' roll allowed the "crossover" of black music into the mainstream popular music market through white performers. David Brackett describes the legacy of that movement as evidenced by the continuation of the "crossover" phenomenon: "The crossover process functioned much the same [in the 1980s] as it had since the inception of separate charts for 'popular,' 'country and western,' and 'rhythm and blues' in the 1940s. That is, the 'black' chart functioned as a 'testing ground' in relation to the 'Hot 100,' revealing extraordinarily popular songs that might have broad enough appeal to cross over to the mainstream." Moreover, the index for mainstream appeal was partially configured by "the expectations about genres and audiences that circulate between industry employees, writers, musicians and fans have the power to affect the way in which the chart performance, and hence the 'popularity,' of different genres is represented."[47] Barry Shank also interrogated the various meanings for "crossover," from integrative promise to cultural dilution, finally demonstrating that both views may be too limiting owing to the fluidity of both racialized ideologies and musical formations.[48] However, Shank rightly suggests that "crossing over" has the potential to complicate racialized thinking by ensuring that musical meaning is not hijacked by the often racialized notions about musical genres held by audiences who inhabit divergent listening contexts, each creating often radically different interpretations of "what the music means."

But, in fact, rock 'n' roll was aggressively promoted to white teenagers through the recordings and appearances by white performers such as Presley, Lewis, Perkins, Charles "Buddy" Holly, and Johnny Cash, followed by a wave of teen idols such as Pat Boone, Dion DiMucci, and Fabian Forte, who were white surrogates for their black models.[49] Pat Boone's covers of Little Richard and Fats Domino songs were not meant to displace their recordings in African American record players but, rather, were meant to place a "safe" version of black music on white American teenagers' turntables.

Though Chuck Berry and Little Richard crossed the color line by posting hits on the national pop charts, black musicians, by and large, continued to face subordinate conditions in the marketplace.[50] The oft-repeated quote of Sam Phillips claiming he could make a fortune if he were able to find a white singer with a black vocal sensibility resonates here.[51] Indeed, Chuck Berry's extraordinary success in the late 1950s points to the possibility of hearing rock 'n' roll as black music, even as he was explicit about his belief that his ability to use "proper diction" helped him achieve success on the pop (white) charts.[52] Berry's early recognition of the racialization of rock 'n' roll as a white musical genre helps explain his careful cultivation of a de-racinated vocal style on his recordings. His vocal style cloaked his miscege-national threat from white teenagers' parents as he sang directly to adoles-cent sexual desire, rather pointedly in light of his legal problems involving relationships with young, white women.

While few rock scholars would disagree with Greil Marcus's assertion that "most of the first rock 'n' roll styles were variations on black forms that had taken shape before the white audience moved in," Chuck Berry's first na-tional rock 'n' roll hit was a reworked country fiddle tune, "Ida Red," which he renamed "Maybellene."[53] According to Berry's pianist, Jimmy Johnson, a cosmetics article spotted in the studio inspired the new title—perhaps a Maybelline product—further implicating the role of commercial culture on rock 'n' roll. For the record, Berry claims the title came "from a storybook of animals who bore names," including a cow named Maybellene.[54] An early rock 'n' roll style, rockabilly was named in recognition of the close relation-ship between country music and rock 'n' roll. Early rockabilly stars such as Johnny Cash and Jerry Lee Lewis transitioned easily to the country-and-western, or country, genre. Rock 'n' roll's inherent cross-cultural hybridity contributed to white parental fears of cultural miscegenation and the cor-ruption of white middle-class youth. However, much of this anxiety was di-rected toward perceived increases in adolescent insubordination to parental authority, masking the racial undercurrents of their concerns.

Rock musicians in the mid-to-late 1960s performed their own sets of cross-cultural moves, merging a core set of idiomatic musical gestures that defined rock with other musical styles. Rock groups' experiments with other musical genres and traditions radically altered the ways in which rock was conceived and discussed. Psychedelic groups integrated instruments from Asia and Africa for their "innerwordly" explorations, following their use by mainstream pop groups such as the Beatles and the Rolling Stones, while art-rock groups such as Soft Machine, Frank Zappa and the Mothers, Pink Floyd, and Gong were fusing avant-garde art music, rock, and free jazz aesthetics.

As I have mentioned, the Beatles' *Sgt. Pepper's Lonely Hearts Club Band* was a watermark recording that signaled rock musicians' development of a musical aesthetic that, despite incorporating a wide variety of musical traditions, including South Asian, proved popular with mainstream rock audiences and rock critics. The increasing influence of non-Western music in George Harrison's guitar work, in particular, familiarized Western pop music audiences with Indian music sensibilities. The music industry's awareness of how diasporic communities, global-hopping "first world tourists" (even if only from their television sets and Martin Denny recordings), and an emergent sense of a "shrinking" planet (cf. the popularization of Marshall McLuhan's conception of the "global village," increased telecommunication systems, and the growing power of supranational financial and political organizations) formed a considerable new market while enabling new consumptive patterns unfettered by national boundaries, style or genre borders, and even language barriers. The music industry's efforts to mark out this emerging market eased the financial concerns of musicians whose desires to explore non-Western and nonpopular music, including collaborations with non-Western musicians, were energized as well as enticing mainstream pop listeners to accept exotic soundings *as music.*

By 1967 a number of pop musicians were blurring the separation of high art and pop music with, on one hand, bands like the Doors singing Bertolt Brecht and Kurt Weill's "Alabama Song (Whiskey Bar)" on their eponymous 1967 debut recording and, on the other, the Nice performing renditions of Tchaikovsky's *Pathetique* Symphony no. 6 in B Minor. Later, in the 1970s, bands such as Sky, led by the classical guitarist John Williams, would merge jazz, rock, and classical music sensibilities.

In 1966 the Paul Butterfield Blues Band recorded *East-West* (Elektra), in which the title composition was a fusion of South Asian raga and African American blues distilled through a hard rock crucible. There is a live release culled from keyboardist Mark Naftalin's own archival tapes of previously unreleased versions of the piece, which even more clearly reveals the band's integrative musical sensibilities. The guitarist Sandy Bull incorporated non-Western instrumentation such as the *oud* in his recordings of the 1960s. His debut recording, *Fantasias for Guitar & Banjo* (Vanguard 1963), is prescient for many of the musical fusions that would become commonplace within a few years. A talented multi-instrumentalist, Bull performed on a wide variety of instruments (banjo, oud, guitar, mandolin, dulcimer), accompanied on some recordings by the jazz drummer Billy Higgins. His merging of Middle Eastern, blues, gospel, and various folk styles is an underacknowledged early fusion-world recording that remains musically compelling today. I recognize there have been a number of composers in the European concert music tradition who had also been interested in non-Western music, from Béla Bartók's ethnomusicological interest in the music of the Magyar to Henry Cowell's interest in Indonesian gamelan, among others. However, I mean to draw attention to the ways in which musicians who were considered "popular" or "pop" began to draw on the music of non-Western traditions.

Yet rock musicians did not encounter the same resistance from rock critics and audiences as their jazz compatriots. This imbalance has much to do with rock's racialization as a white musical idiom, which essentially left rock music "unmarked." Rock's whiteness figured the genre as a universal musical idiom that, as expressed in the acknowledgment by fans, critics, and musicians of rock's inherent hybridity, was free to roam the world in search of beguiling sounds and musical practices that were denied music that was racialized as a black musical tradition (or Latina/o, or, indeed, any nonwhite cultural or ethnic group). Rock artists have been freer in their ability to appropriate other musical idioms, facing far less critical opprobrium in their musical mixtures than jazz or funk artists, for instance (while I recognize that there are constraints and restrictions to this maneuver, it is rock musicians' freedom relative to jazz musicians that I wish to emphasize; furthermore, rock musicians, like jazz artists of an earlier time, had little to lose and everything to gain by striving for virtuoso status). This was undeniably part of rock's attraction for Tony Williams, as we will see.

Peter Wicke argues that the emergence of rock 'n' roll as a distinct genre occurred within a context of 1950s U.S. youth caught in the contradictions of, on one hand, an educational system bent on producing docile managers and obedient workers for the future and, on the other, a culture industry that promoted individualistic pleasure as a goal in itself. Wicke argues further that the "conservatism of country music on one hand and the rebellious energy of rhythm & blues on the other became the essence of rock 'n' roll," energizing the contradictions of these youths, who witnessed "prosperity and consumption as the essential conditions of a meaningful life, but no longer believing in such a life." Rock 'n' roll "reduced [this contradiction] to a musical formula, expressing both the noisy rebellion and the secret conformity" the youth of the time embodied.[55]

Indeed, rock music steadily displaced other types of music from the "top of the pops," partly as a result of a growing youth audience that had plenty of free time and discretionary income. This age group in the 1960s, made up of the so-called baby boomers, was not the first youth subculture identified by the music industry as a group of potential consumers. An earlier modern mass youth culture came into existence in the so-called jazz age of the 1920s, when an unprecedented number of young people had access to sizable amounts of disposable income and leisure time. The culture industries, accelerating a phenomenon begun during the imperial era, when global trade moved products from the colonized periphery to the cosmopolitan market center, increased the commodification of culture, turning artistic endeavors into products, including music. Even after the ebullient decade of the 1920s, the teenaged bobby soxers of the Depression-era 1930s were targeted by a popular culture industry that realized that the "continually new" was not only available in terms of products but of audiences, as well. There are, of course, significant differences between each teen subculture in terms of specific historical and cultural contexts, but the similarities between them—discretionary income, a commodified form of "teen rebellion," identification with popular culture entertainers, and a desire to mark off a teenage space separate from parent culture and larger social constraints—signaled the growing centrality of popular music's role in forming a recognizable youth identity. The music and mass communications industries interpellated teen audiences with increasing sophistication while contributing to the ways in which youth identity was constituted through consumerist culture.

By the late 1960s, however, rock musicians were reshaping popular music by expressing more than adolescent themes and obsessions in their music—a shift reflected in the increasing use of *rock* as opposed to *rock 'n' roll* as a descriptive term for the music.[56] Additionally, the change from *rock 'n' roll* to *rock* foreshadowed the shift to identity-driven political movements as race, gender, and sexuality displaced the mass movements, such as those protesting the Vietnam War and the coalitional countercultural activities of the late 1960s, which no longer seemed to hold their explanatory or representative power. In fact, despite Nick Bromell's keen observations of rock's utopian sensibilities throughout the late 1960s in *Tomorrow Never Knows*, Bromell fails to recognize the economic inequalities that the racialization of genre enabled among groups of musicians, notwithstanding Hendrix and his white middle-class rock fans.

The changing relationship between racial politics and popular music can be lightly sketched by comparing the 1969 Woodstock festival and the 1972 Wattstax concert. Woodstock was celebrated as a utopian Garden, as Joni Mitchell's song so famously described it, a paradise where Sly and the Family Stone, a funk-rock band in which black musicians and white shared duties across gender lines, embodied the countercultural values of racialized and gendered equality, and Hendrix's diving glissandi and electric screams deconstructed the U.S. national anthem through distortion and feedback, reasserting the song as a countercultural sign. Three years later, Wattstax was a celebration of blackness, a point the filmmaker Mel Stuart emphasized in segments of commentary from ordinary black citizens and Richard Pryor placed between footage of the exclusively black musical acts, punctuated by Isaac Hayes in gold chains symbolizing black oppression in the festival finale. Stuart's film forces us to notice the difference in audience participation for "The Star Spangled Banner" and "Lift Every Voice" at the music festival, underscoring the offstage commentators' disappointment in the continued economic, social, and educational inequality between blacks and whites despite the Civil Rights Act of 1964.

Still, by the mid-1960s rock clearly outsold and out-hyped other forms of popular music. Throughout the period the music industry played a part in forming a growing audience for rock music from a group who might have previously been disposed to jazz, as youthful audiences responded to the transgressive and libidinous energies in rock that their parents had heard in jazz. The construction of a market-driven culture industry dictated (apparently) new forms of (in reality) old products, as Adorno criticized.[57] One of the self-perpetuating effects of the continual renewal of popular music forms was that diverse audiences projected their sense of self onto popular music performers and genre-defining performative gestures, basing their projections on delineations shaped, in part, by the music industry.

Yet by the late 1960s, rock musicians did more than simply sell vast sums of recordings to unsophisticated listeners or represent "teen rebellion." They became spokespeople for a radical youth counterculture advocating serious political and social agendas in more confrontational ways than those articulated by earlier youth subcultures such as the flappers or even the beatniks—groups who seemed less committed to radical social change, at least to the fans of then-underground acid rock bands like the Grateful Dead or mainstream popular bands such as the Rolling Stones. As Ralph J. Gleason would write in 1967, "The most immediate apparent change instituted by the new music [acid rock] is a new way of looking at things. We see it evidenced all around us. The old ways are going and a new set of assumptions is beginning to be worked out. I cannot even begin to codify them. Perhaps it's much too soon to do so. But I think there are some clues—the sacred importance of love and truth and beauty and interpersonal relationships."[58]

This idea of radical social transformation through musical change—as well as the role of the individual, rather than the collective, in such transfiguration—would have a significant impact on early fusion musicians.

Ain't Jazz, Ain't Rock . . .

> Most critics use formal criteria in evaluating music, but you can't discuss the "harmonics of funk." It doesn't apply. You have to evaluate funk on the level of emotions, the projection of emotions, maybe rhythms. We just don't have the terminology to discuss funky music critically. —Herbie Hancock

> Yeah, [playing funk] is hard to do, real hard. —Herbie Hancock

"Playing funky" has long registered the racialized meanings attached to black music. At the beginning of the twentieth century the legendary cornetist Buddy Bolden composed a tune known as "Funky Butt," among other titles, and its suppression by New Orleans police, who, according to the clarinetist Sidney Bechet, "whipped heads" whenever it was performed, indicates the term's volatile signification.[59] Funk, referring to bodily fluids and excretions, was explicit in its evocation of embodied activity, often hypersexualized and racialized—to "get funky," then, was to be overcome with black physicality. Funky was used to describe early jazz, as well as nineteenth-century minstrelsy songs, and the attachment of physical pleasures—dance, sex, and other forms of physical activities—to the music underlined both its transgressive and its nonintellectual purview. The recurrent crises around popular music have some of their roots in the construction of black music as a space of transgression. The devalued position the music genre named funk occupies in dominant music discourse, scholarly and popular, is indicated by the relative paucity of texts devoted to serious discussions of its history, aesthetics, or cultural meanings, particularly in light of the vast and growing amount of literature devoted to Afrodiasporic music in general.[60]

My central point is that funk musicians in the 1970s were partially shaped by the longer histories of "funky music" in the United States and, assisted by the creative possibilities that technology granted them, created an aesthetic that not only renewed ties to an African heritage but also made "cultural moves," to borrow Herman Gray's provocative term for an expansive vision of black cultural production, toward a future free of the various discursive and material constraints they faced at the time. While Gray is primarily concerned with twenty-first-century artists, his argument that "contemporary black cultural politics must get beyond the nostalgic paradigms and moral panics about representation, inclusion, and the threats of technology" motivates this brief look at 1970s funk (and, in fact, guides my concern for situating race in music beyond essentialist celebration or condemnation, broadly speaking).[61] In other words, black funk musicians used funk music to revitalize moribund connections to Africa and preslave pasts while looking to futures beyond contemporaneous conditions of racial discrimination. Indeed, they were active participants in contemporary music-production techniques, freely engaging the technological tools of the time to enhance and extend black histories into an imagined future in which black bodies not only participated in space exploration, for instance, but also imagined space travel as a means to diminish, if not eradicate or reverse, the various meanings *funk* might register in its relationship with blackness.

Most contemporary popular music audiences hear funk as a genre fashioned by James Brown and his band's transformation in the 1960s of earlier rhythm-and-blues shuffle rhythms by placing an emphasis on the first beat (also known as the "downbeat") or, as James Brown expressed it, "the one," as well as maintaining a hyped up backbeat. Drummers, while emphasizing the downbeat, incorporated the square rhythmic underpinning of a rock steady hi-hat against R&B's more swing-oriented backbeat, accentuating funk's polyrhythmic complexity. More important, it was a musical idiom that emphasized polyrhythmic interplay not only between percussion instruments but by organizing the entire musical ensemble—including the electric guitar, organ, horn section, and, the instrument that would come to define much of the sound of 1970s funk, the bass guitar—as a "rhythm machine." Sly and the Family Stone's bassist, Larry Graham, is widely credited with inventing the "slap bass" technique, "slapping" the bass strings with his thumb and "popping" the strings with his fingers to create a percussive sound, supplementing rhythmic value to the melodic and harmonic capabilities of the instrument. There were other influential bassists, such as Bootsy Collins of George Clinton's Parliament-Funkadelic (as we will see later, the fusion bassist Jaco Pastorius dramatically transformed the rhythmic orientation of this technique by using it thematically, as well).

By the 1970s, funk was a musical genre created by, marketed to, and popular with an urban African American audience, sounding out the social realities brought by urban "renewal," white flight to the suburbs, and the political sensibilities that emerged in an increasingly pessimistic post–civil rights era. Funk musicians played with urban African American codings and interacted ironically with dominant understandings of black urban experience. However, I want to avoid reducing funk's politics to what Matthew

Brown terms "politics at the gestural level" and rendering its aesthetic dimension as little more than a shout-out to its advanced polyrhythms or its seductive charms as a "groove" music.[62]

To be sure, funk, like jazz or the blues before it, was marked by the primitivist and hypersexualized meanings attached to black cultural life by dominant white readings. Importantly, though, funk remained distinct from jazz by refusing to attenuate those readings by reducing or obscuring the blackness of the music's sonic or discursive signifiers in order to achieve mainstream cultural legitimization. Rickey Vincent cogently describes funk as "an aesthetic of deliberate confusion, of uninhibited, soulful behavior that remains viable because of a faith in instinct, a joy of self, and a joy of life, particularly unassimilated black American life."[63] Indeed, funk musicians foregrounded difference through displays of black flesh on record covers and advertising posters, by embracing black sexuality and physical pleasure, and by otherwise celebrating the black urban experience while critiquing structural and systemic modes of oppression. Gina Dent argues that black pleasure as expressed through and by black music engages a political stance in which black bodies mobilize a counternarrative to those of victimization and humiliation.[64] In this light, "gettin' down" and "gettin' it on" were more than salacious calls for sexual play but functioned as entreaties for the vitalization of a black politics through an engagement of black aesthetics. Being funky was a political as well as aesthetic decision, as James Brown's "Say It Loud (I'm Black and I'm Proud)" testified in 1968.[65]

Vincent argues that funk music was "the successor to the soul music of the 1960s in terms of its representations of popular black values—particularly those ideals of social, spiritual, and political redemption."[66] Vincent explains that as the optimism of the 1960s civil rights movement decreased in the 1970s across black communities and political groups throughout the United States, the cheerful, upbeat sounds of soul music were displaced by the harder-edged sounds of funk. Brian Ward supports Vincent's assertions by detailing the ways in which the move from soul music to funk occurred in a historical context in which the liberal promises of black integration after the passage of the Civil Rights Act of 1964 were increasingly dashed by continued educational, employment, and housing inequities between whites and blacks in the United States.[67] As James Brown exhorted audiences in 1974, "People, we got to get over before we go under," further advising them to "turn on your funk motor, get down and praise the Lord, get sexy, sexy, get funky and dance," advocating a politics of funk, if you will, in a period of economic "stagflation" linking economic empowerment to a black erotics.

Musically, funk bands such as the Bar-Kays, ConFunkShun, Lakeside, Cameo, and Kool and the Gang moved black popular music away from mainstream notions of consonant harmonic and melodic elements and toward the gritty, even "greasy," sounds of 1970s urban black life as announced by the band Tower of Power on its 1970 debut recording, *East Bay Grease*. It is no coincidence that soul music parlayed a strong connection to gospel into a commercial idiom that sounded more conciliatory to integrative desires than to the black nationalist ideals of the black power movement lauded in funk anthems such as the Isley Brothers' "Fight the Power."

Yet, like jazz and rock before it, funk's hybrid roots were obscured by its rhetorical positioning within a given racialized culture. While funk was mobilized in various popular culture forms that highlighted black difference—notably in the so-called blaxploitation films of the era—it was a form influenced by, and influencing in its own turn, musical worlds beyond its nominative home culture. In fact, Vincent spends considerable space on Jimi Hendrix and other black rock musicians in his book, signaling the cross-genre nature of 1970s funk. As George Clinton of Parliament-Funkadelic fame admitted, "The Beatles are my all time favorites," and, like Tony Williams, he admired Detroit's hard rock band the MC5, in addition to contemporary "prog rock" bands such as Yes and Emerson, Lake and Palmer.[68] It was not only that white musicians could "bring the funk" but also that groups such as the Beatles and other progressive rock bands hipped black funksters to the pleasures of psychedelia and the possibilities recording technology and the performance equipment used by rock bands enabled. Funkadelic Billy "Bass" Nelson admits that having to borrow the Marshall stacks and fiberglass drums of the white funk-rock band Vanilla Fudge, when Funkadelic's equipment failed to arrive for a gig opposite them, persuaded the band to change "from rhythm and blues, Motown wannabes into what we evolved into: the real Funkadelic."[69] Beyond mere instrumentation, George Clinton and his P-Funk amalgamation played with the sonic and mind-warping possibilities of the studio, and the sound of funk for many bands was a noticeably sophisticated blend of technological and rhythmic acuity.

The music by groups and artists such as Sly and the Family Stone; Stevie Wonder; George Clinton's Parliament-Funkadelic; Earth, Wind, and Fire; the Bar-Kays; and the Ohio Players circulated as musical and figurative manifestations of an Afrodiasporic tradition that was not simply historical but a vital part of the contemporary soundscape. Musically, while funk bands emphasized the fundamental James Brown rhythmic vamps that formed the foundation for complex overlayings of polyrhythms and melodic material, like their rock counterparts they developed individualized sounds through a careful manipulation of electronic instrumentation and gear, fetishizing specific instruments, playback, and recording systems, as the often extensive equipment listings on recordings of the time attest.

As post–civil rights era hopes were challenged by continued structural oppression and racist policies in the United States, funk musicians looked to Africa as an imagined repository of black cultural authorization but gave it a sounding out that used the latest studio and playback technologies. While instruments such as *mbiras* and *djembe* drums, as well as the wearing of *dashikis*, demonstrated the connections to Africa felt by funk artists and their audiences, even if in primarily imagined expressions, traditional instrumentation was buttressed by their creative interplay with technology, using speaker systems, effects processing, and mixing options to produce music that would have been unrealizable without the electronic gadgetry. These emerging musical practices, including the use of Afrocentric artwork and fashion in promotional photographs, album artwork, and live performances, supported these young musicians' desires to reconnect with working-class black communities through a fashionable blend of black pride and musical technique.

It is no coincidence, then, that a strong element of *avant la lettre* Afrofuturism was prevalent in funk. Egyptian iconography vied with stylized space suits, and pyramids served as backdrops to hovering spaceships in the stage spectacles of live performances and album covers. *Afrofuturism* is a term used to describe a number of African American artists, writers, filmmakers, and musicians, whose works complicate and comment on blackness through the engagement of science, technology, and, often, science fiction literature and iconography.[70] As Matthew Brown argues, "Nineteen-seventies frustrations led to more mediated beliefs in this homeland; rather than a nationalism that pointed either to Africa or to a secure community in the U.S., Funkadelic album cover art on *One Nation under a Groove* (1978) presents 'Afro-nauts' leaving earth and colonizing outer space."[71] Accordingly, Clinton's evocation of a Mothership connection to the Parliament-Funkadelic aggregation played on science fiction imaginings, while other groups, including the Bar-Kays; Earth, Wind and Fire; and the Commodores, performed in space-age costumes. Even Marvin Gaye released a 1978 single, *A Funky Space Reincarnation*, which effectively linked science fiction themes within a funky, streetwise perspective. Drawing on African imagery and futuristic science fiction imaginings for their album covers and stage shows, many funk bands imagined a "funky" black presence that projected Afrocentric cultural values into a technological future.

Yet, while funk allowed black musicians to claim a connection to Africa—even if only to an imaginary, fantastic Africa—and was used to broadcast Afrocentric political views, nonblack musicians are an important part of its history. The white guitarist Joe Medina was a member of the so-called Funk Brothers, the name given to a group of studio musicians used by Motown, playing a seminal role in the constitution of the label's mainstream commercial style of black music. Sly and the Family Stone, heralded as one of funk's founding bands, featured an interracial membership, and the success with black audiences experienced by white funk groups such as the Average White Band, whose very name played on the racialized assumptions of genre, was evidence of the cross-cultural legacy of funk. Tower of Power was founded by the saxophonists Emilio Castillo and Stephen Kupka, neither of whom are African American but whose band became one of the more successful funk bands of the era.

This proto-Afrofuturist turn to outer space and science fiction was not restricted to funk musicians of the 1970s. The fusion drummer Lenny Williams produced a number of science fiction–inspired recordings, including the concept album *The Adventures of the Astral Pirates* (Elektra 1978), and during his most well-known fusion association with Return to Forever, he and his fellow band members had also turned to science fiction for inspiration. Even earlier, the jazz musician Sun Ra based his own cosmology on a number of themes that would be taken up by Afrofuturists, predating the term and its ideological formation in the 1990s. Hip-hop artist Afrika Bambaata espoused a similar theme of global and extraworldly universalism that included a technologically based utopianism. These proto-Afrofuturist approaches shared a desire to position black bodies within discourses of African cultural legacies, as well as to articulate desires for a place in the future as represented in space exploration, computerized networks, and technological advances writ large. As I will detail later, Herbie Hancock engaged these ideas in his fusion music of the 1970s, intentionally confronting the broken middles among race, genre, and technology.

As I have noted, although *funk* may refer to a particular musical genre developed in the late 1960s, *funky* has long been used to describe various black musics, including jazz. The use of *funky* within jazz is often traced to its use to describe the pianist Horace Silver and the hard bop movement in which he was first recognized. To give some sense of the relationship hard bop shares with fusion, including both styles' evocation of "funk," let us backtrack momentarily to the beginnings of bebop. While big band swing ensembles were giving way to jump blues, at least on black jukeboxes in the late 1940s, what was to become known as bebop was being created by young jazz musicians, motivated in part by the same reason fusion musicians would list a quarter of a century later: a creative urge to revitalize a form of music that had grown moribund and overly commercial (at least, to their ears) but to which they still felt a strong connection. As bebop grew beyond musicians' jam sessions, its audience, like the earlier "hot" jazz aficionados, seemed more interested in the transgressive social aspects of the music rather than an enrichment or deep appreciation of jazz culture.[72] In reaction, as bebop became integrated into the mainstream of jazz—indeed, as it arguably became the lingua franca of mainstream jazz—a number of jazz artists turned away from the intellectualizations of bebop toward a jazz that was oriented, once again, to black dance floors.[73] David Rosenthal described the predicament many jazz musicians faced in the 1950s: "The problem in the early fifties was: where do we go from here? Bebop, which had begun as a promise of freedom, had turned into something of a straitjacket, an increasingly codified form of expression. . . . R&B might be a source of new ideas, but it was too limited to satisfy jazz musicians as a regular context."[74]

Many hard bop artists—including Sonny Stitt, Jackie McLean, and John Coltrane—had, in fact, first performed professionally in rhythm-and-blues acts. In contrast to bebop musicians' self-conscious alignments with fine art and their public disdain for commercial considerations, which, as Scott DeVeaux argues in The Making of Bebop, were part of their own mythologizing project, hard bop musicians often performed in both rhythm-and-blues and hard bop jazz groups. Jackie McLean, a self-described bebopper, speaks to the illusory limits of genres: "I played in rhythm and blues bands when I went to North Carolina in 1953 to try to go to school again, and I stayed down there for a year, and yeah, it helped me. It influenced me. . . . I certainly, myself, thought along heavy blues lines, blues feeling, and my concept of it, so I just think it had more of a gospel feeling to it, a sanctified feeling to it mixed with all the other ingredients that Bird [Charlie Parker, bebop alto saxophonist], Bud [Powell, bebop pianist], Thelonious [Monk, bebop pianist] gave us."[75]

Artists such as Horace Silver, Eddie Harris, Jack McDuff, Jimmy Smith, and Lou Donaldson responded to bebop's intellectualism and increasingly rigid codification by creating an instrumental body-oriented jazz that emphasized danceable rhythms. Their blues- and gospel-based melodic and harmonic material was linked to a conscious desire to redirect jazz back toward black audiences, who were seen as abandoning jazz for the pleasures of rhythm and blues. Hard boppers blended the roots of African American musical idioms—the blues, work songs, and gospel, in particular—with bebop's improvisational innovations.[76]

This self-conscious return to the African American roots of jazz music was marked by performative displays of blackness. Hard boppers' "funkiness" was expressed musically by quoting black gospel and spiritual elements along with a renewed interest in blues forms. I do not mean to suggest that bebop musicians abandoned the blues. Bebop musicians did, in fact, manipulate the blues, complexifying the form through the use of, among other things, substitute harmonies and rhythmic displacements. I do mean to suggest, however, that hard bop musicians engaged a more "roots"-oriented approach to the blues. Eric Porter notes that "many be-boppers saw the blues as a symbol of the limitations placed on them as musicians and as African Americans . . . symboliz[ing] both the primitivist expectations of a white audience and the demands of a culture industry that wanted to pigeonhole black music."[77] By contrast, hard boppers openly flaunted their blues orientation by emphasizing, for example, short, rhythmic riffs, rather than long, complex lines, and a danceable backbeat rather than the rhythmic displacements of bebop drummers. Hard bop musicians also strayed from bebop's subversion of popular song harmonies, choosing instead to play on modal and pentatonic harmonic structures.

Songs like Bobby Timmons's "Moanin'" and Nat Adderley's "Work Song" were typical hard bop reengagements of earlier black music traditions. While bebop musicians marked out a space for African American high cultural status, hard bop musicians thumbed their noses at such pretense. Deplored by middle-class blacks interested in political and economic uplift, hard bop musicians' use of black slang was their means of demarcating "soulfulness" and the authenticity of hard bop's roots. Using black vernacular in titles such as "Moanin'," "Strollin'," "Pentecostal Feelin'," "Dat Dere," and "Messin' Around" was a way to actively reengage working-class African American culture, explicitly coding black vernacular speech as a signifying ground on which their music was created, performed, and heard. As a generic marker, hard bop was also less parochial than other jazz styles, encompassing everything from the funky "soul jazz" organ trios of Jimmy Smith and Jack McDuff to the more mainstream jazz bands of Art Blakey's Jazz Messengers and the 1950s Miles Davis groups.[78]

But, like many popular jazz styles, hard bop was met with critical opprobrium. In his essay "The Funky-Hard Bop Regression" Martin Williams wrote, "The gradual dominance of the Eastern and then national scene in jazz by the so-called 'hard bop' and 'funky' school has shocked many commentators and listeners. The movement has been called regressive, self-conscious, monotonous, and even contrived."[79] Contrary to critical efforts to foreground hard bop's commercial success as a means to dismiss the style, the music was embraced by some in the black community as a way of affirming black political empowerment. In the words of a Harlem record storeowner, "I think most of that soul music is now being manufactured rather than felt but at least this is one time in jazz history when the Negroes are popularizing their own music. It would take a lot of courage for Stan Kenton or Shorty Rogers [both white jazz musicians] to call one of their albums *The Soul Brothers*."[80] Although hard bop hits like Lee Morgan's "Sidewinder" (1963) and Herbie Hancock's "Watermelon Man" (1962) helped keep jazz in the popular mainstream, however, the politics of dance and the body failed to register with dominant critical discourse as little more than lightweight entertainment. The dance club and mass popularity, for all its valorization in big band swing discourse, engendered very little prestige elsewhere in much of the mainstream jazz criticism of the postwar period.

Like hard bop, funk music was antithetical to middle-class black aspirations. It represented the same move "backward" in its celebration of black physicality that a black politics of uplift had continually struggled against in a variety of popular culture forms, from minstrelsy in the nineteenth century through the use of jazz as a space of (white) transgression. This debate took a slightly different tangent in the 1960s, when critics such as Amiri Baraka decried the antagonisms the black bourgeoisie felt toward the blues at the time. The issue of black representation in popular music remained a volatile issue within the black community in the 1970s. The funk diva Betty Davis, at one time married to Miles Davis, had her concerts boycotted by black religious organizations and the National Association for the Advancement of Colored People (NAACP) publicly denounced her single, "If I'm in Luck I Might Get Picked Up," from her 1973 debut album.[81] Yet, as Scot Brown notes in his study of the Dayton, Ohio, music scene that spawned the seminal funk band Ohio Players, funk music's formation was largely the result of the increased economic resources of working-class blacks throughout the 1960s: "The availability of relatively high-wage working class jobs in

Dayton, from the World War II era through the early 1970s, gave families resources to purchase instruments, vehicles for transportation, and sound equipment."[82] The distinction between African American middle-class and working-class aspirations of the era is seen in the ways jazz moved toward the symphony hall while funk remained decidedly popular and populist in its appeal. I want to draw attention, however, to the fact that, like earlier blues, rhythm-and-blues, and hard bop musicians (and unlike, say, black minstrels and vaudevillians), a career in funk music held out the promise of upward social mobility from the working class while still acknowledging, even honoring, those roots.

This upward mobility came at a price, however. The simultaneous commercial success with mainstream audiences of the film *Shaft* (1971) and Isaac Hayes's soundtrack cemented the relationship between funk music and representations of "the street." This link between sound and image has continued to provide the U.S. popular imaginary with authenticating tropes of black urban grittiness represented through a black hypersexual and violent pathology—all supported by a funky backbeat, syncopated wah-wah rhythm guitar, and aggressive bass lines (its continuing resonance is witnessed by the fact that funk has not yet been entirely displaced by hip-hop or rap in movie or television soundtracks as a sonic signifier of a particular kind of urban, "street" blackness). Yet films such as *Shaft* also resonated with black audiences, who read these films as affirmations of black (male) superiority and power against (white) oppression. Through their relationship to these films, their images and their narrative thrust, funk music provided a rich intertextual linkage, reinforcing not only funk's blackness but also its confluence with the black power ideological currents of the era.

To return to fusion: Herbie Hancock was explicit about the division between older, jazz-oriented understandings of *funky* and more contemporaneous ideas about the term, declaring, "Well, [Horace Silver performed] some of the first funky piano playing, though it's applied towards a jazz sound in the rhythm section. That kind of playing overlaps what I'm talking about, but they're not the same thing. Horace is within the jazz framework, and I'm closer to the R&B framework. There's a stylistic difference, even though there's a common ground."[83] Hancock underlined rhythm's fundamental place in understanding funk, declaring, "There's another reason for my present style: I haven't found a way to do more advanced things harmonically without losing the funkiness of it. That's why I don't like a lot of jazz/rock fusion music. They lose the funkiness because they put more emphasis on harmony than rhythm."[84] As Hancock also notes, while there are shared elements among the various kinds of musical funkiness, there are distinctions in kind, as well. For example, as I have mentioned, similar to their peers in the rock world, funk musicians were also exploring and utilizing the latest studio technology. Additionally, where rhythm and blues was built around star vocalists backed by anonymous studio bands, funk musicians were more likely to be members of self-contained bands, performing and recording songs they composed and arranged themselves—similar, again, to the rock bands of the era.

I want to conclude my admittedly too-brief look at funk to suggest that privileging "the one" can be conceived of as more than a call to a particular musical groove. Looking at the 1970s helps us consider the ways in which funk musicians—jazz, pop, or otherwise—transformed the meanings blackness registered in the popular imaginary through their reconceptions and performances of an aesthetic that recognized and paid tribute to Afrodiasporic connections at a time when black sociopolitical movements were challenging the subordinate, even degraded, status of blackness itself. As Tony Bolden notes, "James Brown's 1972 hit single 'Make It Funky' codified a clarion call within a wide spectrum of black (organic) artists and intellectuals, just as Duke Ellington had theorized self-reflexively in his 1932 recording of 'It Don't Mean a Thing (If It Ain't Got That Swing).'"[85] Importantly, funk musicians reached out beyond the borders of the United States—indeed, of the planet—as a means to locate their music and aesthetics within a broader space than allowed by the commercial genre considerations dictated by historically racist music industry practices. In this light James Brown's call to "hit on the one" also points to the connections among Afrodiasporic musical practices, a unified yet dispersed and diverse grouping of musical traditions that ranges from BaBenzélé hunting songs to Pentecostal gospel, through Brazilian samba and Puerto Rican plena, as well as can be heard in Trinidad and Tobago's soca and Jamaican reggae. As Radano argues in *Lying Up a Nation*, black music, as a category, was constructed out of a complex set of possibilities, arriving at the end of a long discursive trail marking the distinctions between white and nonwhite musical traditions, particularly as demarcated in the "new world" of chattel slavery of African-descended peoples.[86] Pointedly, Brown's calls emphasizing "the one" speaks to the multiple historic and aesthetic connections among the widely scattered musical cultures created by blacks in contact with other cultures and out of which Brown, Stone, Clinton, and other funk musicians performed and celebrated.

three

Well, just the notion of a folk singer flirting with jazz is seen as presumptuous rather than someone enthusiastically exploring her potential. — **Joni Mitchell**

[The] problem is to take the knowledge of progressive pop writing and apply it to this old form. — **Joni Mitchell**

Since fusion was, by and large, created by young jazz and rock musicians seeking various musical and aesthetic ends, I want to spend a little time thinking about the age-oriented dimension to genre and its contribution to the antagonisms and misunderstandings faced by fusion musicians from their critics and the music industry. Age was a volatile signifier in the late 1960s and 1970s. *The generation gap* was a phrase that was coined during this period and indicated the intensely felt distance between the so-called baby boomers and their parents. In this context, as jazz began achieving high cultural status, it became increasingly associated with a middle-aged, middle-class audience positioned in antagonistic opposition to the youth of the time, especially those involved in the countercultural and socially progressive movements of the era.

Richard Merton, in his comment on Alan Beckett's analysis of the Rolling Stones, in the pages of the *New Left Review* in 1969, captured the sense of the times:

> The reason why an appraisal of the [Rolling Stones] has some importance is this. Britain today is a society stifling for lack of any art that expresses the experience of living in it. Our theatre is a quaint anachronism, our novel is dead, and our cinema a mere obituary of it. Perhaps the only art form which has an authentic expressive vitality in England is pop music. It at least reflects back to us the immediate constituents of experience, even when it does not illuminate them. It is no accident

that it is the one product of contemporary British culture which has any international currency.[1]

Rock was alive, the "art that expresses the experience of living." Jazz, on the other hand, by joining itself to high culture, was thought of as a "quaint anachronism" by the youth of the time. Or, as Christopher Sandford, the biographer for Keith Richards of the Rolling Stones, enthused, "To a generation starved of its own music and force fed trad [jazz], the [Rolling] Stones were manna."[2] This sense of an old world falling away and a new one being born was prevalent in the late 1960s, and fusion was one manifestation of the "new world" that many in the counterculture believed was just around the corner.

In a similar sense Miles Davis was well aware of the relation between age and genre that limited musicians and their ability to connect to particular audiences. While jazz had once offered him the chance to position himself as an artist, by the late 1960s he felt the need for creative change. However, his music career still functioned within a commercial system that confined his talents to already-attained glories. More pointedly, Davis saw fusion as a way to cut across generational as well as racial borders: "It was with *On the Corner* [1972] and *Big Fun* [1969–72] that I really made an effort to get my music over to young black people. They are the ones who buy records and come to concerts, and I started thinking about building a new audience for the future. I already had gotten a lot of young white people coming to my concerts after *Bitches Brew* and so I thought it would be good if I could get all these young people together listening to my music and digging the groove."[3]

While Davis's concern for "building an audience for the future" may have had economic, as well as aesthetic, impetus, he also argued here that his music was a way to "get all these young people together." Davis's effort to accomplish this, however, was hampered by his record label. He details how Columbia misrepresented his creative work as jazz instead of the "new music" he was creating for young black listeners:

> Columbia released *On the Corner* in 1972, but they didn't push it, so it didn't do as well as we all thought it would. *The music was meant to be heard by young black people, but they just treated it like any other jazz album and advertised it that way, pushed it on the jazz radio stations. Young black kids don't listen to those stations; they listen to R&B stations and some rock stations. Columbia marketed it for them old-time jazz people who

couldn't get into what I was doing now in the first place. It was just a waste of time playing it for them; they wanted to hear my old music that I wasn't playing anymore. So they didn't like On the Corner, but I didn't expect that they would; it wasn't made for them.[4]

The disparity between Davis's intent and Columbia's marketing speaks to the broken middle that fusion music inhabits. While Davis explicitly created music that would appeal to black youth and was no longer interested in appealing to "them old-time jazz people," Columbia, locked into its perception of Davis as a jazz musician, proved unable or unwilling to reconceptualize the marketing of his music. Davis defended his choice to fuse various musical idioms by pointing to the openness of a younger generation of listeners: "The kids, they are so great—they can dig what we're giving them. The rest of the people give them shit. They give them the same old fucking thing to be comfortable. That's the reason we're playing, not to be pop stars. . . . I haven't sold out to the fucking kids. I don't sell out to nobody."[5] Davis was not simply being polemical or provocative—he put his money on the table. In 1971 Davis phoned his agent, Jack Whittemore, from Paris and ordered Whittemore to take half of Davis's performance fee for the Philharmonic Hall in New York City and purchase tickets. He then instructed Whittemore to distribute those tickets for free to young black people who could not otherwise afford them.[6]

Davis's stance underscored some fusion musicians' insistence that fusion was a new idiom, distinct from jazz. Leonard Feather discerned the challenge fusion represented to musical categories, noting how Davis was "creating a new and more complex form, drawing from the avant-garde, atonalism, modality, rock, jazz and the universe. It has no name, but some listeners have called it 'Space Music.'"[7] While Betty Mabry opened Davis's ears up to rock music (or pop music as Davis called it, insisting that "rock is a white man's word," explicitly recognizing the racial politics of genre naming),[8] Davis was defiant in his move toward the popular music of the day, declaring, "The critics were getting on my nerves, saying that I had lost it, that I wanted to be young, that I didn't know what I was doing, that I wanted to be like Jimi Hendrix, or Sly Stone, or James Brown."[9] Davis and his younger musical colleagues such as the guitarist Larry Coryell and the vibraphonist Gary Burton did not want to merely imitate popular musicians but were actively creating a "new music" that borrowed elements from a variety of artists and traditions.

Ironically, fusion was, on the one hand, largely a concern for jazz partici-pants and observers even though they largely denied its value or any valid connection to "real jazz." On the other hand, despite rock and funk crit-ics and musicians' interest in augmenting commercial success with the high cultural cachet jazz might bestow, the largely instrumental output of fusion bands remained outside the tastes of rock's and funk's mass audi-ences, which overwhelmingly favored vocal music. With the notable excep-tion of successful crossover recordings such as Miles Davis's *Bitches Brew*, Mahavishnu Orchestra's *The Inner Mounting Flame*, and Herbie Hancock's *Head Hunters* (with implications that will be considered more deeply below), rock and funk writers were far less interested in following this "ain't jazz, ain't rock" music, as their virtual silence during this period regarding Joni Mitchell attests. However, just to be clear, despite my spending consider-able time in the text considering the relationship of these musicians to jazz discourse, their inclusion into a jazz history is not my primary concern. In-deed, as DeVeaux notes, "With the possible exception of those in the fusion camp (who are more often the targets of the debate than active participants in it), no one disputes the official version of the history. Its basic narrative shape and its value for a music that is routinely denied respect and institu-tional support are accepted virtually without question."[10]

While it is arguable that no one except fusion musicians and listeners "disputes the official version" of jazz history, my interest continues to be in thinking through the way fusion music sounded out the broken middle, per-forming the endless possibilities of variation and mixture between genres and testing the limits of their artistic engagements against the assumptions and expectations of fans and critics. Though fusion is now seen as one of the more commercially driven of jazz's substyles, most of the early fusion groups remained unknown and largely unheard outside of private jam ses-sions and infrequent live performances. "Commercial success" was hardly a phrase one would use to describe early fusion bands from the mid-1960s until 1970, with the release of Miles Davis's *Bitches Brew*. But partially be-cause of the commercial success of *Bitches Brew*, the stigma of commercial-ism attached itself to fusion quickly and decisively. Indeed, Leonard Feather saw the arrival of fusion as the epitome of commercial interests dominating artistic ones at the time. "If the year 1970 is remembered in connection with any outstanding event in the history of jazz," wrote Feather, "musicologists may recall it as the Year of the Whores. Never before, no matter how grievous the economic woes of jazz musicians . . . at any prior point in jazz time, did so many do so little in an attempt to earn so much."[11]

Even so, fusion was hardly mainstream popular music in the 1970s, and apart from a handful of bands, fusion musicians never achieved mass audience recognition, much less acceptance, and posted fairly modest material gains, for the most part, compared to other genres of popular music. While it is true that Herbie Hancock's *Head Hunters* (1973) was awarded platinum status (sales of a million units), Jeff Beck's *Blow by Blow* (1975) and *Wired* (1976) each exceeded the two million unit mark, and, as Annette Carson asserts, "until Kenny G appeared on the scene, [Beck's recordings] represented the highest charting instrumental albums ever recorded."[12] Yet because Beck is seen primarily as a rock guitarist, his work is often overlooked as fusion performances even though both recordings featured all-instrumental programs, including Stevie Wonder's paean to Thelonious Monk, titled simply "Thelonious," and Charles Mingus's "Goodbye Pork Pie Hat."[13]

Still, it is meaningful that musicians such as Hancock, Beck, Davis, and McLaughlin—musicians who gained the most economically during this period through their association with fusion—were fairly singular in terms of achieving financial success and that their marketplace achievements were overshadowed by rock and pop music stars of the period. We should also remember that the more successful bands, such as Blood, Sweat & Tears or Chicago, featured vocals and, perhaps because of their success in the mainstream popular music market, would eventually be thought of more as rock bands than as jazz or fusion bands.

In fact, part of jazz musicians' antipathy toward rock was a result of the huge largesse given by record labels to the rock stars of the era. The 1970s was a time of unprecedented music industry profits, and rock stars were among the most visible beneficiaries of the growing monopolization of the industry.[14] As rock music nudged other types of popular music aside, jazz musicians and listeners were left wondering why the music they believed was superior was beleaguered by attacks of irrelevance and highhandedness. In truth instrumental jazz had never really been popular after the Second World War except, perhaps, for the funky organ trios of soul jazz (and they rarely made the mainstream pop charts) and had, since bebop's heady days of the late 1940s and early 1950s, been increasingly seen as culturally significant but commercially irrelevant by music industry insiders, as well as general audiences.

Another reason we may remain skeptical about fusion's purported economic incentive is that many early fusion musicians incorporated avant-garde techniques borrowed from European art music—an unlikely strategy for commercial success. And even when fusion became an "above ground" success with the release of Miles Davis's *Bitches Brew* in 1970 and, even more evidently, with the release of Mahavishnu Orchestra's *Inner Mounting Flame* a year later, fusion recordings' combined revenue gains for the music industry were relatively insignificant in comparison to the sales numbers for rock, funk, and top-forty acts. Many of the biggest fusion bands in the 1970s, including Mahavishnu Orchestra, Weather Report, and Return to Forever, while signed to major international record labels, built audiences the "old-fashioned way," through live performances in a variety of rock and jazz venues.[15]

Yet even if one wanted to insist on fusion's overall commercial success vis-à-vis mainstream jazz as a reason to exclude fusion from serious consideration in the official history of jazz, a quick comparison with earlier jazz history quickly disposes of the charge that commercial success automatically spoils the artistic value for a style as a whole (again, if one thinks of fusion as a jazz substyle, even if tangential to a central core set of practices and aesthetics). For example, big band swing's market dominance for a period did not exclude it from becoming part of the jazz mainstream (except, of course, to moldy figs) and, in fact, played a major role in transforming jazz music from a vernacular or "merely" popular musical style into a sophisticated, even urbane, musical idiom, worthy of serious critical evaluation. Stuart Nicholson makes an important point when he argues that while swing was a commercially successful style of jazz, jazz scholars have focused their attention on artists such as Duke Ellington or Benny Goodman without Ellington's or Goodman's creative work being negatively affected by their association with other big band leaders who are seen as the era's lesser lights, such as Guy Lombardo or Kay Kyser.[16]

Swing masters such as Ellington, Basie, or Lester Young operate on a completely different discursive level from Lombardo or Kyser—a level, no matter how famous or popular, as Lombardo and Kyser undoubtedly were, either could hope to attain. Bebop musicians may enjoy the prestige of being part of a process to raise jazz to an art form in the late 1940s, but it should also be remembered that John Hammond began producing a series of "Spirituals to Swing" Carnegie Hall concerts in 1938; and serious jazz criticism was a part of the jazz scene by the mid-1930s, when Hugues Panassié wrote *Le jazz hot*. Bandleader Paul Whiteman's efforts to make "a lady out of jazz" occurred in the 1920s, two decades before beboppers began deconstructing "rhythm changes," and even Norman Granz's Jazz at the Philharmonic series, which began in the bebop era, formed ensembles from jazz musicians of various eras and styles for its "public jam session" format. Yet through every era, despite its commercial use in Hollywood soundtracks or in the accompaniment to pop singers such as Frank Sinatra, jazz steadily moved up the cultural ladder.

However, even as Nicholson correctly argues that "[fusion] realigned jazz alongside popular culture, a position it has historically strayed from at its peril," fusion remained an "ain't jazz" music.[17] Yet this matters only if one insists on aligning fusion with jazz. As I have noted, free jazz musicians and increasingly mainstream jazz ones, as well, were relying on the patronage of elite and professional-class audiences and institutions as a consequence of jazz music's moves away from the social milieu in which it had grown and gained mass popularity. For many jazz artists this meant moving from mass white audiences to elite institutions for support. However, from the viewpoint of rock musicians and listeners, fusion aligned rock with the posturing airs of jazz, threatening to transform rock from an "electric folk music"—a voice of "the people"—into an arty, even pretentious, idiom. Listeners who privileged rock's physicality and libidinous energies bemoaned rock musicians' growing affectations as pretense and feared the loss of authenticity. But there were also large numbers of rock listeners who welcomed the growing sophistication—as long as the connection to earthier sensibilities were not severed to accomplish it. In 1969 Oxford University Press published *The Story of Rock*, a defense of rock as "folk art (as opposed to fine art)," by Carl Belz, a professor of art history at Brandeis University. Jon Carroll, writing a review of the book for *Rolling Stone*, sounded remarkably like his peers in the jazz world with his confession: "Personally, I remain unconvinced that rock should strive to be fine art, although the increasing self-consciousness of the musicians may make it inevitable. It is our last spontaneous art: it would be a shame to lose it, whatever the aesthetic benefits."[18]

Nicholson detailed the range of music found in the rich oeuvre of the influential fusion band Weather Report: "Despite being routinely described as a 'jazz-rock' band, their stylistic outlook was extremely broad, perhaps the most inclusive in jazz. Their range extended from classical influences such as the French impressionists to free jazz, from World music to bebop, from big-band music to chamber music, from collective improvisation to tightly written formal structures with no apparent meter to straight-ahead swing."[19]

While Weather Report is singled out here, active involvement in blending various musical idioms was a primary marker of fusion bands. Weather Report's musical juxtapositions exemplified the eclectic aesthetic of fusion bands, transforming the various musical cultures as they were brought into contact with one another. Tellingly, Nicholson does not mention rock, funk, or the active use of electronics the group also employed, perhaps seeking, instead, to justify Weather Report by association with "legitimate" genres and implicitly speaking to the devalued status of nonjazz popular music. In truth, as the cofounder and keyboardist for Weather Report, Josef Zawinul, insisted, "I'm not a great fan of rock 'n' roll. Never was. But I like one thing about rock 'n' roll, man, and this is the fire and the energy. And I think that's what was missing in the jazz of the followers."[20] Zawinul clearly saw himself and his fellow fusion musicians as pathfinders who were capable of injecting passion back into jazz distinct from the energetic experiments of free jazz, aligned as fusion musicians were with the tastes of young popular music audiences.

The music critic Francis Davis asked pointedly in the 1980s, "Is [Miles] Davis admirable, as his apologists would have it, for refusing to rest on his laurels—for keeping up with the latest black musical and sartorial fashions? Or is there something pathetic about the sight of a sixty-three-year-old man in clogs, parachute pants, and jheri curls shaking his fanny to a younger generation's beat?"[21] Like many jazz critics who criticized Miles Davis for his "electric turn," Francis Davis placed much of the blame on the trumpeter's seduction by a corrosive youth culture. However, Miles Davis taught the bassist and producer Marcus Miller that musicians have to learn to trust their own aesthetic instincts because critics "only know what you've already done; they have no idea of your goals."[22] Miles discussed his aesthetics of continuous change:

> Those were all young guys [he is referring to his 1960s quintet with Shorter, Hancock, Carter, and Williams] and although they were learning from me, I was learning from them, too, about the new thing, the free thing. Because to be and stay a great musician you've got to always be open to what's new, what's happening at the moment. You have to be able to absorb it if you're going to continue to grow and communicate [through] your music. And *creativity and genius in any kind of artistic expres-*

sion don't know nothing about age; either you got it or you don't, and being old is not going to help you get it. I understood that we had to do something different.[23]

Although Miles was referring to his use of free jazz in the 1960s and Francis Davis was pointing to the trumpeter's final years when he was covering Cyndi Lauper's hit "Time after Time," their quotes point to the continued controversy fusion aesthetics ignited more than a decade after Davis had released *Bitches Brew*. Part of the critical disparagement, as Francis Davis's comments reveal, rested on the idea of a sequence of idiomatic development in an oral tradition that assumed that knowledge passed from master to apprentice. But when Miles Davis pointed Herbie Hancock to the electric piano at the *Miles in the Sky* recording sessions in 1968, it was partly a response to the influence of some of the younger people around him, notably his then-wife Betty Mabry and Tony Williams, both of whom had been enthusiastically urging the trumpet master, who was roughly two decades their senior, to listen to artists such as Jimi Hendrix, Sly and the Family Stone, and the Beatles. As his quote above makes clear, Miles Davis remained open to the younger members of his band, joining them in exploring new ways of creating music rather than being preoccupied with leading young acolytes toward established ideals of jazz mastery.

Significantly, while critics such as Francis Davis argue that this reveals how Miles Davis was following, rather than setting, trends, Miles's confession aptly supports the idea that no "new" music is generated ex nihilo—musical practices emerge from networks of musicians' practices, audience participation, and critical awareness. Enveloped within a network of relationships with younger musicians, coupled with his willingness to cast aside routine, Davis was able to participate in, rather than lead, a movement merging jazz with other popular, and nonpopular, musical practices.

Yet Miles Davis is often the focus of any attention to fusion owing in large part to the music industry's cultivation of celebrity, which worked in tandem with a historical narrative reliant on a succession of male instrumentalists as central to jazz techniques, practices, and meanings. Even so, to be sure, Davis was more willing to engage different music as a mature artist than are most musicians in any idiom.

Without the attention Miles Davis brought to fusion, the music may not have received the wider exposure and serious critical engagement it did in the early 1970s. The "jazz fusion" entry for the *Pop, Rock, and Soul Reader* consists entirely of relevant passages from Miles Davis's autobiography, some of which are reproduced here. There is passing mention of a number of bands and artists—most of whom performed in Davis's bands—but it clearly positions Davis as the "leader in this new development."[24] Yet, like bebop before it, young, relatively unknown musicians were creating fusion music away from the glare of public scrutiny. Davis's established credibility as a jazz musician meant little to fusion's legitimacy—though it helped—and the validity of his post–*Bitches Brew* music was debated by the critical jazz establishment for the remainder of his life, as evidenced by Francis Davis's remarks.

Miles Davis realized that "some people . . . felt that I was trying to do too much, trying to do too many things. They felt I should just stay where I was, stop growing, stop trying different kinds of things." But he was equally convinced that he needed to continue exploring new avenues: "I *had* to do what I was doing if I was going to keep thinking of myself as a creative artist."[25] His continuous searching was his way of engaging the broken middle—the emergent, unstable space between art and commerce, popularity and sacralization, relevance and historical figuration, movement and stasis. Situating his music in this broken middle accomplished more than simply undermining music industry practices or ostracizing jazz critics. It also pointed to the deep connection between age and musical genre as understood at the time—an era of heated discourse about a generation gap between adults and youth, as the Youth International Party founder Jerry Rubin's warning, "Don't trust anyone over thirty," signaled at the time.

Gary Burton, a child prodigy on the vibraphone, underlined the relationship between rock and youth at the time: "I'm young, and I like being young. I feel like having long hair. I enjoy rock music and feel it has an important role in the future of music. It's alive and timely. But I'm not trying to 'prove' anything with my music or group. *I am only concerned that we play what we are*."[26] Burton's declaration of fusion as an honest articulation of "who we are" indicated the importance of rock music to a growing number of jazz musicians of his age. Burton was even more unequivocal about the relative attractions jazz and rock held for these young musicians, declaring that rock music is "the most alive and timely music around today—jazz seems to me one of the most slack and dated."[27] This did not mean, however, that Burton or his generational cohort of jazz musicians was unable or unwilling to perform straight-ahead jazz. In fact, rock musicians of the time such as Keith Emerson or Bill Bruford listed jazz musicians as major influences, often performing music readily heard *as jazz*.[28] While many of the fusion musicians in the 1970s did not automatically equate hipness with mainstream jazz, they didn't deny its virtues, either, as their early careers in straight-ahead jazz ensembles demonstrated.

By 1967, when he and Coryell formed a quartet, Burton had already performed and recorded with established jazz artists such as the tenor saxophonist Stan Getz and pianist George Shearing. He had also led recording dates of his own for the Radio Corporation of America (RCA), including protofusion efforts *Tennessee Firebird* and *The Time Machine* (both titles 1966). Coryell had also recorded or performed with a number of established jazz artists such as Chico Hamilton, Chico O'Farrill, Clark Terry, and J. J. Johnson. Other young fusion musicians such as the saxophonist Steve Marcus and flutist Jeremy Steig enjoyed their first professional engagements in elder jazz performers' bands. And, as befitting Miles Davis's age and status, many of fusion's future stars would come out of his various fusion bands, as well.

Contrary to later accusations of "selling out" by jazz critics, Burton was taking a calculated economic risk when he began merging jazz and rock, admitting, "When I started the group, it was very unusual to be away from jazz into pop rhythms. Our motivation was to give us something else to play. [Bassist] Steve Swallow and I were very worried when we started that it might hurt our popularity because our audience then was right into jazz—and there was some resentment when we changed."[29] Jazz musicians were transforming jazz in a number of different ways, and the young bandleader's concern about his audiences reflected the tensions these changes were placing on artists as well as listeners. Michael Zwerin's liner notes for *Duster* positioned fusion as a broken middle sitting between a free jazz avant-garde and a conservative mainstream in the changing topography of late-1960s jazz: "Jazz, rock and a lot of other things are currently colliding. *A new music, for which there is as yet no name, is being born.* At the same time, jazz as we have known it in the past is going two ways of its own. First, there are the free players, the so-called 'New Thing.' . . . Secondly, there are those who follow established idols, mimicking their personal as well as musical styles. These people do not question the established rules which made sense but are now archaic."[30]

Burton, quoted in the same liner notes, insisted that he "would prefer not to have our music claimed as jazz, or rock, or anything. It has a variety of elements in it, the most important being improvisation," voicing the distrust of labels many musicians hold, regardless of the particular generic bin they are eventually assigned.[31] Still, Zwerin's accusation that "established rules" in jazz had grown "archaic" resonated with Burton's insistence that jazz had become "slack and dated."

The Gary Burton group released one of the first fusion recordings, *Duster*, in April 1967 — the same year the Beatles released *Sgt. Pepper's Lonely Hearts Club Band*. While the Free Spirits recording *Out of Sight and Sound* preceded *Duster* by a year and is often cited as one of the first recordings to feature a blend of rock and jazz, Burton's recording can be more readily heard as setting fusion's course.[32] Burton hired Roy Haynes, a well-respected straight-ahead jazz drummer Burton had worked with in Stan Getz's quartet, as well as Steve Swallow on bass and Larry Coryell on electric guitar. Coryell's sound, in particular, places *Duster* outside of mainstream jazz sounds of the time. His use of distortion, for instance, was a marked distinction from the jazz guitar stylings of Wes Montgomery or Tal Farlow. Coryell, however, did not play rocklike blues licks but explored the harmonic and rhythmic possibilities with an approach more like a jazz musician. In other words, Coryell's guitar *sounded* like "rock" but his thematic and improvisatory lines and developmental ideas echoed those used in post-bebop jazz.

The group's musical practices such as the use of odd meters, long unison lines that obscured bar lines by emphasizing irregular beats, and an eclectic approach to album programming, placing compositions that would not seem out of place on a more straight-ahead recording next to ones that would have been appropriate on a free jazz date, would come to characterize early fusion. Songs such as "One, Two, 1-2-3-4" and "General Mojo's Well Laid Plan" from *Duster* announced fusion's formation in a couple of ways. First, as I have mentioned, Coryell blended a rock-influenced guitar sound with the fleet-fingered single-note lines of a jazz musician. Second, and perhaps more controversially in retrospect, Coryell's rhythmic "comping" (accompaniment) was informed by hard rock and funk, as well as jazz, matching Roy Haynes's interweaving of square rock rhythms and more swinging jazz rhythms.

Burton's group not only emulated the sound of rock but some of the performative aspects of rock music, as well. In the early 1960s, before the dashikis of free jazz musicians and the denim of fusion artists, jazz artists sported crew cuts and wore dark suits and ties, perhaps best exemplified by Miles Davis during his Brooks Brothers phase.[33] Growing long hair and adopting the more casual attire of rock bands for their live shows, the Burton group's onstage demeanor resembled a rock band more than a jazz band. They also parodied rock acts such as the Who and Jimi Hendrix, who burned and destroyed their equipment at the finale of their appearances, by dismantling their gear and leaving it in a pile in the center of the stage before disappearing offstage. When asked about the controversy the group's performance style aroused in the jazz press, Burton responded, "People said I was doing it to attract attention and go commercial but that soon died away as others started doing it. . . . One reason why jazz isn't more popular with young audiences is that it's hard for them to identify with forty-ish musicians in tailored suits. They could loosen up some."[34] The rock critic Paul Williams agreed, writing in a 1966 *Crawdaddy!* editorial that rock music was "the most exciting and alive music in the world today, music that is alive . . . because of its fantastic inventiveness, its ability to assimilate widely different styles of music, its freshness and awareness of a world other forms of music seem ready to desert."[35]

As Burton's response makes clear, fusion's early practitioners viewed mainstream jazz musicians as out of touch with young audiences, deserting "freshness," to use Williams's word, in order to protect their newly earned cultural capital. Moreover, while soul jazz musicians continued to evoke the sweat-filled dance floors of the juke joint, high-profile engagements at a jazz club such as the Village Vanguard were sedate affairs compared to the Dionysian rock concerts at halls such as the Fillmore East. The playful performativity of early fusion shows countered the claims to high art that performers in mainstream and free jazz were contentiously proclaiming at the time.

Coryell performed and recorded with another group of young musicians who were attempting to meld rock and jazz aesthetics into a vibrant new music. Steve Marcus, a saxophonist who had performed in Stan Kenton's and Woody Herman's big bands, led an informal jam session that included Coryell, the pianist Mike Nock, Chris Hills, and Bob Moses. Nock recalls, "Our music was inspired by the Beatles, the Byrds, the Stones, and Coltrane's 'free style.' *It was also a protest against a lot of the conservatism that was so prevalent in jazz even then.* I wanted to play a simple kind of music that grooved me, in those days we didn't think of it as 'jazz-rock,' it was just the music we wanted to play."[36]

Fighting the conservatism that they believed was calcifying jazz music was as much a part of fusion musicians' impetus for their music as it was for free jazz musicians. Marcus's informal jam session group formed the Count's Rock Band, and its first recording, *Tomorrow Never Knows* (1968), turned the title song, a Beatles composition, into a "free jazz meets acid rock" vehicle that illustrated the way in which the harmonic sensibilities of jazz could merge with the volume and rhythms of rock. It also indicated how the higher volumes and electronic timbres of rock music could be translated into the aggressiveness of free jazz "squonking." Another band, Free Spirits, consisting of Coryell, tenor saxophonist Jim Pepper, guitarist Columbus "Chip" Baker, bassist Chris Hills, and drummer Bob Moses, was part of a larger collective of young musicians who participated in exploding the borders between jazz and rock music. The pianist Warren Bernhardt, a member of the collective, recalled,

> [Jazz-rock jams held at a club called L'Intrigue] went on for about a year—certainly until well into 1966. To me that was the beginnings of jazz-rock; to my knowledge there was no one else combining rock and jazz improvisation at that time, combining styles like that. It was a whole different spirit, very much the spirit of the sixties. We started growing our hair long and all that kind of thing. LSD was part of the scene. The music was adventurous and maybe a little chaotic—there was some free [jazz] mixed in there too—they were exciting times![37]

Bernhardt's recollection points to the relationship between rock music and the use of psychedelics such as LSD at the time. Nick Bromell discusses the difficulty the link between drugs and the counterculture presents to academic researchers in his trenchant work on the relationship between 1960s rock music and drug experiences by recalling both Jim Miller's apology for omitting the "carnivalesque atmosphere of confusion" surrounding the creation of the Port Huron Statement and David Farber's cautionary warning to other historians of 1960s youth movements about including the impact of drugs in their analyses.[38] Bromell writes, perhaps defensively, "Yet while what follows is certainly not a 'study' of rock and drugs, I have to trust that it will not be confused either with an intergalactic message sent back to us from Timothy Leary in orbit nor mistaken for the mumbling of that hollow-eyed '60s burnout who's still at his post on a corner of Telegraph Avenue in Berkeley."[39] While Bromell's emphasis is on how drugs affected white, middle-class suburban youth of the period, his assertion that the psychedelic drug experience had a major role in the cultural milieu of the 1960s is difficult to deny.[40]

As Bromell notes, psychedelic drug experiences "are *so discontinuous* with ordinary consciousness" that they transformed musicians and their music, insisting further that psychedelic drug use is "only half the story [of the youth counterculture of the late 1960s]. The other half is rock."[41] Further,

Bromell argues that because of their desire to make their individual, internal psychedelic experiences part of a collective, even communal, experience, the "rock audience's medium of self-expression [was notably] *electric music*."[42] Electric music was the sound of the discontinuity from ordinary consciousness broadcast to the larger world outside of one's own "head." Electric music manifested this disruptive aesthetic by bringing an *electronic* noise into the studios and performance spaces shared by musicians and audiences. Jimi Hendrix, hard rock avatar of the late 1960s, often called his compositions "electric church music," articulating the artful blend of music, spirituality, and technology embraced by the drug culture of the decade.[43] The psychedelic injunction to "turn on, tune in, and drop out" points to this desire to use drugs (turn on) in order to access an alternative and, implicitly, better reality (tune in) and then to use that new knowledge to "drop out" of normative social relations in order to realize a new, better world. While certainly utopian, the idea that there was a socially progressive and productive use for psychedelic drugs was ubiquitous in the late-1960s counterculture.

In citing his engagement with psychedelics, the pianist Warren Bernhardt acknowledged the effect drugs had on his musical choices as part of a radical reconceptualization of musical aesthetics. As LSD opened the ears of the group of musicians he jammed with at L'Intrigue, ideas regarding the boundaries between genres shifted, allowing the "adventurous and chaotic" music to occur. One early fusion group, Jeremy and the Satyrs, led by flutist Jeremy Steig, utilized electronic equipment to merge avant-garde music with a nascent fusion aesthetic. Bernhardt remembered: "We all had tape recordings of random sounds and at any point in our performance we would play them. Sometimes everybody's tape sounds were playing at once. It was crazy. I remember when we played the Village Vanguard opposite Freddie Hubbard, who was straight-ahead hard bop, we drove [the owner] Max Gordon crazy—he hated us. *It was because we were doing things jazz groups weren't supposed to do!* The year before I'd been playing for Gerry Mulligan and when he heard the group he refused to speak to me!"[44]

Young "fusioneers" did not just use musical strategies from a wide variety of sources in order to challenge musical convention. The influence of the 1960s counterculture was also important—the freedom to do things "jazz groups weren't supposed to do" was a powerful incentive for fusion musicians. In 1965 another group of musicians blending jazz and rock began congregating at Mike Mainieri's Guru Music offices in New York. Mainieri, joined by Jeremy Steig and the Satyrs, began his fusion experiments along with pianist Warren Bernhardt, bassist Hal Gaylor, drummer Donald McDonald, and guitarist Joe Beck—a group whose membership would soon include guitarist Sam Brown, bassist Chuck Rainey, and vocalist Sally Waring. This group of musicians recorded an album under Mainieri's name, *Journey Thru an Electric Tube* (1967), a title indicative of the music's attitude. Mainieri describes these jam sessions: "Some nights only a few stragglers would arrive, but there would be many nights twenty or thirty hippies would play, sing, and dance until we shook the 1950s out of our skins. The musical ideas were launched from single sketches and vamps that would sometimes last for nearly an hour, changing shape, tempos, and soloists, depending on who suddenly fell by or split."[45]

"Shaking the 1950s out of our skins" was a defining motto for many of these fusion pioneers. A key difference, however, between earlier jazz musicians and these young artists in the 1960s was that rock music represented freedom from artistic limits, as well as from middle-class mores. Whereas the Beats had heard jazz as the nonconformist soundtrack for their attempts to "shake the 1950s out of [their] skins," jazz was perceived by these young musicians as the realm of the conservative, a tired and nonreflexive response to a world that no longer held social relevance for them.

In the March 7, 1968, issue of *Down Beat* Coryell and Burton took part in a joint "Blindfold Test." After listening to the Beatles' "Fool on the Hill," Coryell offered, "[The Beatles] are still the best of the rock 'n' roll groups. One good thing about them is that they always stuck to rock 'n' roll, or non-jazz. I really don't believe in mixing the two."[46] Coryell's response echoed the words of one jazz critic, Joe Klee, who wrote two years later: "Most 'jazz/rock' bands fall into one of two categories. Either it's a jazz band trying to play rock without any real affinity for or identity with the idiom, or it's a group of rock musicians whose conception of jazz has not progressed far beyond Basie riffing and watered-down copies of the great creative jazz soloists."[47] Ironically, as noted above, Coryell had participated in some of the first recordings to blend jazz and rock only a year earlier. Indeed, Coryell has also recalled, "We were saying, 'We love Coltrane but we also love the Beatles. We love Miles but we also love the Rolling Stones.' We wanted people to know we [were] very much part of the contemporary scene but at the same time we had worked our butts off to learn this other music [called jazz]. It was a very sincere thing."[48] His ambivalence reflects the entrenched view that jazz and rock were deeply incompatible genres, as measured by performance standards and practices at the time—even by young musicians who were troubling the jazz/rock divide.

Not all younger jazz musicians were enamored of rock music or interested in blending jazz and rock. In a 1976 *Down Beat* profile Brian Torff, a twenty-one-year-old bassist, was adamant about his choice to perform on the acoustic bass: "The repercussions of [young bass players choosing to play acoustic rather than electric basses] could be the polarization of rock and jazz and the entire fusion movement's dissipation. Right now, we [acoustic instrumentalists] are in the minority. The hot groups—Weather Report, Return to Forever—maybe they're just fads. I know they can play acoustic instruments, and they will should the [music] industry revert to its former attitudes."[49] The implication, of course, is that those "former attitudes" were grounded in higher musical standards than those performed by fusion musicians. Clearly, the issue of whether jazz could avoid being tarnished by its growing relationship with rock did not depend entirely on the age of a musician or the idea of an aesthetic "generation gap" but would also rest on the issue of musical competency. It was incumbent on these young musicians to find a set of criteria that addressed the unique set of musical competencies required to create a music formed from idioms that required such distinct sets of musical skills that they were seen as incompatible or mutually negating.

Bill Chase, the leader and trumpet player in the big band rock ensemble Chase, voiced views similar to those of Coryell and Klee about the relationship between jazz and rock:

> I can imagine how it must bug rock players, who try to get into jazz but can't swing, to hear a jazz musician playing bad rock. I've heard a lot of rock groups that impressed me until they stepped outside the boundaries of rock and tried to play jazz. Then they lost it completely—their momentum, their audience, and my respect. Because they're attempting something they're not equipped to do. Jazz has to be deep-rooted. So if you're playing jazz, it's got to be good jazz, with good time, swing . . . everything. If you're playing rock, it has to be good rock. So the group [Chase] is really a challenge. We have to be purists in both idioms yet be able to cross over.[50]

Chase's recommendation that musicians be accomplished in both jazz and rock illustrates the dilemma these young fusion musicians faced. His comments hint that the technical demands required to produce "good jazz" might prove antithetical to those required to produce "good rock." Why, then, would Chase choose to merge jazz and rock? Admitting that he was originally "cold to rock," Bill Chase, like many jazz musicians of the time, changed his mind about the musical possibilities in rock after he heard the Beatles. Further, as with his peers, Chase admitted that his new musical direction was based on a sense of freedom: "I'm very happy about where music is at right now, I really am. There's so much more freedom to do what you want without offending people."[51] Aesthetic freedom was the "authenticating" gesture of fusion even as fusion musicians challenged idiomatic orthodoxies.

Although the Count's Rock Band, led by Steve Marcus, successfully "jazzed" rock songs (the Beatles' "Tomorrow Never Knows," Donovan's "Mellow Yellow"), the rock era of the 1970s was shaped by the transformation in popular music as a whole that occurred in the 1960s.[52] Tony Williams argued as much: "The '70s for a lot of people were a reaction to the '60s," and part of his own reaction was sounded out through his fusion band, Lifetime.[53] It is true that mainstream jazz musicians such as the guitarist Wes Montgomery still took pop songs and "jazzed" them. In 1965 Montgomery recorded a collection of contemporary pop tunes entitled *Goin' Out of My Head*, which was so successful that he recorded similar albums such as *California Dreamin'*, *Tequila*, and *A Day in the Life*, the best-selling jazz album of 1968.[54] These albums inspired efforts from other mainstream jazz artists, including Duke Ellington, Count Basie, and Woody Herman.[55] But unlike the Tin Pan Alley songs that had proven such protean vehicles for jazz improvisers in the past, reharmonizations of rock songs often sounded overly precious, lacking the rawness that rock music privileged. No longer were the ii-V-I progressions or harmonic substitutions on which jazz musicians displayed their craft available in the three-chord, and sometimes single-chord, rock songs of the 1960s.

By the late 1960s, the rise of singer-songwriters such as Bob Dylan and rock groups who wrote their own songs such as the Beatles signaled a change from older models of pop music industry production. But the genre distinctions that were partly derived from early sheet music publishing categories remained, even if the days of Tin Pan Alley and the Brill Building had passed.[56] Many of the songs on national and international charts were directly associated with singers and bands whose recorded arrangements often became the canonical exemplars of a given rock song. The rise of the self-contained band—bands who composed and arranged their music and increasingly produced or coproduced their own recordings—gave rock musicians the weight of authenticity, but, arguably, much of their gravitas was derived from a mass audience of pop music consumers, a group whose aesthetic judgment has rarely been the standard for evaluating "cultural excellence." In any case, while Montgomery enjoyed financial success with his recording of the Beatles' "A Day in the Life," his recordings were not aimed at, nor popular with, teenage rock audiences. His recordings were the jazz answer to Nashville's Chet Atkins, both men framing inventive guitar work accompanied by string sections and background singers on recordings produced for mainstream pop audiences, with their musical abilities lending a sophisticated sheen to select popular rock songs of the day.

In fact, fusion musicians argued for a definition of virtuosity different from the bebop standard held in mainstream jazz. Mike Nock described the specific musical aesthetic that the fusion band Fourth Way was interested in pursuing at the time: "Our idea was to play free contemporary jazz over modal rock grooves." [57] Fourth Way's protoworld fusion blend of jazz, Asian and African traditions, rock and funk, and acoustic and electronic instrumentation suggested the far-reaching possibilities of fusion. As a corollary to the use of electronic music technologies, as well as non-Western instrumentation, timbre became the terrain on which fusion musicians marked their use of rock, experimental new music aesthetics, and traditional or folk music traditions. It is small wonder that they were interested in rock, a musical idiom that is fundamentally dependent on sound recording, storage, and reproductive technologies for its sounds and its meanings. [58]

Rock groups of the 1960s and 1970s were also exploring the uses of technology—early synthesizers, computers, and various processes of analog tape manipulation—that had previously been the nearly exclusive interest of a small group of experimental Western art music composers such as Milton Babbitt, Iannis Xenakis, and Karlheinz Stockhausen. Groups such as Pink Floyd borrowed recording and performance techniques, especially prominent in their early recordings, from avant-garde concert music. Finally, the emergence of "progressive rock" in the late 1960s, with its self-conscious use of baroque- and romantic-era European concert music techniques and compositional strategies, also spoke to the growing affiliation between rock and other types of music. [59]

However, it was the increased timbral expressiveness facilitated by synthesizers and other electronic instrumentation that motivated rock artists' interests in "other worldly" soundings, which were deeply influenced by psychedelic drug use. Instrument designers such as Robert Moog, Don Buchla, and Tom Oberheim responded by producing sophisticated but relatively inexpensive electronic keyboard systems, and their effect can still be heard in recordings today. Fusion musicians were similarly interested in using the studio as an instrument, taking their cues from rock production techniques in creating alternative sound worlds, both realizable and unrealizable in "real life."

Rock musicians trade in exaggerated, emotionally charged gestures, and their proclivities for spectacle and melodrama are widely acknowledged.[60] In musical terms rock musicians applied electronics as part of a reframing of virtuosity. The composer Robert Worby explained the effect of Jimi Hendrix's pioneering electric guitar virtuosity on audiences: "the intense power of volume, distortion and howling feedback created a visceral sensory overload resembling total body immersion, a heightened drug experience or passionate sexual activity."[61] It is this linking of the physical and the musical via electronic technologies that is part of the deeply transformative effect of rock music on contemporary music culture. Indeed, one of the most readily identifiable distinctions between musicians who use electric instruments from musicians who perform on acoustic instruments is the use of intentional distortion. As Worby explains, "Distortion, resonance and feedback (technically all very closely linked) are the powerhouses of rock music's guitar technique."[62]

Steve Waksman details the ways in which distortion plays a fundamental role in black electric guitar aesthetics, juxtaposing, for example, the African American blues guitarist Buddy Guy's exploration of the limits of electric amplification to the European American guitarist Les Paul's concerns with tonal purity. Waksman's contention that Guy's use of volume and distortion "was the result of an aesthetic preference for sounds that cut against the grain of a smooth musical surface" speaks to the ways in which distortion announced a "sound that could not be readily assimilated."[63] The eventual "whitening" of rock music, especially as embodied in the iconographic male lead guitarist, speaks to the ways in which the blackness of certain musical sounds and practices has often been obscured and transfigured as they traveled from black to mainstream culture.[64] Steve Waksman observes that, in the end, Hendrix's electric church music was "not the assertion of difference but its transcendence through the overpowering influence of electronic sound."[65] Musically, as Miles Davis later confessed, it was Jimi Hendrix's *sound* and not the musical forms Hendrix used that motivated Davis, in part, toward fusion music.[66] Waksman offers support: "However innovative the *sound* of Hendrix's music may have been, its form typically stayed close to standard blues models."[67] Indeed, Hendrix's interest in new soundings pushed the limits of technology and helped popularize the use of distortion and feedback as "musical noise." Davis was clearly not interested in "standard blues models" — his interest lay in the broader sonic possibilities electronic musical equipment could lend his music, such as when he expanded the sound of his trumpet through the use of a wah-wah pedal during experimental rock-funk jams.

Additionally, the recording studio and its attendant technology allowed musicians to increasingly manipulate recorded events ex post facto. The ideal in mainstream jazz recording, however, was to make the recording process as transparent as possible in order to best capture the spontaneous, improvised creation of "the shared moment" between musicians. Though there were instances of recordings of otherwise unrealizable performances such as Sidney Bechet's "Blues of Bechet" (Victor 1941), in which Bechet overdubbed a number of different instruments to achieve a "one-man band" recording, the ideal of jazz recordings as the transparent transfer of live music to a listener has been a foundational assumption in jazz recordings' use as historical documents and pedagogical tools. But, for example, Miles Davis's fusion albums of the 1970s radically upended those ideals by being produced, in large part, by the engineer and composer Teo Macero's splicing together disparate recording sessions into single, coherent tracks.

By the late 1960s, rock musicians were even less interested in capturing actual live performances than their predecessors in the Sun and Chess recording studios or the more recent and harmonically rich sound world of Brian Wilson's Beach Boys recordings and the sonic fantasias of Phil Spector's famous "Wall of Sound" productions. As Theodore Gracyk argues, rock musicians had embraced modern recording and sound technologies *as an aesthetic choice* from the beginning, as evidenced by the reverb-drenched vocals of the 1950s Sun Studio recordings of Elvis Presley. Indeed, rock musicians were never interested in merely capturing a live performance on tape but were always actively aware of the creative possibilities recording technologies gave them, challenging older ideas about authenticity and the value of live performances. As Virgil Moorefield illustrates in his study of the production techniques of Phil Spector, George Martin, and Brian Eno, the argument that "recording's metaphor [is shifting] from one of the 'illusion of reality' (mimetic space) to the 'reality of illusion' (a virtual world in which everything is possible)" can be heard in the rock recordings of the era (and continue to shape rock aesthetics today).[68]

Bromell, describing the Beatles' *Revolver* (Capitol 1966), argues that rock

musicians valued electronic music because it upended authenticity and resonated with the cultural upheavals of the time: "Why did the Beatles become
obsessed with the possibility of taking available technology and effectually
subverting it, ripping it apart and making it do things it was never intended
for? The sound of this song ['Tomorrow Never Knows'] and of so much of
Revolver wreaks havoc with the distinction between the natural and the artificial. It is a 'mind-bending' sound because it invites the listener to enter
an acoustic universe in which familiar signposts of authenticity have been
deliberately removed. Nothing straightforwardly refers to anything one can
recognize."[69]

When young jazz musicians began implementing new electronic instrumentation and exploring the possibilities modern recording and reproductive equipment afforded them, they were clearly aligning themselves with
rock's aesthetic and visceral appeal. Gary Burton admitted that he was after
the "distortion of the sound, not of the music," while Mahavishnu Orchestra's "Sapphire Bullets of Pure Love" is a twenty-four-second exercise in
electronic sounds.[70] In both cases the connection with rock is audible and
enthusiastic. "Sapphire Bullets of Pure Love" also illustrates the links between experimental electronic music and the popular music of the time.

As a corollary to distortion Gracyk links high volume to noise and critique: "The main reason rock is noise, for both fans and detractors, is volume."[71] Some fusion musicians, such as Tony Williams and John McLaughlin, were attracted to the higher volumes of rock as an aesthetic and political
choice. Yet while accepting that Mahavishnu Orchestra's music "was music,
not mere energy/noise," the jazz critic Dan Morgenstern, in his review of the
band's performance at the 1972 Newport in New York Festival, still found
them "too loud": "Why, when playing an acoustically sensitive hall like
Carnegie, [does the Mahavishnu Orchestra] turn the damned sound up so
bloody loud? Or is it that these musicians can't hear any more how loud they
are? A pity if true."[72] Still, the appearance of the Mahavishnu Orchestra at a
nominally jazz festival reveals the close links fusion bands held to the jazz
world despite critical antipathy.

Why *did* fusion bands such as the Mahavishnu Orchestra turn up the volume? Rock music's loud volume is often tied to larger social effects: reflection of the increased volume of modern quotidian life; expression of the
alienation and frustration of postindustrial anomie; or the propulsion behind the Dionysian rituals of the rock concert. While there is merit in much
of these perspectives, I want to focus on how fusion musicians used volume
in ways distinct from rock and jazz bands.

As Burton's comments indicate, rock fans heard straight-ahead jazz as a cool, emotionally detached, even intellectual, music. "Hot" styles such as New Orleans jazz, while clearly charged with passion, sounded old-fashioned to 1960s rock audiences, who might hear the fervor of New Orleans musicians for mere sentiment. Free jazz, for all its frenetic energy, paled next to the extreme volumes of rock bands. However, increased volume was not simply a reflection of the times for fusion musicians but a way to inject passion and emotion into an instrumental music that favored long thematic lines and complex polyrhythmic interplay, music performed by bands that often lacked a charismatic lead vocalist, the key to mass audience acceptance. Volume, rather than a human voice and the explicit meaning lyrics can enable music to convey, was a key to gaining a youth audience's attention, allowing the musicians to hold center stage. Volume, therefore, provided intensity, energy, and a focus beyond the lyrical, sustaining listeners who were drawn from a broad range of listening habits, including mainstream popular music fans, who might not otherwise be interested in purely instrumental music. One might also venture the notion that big band swing's ability to connect with a mass audience was partly due to advances in microphone, amplification, and broadcasting technologies, as well as the energy conveyed by the loud volume a large ensemble, especially one endowed with those technologies, was able to project.

Still, unlike the softer volume of an acoustic band performing at an intimate jazz nightclub, fusion audiences were unable to converse, the volume of the music only allowing communion between audience and musicians, which promoted a different register of interaction between them in qualitatively distinct ways from other musical genres. Gracyk suggests that "loud music can break us out of our sense of detached observation and replace it with a sense of immersion. . . . Where traditional aesthetic theories have often offered an ideal of disinterested contemplation or 'psychical distance,' the presence of noise can overcome the respectful, reverential aspects of distancing."[73] Fusion musicians used high volumes as a "de-distancing" tactic, forging an affective encirclement of sound between band and audience. Williams and Hancock were both explicit about desires for the type of connection with their audiences from which they believed conventional jazz performances had strayed—perhaps best exemplified at the time by the Modern Jazz Quartet in its formal tuxedos and reserved stage presence. Indeed, Waksman's assertion that "it was precisely this noise [loud distorted guitar sounds] that guitarists used to forge new affective alliances between audiences and performers," supports the view that fusion musicians such as McLaughlin and Williams appropriated rock's volume and distortion not only for aesthetic reasons but for deeply affective ones, as well.[74]

Perhaps, however, more than electronic instrumentation and loud volume, the use of rock and funk rhythms proved the most controversial aspect of fusion. While technology and volume can be arguably linked to mainstream jazz musicians' use of broadcast radio and early adoption of the recording studio, and the invocation of a trumpet or saxophone player's ability to perform loudly linked emotional intensity to volume, rhythm has been a defining element in jazz, particularly since the so-called swing era of the 1930s and early 1940s. Moreover, while various rhythmic orientations have occurred throughout jazz's history, jazz critics characterized funk and rock rhythms as primitive in comparison to swing and bebop rhythms. Joachim Berendt maintains precisely this view in The Jazz Book: From Ragtime to Fusion and Beyond: "Even though the rhythmic patterns produced by seventies jazz-rock drummers went considerably beyond rock rhythms, they were a step backward compared with the complex and multilayered rhythms of modern jazz. Their symmetry and two-beat regularity seemed rigid and schematic."[75] In his book The Jazz Tradition Martin Williams tersely appraised Miles Davis's fusion group: "Of Davis's subsequent flirting with rock rhythms and his avowed determination in the early 1970s to lead the best jazz-rock fusion group in the world, perhaps the less said the better. Except perhaps that, aside from moments by Davis himself, these performances seem failures to me, and failures partly because of the static nature of the rhythms, and consequently the music, involved with them."[76]

Fusion's detractors heard the rock and funk rhythmic patterns used by fusion rhythm sections as forsaking jazz's authentic rhythmic feel known as "swing." As Duke Ellington famously put it, "It don't mean a thing, if it ain't got that swing." Swing, however, as a rhythmic quality, is not easily defined, nor is it present in all the music that mainstream jazz discourse designates as "real jazz." To clarify how fundamental rhythmic purity functioned in the 1970s, I offer here a Bob Rusch review of Hank Crawford's I Hear a Symphony (CTI/Kudu 1976): "For reviewers' servicing, CTI gets Cadence's vote for 'Supreme Pain in the Ass.' They have managed this month to slum and send us HANK CRAWFORD'S I HEAR A SYMPHONY (KUDU 26). It's only heard by him and CTI; certainly the people who do the disco dance to this will doubtfully be hearing anything. There are short spaces of pleasant work between the wa-wa, funk, James Brown grunts and soul hipness — rhythmic but dull."[77]

What does Rusch make of hard bop's "backbeat" sensibilities? Or the fact that many fusion bands used complex meters, even polymeters, in rhythmically nuanced ways? Additionally, Berendt's and Rusch's implication that rock and funk rhythms are less complex than jazz rhythms may betray musical tastes posing as formal analyses. The pianist Mike Nock offers an experiential rebuttal to their view: "I remember a night when Steve Marcus played me a choice selection of Beatles music, it had a profound effect on both of us. I was playing all this musicians' music, not really getting off on it. Then I heard a James Brown record and it floored me. I'd been in the jazz syndrome and you can't find jazz musicians to play that kind of time [rhythm]. They think it's beneath them, yet they can't play it.[78] As Nock's comment indicates, though difficult to execute, jazz musicians and critics deemed funk rhythms simple and musically unchallenging given funk's status in the dominant musical hierarchy.

Unlike free jazz, fusion was not only accessing high art aesthetics but was explicitly engaging "low" cultural forms and audiences. Rock and funk rhythms highlighted fusion's explicit moves back to the streets and roads—the popular—and threatened mainstream jazz musicians' and critics' moves toward the symphony halls and recital rooms of "legitimate" culture.[79] The musical explanations given by jazz apologists who judged rock and funk rhythms simplistic hoped that jazz would mirror the promotion of Western concert music to art, which had culminated in the sacralization of symphony hall culture in the nineteenth century (and would bring jazz to New York City's Lincoln Center a hundred years later).[80] Rock and funk rhythms also tied fusion musicians to youth culture, a formation denied legitimacy or power. Importantly, youth culture appears in the public sphere through the marketplace, a devalued space for high cultural work.

Rock and funk rhythms were heard as noncerebral, body-oriented rhythms—a space of sensuous pleasure rather than intellectual rigor—by celebrated jazz critics such as Martin Williams, further attenuating fusion's legitimacy. The body was viewed by many jazz critics and jazz musicians as a location best avoided except from within a heteronormative, masculinist, black/white binary, an orientation that was further obscured by colorblind, meritocratic rhetoric, as the writings of Winthrop Sargeant and Martin Williams indicate.

Philip Brett asserts that musical pleasure, "nonverbal even when linked to words, physically arousing in its function as initiator of dance, and resisting attempts to endow it with, or discern in it, precise meaning, it represents that part of our culture which is constructed as feminine and therefore dangerous."[81] The performative body—racialized, gendered, and sexualized—was indeed a dangerously loaded nexus of counterperspectives to critical jazz discourse, which hoped to keep the body from reentering the bandstand as jazz moved from a music for dancing and partying to a music of contemplation and aesthetic appreciation. Fusion musicians, in their use of rhythms embedded within a genre logic that reflected the racialized and gendered devaluation of embodied performance (dance, for example) and a cultural hierarchy that displaced bodies from "higher" forms of music, confronted music critics with an array of contestations centering on the distinctions between mind and body, black and white, male and female, and high and low culture.

The two biggest groups, I thought, were Cream and Jimi Hendrix's band. But before that, I was in love with the Beatles. I was a real Beatles fanatic. — **Tony Williams**

Well, jazz is such a bad word, and rock is such a bad word. All those things are so limiting, and commercial music is such a bad word, all the words are really bad. And there's another sound that's going to happen and that's what I want to be a part of.
— **Tony Williams**

In 1969 the African American drummer Tony Williams, white British guitarist John McLaughlin, and African American organist Larry Young (later, Khalid Yasin Abdul Aziz) jammed together for the first time. Soon they would form the early fusion band Lifetime. In the years after the original Lifetime disbanded, Williams was asked repeatedly about his association with McLaughlin, who had subsequently achieved global stardom as leader of the archetypal fusion band the Mahavishnu Orchestra. Williams, noting interviewers' lack of interest in Lifetime's largely forgotten organist, responded pointedly, "What about Larry Young? He was the genius of that band," implicitly challenging the conventional view by jazz critics of fusion as a benighted musical genre performed by musicians who either lacked the skills to perform "real jazz" or, if competent as jazz performers, were cynically seeking the higher monetary rewards of rock music.[1] Lifetime used rock music to question and complicate the meanings jazz held as popular music, as well as its emergence as art music.[2]

Williams's question, as well as the music of his fusion band, Lifetime, contested the link between racialized bodies and genre, implying that McLaughlin's heightened visibility and critical acceptance ran along racialized, and not merely aesthetic, lines. Further, Williams perceived a racial component to the musical choices made by audiences:

White people, when they go and want to listen to something, they listen to it to identify with it, just like everybody does. . . . You know, they . . . want to see something that they feel they could be a part of; you know, they could be up there singing, that could be them up there playing the guitar.

If they go see a black person, they can't do that, because they can't imagine themselves being black.[3]

Rather than take up the question of whether or not Williams was correct, I want to direct my inquiry toward the relationship between Williams's listening practices and the racial dynamics of genre on his own music making. (Ironically, McLaughlin's explosive fretwork provided much of Lifetime's emotional heat, and the dramatic dialogue he and Williams shared carried over into McLaughlin's later collaborations with the Mahavishnu Orchestra's drummer, Billy Cobham.) When Williams recognized an affiliation between audience member and band member, he was implicitly problematizing his own relationship to the Beatles. How did he identify with the Beatles? Did he think he could perform rock music because he was a "rocker," too — just like the Beatles? Can fusion be heard as a strategy by Williams to make visible the racial assumptions behind genre categories? Was it his desire to transform the racial logic of genre into something more representative of the diversity subsumed under rock's banner of (white) universalism, or, indeed, of jazz's "colorblind" universalism as announced by jazz critics such as Leonard Feather, Martin Williams, and Gene Lees? While the idea of the jazz bandstand as a demonstration of democracy was an ideal, some jazz critics longed for the days before militant free jazz musicians polarized jazz audiences. These writers invoked a nostalgic return to a time when, as Leonard Feather put it, "blacks and whites congregated [at] Harlem rooms without fear of violence."[4] Was fusion — the "sound that's going to happen" — Williams's way of getting past all the "bad words"?

One of Williams's primary motivations for merging rock and jazz was to reach beyond conventional genre categories, evincing the naked, perhaps naive, optimism fusion held for its early practitioners. In the late 1960s, after gaining international prominence in Miles Davis's "second quintet," Williams began to search for other young jazz musicians who shared his appreciation for rock musicians such as Jimi Hendrix and the Beatles. Only seventeen years of age when he began performing with Davis's band, Williams was partially responsible for incorporating elements of the "new thing" (free jazz) into Davis's music. But Williams also claimed his musical roots traversed both rock and jazz: "I had been listening to and enjoying Jimi Hendrix a lot. I also liked Cream and the MC5. My drumming had become more aggressive and that was the direction that I wanted to follow."[5] His confession was received differently from those of previous generations of jazz musicians, who were often able to express their admiration for non-jazz popular music without encountering the disapproval rock fans faced from jazz critics and fans. Significantly, Williams formed R&B and doo-wop groups during his youth. These groups were conceived along the lines of the Coasters and the Orioles and included the performance of choreographed dance routines. Though Williams's singing in Lifetime may have surprised many of his jazz fans, he had notably been the lead singer for a group called the Monticellos.[6]

Williams was introduced to jazz through his father, the saxophonist Tillmon Williams, who not only played jazz recordings at home but also took the younger Williams on his rounds of jam sessions and professional club dates. Meanwhile, Tony Williams also enjoyed listening to Top 40 radio with his friends, singing and dancing with them in popular music groups, and, like many teenagers throughout the United States, routinely viewed the nationally televised broadcasts of Dick Clark's *American Bandstand*. Though he would eventually merge rock and jazz, the two genres were discrete soundscapes during his youth, as Williams explained: "For a long time I realized that I had been living in two worlds. I was living in one world where I was making friends in grammar school and in high school, going to parties with them, listening to rock and hanging out on corners. And then I got a chance to go out with my father and play. I'd be with him and all the older musicians, his friends, and they took me into their scene and showed me what they had. So, it was two worlds all the time for me."[7]

Williams may certainly have been a unique musical talent, but his sound world—multiply located, temporally displaced, and technologically mediated—was not unlike that of most other "baby boomer" music fans. Williams's access to music from a wide variety of places and periods partially defines the soundscape of his generation, and his ecumenical appreciation for the music of Billy Eckstine, Frank Sinatra, Max Roach, Art Blakey, Karlheinz Stockhausen, and Igor Stravinsky, as well as the Beatles, Jimi Hendrix, and the MC5, was considered routine connoisseurship. Moreover, economic interests, consumer curiosity, and the degree of displacement from "origin" to "consumption" often transformed the contexts of musical traditions or idioms for these young listeners.

But when Williams described his continuous crossing between various musical idioms as a result of modernity's profuse soundscape—"There's so much [music] that I can't remain narrow"—he was not speaking merely as a consumer.[8] When he was twelve years old, Williams sat in with Art Blakey's band. As a seasoned drummer of fifteen, Williams had rapidly gained professional experience by performing mainstream jazz with older Boston musicians such as the pianist Leroy Fallana and the organist Johnny "Hammond" Smith. He was also simultaneously involved in more experimental music: "I started working with [saxophonist] Sam Rivers. We worked in the Club 47 in Cambridge [Massachusetts] and that's where we first met. . . . Sam and I and [the Boston Improvisational Ensemble] got together and we'd play. They'd put graphs up on the wall, and we'd play to that and then they'd put numbers up and we'd play to that, and we'd play to a time clock, in all kinds of variations, different variations, and from that we went to other things."[9]

Williams later continued similar work with the notable experimental jazz musicians Eric Dolphy (saxophone) and Cecil Taylor (piano), but in 1962 Williams's first move away from his family home in Boston was to New York City as the drummer in the alto saxophonist Jackie McLean's hard bop group.[10] Williams ended his short journeyman period a few months later when he joined Miles Davis's quintet, one of the most commercially and critically successful jazz groups of the time.

In 1963 the founder of Blue Note Records, Albert Lion, offered Williams the chance to record, and his debut recording, titled Lifetime, was one of Blue Note's first avant-garde releases. This album lent Williams's steadily growing body of recorded work an impressive range, especially for someone not yet twenty years old. Williams composed all the music for the sessions, leading a band of older musicians that included Rivers and the vibraphonist Bobby Hutcherson. Despite his young age, Williams was committed to a high standard of musicianship, and that commitment was noted by Miles Davis, who claimed that Williams "was the only guy in my band who ever told me, 'Man, why don't you practice!' I was missing notes and shit trying to keep up with his young ass."[11]

Though he dropped out of high school in order to join McLean's band, once settled in New York City, Williams contacted the Manhattan School of Music, inquiring after a teacher. He was referred to Monica Jakuch, who taught him European common-practice art music theory and harmony. Later, he privately studied twentieth-century theory and compositional techniques with Art Murphy. When Williams moved to California in the 1970s, he continued his music studies with Robert Stine, a music professor at the University of California at Berkeley (UCB). When Stine eventually left for a university post elsewhere, Williams continued his composition classes with Robert Greenberg, then a graduate student at UCB. He also studied briefly with Olly Wilson, the noted African American art music composer. At the end of his life Williams was studying privately with David Sheinfeld, a former first violinist with the San Francisco Orchestra. In one of his last interviews Williams explained his reasons for taking music lessons despite his professional status and critical acclaim: "I remember when I started taking serious compositional classes, people were always asking me why I was doing it. They seemed to believe that since I had a record out I didn't need to do anything else. I don't understand that attitude at all. To me, being a musician is like being a doctor. You've got to keep up with all the changes, and the more you learn about your profession, the better off you are."[12]

His equal interest in popular *and* "serious" music shaped the dialogical ground on which Lifetime's music was created, performatively mapping the correspondences, as well as the incongruencies, among various musical worlds. Yet Williams's ambivalent attitude toward the discrepant rankings among rock, jazz, and Western art music indicate some of the tensions he felt between popular tastes and broader aesthetic evaluations. On one hand, Williams held certain rock musicians in the same high regard as jazz and Western concert music musicians. On the other, he recognized the formation of a number of cultural hierarchies, the dominant of which held the Western concert tradition to be the standard for musical evaluation. When Bill Milkowski asked whether his early association with Sam Rivers affected his decision to explore free jazz on his early recordings for Blue Note, Williams responded: "No, those [recordings] were coming out of my experience with a lot of things—my love for Ornette Coleman's music at the time, Cecil Taylor's music, Eric Dolphy—all the things that I had heard that I was really involved in. I was listening to a lot of Bartók at that time, every day. [Karlheinz] Stockhausen and a lot of Stravinsky, too. *So the influences were wide-ranging.*"[13]

Williams's efforts to master Western concert music were a comment on his predicament: Williams pointed to his familiarity with Western concert music, as well as his participation in avant-garde music, not necessarily to legitimize his fusion music but to legitimize his own musical authority. But using Western art music as a standard proved problematic. Despite explicitly rationalizing Lifetime's eclectic gathering of musical practices as a means to equalize an array of musical traditions, the band members' music remained linked to older arguments dictating artistic rankings and evaluations imported from Western art music aesthetics—an aesthetic world unfamiliar, even arguably antagonistic, to non-Western and non-art music practices and practitioners. However, because Lifetime and other early fusion bands pursued their visions largely without commercial success throughout this period, they implicitly negated criticisms of any pandering to "lowered" musical tastes. Indeed, Williams's explicit admiration for both Bartók and the Beatles simultaneously made him suspicious of, as well as vulnerable to, Western high art *and* pop music conceits.

On the surface Lifetime resembled a typical "soul jazz" organ trio of the time. In the early 1960s organists such as Jimmy Smith, Jack McDuff, Jimmy McGriff, and Shirley Scott combined elements from R&B and jazz, helping to create a hybrid genre called "soul jazz," and were among the most popular acts in jazz among listening audiences, if slighted critically. While soul jazz artists troubled the conventional view of jazz as an increasingly complex idiom by their unabashedly candid "return" to the blues, fusion musicians challenged jazz conventions even more fundamentally by not only borrowing the "power drumming" (as described by Williams)[14] from rock but also the electric instrumentation and amplification systems as well, calling into question the centrality of "swing" rhythms and the primary position of acoustic instrumentation to jazz discourse as elucidated by writers as diverse as Amiri Baraka and André Hodeir.[15]

When Lifetime was forming, an exchange between Dan Morgenstern and Alan Heineman in the pages of *Down Beat* concerning the addition of rock groups (and, more notably, their fans) to the 1969 Newport Jazz Festival spoke to the antinomies between the adherents of both genres.[16] Lifetime's fusion music also questioned the elevation of jazz to an art form as an unalloyed benefit, countering it with an explicit populist aesthetic and performative agenda; yet, as previously noted, Williams would later support his artistic choices, in part, by registering his proficiency with Western art music.

Williams's defensiveness ("jazz is such a bad word, and rock is such a bad word," etc.) was provoked by his awareness of the relative status of the various genres Lifetime was seeking to merge. Genre categories are "bad words," in part, because they constrain musicians; still, ask any musician what music she or he composes or performs and the musician will most likely answer with genre names, even if used negatively or ironically. As discussed earlier, performing their duty as discursive shorthand, genre names read less as empty, floating signifiers than as active, invested signifying practices. Genre names are doubly powerful for being ambiguously reductive owing to, in some part, the music industry's need to remain flexible to market trends and fluctuations. As such, genre terms remain volatile signifiers, fueled by vernacular practices and music industry requirements.

Beyond the question of genre cataloging though, music critics, listeners, and producers also use the often implicit racialization of various genres to deflect criticism or confirm artistic legitimacy for a given genre. (Such discussions are certainly not limited to racialized ideas concerning legitimate performers or performance styles, but I will limit my remarks to this particular aspect.) This racial code, if you will, recognizes or fails to recognize specific genre crossings, reserving special attention for the proscription of the types of performative bodies considered legitimate for the public performance of specific types of music.

Although Lifetime may not have broken the links between race and genre, however, Williams and his musical cohort helped forge a new idiom that made those links more visible, forcing a confrontation among critics, listeners, and musicians that resonated along the always-shifting borders of jazz and rock. In this context it is helpful to remember that while jazz artists often cast fusion as a "crossover" attempt by jazz artists to enter the pop mainstream—an accusation resonating with all of the term's implications—fusion musicians were not the first jazz artists to cross genres or to participate in nonjazz music.

In fact, as Reebee Garofalo has noted, the music industry term *crossover* describes the movement of musicians in a subsidiary market marked by race, such as when, for example, R&B artists "cross over" to mainstream success in the pop market. African American musicians, having proven their commercial appeal in markets targeting African American consumers, might then attempt to "cross over" to (white) mainstream success or, more accurately, were promoted by their record labels to the mainstream market. As Garofalo points out, white musicians compete primarily in the mainstream pop market—with the phrase *mainstream pop* itself being a generic codifier for the market for white consumers. In the 1950s, for instance, white performers and their management rarely saw any reason to invest capital and effort into cultivating a black audience, which could readily hear them on national radio and television broadcasts. Thus, for example, the sales figures for Willie Mae "Big Mama" Thornton's 1953 hit R&B single "Hound Dog," marketed as a race record to African American audiences, fell short of Elvis Presley's 1956 cover version sales, marketed as Presley was to a national popular music audience. As rock 'n' roll was transformed into rock, the rise in rock's cultural capital, and its concomitant racialization as a "white music," went hand in hand with broader aesthetic and cultural divisions to which the increasing absence of black rock musicians became another tragic, if unsurprising, adjunct.[17]

Yet exceptional black musicians continued to impact rock music in revolutionary ways — try to think of rock music, particularly hard rock, without Jimi Hendrix and his exemplary guitar technique, his use of technology, and his fashion style. In a similar sense much of contemporary popular music would sound drastically different without Latin or gay dance and club subcultural influences and creative energies. The continuing use of euphemistic terms such as urban contemporary to designate racially inflected market segments indicates the ongoing efforts to market particular artists into specific genres (in this case, "urban contemporary" refers to a radio format of modern R&B and hip-hop music targeting a primarily black audience).

Jazz musicians have always had open ears, using other idioms as inspiration for their own innovations. But while an early jazz musician like Ferdinand "Jelly Roll" Morton could boast about his familiarity with classical music, Tony Williams was not seeking to align jazz with high culture. Rather, he was linking jazz to a musical genre — rock — that was problematic, particularly for African American jazz musicians. Yet, as I have noted, rock, rather than jazz, was increasingly displacing cultural hierarchies among the literati and artistic avant-garde by the late 1960s, while jazz musicians and critics were concurrently promoting jazz as art music and castigating rock as mere commercial pabulum.[18] Indeed, jazz was heard by many jazz critics and musicians as the embodiment of a colorblind American democracy in sound, a "classical music" created in an autonomous art space devoid of racial and ethnic affiliations.[19] Most important, however, because rock music was identified with white popular audiences in the late 1960s, when Williams chose to merge his jazz sensibilities with rock, he highlighted the relationship between race and genre.[20] He and other black fusion artists, such as Miles Davis and Herbie Hancock, grappled directly with the fact that even as genres evolve, mutate, develop into, and recoalesce into new categories in relation to the prompts and responses of the music industry or a listening audience, race plays an important part in allowing or disallowing particular bodies to perform one type of music or another.[21]

For their part the members of Lifetime merged elements borrowed and transformed from jazz aesthetics and rock music, moving beyond the black/white binarism through which critical jazz discourse often framed discussions of ownership, authority, and belonging in relation to either genre or aesthetic approach. I am thinking here of a long history of debates within jazz regarding authentic practitioners of the music. These debates range from the Original Dixieland Jazz Band leader Nick La Rocca's claim that African Americans had nothing to do with the creation of jazz to the British critic Stuart Nicholson's recent assertions that the future of jazz is located in northern Europe. A sizable cohort of critics and writers have made various assertions regarding African American claims as authentic jazz practitioners, ranging from the essentialist views of early jazz observers such as Alexander Ansermet to more recent claims for the imprimatur of African American culture from Stanley Crouch. I am not focused on this particular argument at this point except to note that fusion musicians, like jazz musicians of other eras, were compelled to address issues of authenticity and authority within a racialized context.

Indeed, Lifetime's performances embodied the contradictions in the conventional assignments between race and genre. Additionally, Williams's attraction to late-1960s psychedelic rock made his transition from Miles Davis's drummer to fusion pioneer problematic, even for sympathetic jazz listeners. While his drumming style in Davis's group was often described as aggressive by jazz writers, Williams's fondness for the Beatles, Hendrix, and the MC5 was even more readily apparent in Lifetime and showcased his wide range of musical interests, as well as his drumming skills.[22] The protopunk drumming of "Right On," for example, sounded out the contradictions and correspondences between jazz and rock, marking out different measures of the distance between the two idioms.

Because rock music was racialized by the late 1950s as a white popular music idiom, when Williams and Young chose to merge jazz sensibilities to rock, they highlighted the relationship between race and genre. Rock's construct as white music was something against which Williams would continually struggle. However, by including Jimi Hendrix in his roster of influential rock musicians, Williams also called on his listeners to reexamine rock's relationship to black musicians' bodies, practices, and aesthetics. In addition, Williams's explicit naming of particular rock artists also indicated the nonarbitrary nature in his decisions to use—or not use—various elements from rock and jazz. Still, while musicians such as Ike Turner, "Little" Richard Penniman, Charles "Chuck" Berry, and Antoine "Fats Domino" Dominique had provided the foundational recordings of rock 'n' roll, by the 1970s rock music was widely viewed as a genre performed primarily by white musicians for white audiences.[23]

Williams voiced the same motivations for merging rock and jazz as did Larry Coryell, who traced fusion's origins to an equal appreciation for the music of both John Coltrane and the Rolling Stones by young jazz musicians. Both musicians viewed fusion as the union of rock music's expressive energies and accessibility with jazz's more formal complexities and performative demands. In a manner similar to Travis Jackson's characterization of the saxophonist David Murray's and the drummer Steve McCall's reorientation of a jazz tradition, Williams read the past of jazz and rock in a way "that escapes the confines of seeing tradition as static or compelling relentless innovation in favor of seeing it as an opening of the way to both the past and the future."[24] Similarly, in his blending of the two traditions, Williams helped initiate new ways of hearing and performing jazz and rock. Still, fusion musicians would have to gain a popular audience before they could transform listening habits, genre categories, or music industry practices.

In fact, Lifetime initially puzzled jazz audiences. In a 1970 interview Stu Woods reminded Williams of a Lifetime performance when, following an intensely played set, the audience just sat there, stunned, responding wanly with "some timid applause." Williams, acknowledging the audience's muted response, replied with an anecdote of his own, recalling a concert where he "was off the bandstand before they started clapping. I was at the bar getting a glass of water and then the applause started. That was really a bring-down."[25] The energy with which Lifetime forced the issue of volume, rock's aggressive style, and the use of electric and amplified instruments stood in marked opposition to conventional jazz music, and Lifetime's challenge clearly overwhelmed jazz audiences of the time.

And so, Lifetime hoped, the audiences would begin to change in tune with the music. In a 1970 *Melody Maker* interview Richard Williams noted that when he went to hear Lifetime at Ungano's, "the place was packed with young people who looked like rock fans." When asked about his motivations for playing venues more closely associated with rock, Tony Williams countered, "The music hits the kids at the level that they get tired of crap. So many rock groups sound the same—trite, terrible, and just plain silly, man. And people, whether they know it or not, want to hear something better. At Ungano's it's a different audience from, say, a place like [the jazz club] Slug's."[26]

Here Williams is positioning Lifetime—and, by extension, fusion writ large—as a music for rock fans searching "to hear something better." Jazz fans were not necessarily Lifetime's target audience. Williams's early disappointments with jazz audiences were not simply a result of a preoccupation with *popularity* but an indication of his *populist* concern about reengaging a popular audience of his peers. On the one hand, as mainstream jazz moved into the cocktail lounges of Las Vegas and Atlantic City, as well as the tourist clubs of Manhattan, jazz came to be perceived by fusion musicians as relinquishing much of its social vitality to rock. On the other hand, mainstream and avant-garde jazz artists initiated tenuous connections to elite culture as they gained arts council funding, concert hall engagements, and, later, academic posts, moving jazz further along a path that Williams described in 1976:

> Twenty years ago, jazz was being made for a very happy audience and writers and scholars who didn't play music came along and told people that this music was an art form. That's fine, because that's what many of the musicians wanted it to be regarded as. But what it did was to make everyone conscious of it as an art form. The same thing that happened to classical music almost happened to jazz; *it almost became sterile with people playing only for very elite purposes.* The approach was no longer human at times. What's happening now is that it's becoming more human [through fusion]. Most people don't know anything about the technical possibilities inherent in playing jazz—and they don't want to know.[27]

Sounding remarkably similar to Dizzy Gillespie, who once commented on dancers' ignorance of "ruptured 129th" chords, Williams admits to his concern for connecting with popular audiences. In fact, communicating with a youthful audience was a key part of Lifetime's aesthetic program, and the band members' unapologetic efforts to attract young audiences were initiated at a time when, as noted above, jazz musicians were beginning to slowly gain inroads to cultural and institutional legitimacy.[28] Fusion musicians' efforts to regain popular appeal for jazz, particularly among young people who did not necessarily identify themselves as jazz fans, were met with indifference or antipathy by two otherwise distinct groups. One group—which was represented by jazz critics associated with *Down Beat* and similar mainstream jazz-oriented publications—remained committed to viewing jazz music as either an art music or as part of a broad stream of African American vernacular practices. On this particular issue they were joined by the second group, which comprised Afrocentric or black nationalist jazz critics and musicians such as Bill Dixon, Archie Shepp, and Charles Mingus. These two circles each claimed to be untainted by commercial interests, and they were each equally sensitive to any implications of exploiting jazz musicians for corporate interests.

Yet, to give one example, when faced with the dominance of white musicians in the mainstream market, bebop musicians in the 1940s, as Scott DeVeaux argues, responded with "an attempt to reconstitute jazz — or more precisely, the specialized idiom of the improvising virtuoso — in such a way as to give its black creators the greatest professional autonomy *within* the marketplace."[29] Bebop musicians, in other words, were not exclusively concerned with their status as artists in the public sphere. They were motivated in part by economic concerns, as well as a sensitivity to their positions as artists and entertainers. By the early 1970s the recurring debates within jazz regarding the dialectic between art and commerce — an entrenched cultural argument that swing, bebop, and cool jazz musicians all confronted at one time or another — were being revitalized by Williams and his young cohort of fusion musicians.[30]

Despite the validation that his studies of Western concert music may have granted him, Williams heard rock music as a primary source of artistic freedom, personal expression, and aesthetic pleasure. After leaving one of the world's most high-profile mainstream jazz groups, Williams was insistent about his need to create a different kind of music. He titled Lifetime's debut 1969 recording *Emergency!* because it was "an emergency for me to leave Miles" and, more important, to mark his desire to "play an emerging music that was my own."[31] After all, as he asked rhetorically throughout interviews of the time, hadn't he already been the drummer in one of the best acoustic jazz quintets? He decided to form an organ trio but with musical goals markedly different from the ones soul jazz organ trios had pursued: "I use electric instruments because it's there; *it's another sound*. I can't play the same thing all the time; after playing with Herbie [Hancock] and Wayne [Shorter], I can't play with any horn player right now. After playing with Miles there aren't any trumpet players for me to listen to right now, so I go somewhere else for something else. I try to be stimulated."[32]

As I have noted, one of the key aesthetic motivations for Williams's electric "turn" was his fondness for Hendrix, Cream, and the MC5, thus indicating the distance between his professional jazz efforts and his private listening habits. Lifetime's aesthetic was forged in the very "contradictions" between jazz and rock, partially shaping the ways in which fusion measured, and attempted to bridge, that gulf. For Williams, as well as other young jazz

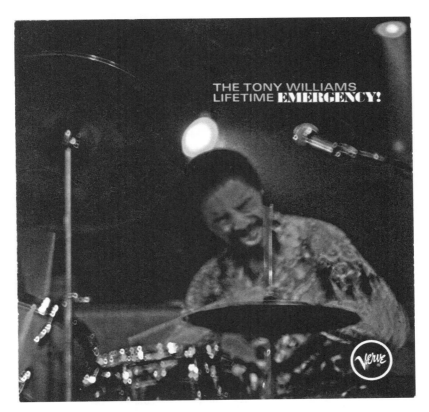

The Tony Williams Lifetime *Emergency!* front cover.

musicians, their readily acknowledged artistic debt to contemporary rock music marked them as participants in a discussion borrowed from rock aesthetics, which, as Keir Keightley argues, "involves the making of distinctions within mass culture, rather than the older problem of distinguishing mass from elite or vernacular cultures. *Rock's values and judgements produce a highly stratified conception of popular music*, in which minute distinctions are seen to take on life and death significance. Taking popular music seriously, as something 'more' than mere entertainment or distraction, has been a crucial feature of rock culture since its emergence [in the 1960s]."[33]

Such intrarock discussions displaced the high/low cultural wars by rejecting the assumptions privileging one set of musical practices "above" others. Rock audiences of the late 1960s largely rejected earlier entertainment ideals, valuing, for example, authenticity above showmanship. Though this was largely rhetorical—witness the emergence of psychedelic light shows and other manifestations of rock spectacle—these moves occurred largely out of earshot of the symphony hall and the jazz club. Williams, for his part, participated in these intrarock polemics when he discussed his preference for the Beatles or Jimi Hendrix (as opposed to naming, for instance, the country-rock group the Byrds or a more mainstream popular group such as the Association). As Gracyk and Wicke argue, rock artists of the 1960s such as Hendrix had helped transform what had been viewed by music critics and scholars as a teen entertainment idiom, rock 'n' roll, into a more serious musical endeavor, rock. These musicians facilitated this transformation by addressing increasingly mature themes, incorporating sophisticated musical techniques (including elements grafted from the avant-garde art music world), and, in Hendrix's case in particular, exhibiting an instrumental virtuosity in an otherwise largely nonvirtuosic musical tradition (for the most part, rock discourse on authenticity stresses a certain lack of technique but, like any other idiom, maintains various internal markers to register technical competence).[34]

In fact, the Beatles and Hendrix represented a nascent aesthetic sophistication in rock music—if not exactly on par with Euro-American art music masters, then certainly "more than" pop. As they and other rock musicians began to self-consciously position themselves as "legitimate" artists, their moves were reinforced by rock journalists such as Robert Christgau, Greil Marcus, Lester Bangs, Cameron Crowe, Dave Marsh, and Ben Fong-Torres, each of whom treated rock music to serious analysis, contributing to a burgeoning rock discourse constructed by *Rolling Stone*, *Creem*, *Crawdaddy!*, and numerous other trade publications that emphasized rock's critical, even intellectual, aspects.

But evaluating differences in popular music culture was nothing new to the jazz world. Jazz listeners had split hairs over jazz minutiae for decades. Rock musicians' moves to self-consciously position themselves as "legitimate" artists were reinforced by an increased attention to their lyrics and music by journalists, echoing the expert-fans of jazz discourse. Similar to the ways in which serious jazz listeners consumed jazz, as Keightley's argument implies, Beatles and Hendrix fans and critics represented an aesthetic sophistication in rock music *consumers* as well as creators.

Evaluating differences in rock music culture also mirrored the distinctions jazz critics hoped would prevail for jazz over other types of popular music, elevating jazz into a type of "classical music," privileging or discrediting different styles of jazz thought to detract from, in their view, an unimpeachable goal. Again, Williams's own ambivalence was marked by his commitment to private classical music theory and composition lessons and his attraction to rock music's expressive powers and non-elitist appeal.

Williams insisted: "So anyway, the energy of the music is happening, but it's rock & roll. . . . Because I'm a drummer, I'm attracted more to [rock's] power kind of drumming, and the emotional kind of drumming."[35] "Spectrum," from the band's debut, illustrates his conception of power drumming, beginning with the band's powerful unison entry into the composition. McLaughlin and Young perform a soon-to-be-typical fusion unison line: angular, intensely abstract, abrasive yet technical, and virtuosic. Similar in rhythmic and thematic intensity to a bebop "head" (theme or melody) such as "Shaw 'Nuff," Lifetime performed as a single, multiheaded organism (again, comparisons to Parker's and Gillespie's unison reading of the main theme on their original "Shaw 'Nuff" recording are apt).

Periodic rhythmic breaks appear between segments of the main theme. McLaughlin takes the first solo, a remarkably cogent improvisation that builds on fragments of the main theme. The band reiterates the "head" before Young takes his solo. Underneath Young's abstracted rhythmic ideas, Williams builds his emotional power slowly, relying on steady swing cymbal work. Young spins long filigreed lines as Williams's intensity increases beneath the organist's soloing. Young and Williams converse through an extended antiphonic section. McLaughlin is silent for much of Young's solo, entering briefly before Young ends his solo and the band reiterates the main theme. After this restatement of the theme the trio moves into a blues-rock rave-up cadenza, giving the leader a chance to solo before McLaughlin signals the last unison rendition of the main line to end the track decisively.

Still, many of the jazz musicians with whom Williams was playing at the time were dismissive of his interest in pop and rock music, thereby partially motivating his departure from Davis's band. Williams was clear about one of the reasons his professional peers remained unconvinced about the value of rock music: "Well, it's because I'm a big fan of the Beatles. When I say that, people get nuts. I had this Beatles poster in my apartment years ago and people would come and visit and they'd see this poster and say, 'Man, why do you have that on your wall?' You know, I'm supposed to be this 'jazzer,' and I'm listening to the Beatles. But the thing is, it's the context that people don't want to deal with. When the Beatles hit, I was still 17, 18 years old. That was part of my generation's music."[36]

His peers in the jazz world were older, not "part of Williams's generation," and his efforts to recognize rock music as having artistic value were often rejected by them. At the time, the jazz and rock worlds seemed so distant—at least from a jazz musician's perspective—that many of Williams's jazz contemporaries rejected offers to join him in his fusion explorations. For example, the African American guitarist Sonny Sharrock, who was a mere five years older than Williams, turned down an offer to be in Lifetime with the reply that he didn't play rock.[37] For the most part jazz musicians had been feeling the encroachment of rock musicians on their former dominance of the popular music market and found little comfort in Williams's efforts to reconcile jazz and rock music. The bassist Ron Carter, Williams's former partner in Miles Davis's rhythm section, voiced some of these concerns in a 1969 conversation with the drummer Art Taylor. I quote Carter at length in order to indicate the range of concerns some jazz musicians held at the time with regard to rock:

> In my research I have found that most of the current rock beats are nothing but very poorly executed New Orleans jazz drumming. . . . If you listen to the record [drummer Billy Higgins] made, *The Sidewinder*, with [trumpeter] Lee Morgan, it sounds like a rock beat. It is not rock. It is only classified as rock for the commercial value of the term. The guitar players who make jazz records or the jazz bands who hire guitar players to get a rock flavor are playing all rhythm-and-blues licks, which is not rock. Rock today, as the public knows, is nothing but watered down, original B. B. King and Blind Lemon Jefferson. The original field hollers that were stolen by Alan Lomax and released on Vanguard Records in the

fifties, jail cries that they played, the seven-bar and thirteen-bar blues, Leadbelly and all those cats, are being transferred into white rock bands. All they do is play it louder and much poorer for commercial reasons. I feel that jazz players are not playing rock as the market understands it, but that's what they are going into due to the commercial potential of the term rock.[38]

Carter's views regarding fusion musicians' economic motivations and their lack of jazz skills—derived partially from his definitions of rock, R&B, and jazz—exemplify the contentious debates of the time between older and younger jazz musicians. For older jazz musicians such as Carter, economic values trumped the social values Williams noted when he pointed to the Beatles as an indicator of the then-current connections between youth culture, psychedelic rock, and countercultural values.[39] However, the central arguments centered on the economic; mainstream jazz musicians and listeners maintained the view that fusion musicians were little more than musical mercenaries with more interest in earning money than preserving artistic integrity. Yet, as I will argue below, rock music of the late 1960s grew increasingly linked to countercultural political thought, and in a close resemblance to the more overtly politicized rock musicians he admired, Williams's efforts to meld jazz and rock were motivated by aesthetic and social concerns, as well as economic ones.

When asked why he chose a career in jazz although he grew up a rock fan, Williams was explicit about his decision: "The reason . . . is because in 1954 and '55, the only interesting things about playing music were in jazz. Jazz was more adventurous. In 1954, you had the Everly Brothers, who I loved; Frankie Lymon and the Teenagers; you had Elvis, you had all these kinds of things in the pop world. But there were no bands. Drumming was not something that was exciting in that kind of music."[40]

It can be argued that economic considerations also helped propel Williams toward a career in jazz rather than rock, as might have easily happened given his early rock band experiences and interest in the Beatles and Hendrix. Importantly, his father's network of jazz musicians, club owners, and other players in a local jazz scene helped to facilitate his early professional formation as a jazz musician. For all his activity as a young rock musician, he and his rock band mates were less professionally organized, less connected to the professional music industry, and less likely to find gainful employment.

Still, by the time he formed Lifetime, Williams pointed to various rock artists' music in terms of musicianship and complexity: the Beatles, along with their producer, George Martin, drew on a wide variety of musical idioms, including Western art music, older styles of British and American popular music, as well as more obvious rock influences such as the blues, R&B, gospel, and country and western; Jimi Hendrix's mastery of the blues did not preclude him from becoming a pioneering guitarist who became famous for his experiments with feedback, distortion, and sound-manipulating devices (like the wah-wah pedal and fuzz box), along with his penchant for aggressive dissonance and volume; and Cream was a band of rock virtuosos who signaled the arrival of a growing number of technically proficient rock musicians (especially if one recalls the bassist Jack Bruce's professional apprenticeship in straight-ahead jazz groups). Growing contingents of rock musicians, including Stevie Winwood of Traffic and flutist Ian Anderson of Jethro Tull, were drawing on a number of aesthetic and musical traditions, ultimately gaining some measure of critical legitimacy for their efforts.[41] As a professional musician whose categorization as a black jazz musician held specific sets of meanings in economic as well as aesthetic terms, Williams shouldered concerns about artistic value based on the racialized implications of transgenre mergings.

Lifetime's blending of rock and jazz practices was an "opening of the way" performed in the broken middle between the two musical traditions. In this way Lifetime participated in the identity politics of the period. They modeled Stuart Hall's "new ethnicity" *avant la lettre*, performatively enacting an idiosyncratically affiliative identity.[42] Rather than forge an identity between any two groups marked as distinct from one another with absolute or *necessary* entailments to past histories of confluence or conflict, their music retained a sense of contingent mergings, sounding out the abandonment of necessary legacies and entanglements, lithely moving between musical traditions, touching on yet adhering to none. In spite of a rhetorical construction of separate music worlds, Williams, McLaughlin, and Young felt free to imaginatively combine rock, jazz, and any other musical tradition or set of practices.

Importantly, Williams's initial motivations for performing jazz (e.g., its aesthetic and technical sophistication) had been transferred to rock. By citing his appreciation for the Beatles, Jimi Hendrix, and Cream, Williams was challenging the notion of the superiority of jazz over other popular music in musical terms, and, by drawing inspiration from a "white" music, he helped to position fusion music as a powerfully syncretic force. Such moves were countered by contemporary mainstream critical jazz writings. For example, displaying the posture of mainstream jazz critics of the time, Dan Morgenstern, editor of *Down Beat* in 1969, wrote about the year's New-port Jazz Festival: "Hopefully, the loyal jazz fans have not been alienated. A good program should bring them back next year. By all means, spice it up with valid things, like real blues and r&b, but leave rock where it belongs: in the circus or the kindergarten."[43]

But, as mentioned earlier, when Williams began his fusion experiments in the late 1960s, rock musicians were reshaping popular music by express-ing more than adolescent themes and obsessions in their music, gaining cultural legitimacy in ways jazz music had only begun to acquire itself, while simultaneously eclipsing jazz in the marketplace. Though it is true that jazz artists such as Quincy Jones kept mainstream jazz ubiquitous in movie and television scores, and that a minority of jazz artists found increasing insti-tutional support at this time, thus eventually gaining critical legitimacy in the academy (even if kept at an arm's distance from "legitimate" music), the music industry and popular audiences turned a deaf ear to many jazz musi-cians' creative work, leaving jazz critics to lament jazz's imminent passing. While most jazz musicians rarely believed they would become wealthy pop stars, I want to note here the effects of rock music's rise in cultural capital on jazz musicians' economic status. This linkage was not only apparent to jazz musicians but was felt by the jazz world writ large.[44]

Recognizing rock musicians' increasing cultural reach, as well as ac-knowledging publishing market realities, *Down Beat* soon featured rock mu-sicians in cover stories and interviews, as well as rock recordings and live shows in its review sections. Still, a certain hesitancy can be noted when Morgenstern opened up *Down Beat*'s editorial policy in the June 29, 1967, issue, writing that the magazine, "without reducing its coverage of jazz, will expand its editorial perspective to include *the musically valid aspects of the rock scene*."[45] Ironically, Morgenstern viewed jazz's entry into the rarified space of high art as foreclosing jazz's ability to be a "social force . . . [which once] taught us how to live in peace and harmony with each other" at a time when mainstream jazz had been positioned as a democratic space by observers such as André Hodeir even as that ideal was being contested by writers such as Amiri Baraka (writing as LeRoi Jones).[46] This was by no means the only view, but it was an ideal held by many in the jazz world at the time, a perspec-tive that fit neatly into the era's liberal politics. Indeed, the integrationist appeals of the late 1960s by critics and fans were advocated by those who became increasingly defensive in their appreciation for jazz music and musicians of all skin colors, particularly in the face of growing black nationalism in certain jazz circles.[47]

But positioning jazz as art music tends to erase the struggles of black musicians for artistic recognition. Arguments used to support jazz's move up the cultural hierarchy were often based on an assumption of the bandstand as a space of deracinated meritocracy, thereby effectively eliding discussions about black participation in high culture—indeed, ignoring high modernist culture as partially constituted by black artists and aesthetics. Yet racial biases off the bandstand continued to dictate the terms of critical value, institutional legitimation, and economic compensation for jazz musicians positioned in particular racialized ways (e.g., economic differentials for black and white band leaders or musicians).[48]

Both fusion and free jazz artists recognized this situation but used different strategies to overcome their marginalization. Moreover, claims of jazz's status as an art music elide the ways in which jazz remained connected to the marketplace, dependent on recording technologies and mass-market distribution circuits—it had not yet become sponsored by commissions and grants in the manner of art music. On the one hand, art status did not alter jazz musicians' continued disbarment from elite positions, for the most part, even within the institutions that arbitrated the distribution and compensation for their recordings and public performances. On the other hand, rock musicians were linking their music to a broad range of social and political issues by 1970 and were being figured by rock discourse as political subjects brandishing a slate of radical challenges to social and political norms.

The band's adoption of electric, amplified power and an extroverted emotionality, demonstrated largely through loud volumes and displays of technical virtuosity, fueled jazz listeners' antipathy toward the band's music, which often rested on an assumption of rock music's lesser technical demands. But as Gracyk argues, rock's rhythms are "neither primitive nor simple, nor primordial nor mechanical. The poverty of Western thinking about rhythm, coupled with common prejudices and stereotypes about popular culture, obscures the diversity and role of rhythm in rock music."[49] In other words, rather than abandoning jazz's complexity, Williams was trading in one way of addressing rhythm for another, no-less-complex, manner of drumming.

This view, however, was not shared by jazz musicians and critics at the time, as Ron Carter's remarks above indicate.

Lifetime embraced rock's willingness to use whatever tools technological advances in recording and sound reproduction had to offer. Moreover, in contrast to jazz critics who often criticized electric instrumentation as emotionally "cold," Williams's interest in electric instrumentation was visceral: "I started hearing a lot of electricity. The first thing I can remember . . . was Jimi Hendrix's first record, and the sound of it . . . with all that electricity. . . . I mean, not presence electricity, but *the amplified electricity, the sound of the guitars, and that started to excite me, and I wanted to hear more of that.*"[50]

Williams's excitement—desire hyperventilating at the sound of electric guitars—registered itself in a time-honored rock 'n' roll way: by cranking up the volume. As we have seen, Lifetime performed at volume levels uncomfortable for many jazz fans. The liner notes to Lifetime's second recording, *Turn It Over*, emphasized the role volume performed in the burgeoning fusion aesthetic by stating in bold capital letters, "PLAY IT LOUD" and "PLAY IT VERY VERY LOUD." Williams and his fellow band mates utilized volume to announce their break from conventional jazz aesthetics, incorporating rock's electric amplification and sound-modifying technologies to signal their excitement about fusion music. Moreover, Williams's intentionally hard-to-decipher liner notes stood in marked contrast to listening to the recording at a loud volume—an indication that the music mattered more than the writing. Conventionally, liner notes and credits are written to give information rather than obscure it. By intentionally printing the credits in a difficult-to-read manner, while highlighting the volume at which the recording should be played, Williams (who is listed as one of the graphic designers) challenged many period listeners' practices of reading liner notes as part of the act of music consumption. With this liner note design Williams seems to suggest that it is relatively unimportant to know who is playing or what he is playing, but it is important to "play this record very loud."

This appeal to an increased volume also registered the band's commitment to a politics of pleasure similar to the one enunciated by the MC5, which has been compellingly analyzed by Steve Waksman. Briefly, the MC5 called on rock audiences to abandon bourgeois rationality's distrust of the body through the use of volume, noise, and electric instrumentation in rock performance spectacles. Similarly, Lifetime also used loud volume as an audible signifier focusing attention back on the body. Unlike the MC5's stated purpose of liberating white bodies from bourgeois convention, however,

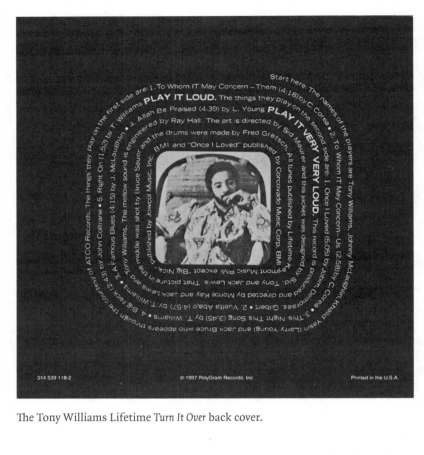

The circular text, reading from "Start here" around the spiral, reads:

Start here. The names of the players are Tony Williams, Johnny McLaughlin, Khalid Yasin (Larry Young) and Jack Bruce who appears through the courtesy of ATCO Records. The things they play on the first side are: 1. To Whom IT May Concern – Them (4:18) by C. Corea • 2. To Whom IT May Concern – Us (2:58) by C. Corea • 3. This Night This Song (3:45) by T. Williams • 4. Big Nick (2:44) by John Coltrane • 5. Right On (1:52) by T. Williams **PLAY IT LOUD.** The things they play on the second side are: 1. Once I Loved (5:05) by C. Corea • 2. Vuelta Abajo (4:57) by T. Williams • 3. A Famous Blues (4:15) by J. McLaughlin • 4. Allah Be Praised (4:39) by L. Young **PLAY IT VERY VERY LOUD.** This record is produced and directed by Monte Kay and Jack Lewis and engineered by Ray Hall. The art is directed by Sid Maurer. All tunes published by Lifetime Kaymont Music BMI except "Big Nick," published by Jowcol Music, Inc. BMI and "Once I Loved" published by Corcovado Music Corp. BMI and the drums were made by Fred Gretsch. The mellow sound is engineered by Lifetime. Tony Williams. That picture in the middle was shot by Bruce Sauer.

314 539 118-2 © 1997 PolyGram Records, Inc. Printed in the U.S.A.

The Tony Williams Lifetime *Turn It Over* back cover.

Lifetime's loud volume and use of noise served as a locus of unresolved tensions in terms of the ownership and individual autonomy of black musicians' creative works. As Williams noted in a 1979 interview, critics and fans own "these records of me with Miles [Davis], for example, and they gave me their approval, so I 'belong' to them on those records. I'm up there in their special section, and they go up and pick me out. They've *bought* me, so to speak. Well, if they feel that way about the music, then they resent it if you change."⁵¹ Williams's reference to being "bought" and, by extension, "owned" by consumers resonates audibly against the historical backdrop of African American slavery in the United States, underscoring the constraints of genre on musicians.⁵² His attention to audience "approval" betrays the terms of the relationship, and one way to assert artistic autonomy was to play music no one wanted to hear at volumes they could not help but hear.

Yet musicians received mixed blessings with the emergence of recording and sound reproduction technologies. As I have noted, musicians were able to reach potentially larger audiences by dislocating bodily presence from musical performance, effectively "performing" through recordings. This benefit had economic as well as aesthetic demands and rewards. As the number of recordings superseded live performances circulating in the marketplace, musicians were increasingly locked into particular ways of performing music. One need only think of current listening habits dominated by reproductive processes rather than live performances to recognize the economic implications for professional touring musicians who must reproduce recordings for audiences who have grown attached to specific recorded versions of musical compositions.

Musically, Lifetime's second album, the 1970 *Turn It Over*, was an even more confrontational recording than its 1969 predecessor, *Emergency!*, performatively critiquing both listeners' and critics' assumptions of ownership in all its figurative and sonic excesses. *Turn It Over* outlined an openly aggressive turn by the band toward its critics and signaled its interest in a new audience of rock fans. As Williams admitted later, the recording was partly a reflection of the social turmoil of the time:

> Most people forget [the social and political upheavals of the early 1970s] when they talk about [Lifetime] or even the state of jazz at that time. There was a lot of tension and anxiety about what we were doing. Our music wasn't always accepted and it was tough to deal with that. *The title was about turning over society. It was my version of* [MC5's] *Kick Out the Jams.* The album art [on *Turn It Over*] was black, the liner notes were very hard

to read—it was just aggressively antagonistic. That was the whole idea behind that record.[53]

As a fan of the MC5, Williams was conceivably aware of this band's association with the white radical group the White Panthers. The White Panthers, a group modeled somewhat loosely on the Black Panthers (declaring, for instance, in its own manifesto the "full endorsement and support of [the] Black Panthers' 10-point Program"), espoused a radical, anarchic political position as evidenced on the inner sleeve of the MC5's debut album, *Kick Out the Jams* (Elektra 1969). John Sinclair, credited with "Guidance" on creating this album, wrote the liner notes and was the most articulate voice in delineating the MC5's politics. He was well known in the rock music world as a political activist—some would say a provocateur—and he was sentenced to ten years in a federal penitentiary for possession of two marijuana cigarettes. A fan of free jazz as well as hard rock, Sinclair continued to write free jazz and rock record reviews from Marquette Prison in Michigan. One article was a manifesto entitled "Self Determination Music," wherein he outlined some of the social and creative implications for musical production in a system in which musicians owned the means of producing and distributing their creative work. Here he also demarcated an "authentic" revolutionary music opposed to a commercial mainstream. While his ideas were not entirely singular in the early 1970s, his influence, along with the MC5, struck a resonant chord with the nascent punk rock movement that emerged later in the decade. His slogan, "Music is revolution," also connected with the political aims of African American free jazz artists, and he often connected hard rock, free jazz, and revolutionary politics in his radical political writings.

Williams's own revolutionary leanings were far less direct or explicit. His politics were directed primarily toward Lifetime's musical mixtures. Lifetime was never a politicized band in the manner of the MC5 (or, indeed, the Beatles), subsuming its political views in an aesthetic contestation of conventional musical practices, categories, and institutions. In this way Lifetime presaged the so-called identity politics of the late 1970s, abandoning the large-scale revolutionary aims of some radical groups for the more limited agenda of reshaping social relationships in local, intimate spaces while remaining increasingly aware of global connections.

Williams was in fact pessimistic about political solutions and processes, admitting when asked about "all the strife going on with his people" that "we're not going to see [positive social change]; we're going to be long dead. All we can do is hang in there and keep fighting."[54] Despite this point of view, however, Williams went on to state unequivocally, "I don't play political music. Music is hipper than that. When cats in the press ask, Does your music express your people's conflicts? I say no, it's just there. Anything I do politically is too personal. I don't need to use my music to do that. That's cheating. I really don't dig political music, using music."[55]

Williams uttered these words at a time (the mid-1970s) when his musical contemporaries on either side of the jazz-nonjazz borders were challenging the division between musical and political activities. Jazz artists such as Charles Mingus and Archie Shepp offered social and political commentary along with their music while musician-led organizations such as the Association for the Advancement of Creative Music, Sun Ra's Arkestra, and Charlie Haden's Liberation Orchestra exemplified alternative social formations. Rock musicians such as Sly and the Family Stone, Jimi Hendrix, and the MC5 were explicit about their radical political and social views and donated public performances to political organizations.

In what manner did Lifetime mean to "turn over society," then? Williams, McLaughlin, and Young highlighted how volatile interracial and transcultural mixtures remained (in spite of advances in U.S. public policy, such as the passage of the Civil Rights Act of 1964) without explicit political platforms or manifestoes but, rather, through embodying transcultural mixture as members of a racially integrated band creating a transgeneric music. In the politically charged cultural landscape of a post–civil rights America, hiring McLaughlin (and, later, the white English bassist Jack Bruce) proved controversial. As a white Englishman deeply involved with Williams's music, McLaughlin provided a lightning rod for the debates surrounding black creativity and the desires of black artists such as Williams to lay claim to broader, even universal, aesthetic legitimization and audience appeal. Williams heard about the guitarist through the bassist Dave Holland, who knew McLaughlin from their time spent sharing bandstands in England.[56] Later, Williams claimed McLaughlin "was the best around at the time [and] . . . I knew he had [the] capability to play exactly what I was looking for."[57] The electric guitarist, whose style was influenced by John Coltrane and blues guitarist Muddy Waters, fit in well with Williams's agenda to distance himself from mainstream jazz music, as well as give voice to the "excitement" he heard in Hendrix.

Instead of critical acclaim, however, Williams faced the same questions confronted by his former employer, Miles Davis, as well as Hendrix, about leading a racially mixed band. Neither the rock nor jazz worlds seemed comfortable with the racial politics of mixed-band membership, especially if the leader of the band was black. Williams acknowledged as much:

> Somebody came back to me and said, "What are you doing about white guys in your band?" That's such a drag, because like I told other people, it's such a thing now, I'm really in the middle of everything. On one side, I've got black militants, you know, and it should be all black, and the rock musicians don't really consider us rock. You know, we're not trying to be rock. They think we're trying to play up to them, and we're not. And I'm not trying to get away from jazz because I want to make money, and that's not it either. I've got all these things coming down on me.[58]

Williams was obviously distressed about the reaction to Lifetime by black nationalists, as well as white and black jazz critics and audiences. When black nationalists confronted Williams about hiring white musicians, it revealed how audiences had internalized these constructs regarding the correspondences between idiom and musician, supporting Williams's claims about the relationship between race and genre, audience and musician. Lifetime's eager embrace of a "postethnic" aesthetic was a way in which the band members tried to reconfigure racial and ethnic difference(s), though, at the time, their efforts were anathema to black nationalists and cultural conservatives alike.

Musically, whereas *Emergency!* was psychedelic in orientation, with compositions such as "Where" and "Vashkar," *Turn It Over* was a restatement of Lifetime's affinity for hard rock, in unequivocal terms, with cuts such as "Right On" and "A Famous Blues." The opening tracks, versions of Chick Corea's "To Whom It May Concern—Them" and "To Whom It May Concern—Us," were arranged to immediately alert listeners to Lifetime's unapologetic moves toward rock. McLaughlin's guitar tone and choice of solo material did not reference jazz guitarists such as Charlie Christian or Tal Farlow so much as contemporaneous rock guitarists such as Jimi Hendrix, if rendered in a different harmonic context. For example, Williams's composition "Right On" highlighted the ways in which rock and jazz could meet as Williams goaded McLaughlin and Young into increasingly frenzied choruses.

Their version of the Antonio Carlos Jobim bossa nova composition "Once I Loved" displayed Lifetime's merging of rock and experimental music. Williams only provides vocals on this track. The track begins with Larry Young sustaining notes in the upper register of the organ accompanying tape distortion, guitar, and microphone feedback and amplifier noise, with

McLaughlin inserting intermittent chords. It is almost a full two minutes before Tony Williams sings the lyrics in English forlornly, "Once . . ." while the high-pitched background continues. McLaughlin provides harmonic support, moving through the changes while Young maintains long treble tones. Finally, a few minutes later, Williams sighs, "Love." The track seems to flutter away, another truncation. It ends abruptly, sounding as if the song was ended more by happenstance—the end of a tape reel, perhaps?—than by intent. A listener might hear this as a sonic foregrounding of Lifetime's own premature ending, if not a premonition of Larry Young's disappearance from jazz history.

"Once I Loved" is followed by "Vuelta Abajo," a Williams composition that immediately places Lifetime back in a sonic space familiar to Cream fans with its bass riffing, guitar histrionics, and volatile drumming. The next track, McLaughlin's "A Famous Blues," with its barely audible whispered vocal track running beneath the lead vocals, conjured psychedelia once again, and Williams's solo midway through the piece showcased the leader's technical skills. As fusion contested the assumptions in the relationship between genres and audiences, it is small wonder that Lifetime's record label, Polydor, failed to market the band successfully, promoting Lifetime to a jazz audience indifferent, and often hostile, to the band's fusion agenda.

In the end Williams was explicit about how Lifetime's fusion agenda might be conceived as a way of "turning society over," arguing, "[I plan] to show people that the music isn't dead. Try to bring back the vitality that has been lost. They've made jazz an art form, put it in concert halls, made it intellectual, and that's one way they killed it. So did the rock [critics]."[59] In effect, Williams, echoing Jon Carroll's review of the *Art of Rock* in *Rolling Stone* magazine, was arguing that even as rock became more "intellectual," it risked losing its vitality to affect people along the way. Similar to the MC5 or Hendrix, Lifetime suggested that a politics of pleasure and an aesthetics of noise might prove equally challenging to critical hegemony as overt political action.

Williams's disappointment with the reaction by critics and longtime fans of his work with Miles Davis was "painful," but he was uncompromising about his decision "for not staying in musical areas that *they* felt comfortable with."[60] Lifetime signaled Williams's frustrations about the borders between various musical genres, as he explained in an interview soon after *Turn It Over*'s release: "Five years from now I may just walk on stage and saw a chair in half. Right now I'm using electricity and rhythms that make me feel good. If I didn't feel good I'd never play—I certainly wouldn't play just because somebody wanted to hear me. When what I play stops feeling good, I'm not going to continue."[61]

He admitted elsewhere that he had turned down offers to record because he "didn't want to make records just for the sake of making records, for the romantic feeling of being in the studio," emphasizing a personal criterion for his music.[62] Yet the feeling of being "vilified," as he described it, was difficult to alleviate, and Lifetime became louder, more aggressive, more, well, rocklike in its attempt to "kick out the jams."

Lifetime's alignment with the aggressive styles of psychedelic and hard rock was underlined by the 1970 addition of the British bassist Jack Bruce, whose membership in the successful rock group Cream appeared, initially, to aid Lifetime's crossover to a rock audience. But behind-the-scenes management struggles between various band members' support teams, particularly Robert Stigwood's handling of Bruce, began to wear on the cohesion of the group musically. After another two recordings, Williams disbanded Lifetime and effectively retired from the music business for three years.[63] Another problem, according to Williams, was his own indecisive leadership: "Everyone started to have their own idea as to what the band should be. As young as I was, I didn't have the experience to recognize that. I should have fought to maintain my original vision."[64] Eventually, Williams abandoned the use of Lifetime as a band moniker entirely, noting a personal as well as professional loss: "It just wasn't the same without Larry Young. He was the heart of Lifetime."[65]

While certainly not the first multiracial band, as one of the first groups to be explicit in its attempts to merge rock and jazz sensibilities, Lifetime entered the broken middle, flowing between genres and traditions. For example, each instrumentalist maintains an equal interest in the overall musical texture of McLaughlin's composition "Where," mixing the rock and jazz elements freely in the phrasing of the music. The composition's three verses allow the musical instruments "to speak" with the barest of accompaniment to Williams's vocals, providing a sense of lightness and space and underscoring the softly enunciated lyrics. Each verse asks of a future—where are you/they/I going?—as well as a past—where do you/they/I come from?—sung deliberately and unhurriedly.

An early example of fusion song, "Where" begins quietly as a softly enunciated rhythmic pulse emanating from a disconcertingly unidentifiable source: a drum, a looped mechanical sound of some kind, the B3's rotary speakers—a mix of all three? McLaughlin elicits arrhythmic timbral gestures from his electric guitar as the steady pulse continues underneath. Young is present as a barely registered treble pitch fading slowly from back to middle ground. After a brief opening section notable for its atmosphere of muted psychedelia, McLaughlin hints at the short melodic phrase that defines the composition, signaling Williams, who begins singing shortly after the riff's appearance. His voice is quietly inquisitive, whispery and tentative, "Where are you going?" Williams lets the instruments fill in the final line of the verse, "If anyone asks you, I hope you can say," his voice fading as McLaughlin begins his guitar solo.

As Williams signals a rhythmic shift on the tom drums, the instruments respond emphatically to the lyrical challenge, pushing past Williams's understated singing style by raising the volume and emphasizing their presence through the use of distortion. His drumming, while continuing to enunciate the rhythmic pulse, also plays against Young's ostinato figure while interacting with McLaughlin's soloing. The band's unison performance of Young's ostinato figure signals the end of McLaughlin's first chorus. The band shifts, returning to the faintly psychedelic introductory section as a brief interlude before McLaughlin begins his second solo chorus.

Developing a series of intensely abstract lines against a firmly etched rhythmic drive, articulated directly by Williams's hi-hat and cymbal work, McLaughlin's single-note lead lines reveal some of the speed and technique he has at his disposal. Abruptly, at the end of an undeniably expressive solo, and again in unison, McLaughlin and his band mates immediately return to the opening section's quiet rhythmic pulse and McLaughlin's and Young's open-ended timbral explorations. Soon, Williams sings the second verse, again sotto voce: "Where are they going?"

Young begins his solo at the same lyrical juncture as McLaughlin, responding to Williams's leading "I know they can say" with a strong melodic line. Young's textural organ solo counters McLaughlin, who takes up the song-defining ostinato pattern. Among the recording's many audio shortcomings is this anomaly: Young's organ is mixed in the background of the audio space, causing McLaughlin's rhythmic accompaniment to be heard in the foreground. To these ears the organ solo often sounds like audio bleed from the other band members' recording microphones rather than as an independent discrete track.

Young's second solo chorus begins murkily, his organ remaining hidden behind McLaughlin's abrasive rhythm work. Young begins another line, and McLaughlin momentarily refrains from playing before reentering with more rhythmic intensity, slashing a descending line against Young's more florid soloing. But an arbitrary jump cut, a premature curtailment of a line Young is pursuing, occurs in the middle of the organ solo. Was Young's solo edited down? Yet again—was there a technical breakdown (tape machine, mixing board, tape)? Along with Young's organ framed low in the mix, the truncation of the organist's solo speaks to Young's troubled presence in Lifetime: his literal inaudibility in his position as soloist in an organ trio; his subsequent historical inaudibility alongside the continuing presence of his recordings in the commercial marketplace; and his audio presence as merely one other voice, rather than as the dominant, or even secondary, voice of a nominal organ trio.

The formal structure of recurring elements—dynamically low-key rhythmic pulse used in the introductory section and as an interlude during vocal verses between instrumental solos; the unison performances of the abrupt dynamic variations that signal section changes; the ostinato sequence as accompaniment figure; the feel of a steady, grounding pulse beneath even the most abstract sections—reveals the self-conscious song structure of the recorded track. Clearly, though, the interaction between the band mates is conversational, performing the dialogic implications Monson, Berliner, and Feld credit African American musical practices as privileging, and their abrupt unison changes indicate live signaling—these musicians are playing together in the same room. The arrangements through which Lifetime interwove structural and improvisational elements most closely linked its music to jazz. At the same time, however, the band's open embrace of rhythmic, technological, and sonic elements borrowed from rock clearly marked its music as distinct from jazz.

In each verse Williams asks about pasts and futures, but nonverbal instrumental passages reply, blurring intent, averting answers, offering no finalities. The musicians, struggling with the ineffable, speak through their instruments. McLaughlin described his idea of music *as* the message: "Whatever words I'm saying will never equal what I'm able to say in music. Because I can talk to you about it, but it's like telling you, 'Mmm, I'm eatin' this delicious cake,' you know, [and] the best thing you can do is eat it."[66] In similar fashion "Where" juxtaposed lyrical and instrumental content, articulating the gap between the two modes of musical expression. As each short verse ends, the instruments continue, providing responses to Williams's recurring interrogation into our pasts and our futures. Psychedelic organ timbres mingle with distorted rock guitar, each announcing rock's "answer" to Williams's probing questions about origins and aspirations quietly, though not passively, and announcing Lifetime's belief in fusion music's abilities to sound out the network of links between sounds and social context, creativity and representation, race and genre. After Williams sings the concluding lines—

Where am I going?
Where have I come from?
If anyone asks me
I know I can say

—the instruments reply quietly and, as a slow fade segues into Carla Bley's "Vashkar," instantiate the simultaneous multiple perspectives Lifetime's fusion music articulated, inviting us into the conversation and urging us to provide an answer of our own.

As Williams's obscure liner notes to Turn It Over caution us, we should not miss the music for the words, the temporal flow of pitch, timbre, and rhythm for the discursive formation. And in the denial of overtly political music, Lifetime's music reminds us that we should be wary to claim too easily that fusion's transgeneric mixtures would replace the cyclical arguments regarding authenticity and purity within musical discourse.

Williams remained distressed over the critical reception of his first Lifetime recording, and the second, the confrontational Turn It Over, measured his concern with its deliberately difficult-to-read liner notes and its unapologetic use of hard rock elements such as Williams's bellicose rock drumming, McLaughlin's aggressively angular guitar pyrotechnics, and Young's abstract yet visceral organ work, alongside delicate, psychedelic rock tracks. Lifetime undermined those hard rock elements by blending the loud, electric instrumentation with Williams's soft, airy vocals. His vocals simultaneously disturbed and placated the emotional qualities expressed through each musicians' instrumental dexterity. This was a conscious decision, as he revealed when he was asked if he considered singing in a "more rock-oriented way": "I try to feel like I give all that out on the drums, the way a rock singer does it with singing, like James Brown. The way that I'd like to sing would be more like . . . Frank Sinatra or Tony Bennett. I like the way they sing."[67] Even in the vocals, Lifetime lit out into the broken middle between hard rock and mainstream popular music that leaned toward swing, disturbing conventional ideas about the incompatibility of hard rock and jazz aesthetics. Williams's voice, in failing to displace his own drumming, as well as McLaughlin's dramatic guitar displays and Young's earthy abstractions, gave Lifetime's songs an androgynous edge, placing the group closer to the gender-bending tendencies in 1970s rock, particularly in contemporaneous styles such as glam, than to the stridently masculinist world of jazz from which they had all just emerged.

Frustratingly for these professional musicians, however, Lifetime was not commercially successful, failing to attract much attention at the time. One journalist, Steve Lake, writing in 1974, remembers, "The first album by [Lifetime], a double [LP] called *Emergency* was a real shocker, greeted almost universally with a stunned silence."[68] While Lifetime is now credited with being one of the first fully realized jazz-rock fusion bands, the band—and Williams's own perspective from the leader's position—is important in other ways. Williams described his music in the 1970s as a "reaction to the 60s." As people began to coalesce politically around new social movements on the left and the right and identity politics became an increasingly salient space of political and social action throughout the decade, Lifetime's cultural politics were part of a larger series of cultural debates, including questions regarding cultural plurality, transitory affiliations, and shifting identities.

Indeed, Young's historical marginalization can be mapped onto Lifetime's ultimate failure in the marketplace. Because Lifetime and other early fusion bands pursued their visions largely without commercial success throughout this period, they implicitly negated criticisms of any pandering to "lowered" musical tastes. Still, fusion musicians would have to gain a popular audience before they could "overturn all the bad words" and transform listening habits, genre categories, or music industry practices. In fact, as Williams admitted, "Most people forget that when they talk about this band [Lifetime] or even the state of jazz at that time. There was a lot of tension and anxiety about what we were doing. Our music wasn't always accepted and it was tough to deal with that."[69]

Williams's agenda of cross-genre coalescence speaks to the ways in which fusion music provided one model for engaging difference. The efforts of Lifetime's band members to self-consciously merge their musical tastes and abilities into a broader, more inclusive musical formation were dialogical yet confrontational. By crafting an aesthetic out of "seemingly antagonistic relationships as non-contradictory oppositions," Lifetime challenged the notion of an oppositional white and black "sounding world."[70] Lifetime's transgeneric musical blends disputed cultural hierarchies based on racialized conceptions of "high" and "low" culture—an idea through which later fusion bands would fashion themselves.

By the time I got [to the United States in 1969] I was thinking more seriously about what's real in life, what's the purpose. Of course, there's also a purpose in music. I mean that music has no "message." It is the message. But to discover that is something. Growing up with a European background, you grow up with these intellectual conceptions and misconceptions which can really throw you. —**John McLaughlin**

All I want to do, as far as music's concerned, is to disengage myself from the conditioning prejudices that people place upon products because it's in their interest to. —**John McLaughlin**

Throughout most of the 1970s, John McLaughlin's efforts to merge his spiritual beliefs and musical aesthetics articulated some of the tensions inherent in fusion music. McLaughlin's positioning as a white Englishman complicated the musical and spiritual paths he undertook at the time and expressed fusion music's ambivalent cultural dexterity. What was possible in the cross-cultural collaborative projects McLaughlin initiated, given histories of colonialist desires for colonized bodies and cultures as sites and spaces of pleasure, as imagined repository of "timeless" spiritual knowledge, and as source of economic gain? Even allowing for McLaughlin's innocence, sincerity, and sensitivity to the issues the question raises, historical and ongoing inequalities remain. Are good intentions good enough?

My interest stems from McLaughlin's explicit attempts to connect sounds, bodies, and spiritual, even religious, values in his music, not to suggest that he, or any musician, need rectify historical inequities as individuals. As McLaughlin stated plainly at the time, "Music is spiritual language."[1] He elaborated: "I'm working towards a situation of freedom. My ideal in life is to become completely free and to be able to translate that into musical structure, musi-

cal form, with people who I can be utterly free with. But to be utterly free means you have to have discipline too or it's just anarchistic self-indulgence. And that's what I'm working on [in music] and I think, in my lifetime, I'll get to it. But I also think I'll get to it in life too."[2] In the article from which these quotes come, the critic Bill Henderson noted:

> John [McLaughlin] also makes the connection between improvisation and liberation, spiritual liberation, which obviously is what has turned so many jazz musicians in particular towards [a] spiritual search.
>
> [McLaughlin said,] "Improvisation is very mysterious. If you trace the source of improvisation, you get back to pure being. And in the realm of pure being you're in the realm of religion, of mysticism and philosophy."[3]

McLaughlin placed the source of improvisation "in the realm of pure being," a space free from histories and their implications. However, his idea of improvisation as a "mysterious freedom" operating dialectically between discipline and "anarchistic self-indulgence" was a sign of McLaughlin's wary sense of individual freedom in a tug of war with collective traditions, histories, and cultures. In fact, McLaughlin's presence in Mahavishnu Orchestra and Shakti indicated how ambiguous white interlocution could be against the racial order when utilized to challenge its own position of privilege through notions of peerage rather than a simple reversal of given racial hierarchies.[4] McLaughlin, like other young fusion musicians, felt free to engage difference explicitly, marked by an eclectic aesthetic unbound by genre and increasingly free of geographic and temporal considerations; an interest in connecting with a popular audience; and, central to his music, a sustained engagement with Indian musical and spiritual practices. Indeed, McLaughlin formed an aesthetic aligned with, if not entirely based on, spiritual advocacy. He was candid about his union of music and religious belief, stating, "I am dealing with the soul of music, my relationship with my own soul, my inner communion, the communion with my spiritual teacher (Sri Chomery [sic]), who represents the Divine Being. My primary concern is my inner peace and harmony—the music comes out as a result of this."[5]

George Lipsitz, writing about other cross-cultural musical mergings, focused on the ethical question of power in such cases: "The main problem posed by the inter-cultural collaborations orchestrated by Paul Simon or David Byrne stems from their unwillingness to examine their own relationship to power or to allow for reciprocal subjectivities between and among cultures. . . . Their escapes into postmodern multi-culturalism, however well-motivated, hide the construction of 'whiteness' in America—its privileges, evasions, and contradictions."[6] Lipsitz's point about the ability for whiteness to disappear into sound, into music and into aesthetics, enables us to see McLaughlin's performance of whiteness in submission to Asian spiritual and musical instruction as a questioning of an assumed racial order. Unlike Simon or Byrne, McLaughlin's music was largely a reflection of his discipleship under the Indian guru Chinmoy Kumar Ghose (for the rest of the text, I will use the more common honorific, "Sri Chinmoy"). Lipsitz's concern about the invisibility of whiteness, however, remains salient.

McLaughlin was not alone in pursuing alternatives to conventional Western spiritual practices during the 1960s and 1970s. Studies such as Robert Ellwood's *The Sixties Spiritual Awakening* argue persuasively that the 1960s was a fundamentally spiritual time, affecting the social and political milieu in which traditional as well as "new" religious expression was partly constitutive and challenging assumptions about the 1960s as a deeply secularist time marked by an antagonism to spiritual and religious inclinations.[7]

While rock musicians such as George Harrison brought worldwide attention to Indian musicians and mystics, as well as the links between them, many jazz musicians investigated or espoused non-Christian religious or spiritual beliefs. Dizzy Gillespie, for example, embraced Baha'i; John Coltrane, though nominally a lifelong Christian, explored a number of religious traditions and their relationships to music, including ones from India; Alice Coltrane embraced South Asian spiritual practices, studying with Swami Satchidananda, changing her name to Swamini A. C. Turiyasangitananda, and eventually founding her own ashram in Agoura, California; and artists such as Albert Ayler, who embraced a unique blend of Christian, African, and Islamic musical and spiritual practices.[8] Additionally, there were the "Indo-Jazz fusions" of the Indian violinist John Mayer and the British alto saxophonist Joe Harriott. As Alyn Shipton notes, "Harriott's free-jazz group [included] trumpeter Kenny Wheeler, bassist Coleridge Goode, and pianist Pat Smythe [as well as] Indian musicians Diwan Motihar on sitar, Viram Jasani on tamboura, and Keshav Sathe on tabla."[9] Harriott's album *Indo-Jazz Suite* was released in 1966, though it made little impact on the U.S. jazz scene at the time.

In 1974 McLaughlin's "spiritual ideal [. . .] was] to transcend the human consciousness and become aware of the divine consciousness. That's my goal: to become aware of what I am and who I am and then ultimately to reveal this in music."[10] Indeed, McLaughlin welcomed the chance to perform for popular audiences: "What am I a musician for? I am not a musician for musicians. I am a musician for people who are not musicians. . . . After all, what is my music worth with no one to listen to it? It's worthless. It's essential that people listen. Hopefully their experience can be improved by listening to it."[11] The sacred and the profane, the eternal and the transient formed a broken middle through which McLaughlin's spiritual ideals and musical aesthetics were articulated within consumerist capitalism. How did McLaughlin mean to negotiate the long clutches of race, musical tradition, and historical narrative with claims to transcend "human consciousness and become aware of the divine consciousness," to be "utterly free in the realm of pure being" while participating in the marketplace? Or, was his emphasis on work and discipline, including its opposition to "anarchistic self-indulgence," and his desire for "improving" audiences able to speak productively to the relations between whiteness and cultural hybridity caught within a global market?

By 1968 McLaughlin had been a member of Georgie Fame's Blue Flames and the Graham Bond Organization but enjoyed little financial security. He began work as a studio musician to earn a living wage. But, while studio work was lucrative, he remembers it wearily: "Around '67, I started doing TV shows and really got swallowed up in that, but after a year-and-a-half I couldn't handle it. I mean I recorded with Tom Jones and Engelbert Humperdinck, Paul Anka, Dionne Warwick and Burt Bacharach, a few good people, Astrud Gilberto, but generally, the majority of the time, it was just computer guitar. You know, . . . press a button and get a sound. Whatever they want, you've got to do [it] and I couldn't handle it."[12]

His disenchantment with the life of a studio musician led to studies of Eastern spiritual traditions. However, he was trying other avenues as well, as he once recalled:

> You start out smoking pot and you want to get progressively higher. You start taking speed, methedrine, start mixing a little of this with a little of that. Before you know it, you're skin popping and next you're putting it into your vein. I know. I've seen these things happen to myself. So that was happening to me and I had a few acid trips [. . . and] what acid did for me was make me laugh. Really, it was a joy, just as natural existence is joyful. Graham [Bond] had gotten me interested in occult matters and I began to realize what kind of thing a human being was and what I am. Anyway, I just left the whole thing [quit using drugs].[13]

Viewed against the pianist Warren Bernhardt's memories of the burgeoning fusion scene at Club L'Intrigue, as well as more well-known musical examples from the jazz, country, and rock worlds, McLaughlin's countercultural pilgrim's progress seems less singular. However, while Bernhardt and his peers used psychotropic drugs to expand their sense of the musical, McLaughlin would reject drugs in order to attain the same expansive sense of creativity.

Newly sober, McLaughlin embarked on a period of heightened musical and creative activity that dovetailed with his interest in Sufi and Hindu spiritual teachings. While conventional conceptions of "serene" music are usually described in terms of lyrical themes, impressionistic harmonies, and relatively passive rhythmic pulses, McLaughlin expressed his newfound spiritual vision through high volume and the use of sound technology that other artists such as Jimi Hendrix had exploited in decidedly less saturnine pursuits. Later, in Mahavishnu Orchestra, the rhythmic complexities he found in South Asian music were joined with the aggressive propulsion of hard rock rhythm sections, creating a loosely dynamic yet highly organized ensemble flow. McLaughlin's aesthetic decisions were based on his understanding of the relationship between ephemeral music and material life:

> You put a group of musicians together and you get friction, immediately. But the world is friction. You can't have just total apathetic contentment. There are a lot of "spiritual" conceptions about music, like blissed out and so on. And to me that is completely and absolutely wrong. It's not wrong but if there was no friction, if everything was just beautiful, the music would be like eating plasticine . . . because . . . *the serenity of music is founded upon the anguish of existence.* And the perception and the acceptance and the translation of that will produce serenity. But I think you can only tell serenity as serenity when you hear the background of human existence, full of pain and friction and emotion and evils and problems and inabilities and searching and dead ends.[14]

McLaughlin's decision to sound out his spiritual concerns is evidenced on his first album as leader, *Extrapolation* (Douglas 1968). This recording, produced before McLaughlin moved to the United States and achieved worldwide fame, exhibited his conventional jazz "chops" (technical abilities), as well as his interest in other idioms. The group McLaughlin led on the recording were other young British jazz musicians: Jon Surman (saxophone), Brian Odges (bass), and Tony Oxley (drums).[15] Song titles such as "Spectrum" ("In praise of light"), "Really You Know" ("Speaks for itself"), and "Two

For Two" ("Excursion into freedom") on *Extrapolation* hint at McLaughlin's esoteric spiritual interests.[16]

The tracks segue into one another, loosening the grip of structural cohesion in favor of flow. The intricate theme to "Spectrum," for instance, and its rapid tempo segues almost imperceptibly into the daydreaming cowboy blues of "Binky's Dream." Later, the ballad "Really You Know" is followed by the hyperkinetic "Two for Two," which features a remarkable rhythmic solo by McLaughlin, revealing his debt to rock as well as jazz. *Extrapolation* was largely an acoustic affair with the notable exception of McLaughlin, who performed on both acoustic and electric guitars.

Shortly after *Extrapolation* was recorded, McLaughlin received an invitation from Tony Williams to join Lifetime. Williams had been given a tape of a session with McLaughlin from another drummer, Jack DeJohnette. The session included Dave Holland, who knew McLaughlin from their time coming up together in the jazz scene in England, and an unknown pianist.[17] Hearing the guitarist in a loose jam situation, Williams heard a possible associate who might share his desire to fuse jazz and rock, noting not only McLaughlin's facility but also how, as Stuart Nicholson observed, "power and volume were central to [McLaughlin's] expressionism."[18]

Indeed, the loud volume of rock music was an integral part of McLaughlin's spiritual message. "I now understand that volume is as natural in music as in life," he explained. "Most people are afraid of it, preferring the more comforting softer sounds. But you must not be intimidated by volume. In order to play a complete music, or to appreciate music in all its colors as a listener, you have to be open."[19] Again, I want to highlight how McLaughlin's spiritual odyssey did not negate distortion, volume, and speed and, in fact, propelled his efforts to position those very qualities *as* the "serenity of music against the anguish of existence."

McLaughlin accepted Williams's offer and, on arriving in New York, performed in a Harlem club for his first U.S. appearance. Fellow fusion guitarist Larry Coryell recalls, "I first heard John at Count Basie's with Tony Williams and Larry Young. After 30 seconds of his first solo, I turned to my wife and said, 'This is the best guitar player I've ever heard in my life.' That night, everybody was there . . . everybody from Cannonball's [Adderley] group; I think Miles was there . . . Dave Holland . . . and we were all totally knocked out by that fantastic debut of John."[20] As a result of the engagement McLaughlin not only secured a spot in Tony Williams's new group but was also invited to perform on Miles Davis's next recording date, *In a*

Silent Way. McLaughlin would eventually contribute to a number of Davis's recordings, including *Bitches Brew,* while continuing with Lifetime.[21]

Lifetime gave McLaughlin the opportunity to play with his "favorite organist [and] drummer." He confessed, "The most unexpected thing in my life was for me to turn Miles [Davis] down because Miles was my idol. I'd been listening to Miles since I was 15. I was 27 when I got to America, so I had been into his music for twelve years. I knew the man so intimately and loved him and admired him, and here he was asking me to play in his group, and I had to say no. That was something for me, but it made me very much aware of what I was involved in with Lifetime."[22] It is clear that his interest in spiritual and aesthetic matters overrode economic concerns. Having left the comforts of studio musicianship behind, he was only secondarily concerned with economic gain, which joining Davis's band might well have secured for McLaughlin at the time. Lifetime, however, provided the opportunity to work out the possibilities between spiritual ideals and musical sounds for which he had been searching.

McLaughlin voiced another reason for working with Williams and Young rather than Davis: "Lifetime was a musical thing that I realized was helping me into my own. I stayed with Lifetime, a decision I haven't regretted for a second. With Lifetime it was possible for me to really make a compositional contribution which I don't think I would have had as much of with Miles."[23] McLaughlin had composed a number of interesting pieces for recordings under his own name and would continue to provide music for Lifetime. McLaughlin also recorded the acoustic *My Goal's Beyond* (Douglas 1971) with one side devoted to jazz and the other side to an exploration of fusing Indian music and jazz with the enlistment of Badal Roy on tabla. It also featured his future Mahavishnu Orchestra band mates Billy Cobham and Jerry Goodman, as well as the saxophonist Dave Liebman and percussionist Airto Moreira. Around the same time, McLaughlin recorded a psychedelic-influenced fusion date leading a band consisting of drummer Buddy Miles, bassist Billy Rich, and organist Larry Young, titled *Devotion* (Douglas 1970). Taken together, these recordings indicated the range of musical interests McLaughlin would continue to pursue over the course of his career.

Yet McLaughlin's primary motivation remained "to become aware of what I am and who I am and then ultimately to reveal this in music," a desire to wed music and belief into a coherent expression of revelation and spiritual insight. To this end, while he kept busy professionally, his early years in the United States were also spent studying spiritual matters intensively under Sri Chinmoy. Inescapably, his whiteness stood in stark contrast to the musical and religious worlds McLaughlin was entering. Narratives of wise persons of color selflessly leading naive but honorable white individuals to spiritual or moral epiphany have been used in the service of obfuscating inequitable relations of power, supporting condescending notions of racialized agency, and obscuring the real and symbolic violence done to subaltern epistemologies and cosmologies by white imperialist power. British citizens indulging in South Asian exotica to achieve spiritual or physical nirvana was not a new phenomenon—the act of "going native" a familiar trope in British colonial history. McLaughlin, as a white Englishman, could not fully escape this historical predicament, particularly vis-à-vis his relationships with musicians and mystics of color, no matter the sincerity of his motivations or the quality of his aesthetic cultural productions.

Yet his explicit desire to link his hybrid musical practices and spiritual beliefs lends a different sort of calculation to his music. He recognized that his secular English upbringing was a source of "intellectual conceptions and misconceptions which can really throw you,"[24] notions against which his involvement with Asian philosophy and Indian music occurred. His attentiveness to these issues was at the forefront of his fusion efforts throughout the decade, influencing the direction of his music.

Mahavishnu Orchestra's debut recording, *The Inner Mounting Flame* (Columbia 1971), signaled the arrival of fusion in ways distinct from Miles Davis's *Bitches Brew*. Stuart Nicholson's description succinctly sums up the situation: "For all its innovative importance, *Brew* had often been turgid and congested with discursive melodies and soloing. *Inner Mounting Flame* represents the next decisive step in the evolution of jazz-rock fusion."[25] The success of the album was unprecedented for an all-instrumental jazz recording and helped fuel the music industry's swift appropriative agenda.[26] As the record executive Ricky Schultz admitted, "Partly in response to the success of Mahavishnu Orchestra, Return to Forever, and Weather Report, jazz fusion suddenly had more currency within the [music] industry."[27]

McLaughlin, however, was unconcerned about which genre Mahavishnu Orchestra's music belonged to: "I don't care what people call me. I don't care what they call the music. We just get up there and play. It's like, people ask me what kind of music we play, and I say, 'You listen, then you can call it anything you want.' There are people who consider themselves Mahavishnu Rock 'n' roll Freaks, and that's great. I'd rather play for rock 'n' roll audiences than jazz audiences anyway. Jazz listeners are too narrow, too purist for us. Rock audiences are more open."[28] As with Gary Burton, Miles Davis, and Tony Williams, McLaughlin saw jazz audiences as "too purist," a moribund group whose antipathy toward rock music nursed an outdated sense of currency and awareness. More important, however, McLaughlin was disregarding labels: "I don't care what people call the music."

In light of his comment the popularity of Mahavishnu Orchestra's recordings indicated that interests in jazz and rock did not represent the incommensurable or oppositional positions outlined by the music industry and critical discourse. Mahavishnu Orchestra band members enthusiastically mixed genres, traditions, and sets of musical practices and proved that audiences were far more flexible and wide-ranging in their tastes and listening habits than either music industry executives, critics, or even fans themselves often acknowledged at the time. Mahavishnu Orchestra's debut performance took place at the Gaslight Au Go Go, a club formed only months earlier from the newly merged businesses of the Village Gaslight, which featured folk music, and the rock venue, Café Au Go Go—the new space reflecting the increasingly blurring lines between audiences and musical genres. In any case, though their first appearance was as an opening act for John Lee Hooker, Mahavishnu Orchestra created such a demand that the band was asked to perform at the club "for weeks," according to Bob Belden.[29]

In a similar way to his music, which drew inspiration from a variety of sources, including Spanish flamenco, Hindustani classical music, and African American blues and jazz, McLaughlin searched a wide range of spiritual beliefs, including Sufi mysticism, Tarot, numerology, Buddhism, and Hinduism. As McLaughlin admitted, "I was raised without any religious instruction apart from the dust they serve you up at school. I won't say that it's that way for everyone because I'm sure there are some enlightened teachers in the schools. But for me, the dust was just pushed down my throat and didn't mean anything. And my parents didn't do anything [religious]."[30] Already involved with Hatha Yoga and various other spiritual practices as a way to "transform consciousness without chemicals,"[31] when McLaughlin met Chinmoy in 1971, he asked him about the relationship between music and spirituality, recalling, "[Chinmoy] gave a very long answer, a beautiful answer, pure and simple."[32] McLaughlin found, among many other ideas, Chinmoy's notion of the Master Musician and the ways in which music "embodies the Absolute Supreme" compelling enough to become his disciple.[33] In response Sri Chinmoy gave McLaughlin the name "Mahavishnu" (Hindi

Mahavishnu Orchestra's 1975 *European Tour Official Programme* front cover.

for "creative spirit"), as well as suggesting the name "Mahavishnu Orchestra" for his post-Lifetime band.

As a public acknowledgment of his commitment to his new beliefs, McLaughlin began using the name "Mahavishnu" publicly, performing in white robes, giving compositions such titles as "Sapphire Bullets of Pure Love," "Visions of the Emerald Beyond," and "Vital Transformation," and including Sri Chinmoy's writings as album liner notes. There was a performative component to his blend of music and discipleship: onstage pre-performance prayers and moments of silence, the onstage burning of incense, and the introduction of band members as "brother musicians." Chinmoy's view of music and its role in spiritual enlightenment underscored McLaughlin's own concern about whether "the development of a philosophical, interior way [could] be expressed in musical terms."[34] McLaughlin was equally insistent on the value of the relationship between "interior philosophy" and "exterior musical terms," declaring, "Spirituality is worthless if it isn't practical! Music is my work. I am a musician!"[35] Linking work and discipline to spirituality and music was McLaughlin's continual concern, and he announced his strategy for negotiating the broken middle between musical practices he believed were also spiritual practices and music industry dictates.

The final track of The Inner Mounting Flame, "Awakening," is a succinct study in sounding out McLaughlin's insistence that freedom is found, paradoxically, in disciplined restriction, its arrangement an intense mix of improvisational solo freedom and taut band cohesion. The title speaks directly to rising into consciousness but rather than a gentle emergence, the band explodes from the initial downbeat. The intricate theme reflected the increasing influence of Indian musical practices on McLaughlin's compositions and soloing style. The quick unison lines of the main theme as performed by McLaughlin, violinist Jerry Goodman, and keyboardist Jan Hammer are surpassed in rhythmic intensity by drummer Billy Cobham, often seeming to perform at twice the pulse of his compatriots. As the first soloist, Goodman uses fragments from the ragalike theme to build his statement, and Hammer follows with a concise, lithe solo, using his ring oscillator and modulation wheel to great effect. McLaughlin's incendiary solo follows, only to be surpassed by Cobham's powerfully dramatic drum statement, before the entire group performs the main theme in unison to close. A little over three minutes on the recording, it is a quintessential Mahavishnu Orchestra track, an exquisitely brief summation of the aesthetic the band would pursue for the next two to three years.

McLaughlin openly acknowledged his debt to African American musicians such as Miles Davis and John Coltrane, considering their music sacred. McLaughlin's recording with Carlos Santana, *Love Devotion Surrender* (Columbia 1973), opens with a fusion reading of John Coltrane's "A Love Supreme." The connection to Santana was not purely musical. They were both disciples of Sri Chinmoy, as the album's gatefold photo of the two guitarists standing on either side of a beaming Chinmoy attests. Their interpretation of "A Love Supreme" is a spiritual *cri de coeur*, both guitarists ecstatically energizing the band between Khalid Yasin's (Larry Young) atmospheric organ interludes.

Significantly, Coltrane's influence extended to McLaughlin's attempts to link musical practices and spiritual beliefs. McLaughlin was not alone in naming John Coltrane as a model for explicitly linking musical and spiritual ideas. As Amiri Baraka (LeRoi Jones) wrote in his 1968 book, *Black Music*, "[John Coltrane] is an example of the secular yearning for the complete change, for the religious, the spiritual."[36] McLaughlin was unequivocal about Coltrane's influencing his own belief in the spiritual value of music making: "For a long time I'd been disenchanted with the guitar as far as jazz music was concerned because I didn't feel anyone was approaching the height and inspiration of Miles and Coltrane. This was my own personal feeling. I don't know what it was, but guitar players didn't have it. Of course, Wes Montgomery was great. I loved his music when I first heard him. But when I pursued it further, I couldn't get out of it what I wanted, [which is] what Coltrane and Miles gave me."[37]

McLaughlin was equally candid about his inability to understand Coltrane's recordings such as *Giant Steps* (Atlantic 1959) and *A Love Supreme* (Impulse 1964) when they were first released. Coincidentally, McLaughlin's interest in Indian spirituality and music occurred at the same time as his introduction to Coltrane's music, with his understanding of Coltrane's musical innovations increasing as he became more adept in the musical traditions of India.

McLaughlin cited volume 2 of *The Sufi Message of Hazrat Inayat Khan — The Mysticism of Sound, Music, the Power of the Word, and the Cosmic Language* — as a key element in developing his ideas about the relationship between music and spiritual enlightenment.[38] Inayat Khan was an Indian music master and Sufi mystic who helped introduce the two traditions to Europe and the United States, linking South Asian Indian music and mysticism for early twentieth-century Western ears. McLaughlin explained his dedicating his music to the

Supreme Being as "a matter of determining priorities in life. Because I've determined mine, [which is] opting for living for The Supreme Blessed One, my emotional, spiritual and intellectual pursuits are in accord. I make music easily and link with my audiences. And my direction in music is totally in harmony with the manner in which I conduct my life."[39]

McLaughlin not only performed with Mahavishnu Orchestra under conventional circumstances in front of rock audiences and at jazz festivals, but, as his statement to create music in "harmony with the manner in which" he lived suggests, he performed at benefit concerts, as well.[40] As noted, even the higher-profile Mahavishnu Orchestra engagements began with prayers and dedications to the Supreme Musician, and as McLaughlin admitted at the time, "I think of my music now as an offering to God."[41]

However, Mahavishnu Orchestra's commercial success forced him to contend with the material pressures that record labels, managers, fellow band members, and audiences placed on his music, creating tensions between his spiritual ideals and his concerns as a professional musician. The music of Mahavishnu Orchestra formed around various musical juxtapositions. The band performed meticulous ostinato patterns in polyrhythmically and contrapuntally rich sequences providing improvising band members with complex yet supportive fields, coupling frenetic energy with precise unison band technique, and uncompromisingly loud volumes and rapid tempi set against often-lyrical solos and moments of placid tranquility. When Burt Korall observed that Mahavishnu Orchestra performed an eclectic "mingling [of] jazz, rock, basic blues, electronics, and elements from Western classical and Indian music," McLaughlin replied, "It was inevitable. We have been inundated with music—from everywhere—for a number of years. Media have broken down national-musical boundaries. There no longer are specific types of music, really, only good and bad. The musician's job is to make the blend something of his own."[42]

However, Steven Feld's observation—"commodity capitalism, and particularly monopoly capitalism, promotes musical tokenism"—serves as a needed brake against the rush to claim all the world's music as one's own.[43] McLaughlin positioned himself in the service of the Divine Musician with the "mission to realize his own [and his audiences'] divinity." His ideal was to reach beyond mere form and idiom to "the realm of pure spirit," accomplished through "work—with a capital W."[44] His work ethic was used to learn "from different teachers, from different cultures," adding a bit of advice "to the young musician: Work and Practice."[45] Keeping Feld's warning about musical tokenism in mind, we should note that McLaughlin's admonishment to young musicians to work and practice followed his own ardent studies of Indian musical and religious practices.

McLaughlin's composition sits provocatively against this backdrop as his "The Life Divine" bears a close relation to Coltrane's signature riff in "A Love Supreme." The track follows Coltrane's "A Love Supreme" and "Naima" on *Love Devotion and Surrender*, underlining the deep influence the saxophonist cast on the guitarist. In McLaughlin's live performances with Carlos Santana, both guitarists would join to perform medleys of "The Life Divine" and "A Love Supreme." While clearly an homage to Coltrane, the closeness of the themes resonates against one of the chants of "The Life Divine" riff—"that love divine / is yours and mine"—expressing the monistic unifying thrust of McLaughlin's beliefs. His conviction that humans—indeed, all sentience—are singular expressions of a divine force lent a fundamentally transcendent and universalist glow to his particularist claims and subjective musical expression.

The enormous success of Mahavishnu Orchestra—which surprised everyone, including the band members—gives McLaughlin's positioning an added complexity as economics, racialized conceptions of genre, and the appeal of a predominantly white band to a mainstream audience impacted the band's commercial success. The Lifetime trio, for all of its musical innovations, featured two black members and was promoted in distinct ways from Mahavishnu Orchestra. While Mahavishnu Orchestra was able to "cross over" to coverage in *Rolling Stone* magazine, garnering the attention of a mainstream popular music audience, Williams and the initial lineup of Lifetime (Williams, McLaughlin, and Larry Young) were covered almost exclusively in jazz magazines, leaving a majority of rock fans, a potentially mass audience, unaware of Lifetime's existence. As we saw in the previous chapter, Williams's response to questions from black nationalists about performing with McLaughlin indicates that Lifetime was caught in the authenticating political atmosphere of the era. At the time, Williams's admission of interest and admiration for groups such as the Beatles did not endear him to radical black critics, and rock fans could be suspicious of black jazz musicians' sincerity in appreciating rock music.[46] Mahavishnu Orchestra's debut recording was certainly superior in terms of audio fidelity to Lifetime's *Emergency!* album, but that does not entirely explain Mahavishnu Orchestra's explosive entrance into the popular music world.

Lifetime undoubtedly suffered from management problems stemming from each artist's negotiating contracts through three separate management teams, each team attempting to promote its client above the others, pursuing often-contradictory agendas and creating friction among the band members at times. McLaughlin and Williams both point to management problems as the reason Lifetime was unable to achieve greater success, particularly once Jack Bruce joined as the band's bassist for the second album, *Turn It Over*. Mahavishnu Orchestra harbored interpersonal conflicts, as well, yet despite these conflicts managed to survive for a brief moment as fusion's highest-profile band in commercial as well as critical terms.

Moreover, Lifetime included vocals, a clearer path to mainstream acceptance than the all-instrumental albums of Mahavishnu Orchestra. While, for many jazz critics, Williams's vocals were unconvincing and damaged Lifetime's work, in conventional marketing terms vocal music is easier to sell to mass markets than instrumental music. Moreover, Williams's vocals and their thematic material were not altogether risible in an era awash in psychedelia-drenched lyrics and popular listening sensibilities accepting of vocalists such as Bob Dylan, Jon Anderson, and Lou Reed.

Nevertheless, while Mahavishnu Orchestra more often fully realized the broken middle Lifetime initiated in the breaks between jazz and rock in artistic and creative terms, the financial success of Mahavishnu Orchestra became a flashpoint for jazz critics' dismissals of an emergent musical style. In spite of McLaughlin's call to spiritual ideals, the odor of mercantilism permeated critical perception, and, to be fair, there were a number of jazz musicians who began to incorporate nonjazz popular music in facile attempts to garner larger sales.

McLaughlin's public admission of his status as a disciple of Sri Chinmoy in *Rolling Stone* magazine — "You see, I'm [Sri Chinmoy's] disciple and he is my master. It is through his grace that I am what I am and that I play what I play. I am immersed in him. He's a divine Being, do you understand? Divinity! Perfection!"[47] — stood in sharp relief to his relationship to the other members of Mahavishnu Orchestra. McLaughlin, acting as a vessel of Divine Will, devoted himself to personal spiritual goals and acquiesced to Sri Chinmoy's suggestions and advice. Positioned simultaneously as Mahavishnu Orchestra's bandleader in the public eye — though announcing themselves a band of equals — and as a disciple of Sri Chinmoy, his dual roles lent a certain amount of ambiguity to his leadership, which would be tested throughout this first incarnation of Mahavishnu Orchestra. As the band members began to voice their own desires—desires that were at odds with McLaughlin's spiritual aims—the disparity between McLaughlin's ideals and the rest of the band members' more prosaic concerns became increasingly apparent.[48]

The polarizing effect of McLaughlin's spiritual advocacy unleashed tensions within Mahavishnu Orchestra itself that address the tangled, troubled braid of relationships between musical cultures and the music industry. While McLaughlin continued to publicly announce his spiritual beliefs in concerts and interviews, the other band members were less sanguine about his proselytizing. In a 1973 *Crawdaddy!* interview the band's violinist, Jerry Goodman; bassist, Rick Laird; and, most notably, its keyboardist, Jan Hammer, voiced their dissatisfaction with what they viewed as McLaughlin's heavy-handed spirituality and their public status as sidemen in "Mahavishnu McLaughlin's band." They were pointed in their criticism: they were contributors to compositions for which McLaughlin received all the credit (a complaint that highlights the relative monetary value between composers and performers in terms of royalties—their visibility was not the only component of their dissatisfaction); and McLaughlin's spirituality made him a less-than-fraternal band mate on the road, particularly in his stance as a spiritual leader of sorts. As Hammer put it, "[McLaughlin] assumes that the reason he is promoted like that is not at all commercial. He refuses to see that. The only things he sees in it is that he is here by Divine Right and that he's an enlightened person who is already sort of a guru."[49]

Billy Cobham, however, admired McLaughlin's transformation, acknowledging that McLaughlin openly "talked about the fact he used to be into smoking and drugs and stuff and he did something bold in a way, because he went from there completely over to the other side—no smoking, no drugs whatsoever—totally vegetarian, cleansing his system, and to me that's an indication of someone trying to find peace of mind."[50] Cobham was as surprised as McLaughlin about the unexpected success of Mahavishnu Orchestra and remained pragmatic about the long-term efforts of the band, noting that while he was prepared to go "play the clubs again," he was convinced that the band's problems stemmed from "the basic immaturity of some . . . of the cats [who] feel that they don't get their just deserves when it comes to notoriety and exposure. On the other hand, they don't try to get themselves exposed. . . . It's like they don't try, and when they do try, it's totally out of frustration from waiting for somebody to do something for them."[51]

The constant touring exacerbated the tensions within the band. There were other signs besides testy interviews that indicated a growing divergence between McLaughlin and the other band members. Billy Cobham released a solo record, *Spectrum* (Atlantic 1973), with Jan Hammer the only other Mahavishnu Orchestra member to contribute to the album. When asked why his compositions were never performed by Mahavishnu Orchestra, Cobham replied simply, "Because I haven't submitted any [compositions]. I have nothing really for [the Mahavishnu] Orchestra."[52]

Cobham's willingness to take his compositions outside of Mahavishnu Orchestra was not an option the other musicians seemed prepared, as Cobham indicated, to pursue on their own. Hammer was direct in his assertion that the rest of Mahavishnu Orchestra "made John [McLaughlin] realize that the band cannot run on his compositional ability alone. By that I mean, with him getting all the credit. . . . I came up with many of those melody lines but they were part of his so-called tunes. These things happen. You're rehearsing and these things just come to you very quickly and you don't think of any business part of it because you are making music, but after a year-and-a-half and there are two records out and they have these credits, man, well, you know, you just get turned around."[53]

When Snyder-Scumpy asked Hammer to "find something nice to talk about," Hammer responded tersely: "There's very little nice except for the music. Everything around it is disillusioning."[54] Later, Hammer admitted that the band achieved artistic and commercial success rather suddenly and that the band members, all journeyman jazz musicians unaccustomed to the bright glare of media publicity and critical recognition, reacted in counterproductive ways to the attention, eventually performing their music perfunctorily without the high energy and intensity of their formative period.

According to McLaughlin's official website, the original Mahavishnu Orchestra's breakup occurred when he and Billy Cobham, after a short tour with Carlos Santana supporting *Love Devotion and Surrender*, joined the rest of the band on a flight to Japan. Rick Laird, Jerry Goodman, and Jan Hammer did not speak to McLaughlin. According to Bill Milkowski's liner notes to *The Lost Trident Sessions* (Sony 1999), he found out why they were silent after reading, on the plane, the joint interview with the three of them in *Crawdaddy!* in which they aired their grievances explicitly and candidly (and from which I quoted above). The band broke up less than six months later. On his website McLaughlin notes,

> I don't know why they went "out" like that, but, anyway, they then began making unhappy noises to our manager about the release of the Trident

[Studio] Recordings. I wanted to be democratic about it and put it to a vote. Billy [Cobham] and I wanted an immediate release.

For some reason Jan [Hammer] and Jerry [Goodman] convinced bassist Rick Laird to vote with the both of them against not only an immediate release, but they didn't want to release the album at all, so consequently the recordings stayed in CBS and eventually got lost. We recorded the live album, "Between Nothingness and Eternity," in a Central Park concert to replace the Trident recordings.[55]

The "lost Trident recordings," as they came to be known to Mahavishnu Orchestra fans and record collectors, circulated as bootleg recordings. When two-track mixes of the recordings were discovered in CBS's recording vaults, the recording was officially released in 1999, twenty-six years after Mahavishnu Orchestra recorded the tracks at the Trident studios. The music is more of the incandescent music that shook up the world as the first two Mahavishnu Orchestra recordings but went unheard for more than two decades, long after these recordings would create much impact beyond fans and historians.

On December 31, 1973, less than three years after they formed, the original Mahavishnu Orchestra gave its last performance in Detroit, Michigan. Despite McLaughlin's vigilant adherence to his principles as he saw them, Mahavishnu Orchestra ended in bitter acrimony among McLaughlin, Goodman, and Hammer, in particular. While McLaughlin and Goodman were eventually able to put the past behind them, McLaughlin has continued to speak publicly about his failure to convince Hammer to consider reuniting for performances or recordings. In the end the original Mahavishnu Orchestra's breakup was difficult for McLaughlin, and he admitted, "I got to the point where I was in such an artistic and spiritual upheaval that I had to sever every tie I had to everything. I didn't play for many months. It was almost a year. And then Shakti came out and [was] met with a thunderous burst of indifference."[56]

Shakti connected Hindustani (North Indian) and Carnatic (South Indian) music traditions for the first time in both of the traditions' long histories. This intracultural South Asian merging was blended further with blues and jazz. Lakshminarayanan Shankar, Zakir Hussain, and McLaughlin all cited the common emphasis on improvisation for the music traditions, both as individual musicians and collectively as musical ensembles, as a way for them to connect musically. While always acknowledging spontaneous play as a central element in their aesthetic, they were also unequivocal about the role of discipline and tradition in shaping their expository improvisations and about their interest not only in a musician's technical facility but also in her or his ability to interact with other musicians who were also continually acting and reacting in the moment. Shakti was also a vehicle for McLaughlin and Shankar to pursue their mutual interest in alternative tunings and synthetic scales.

In Shakti's first incarnation (1974–77) the members were, in addition to McLaughlin, the violinist L. Shankar, tabla (drum pair, Hindustani) performer Zakir Hussain, ghatam (earthenware pot, Carnatic) performer T. H. "Vikku" Vinayakaram, and mrindangam (double-sided drum, Carnatic) performer Ramnad Raghavan. Even though McLaughlin was no longer a disciple of Sri Chinmoy at the time of Shakti's formation, his views about the relationship between music and spirituality were little changed, as evidenced by composition titles such as "What Have I Need for This—What Have I Need for That—I Am Dancing at the Feet of My Lord—All Is Bliss, All Is Bliss." (His lessening involvement with Sri Chinmoy was also signaled by his dropping of the name Mahavishnu.)[57] As he confessed in an interview with Joachim Berendt, "I was so lucky to have lessons from Ravi Shankar and other masters of Indian music. I love India, its music and its spirituality, its religions. The spirituality is the music. You can't separate the two—like you can in the West."[58]

While the resonances with orientalist discourses are readily apparent—India as an ahistorical site of "ancient wisdom" is a problematic construct—for the moment I would like to think about McLaughlin's involvement in terms of intercultural gains. In the tensions between colonialist desire that he evokes and the syncretic aesthetic he, Shankar, Hussain, Vinayakaram, and Raghavan created, Shakti's music reflected how their intercultural exchanges ably pried open those possibilities for engagements of various kinds across, between, and through difference, unsettling conventional assumptions about the links among national and cultural identity, genre definitions, and discrepant cultural valuations developed along the fault lines of uneven power relationships. Still, Shakti's efforts were mediated by the transnational culture and media industry and, more distantly, by the history of British imperialism and South Asian musical traditions. While I am not here to suggest that anyone does or does not completely escape these complex weavings of the political and the cultural—particularly as they are mediated through international markets, consumers, and taste regimes, and sifted through the histories of Western appropriation and exploitation of Othered cultural production—McLaughlin's serious engagement of South Asian music as expressed in Shakti was based on the shared concern with Shankar and Hussain in the possible meanings for music beyond mere self-expression or entertainment.

McLaughlin's interest in South Asian music began earlier, in the mid-1960s, when a guitarist friend, "Big Jim" Sullivan, played a Ravi Shankar record for him. Both men became members of the Theosophical Society in London at this time. As McLaughlin confessed, he "couldn't understand [Shankar's music] but there was something which grabbed me."[59] McLaughlin, who had been studying The Sayings of Ramana Maharshi, a Hindu saint, began reading the album's liner notes, recalling, "I read the same things I was reading in that book by Ramana Maharshi, so I realized there is a connection between the music and the wisdom. And I knew I had to listen more in order to understand this connection."[60]

McLaughlin's interest eventually led him to study the vina with S. Ramanathan at Wesleyan University beginning in 1971 (the vina is an Indian string instrument that is a precursor to the sitar in the Carnatic music tradition). McLaughlin met his future Shakti collaborator, L. Shankar, through S. Ramanathan, whose mrindangam player was Shankar's uncle. Shankar recalls their first meeting:

> It was as if we had already been playing together for many years. Until that time, I had worked with many jazz musicians, but they were never able to cross over in to my sphere. I had to do all the bending. When I met John, I was delighted, because he could join me at that point where East and West meet, where the Western musician can meet the Eastern musician and learn. We took lessons from each other constantly, and still do. I work with him learning harmony and jazz; he works with me learning ragas, rhythms, and ornamentation (slides, bends, shakes).[61]

Both Shankar and McLaughlin explain their musical ease together as the result of a deep personal knowledge of the particular musical traditions that each brings to their collaboration, implicitly placing a high value on discipline (practicing, rehearsing) and explicitly on enjoyment—"I was delighted." It is significant that not only was each capable of being the other's teacher but that each was willing to be the other's student. Their exchange of knowledge privileged neither side; rather, their exchange recognized authority and expertise in the other.

Significantly, Shankar, Hussain, Raghavan, and Vinayakaram are all classically trained musicians, each of whom matriculated through a strict system of Indian musical training. McLaughlin, by contrast, is a largely self-taught jazz musician. Their discrepancy in educational backgrounds reversed some of the tensions residing in the intercultural productions between white musicians and artists of color. Despite McLaughlin's dominance of compositional credits (he wrote or cowrote with Shankar most of Shakti's repertoire), listeners hear the privileging of South Asian music in the use of raga-influenced material as the baseline for their musical explorations. Additionally, both jazz and Indian music traditions share the competitively high-spirited but fraternal interplay among soloists, and the musicians' evident pleasure in their musical interactions would become one of the highlights of Shakti's live performances. Shakti also borrowed from Indian music an emphasis on thematic linearity rather than complex harmonies or harmonic progressions and the particular use of microtones, nontempered pitches, and scalar manipulation.

Significantly, Shakti created a rhythmic sensibility that was a then-new South Asian blend of Hindustani and Carnatic traditions. In fact, much of the initial critical dismissal and corporate apathy for Shakti stemmed from the perception of the music as "too Indian." *Down Beat*'s reviewer, Michael Rozek, wrote that he "couldn't hear any sweeping fusion—the Indian influence predominated."[62] Yet, Hussain's father, the tabla master Alla Rakha, told *Folk Roots* magazine, "Shakti was not Indian music, it was not American music. They made something else. Some numbers I like, some numbers I don't like. Zakir, I told him not to do that."[63] Caught in the broken middle, Shakti was a commercial failure at the time. Indeed, McLaughlin acknowledges that his record label, Columbia, and his management thought his decision to form Shakti and abandon his successful jazz-rock career was "a little crazy."[64]

Hussain recalled his father's warning. When his father expressed concern that he would "drift to the other side of the world and sever [his] connection with India," Hussain promised his father that he would return periodically to India. His concert schedule continues to show dates in India, where his repertoire is primarily confined to the Hindustani classical tradition. When Anil Prasad asked how Rakha's own recordings with the jazz drummers Buddy Rich and Elvin Jones differed from Shakti, Hussain replied that his father "had already proved himself as an Indian classical musician. He had been playing for fifty-odd years and had already been accepted as one of the greats. So, for him to interact with somebody posed no danger to him as far as losing his identity. For me, as a young musician of nineteen or twenty, there was more of a danger of that."[65]

Hussain's remarks detail the dangers inherent in intercultural fusions: loss of identity, attenuation of "roots," displacement. Hussain implicitly supported Shankar's and McLaughlin's citation of deep knowledge as a means of maintaining artistic integrity when he defended Rakha against a charge of possible cultural dilution or loss by noting Rakha's lengthy experience and widespread acknowledgment as a master musician. The key issue here—loss of cultural identity—is rescued by the assertion of entrenched musical knowledge. Cross-cultural or hybridized identity, if you will, is enhanced by one's willingness to remain a student, to remain inquisitive and curious, as illustrated in Shankar's and McLaughlin's revolving teacher-student relationship, rendering cultural identity as a locus of play and constant reinvention rather than a shrine to outdated modes of participation, a jam session of ongoing and developing collaborations rather than a conservatory of scripted gestures.

As indicated in interviews, L. Shankar and McLaughlin viewed the engagement with other music cultures as (re)generative rather than as encroaching on the "purity" of any particular culture. Indeed, Shakti did not signal a return to an "authentic folk music" or classical Hindustani music. As John Ephland points out in his liner notes to the compact disc release of Shakti's debut recording, McLaughlin's custom-built guitar embodied the fusion that takes place musically on the album. Inspired by his studies of the vina, McLaughlin instructed the luthier Abraham Wechter to scallop the fingerboard of the guitar in order to give him the ability to replicate the type of articulation he was able to achieve on the vina. McLaughlin also ordered seven additional "drone" or sympathetic strings to intersect the six main strings over the sound hole in order to enable him to play modally with a base drone, as Hindustani and Carnatic music demand. McLaughlin's customized guitar, however, was not a vina, nor was Shakti an attempt to reproduce South Asian traditions. As McLaughlin acknowledged, "One thing I can tell you, they don't want me to play South Indian classical music. What interests them is that I am a jazzman. They're looking to build bridges as I am and they're looking for new influences and new stimuli."[66]

What can we make of Shakti's "East meets West" idea, then? McLaughlin and Shankar were both asked this question. McLaughlin asserted, "I don't believe one can talk about east-west fusions in music. One can only speak in personal terms—that's people. I feel very much at home in India, with Indian people, culturally speaking. I feel very much at home with most people, but the more you understand about their culture and idiosyncrasies, the more at home you feel. For me, that's where the fusion takes place. It's not in the music. If you try to make an east-west fusion you're going to be a miserable failure right away."[67] Shankar was equally firm about what Shakti represents for him: "In my opinion, Shakti is the first group in which the East/West blend was properly represented. It is not me writing the Eastern part and John writing the Western part. We work together. John knows the Eastern system, and I know the Western system. To write better music for Shakti, we had to study each other's systems. So the music is not artificial."[68]

McLaughlin and Shankar both speak of their mutual abilities to understand another musical tradition's perspective in a "natural, not artificial" way. Yet their cross-cultural exchange plays out against an ever-shifting series of promises and perils brought into dialogue in the performance of fusion's broken middle: the promise of mutually respectful abridgments of difference may also move toward the peril of homogenization and cultural loss; the promise of collaboration is shadowed by the peril of appropriation; and the promise of understanding and shared responsibilities is confronted by perilous (and imperiled) histories and legacies of coercions, inequities, and displacements, as well as oppositions, rebellions, and resistances.

McLaughlin was insistent on initiating cultural mixtures along with interior exercises of (re/de)familiarizing oneself with difference and the active taking on of "fragmented individualities," of recognizing that one does not fully apprehend one's own home culture, that knowledge is always partial and incomplete, arguing that he and Shankar were both separated yet "in the same boat, we're searching through each other's cultures. And he needs to, as I need to in his. He has to be able to operate in my medium. In fact, make my medium his medium. *And that's the only East-West fusion of music—inside the musician.* You can't just take saxophone and guitar and tabla and blahblahblah and make an East-West fusion. *Fusion can only exist inside an individual, who works and studies in that culture, until it's natural.*"[69]

McLaughlin's music sounded out transcultural work as interior transformation within the breaches between musical cultures. He openly accepted wider social consequences for traversing the broken middle between South Indian and North Indian music and jazz: "One man can change a whole magazine . . . a record company . . . a radio station. Two men can do miracles. And one hundred men could change the world, if you know what I mean . . . and the world needs it. God, does the world need it."[70]

Shakti sounded out the possibilities that fusion music's eclectic aesthetics presented for negotiating the broken middles between history, power, and ideology through a regimen of study, practice, and work. Shakti serves as a reminder that musical traditions are social constructs, that our ways of creating, recreating, and appreciating music are social and mutable.

John McLaughlin was certainly not the only popular musician to try and connect spiritual beliefs and musical practices during the 1970s. The Beatle George Harrison helped popularize Transcendental Meditation, for example, and a passing knowledge of astrology became common, even among those who claimed disbelief. In 1992 McLaughlin reminisced about the original Mahavishnu Orchestra: "I am convinced now that people shouldn't be bombarded by music. Maybe I did it before but twenty years ago was another era—the Vietnam war and the whole thing [with Max Roach's] 'Freedom Now!' The Black intellectual movement and how it was repressed, flower power, LSD and all of that. Where we were going—it was a very different period."[71] While this interview offers no further clues to McLaughlin's thoughts on the repression of a "Black intellectual movement," his close relationships with young black musicians such as Tony Williams reasonably imply McLaughlin's awareness of the political atmosphere in a certain segment of African American society at the time. He is also explicit about the use of rock's volume and energy at the time as a conscious decision to convince—or confront, perhaps—listeners of the urgency of the times. It clearly remains a significant element of the historical moment for him.

Yet McLaughlin's whiteness separated him from many of his most important musical compatriots—Miles Davis, Tony Williams, Billy Cobham, Carlos Santana, L. Shankar—as well as the various musical and spiritual traditions he studied and in which he participated. Indeed, McLaughlin's attempt to weld his spiritual ideals to his music appears, in some respects, naive and contradictory, given high relief by the economic success of Mahavishnu Orchestra. What does this failure—if, indeed, it is a failure—reveal about his attempt, operating, as he does, within the circuits of a global music industry? Was his spiritual quest to "achieve freedom in real life and in music" so antithetical to the production of commodified musical objects within capitalist (bourgeois, corporate, postmodern) structures of production, distribution, and consumption that it was merely appropriated, recycled, and recontextualized for economic gain? Again, are good intentions good enough?

McLaughlin positioned himself simultaneously inside and outside—within the broken middle—of the very aesthetic practices in which he engaged in order to "become aware of what I am and who I am and then ultimately to reveal this in music." His tenure with Tony Williams and Miles Davis also brought him into contact with the racial politics of merging jazz and rock, a complex set of relations embedded within the larger political and social milieu of the United States in the 1970s. His discipleship under Sri Chinmoy indicated the depth of his sincerity in pursuing spiritual matters. McLaughlin's spiritual and musical quest located him in the broken middle between history and race, a space of "dislocative" tendencies, hybrid loyalties, and factional collaborations—a site, in other words, of doubled meanings and continuous movement between traditions and aesthetic conventions. In short, McLaughlin's activities suggest that good intentions are not good enough—that, in fact, one needs to continuously and conscientiously work (study, practice) and perform (enact, participate) in order to navigate the inherently unstable broken middle between the entangled histories and complicated cultural shifts that transcultural music production entails.

McLaughlin asserted, "You cannot be static. There's nothing static in the universe; it's evolving, so you might as well harmonize with this process, with this law. And I'm really glad it's like it is, because it continually opens up greater possibilities and opportunities."[72] He also recognized, however, that "[before] a new era can be born, the old one's got to fall away, otherwise there's no room for the new to emerge and grow."[73] In this recognition he gestured toward the double-edged process of navigating the broken middle, a space of gains and losses, of compatibilities and incommensurabilities—a meeting place not only for spirits but also for genres, traditions, and cultures.

six
Don Juan's Reckless Daughter / *Joni Mitchell*

I'm not a jazz musician but I need that creative freedom. That's why now I'm being sucked into jazz projects and working more and more with jazz musicians. I find I'm more understood there, and the heavier the player that I work with, the [easier] it is to communicate. Because I'm [musically] illiterate; I don't have the number system, nor do I have the letter chord system. I don't understand it. I'm a painter. I like to speak in metaphor: "play me some semi-trucks going by," you know . . . by emotion and by remembrances. —**Joni Mitchell**

That's one thing that's always been a major difference between the performing arts, to me, and being a painter. A painter does a painting and that's it. You know, he's had the joy of creating it and he hangs it on some wall, somebody buys it, somebody buys it again. Or maybe nobody buys it and it sits up in a loft somewhere 'til he dies. But he's never—I mean, no one ever said to Van Gogh, "Paint us *Starry Night* again, man!" You know, he painted it—that was it. —**Joni Mitchell**[1]

Joni Mitchell (née Roberta Joan Anderson) is a popular music enigma. Her earliest compositions such as "Both Sides, Now" and "The Circle Game" date from the late 1960s, when she was one of many popular folk-oriented singer-songwriters. Her most significant commercial success, however, occurred during her "jazz" period (1974–80), when her song "Help Me" earned her the only top-ten single of her long career, peaking at number seven, while the album from which it was taken, *Court and Spark* (Asylum 1974), reached number two on the album charts.[2] Ironically, as *Court and Spark* initiated her most explicit engagements with jazz, subsequent albums registered increasingly lower sales and critical acclaim throughout the decade.[3]

    As I mentioned in my introduction, my inclusion of Mitchell in a study of fusion music may strike some readers as overly idiosyncratic, so I want to outline my reasoning here to show that my decision was neither arbitrary nor whimsical. As I have also mentioned, rock and soul musicians helped create fusion. A short list of compelling candidates for fusion studies might include, among many others, Frank Zappa, Jeff Beck, Bill Bruford, Roy Ayers, Ronnie Foster, Michael Henderson, Stevie Wonder, Robert Wyatt, Elton Dean, Neil Schon, and Ronnie Montrose. Contemporaneous women musicians such as Flora Purim, Patrice Rushen, Urszula Dudziak, Carla Bley, and Gayle Moran—all of whom performed fusion music—could, by comparison, be more easily heard as jazz musicians (and certainly warrant further study).[4] However, Mitchell's positioning as a female folk-rock musician; her responses to music industry inducements, coercions, and demands; and, most important, her creative work, which not only fused musical genres but also synthesized music, painting, and poetry, uniquely illuminated fusion's negotiations in the broken middles between artistic media, as well as musical genres. Indeed, because her creativity combined musical, lyrical, and visual art, she staked unique claims for fusion.

Mitchell's upbringing on the midwestern Canadian plains may have played into her sense of independence, giving her an expansive and free-ranging imagination that fueled her generic travels. Marshall McLuhan, one of Canada's most famous intellectuals, could have been describing Mitchell here: "The advantages of having no sharply defined national or private identity in Canada appear in the general situation where lands long blessed by strong identities are now bewildered by the growing preformation and porousness of their identity image in this electronic age. The low-profile Canadian, having learned to live without such strongly marked characteristics, begins to experience a security and self-confidence that are absent from the big-power situation."[5] As I detail below, Mitchell drew on this sense of "porousness" to push beyond genre conventions and explore the uncharted broken middle between pop and jazz.

As she confessed in 1972, "I have a house in California . . . [simply] for an address. The house in Canada is just a solitary station. . . . I'm so transient now that even though I have the house in Canada, I really don't feel like I have a home—well, it's home when I'm there, you know, but then, so is the Holiday Inn in its own weird way."[6] Mitchell's constant traveling between California and Canada, as well as among various tour stops, is sounded out in her music—a broken middle through which transition inspires and motivates transformation. Doubtlessly, Mitchell's engagement of the broken middle includes the space between Canada and California, an expanse marked in her 1970s work by notions of a vast primitive northern wilderness, on one hand, and a crowded, frenetic urbanity, on the other. The Canadian literary scholar Northrop Frye suggests that "to feel 'Canadian' was to feel part of a no-man's-land. . . . One wonders if any other national consciousness has had so large an amount of the unknown, the unrealized, the humanly undigested, so built into it. . . . Such a frontier was the immediate datum of [a Canadian's] imagination, the thing that had to be dealt with first."[7] In fact, Canadians' lack of a strong national culture due to its dominance by its southern neighbor, as well as its national mythology as a nation "founded by two nations" (Great Britain and France), is perhaps best summed up by notions of Canadian cultural studies as "an exploration of the multiple passages *between empires*," an idea that resonates with my use of the broken middle to describe the generative spaces between categories.[8]

Mitchell's creative work tested the dichotomy between "art" and "popular culture," simultaneously challenging the music industry's view of her creative output as pop commodity while using jazz as high cultural asset (rather than arguing, as Gary Burton and Tony Williams did, that jazz had lost its relevancy). She admitted to Mary Dickie, "I'm a fine artist working in the pop arena. I don't pander; I don't consider an audience when I work; I consider the music and the words themselves, more like a painter."[9] Mitchell's engagement with jazz would only heighten the stakes for defining the breaches, the broken middles, between art and popular cultures. In a *Rolling Stone* interview Mitchell proclaimed, "People get nervous about that word. Art. They think it's a pretentious word from the giddyap. To me, words are only symbols, and the word 'art' has never lost its vitality. It still has meaning for me. Love lost its meaning to me. God lost its meaning to me. But art never lost its meaning. I always knew what I meant by art."[10] Less populist than Williams or McLaughlin, Mitchell navigated the broken middle between romantic autonomous art tendencies and more mundane commercial considerations, plying the waters between high art aesthetics and a popular music career.

Mitchell's earliest commercial success rested on better-established musicians recording her compositions. In 1967 Tom Rush and Buffy Sainte-Marie recorded Mitchell compositions on their respective recordings, and Judy Collins's version of "Both Sides, Now" from her release of the same year, *Wildflower* (Asylum), was a hit before Mitchell's self-titled debut album was released a year later. Mitchell, aware her songwriting royalties were a significant income source, fought to retain her publishing rights during the negotiations leading to her first major label signing. Mitchell's ability to retain the publishing rights is notable given record companies' usual procedure to procure those rights away from new artists as publishing royalties generate a significant share of the profits for the music industry. Still, Mitchell compared her deal with Reprise to sharecropping "because everything is billed back to you" and remained astounded at "how much money [she has] made given how bad the deals have been."[11]

Nevertheless, her contract with Reprise was unique, particularly for a female musician, and is all the more remarkable given her unproven status as a recording artist. In addition to retaining her publishing rights, she was granted total artistic control, including choice of album artwork and repertoire, from her initial recording. Her paintings appeared as album cover art, and Mitchell's interweaving of painting, poetry, and music articulated the connections among the various modes of artistic expression. The value of her creative work is partially measurable by her wide-ranging influence, from genre-defying Prince's performative border crossings to the mannerist postures of the rock auteur Beck to the jazzed up hip-hop rhapsodies of A Tribe Called Quest's Q-Tip.[12]

As the 1960s progressed, Mitchell's increasingly large, even mass, audience placed demands she found increasingly constraining and threatening. An infamous concert appearance at the 1970 Isle of Wight Music Festival in which an audience member's intrusion on the stage sparked an emotional appeal from Mitchell to respect performing artists indicated the boundaries she believed necessary to erect as an artist working in a "self-confessional" genre. But Mitchell remained focused on aesthetic concerns, insisting that her songs were narratives or character studies rather than purely autobiographical works. Her willingness to continue her fusion experiments, even as the sales figures for her recordings steadily dropped throughout the decade, pointedly displayed a commitment to her aesthetic vision. Her repeated insistence that audiences appreciate her as an "artist" rather than "pop star" often ignored not only her dependence on the "star maker machinery behind the popular song," as she sang in "Free Man in Paris," but also effaced the craft behind the popular song, ironically pointing to her admitted musical "illiteracy."

Mitchell's musical idiosyncrasies, rising in part from her lack of knowledge of standard Western musical theory, framed her efforts as the effect of naive talent rather than the result of deliberate aesthetic strategies and decisions. Her public image as the quintessential "female hippie singer-songwriter" did nothing to help position her as a serious artist. Despite Mitchell's attempts to distance herself from the image of an acoustic guitar-toting naif, the journalist Laura Campbell described Mitchell in 1998 as the "consummate 'hippy chick,' Annie Hall meets urban cowgirl, with a haunting beauty that intrigued many famous lovers, from David Crosby, Graham Nash and Stephen Stills to James Taylor, Jack Nicholson and Warren Beatty," when Mitchell was in her mid-fifties.[13] Mitchell's artistic efforts were consistently heard as ephemeral and naive and, despite her many artistic accomplishments, effectively barred her from serious critical engagement.[14]

Until *Court and Spark* openly contested her generic constraints, Mitchell remained strongly identified as a folk or "folk-pop" artist, a classification that assumed an engagement with song forms and the straightforward melodies and harmonic progressions of folk music traditions, particularly of the British Isles.[15] As with other conventions, from her first recording Mitchell escaped strict adherence to those traditions by consistently playing with folk song forms; creating compositions utilizing her own open guitar tunings; or by moving harmonically or thematically through a composition in complexly idiosyncratic ways. Her lack of formal musical instruction allowed her to explore new possibilities in popular music but placed unusual performance demands on her fellow pop and folk musicians.

Her singular style eventually forced her to consider using jazz musicians such as John Guerin, though jazz critics felt no need to critically engage her music.[16] Increasingly frustrated with the inability of folk and rock bassists to perform contrapuntally or counterthematically, Mitchell heeded the rock session drummer Russ Kunkel's recommendation that she hire jazz musicians.[17] This decision would prove troubling to critics and fans alike. As Mitchell admitted, "Basically, I was kissed off after *Court and Spark*. I cut my players some slack on *Hissing of Summer Lawns*, and they reverted to jazz harmony. Without me harmonizing them, they applied some jazz licks and chords against my harmonies. A lot of people didn't like that."[18]

Mitchell, moving away from the music of a "self-confessional singer-songwriter"—a critical figuration that did not give sufficient account of her eclecticism, in any event, apparent from her earliest recording in which Mitchell merged Gilbert and Sullivan, Celtic mythology, and divorce—embraced elements of jazz music as part of an aesthetic program to articulate concerns increasingly remote from the need to expose her "authentic" feelings as she had on the recording, *Blue* (Reprise 1971).

Musicians who were known primarily as jazz musicians began to appear on her album credits after 1972's *For the Roses*.[19] Though her full immersion in jazz music would register itself on *Mingus* in 1979, she steadily increased her jazz affiliations through association with jazz musicians, song selection (she first covered the jazz singer Annie Ross's "Twisted" on 1974's *Court and Spark*), her increasingly melismatic singing style, which not only drew on jazz singing styles but also began to dismantle the "tyranny of the bar line," and, finally, her explicit citation of jazz music as an influence. Significantly, the appearance of these elements coincided with Mitchell's change in song presentation. As she moved from being a solo performer to being the leader and member of a working band, the influence of musicians such as Tom Scott, Joe Sample, and, later, Wayne Shorter and Jaco Pastorius, was soon heard in compositions that integrated intricate unison passages with open improvisations, musically complementing and commenting on the lyrical content, written in free verse as Mitchell discarded rhyme schemes with their mundane regularities.

This shift in musical and lyrical elements was reflected in the way her music began to sound. A significant partnership grew out of her frustration with bassists who were not "capable of anchoring *and* countermelody."[20] Eventually, Jaco Pastorius was recommended to her. Empathetic to Mitchell's idiosyncratic guitar performances, Pastorius provided contrapuntal counterlines, following and coaxing her vocals while simultaneously supporting the harmonic progressions of her songs. Mitchell recalled, "[Pastorius] kind of blew my mind. He was incorrigible and difficult to deal with, but I was so excited that someone was doing what I had been asking people to do. Here was a kindred person, thinking as I did about the bottom end."[21] In concert they performed *en simpatico* and his natural showmanship, especially featured in an unaccompanied solo spot, were highlights of her Shadows and Light tour. (In fact, Mitchell granted each member a generous amount of time in which to solo unaccompanied.) During these segments Pastorius would perform the bravura bass virtuoso pieces he performed in his regular working band, Weather Report. Mitchell's touring band at this time consisted exclusively of jazz musicians: Pat Metheny (guitar), Lyle Mays (keyboards), Pastorius, Don Alias (percussion), and Michael Brecker (tenor sax). She also sang with a jazz singer's sensibilities, ignoring bar lines for expressive effect and using her vocal range to effectively vocalize instrumental-like lines. The room she allowed for extended soloing for her band members also reveals a jazz sensibility; mainstream popular singers leave little or no performance time for instrumental soloing.

Her performances from this period are strikingly reminiscent of Billie Holiday—the expressive sense of a jazz instrumentalist with an elastic sense of time and an instantly identifiable voice. In fact, collaborations by Mitchell and Pastorius echoed the famous musical dialogics of tenor saxophonist Lester Young and vocalist Billie Holiday, with the two musicians anticipating or finishing each other's lines, a syncopated, improvised *pas de deux*. The two working relationships shared many elements, including an unaffected and intuitive affinity indicated by their spontaneous musical interplay.

The recording Hejira (Asylum 1976) initiated a productive relationship for both partners, and Pastorius's work on this album stands among the best of his recordings, particularly on "Black Crow" and the lead track, "Coyote." "Coyote" showcased their creative partnership best on this album as they reversed conventional performance practices. This is immediately heard in the introductory passage featuring Pastorius articulating the melody above Mitchell's rhythm guitar, effectively reversing standard guitar-bass relationships. As soon as her vocals enter, however, Pastorius immediately drops to a conventional bass range while providing a counterrhythmically inventive response to her theme though his note selection is firmly rooted in the harmonic progression of the composition. In fact, much of the rhythmic drive is provided by Mitchell's steady rhythm guitar strumming, played against Pastorius's facile rhythmic elaborations on the pulse she provides. The only other musician, Don Alias on congas, is mixed low in the track, providing coloration on the pulse but generating little rhythmic propulsion as Mitchell's strumming replaced the drums as the central focus of the rhythm. The guitar thus contained, the bass assumed the lead instrument position, Pastorius drawing on a long tradition of virtuoso bassists in jazz (though few were heard performing lead lines), and virtually alone at the time in folk or rock music. Pastorius's bass work on Hejira is compelling not only because of his rhythmic and harmonic counterpoint but also as a result of his fretless bass's particular timbre, produced in a very specific context of then-current technological horizons.

"Coyote" finds Pastorius now leading, now following Mitchell's thematic material, both of them free yet bound within the limits of the compositional structure and each other's musicianship, underlining Mitchell's admission in the song that she was a "prisoner of the white lines on the free,

free ways." Mitchell's emphasis on the phrase, "free, free ways," speaks to the constraint between the road's lane markers, as well as the entrances, exits, merging lanes, and contact spaces, such as tollbooths, framing the ways in which movement is ordered out of the "chaos" of an unpaved landscape. Roads, after all, do not allow one access to "everywhere" or even "anywhere" but "only there (or here)" along a predetermined path. Even wanderers, Mitchell is implying, have their choices bound by history and convention.

Mitchell linked her creative methodology to one of her musical idols, Miles Davis, and, like John McLaughlin, describes Davis's music as sacred. Similar to Davis's notion of the creative process, she was explicit about forcing musicians to be sensitive to the nuances of the musical moment:

> I not only [cannot] read [musical notation] but I didn't know—and don't to this day—what key I'm playing in or the names of my chords. . . . I approach it very "paintingly," metaphorically; so I rely on someone that I'm playing with, or the players themselves, to sketch out the chart of the changes. I would prefer that we all just jumped on it and really listened. Miles [Davis] gave very little direction, as I understand it. It was just "Play it. If you don't know the chord there, don't play there," and that system served him well. It was a natural editing system. It created a lot of space and a lot of tension, because everybody had to be incredibly alert and trust their ears. And I think that's maybe why I loved that music as much as I did, because it seemed very alert and very sensual and very unwritten.[22]

Miles Davis's practice of presenting new musical charts to his band members at a recording session or altering tunes immediately prior to recording them forced his musicians to be spontaneous and actively listen to the other musicians instead of repeating well-rehearsed "licks" (musical phrases) that often foreclosed active listening among participants. Jazz music is often constructed as the spontaneous expression of its performers, who are reacting in the moment without preconceived gestures, but musicians recognize the often preplanned nature of their improvisations. Mitchell also employed this particular music practice in order to avoid the lifeless gesture that she calls "caricature." Mitchell elaborated in an interview with Bill Flanagan: "Obviously, not all of what a person is, feels, [or] thinks is worthy of putting in a song. You don't have to display your asshole any more than you have to limit yourself to only heroic roles. I guess the best of it would be to chronicle as much as possible the heroic parts of your thinking as well as your frailties, so you give a balanced picture. That's what makes a good part in any art form. Otherwise it becomes caricature."[23]

In other words, she was not avoiding stagecraft or, contrarily, privileging her lack of musical skills in the service of mere spontaneity but was arguing for a balance between being open to the moment of creativity and adhering to preconceived parameters in order to render a balanced yet artistically nuanced aesthetic experience. Again, the resonance with jazz practice is clear. Jazz musicians—and Joni Mitchell—utilize *both* preconceived musical structures, forms, and other types of music knowledge, as well as spontaneous and unrehearsed improvisatory skills to create music both "in the moment" and in written compositions.[24]

Mitchell explained this tension between preplanned structure and improvisational freedom by telling a short story she attributed to Henry Miller. In the story a famous clown forgets his part one evening just as he reaches the climax of his act. As the tension mounts, the audience is spellbound as he stands there, mute. Just as the audience is ready to boo him, he suddenly remembers his part and he receives a thunderous applause from the audience. The next night, he pretends he's forgotten the part again, draws the tension out, and then "remembers" his line with the same result. He continues to do this, night after night, but one night, he finds faking the audience out for the easy applause overly manipulative. He quits and finds work as an elephant boy in another circus. One night, the head clown for this new circus falls ill, and the former clown, now elephant boy, performs the part for him. Hearing the elephant boy receive louder applause than he's ever heard for his own performances breaks the sick clown's heart, and he dies. When the replacement clown hears about the sick clown's death, he quits the circus for good, becoming a wandering drunkard. One day a policeman hits him with his billy club in an attempt to get the old clown to rise and move on to another town. The clown, sensing his death is near, performs his old routine for the policeman. Again, he seems to forget the climax to his act, "remembers" it, and the policeman responds just like the audiences of old, laughing uproariously. With a sense of contentment and satisfaction, the old clown dies.[25]

Mitchell related this story in an interview, expanding on her observation of how, when she first began to achieve mass popularity, audiences began reacting to her own performances with seemingly little critical acumen, unable to differentiate between good and bad performances. The lesson she learned, after reflecting on this type of reaction, even after she exposed her frailties on *Blue*, was that the artifice of authenticity—in other words, inauthenticity—was not necessarily a false experience. In a similar way to her conception of how to prepare oneself for the "magic" of the creative musical moment, Mitchell does not abandon her craft but uses it to recreate moments of "truth." Inauthentic performativity, then, is a methodological tool Mitchell utilizes to create a public persona through which she may readily construct artworks that resonate "truthfully" with audiences.

Mitchell's very "inauthenticity" enabled her to play with the musical structures that dictate idiomatic gestures, audible in her steady distancing from folk and rock music toward the overt introduction of jazz sensibilities in *For the Roses*. Mitchell described her own genre-erasing aesthetic this way, "I didn't develop the chauvinism on a small scale that gives you limitations. There are moments in my life . . . when I think, 'God, I don't have a nationality, I don't have a religion, I don't *belong* to anything.' There are moments when I crave to belong to something. But on the other hand, there's a great freedom with not belonging to anything, there's an open-mindedness with not belonging to anything."[26]

This "nonbelonging" cuts both ways, however. Not only is one freer from normative strictures, but one also lacks a community of support and protection. *Mingus*, her collaboration with the eponymous jazz bassist, composer, social critic, and raconteur, continues to be largely ignored by the jazz establishment. Despite the fact that the recording featured some of Mingus's final work, the album is rarely mentioned by jazz critics. In fact, the silence from the jazz press that greeted the album's release was striking next to the lukewarm reviews it received, for the most part, in the rock press. As I will detail below, the rock and pop reviewers became more estranged with each consecutive recording after *Court and Spark*. By the time *Mingus* was recorded, the few rock journalists still willing to review her output were awaiting another "Chelsea Morning" or *Blue*. Her refusal to accommodate their wishes exacerbated an already testy relationship, and *Mingus* was heard as a pop star's calculated—and failed—bid for artistic legitimacy.

Mitchell shared her perspective regarding the positioning of her music as liminally situated between rock and jazz:

All the time that I've been a musician, I've always been a bit of an oddball. When I was considered a folk musician, people would always tell me that I was playing the wrong chords, traditionally speaking. When I fell into a circle of rock 'n' roll musicians and began to look for a band, they told me I'd better get jazz musicians to play with me, because my rhythmic sense and my harmonic sense were more expansive. . . . Then, when I began to play with studio jazz musicians, whose hearts were in jazz but who could play anything, they began to tell me that I wasn't playing the root of the chord. So all the way along, no matter who I played with, I seemed to be a bit of an oddball.[27]

Her self-described status as "oddball," exterior to "rock" and "jazz," names her alterity, her position within a broken middle between externally imposed strictures. She sings about her liminality in "The Boho Dance" from *The Hissing of Summer Lawns*:

Nothing is capsulized in me
On either side of town
The streets were never really mine
Not mine these glamour gowns.

She continued to argue against what she termed "the hippie uniform of rock 'n' roll," as well as the perception that her abandonment of the "hippie/boho code" meant a compromise of her political and social ideals. Idiosyncratic and headstrong, Mitchell continued to pursue her aesthetic vision despite critical dismissal and the risk of losing mass audience appeal.

Her decision to compose music that lacked regularity compelled an exploration of longer forms. She describes this exploration as a process of "breaking patterns," of becoming "the Jackson Pollock of music. I just wanted all the notes, everybody's part, to tangle. I wanted all the desks pushed out of rows, I wanted the military abolished, anything linear had to go."[28] It was on *Hejira* and *Don Juan's Reckless Daughter* (Asylum 1977) that her music became explicitly structured by free verse, improvisation, and extended forms. Her free-verse lyrics necessitated a break from strophic folk and pop forms because, as she told Anthony Fawcett,

the way I write songs now is around a standard melody that nobody knows, because that way you can get your words to have their organic inflection so that when you emphasize something you go up or you go down. Or if you want to put ten syllables in a line that in the next verse is only going to have three syllables drawn out through those bars, you have that liberty. As a result, you can't write *one* lead sheet and put the four verses on it, every verse has to be written out individually—it's all variation on a theme."[29]

While lyrics play an important role in her music, Mitchell was equally interested in keeping the music itself as interesting and multifaceted as the lyrical content of her compositions. She viewed the coupling of musical and lyrical interests as a "hybrid that allowed for a certain amount of melodic and harmonic movement but with a certain amount of 'plateaus' in order to make a larger statement, to be able to say more."[30] The jazz vocalist Cassandra Wilson, speaking in a joint interview with Mitchell, noted, "There's something about [Mitchell's] phrasing that implies space. It's the most unique phrasing. When I first heard the way that [she] would say all the things [she] would say, and then try to do that—I would try to write poetry and sing it and I would just sort of—I couldn't get it all in! That's a special art. Not everybody has that."[31]

As Mitchell's melodies became more complex, critics and fans began wondering what had become of "melody" in her work. Mitchell responded: "Even though popularly I'm accused more and more of having less and less melody, in fact the opposite is true—there's more melody and so they can't comprehend it anymore. So I'm an oddball, I'm not part of any group anymore but I'm attached in certain ways to all of them, all of the ones that I've come through. I'm not a jazz musician and I'm not a classical musician, but I touch them all!"[32]

Inherent in Mitchell's claim of "nonbelonging" and her stake in positioning herself as marginalized "outsider," in spite of a global fan base, was the lack of critical support as she gradually distanced her music from folk and rock moorings. While Leonard Feather was able to write a cover story for *Down Beat* (which also published a singularly positive review of *Mingus* by Neil Tesser), pop and rock critics were increasingly dismissive of her work. Ariel Swartley, writing in her mixed review of *Mingus* for *Rolling Stone* magazine, asserted, "It's been a long time since her songs had much to do with whatever's current in popular music. (She would prefer we call them art songs.) But then, she doesn't so much come on as an outsider, but as a habitual non-expert. She's the babe in bopperland, the novice at the slot machines, the tourist, the hitcher."[33]

Mitchell, however, argues that rather than "habitual non-expert," she is a "consistent nonbelonger," declaring, "If you want to put me in a group— I tell you, nobody ever puts me in the right group. You want to know what group I should go in? The black press gets it. I'm not a folk musician. I'm a girl who plays acoustic guitar but so does every other rock 'n' roller. . . . I was a folk musician from 1963 to 1965. At the moment I began to write my own music, even though I wrote it on acoustic guitar, I was no longer a folk musician. You know, melodically, folk musicians were playing three-chord changes. *[I had] the desire to write [lyrics] with more content with a desire for more complex melody — [that] was my creative objective. That is not folk music.*"³⁴

Mitchell's insistence on this point is explicit about her distance from the normal associations she evokes and the categories (female artist, folk musician, pop superstar) in which critics and observers situate her. Besides the mixed collection of originals and jazz standards on *Both Sides, Now* (Reprise 2000), it is noteworthy that of the four nonoriginal compositions in her recorded work, three are jazz songs. She covers the Annie Ross and Wardell Gray composition "Twisted" on *Court and Spark* and uses the Johnny Mandel and Jon Hendricks composition "Centerpiece" as an interlude in her song "Harry's House" from *The Hissing of Summer Lawns*.³⁵ On the album *Mingus* she set lyrics to a third jazz composition, "Goodbye Pork Pie Hat," demonstrating a profound ability to merge her own artistic sensibilities with Mingus's unique blues-based elegy to the tenor saxophonist Lester Young. Mitchell's nonbelonging was a result of her search for an equilibrium between "roots and routes," a term I borrow from James Clifford, who, while aptly describing the tensions between localized and diasporic lived experiences, also suggests to me another perspective. This is the perspective of the "never (quite) local, never (wholly) alien," an "un-bounded-ness," continuously ebbing and flowing, or, more accurately, like the smoke in a drafty room, simultaneously cohering and dissipating, registering itself beyond reductive "inside/outside" dichotomies.

Again, Mitchell's childhood in the Canadian plains provides a compelling backdrop through which we might view her self-proclaimed outsiderness. As Carole Carpenter asserts, "Since [Canada] was, for many years, a colony of Great Britain, and increasingly since the 1940s has been an economic colony of the United States, Canadians have commonly looked beyond their borders for their cultural identity."³⁶ I want to be careful not to map "Canadian-ness" too strongly onto my reading of Mitchell's 1970s work, but there is resonance between her aesthetic stance — particularly in her strongly voiced independence from convention — and the sense of Canadian-ness derived, paradoxically, from external sources. In fact, Jody Berland's concerns in *North of Empire* with Canada's position as a "Second World" nation, neither fully postcolonial nor wholly imperialist but a "neither/nor" space formed "from the violent fusions of multiple identities," provides a window into Mitchell's performances of identity through music and imagery.³⁷

While Mitchell utilized jazz musicians such as the pianist-keyboardist Joe Sample, woodwind player Tom Scott, and drummer John Guerin on *For the Roses* and *Court and Spark*, it was on *The Hissing of Summer Lawns* that her jazz affiliations began to reveal their depth and coherence with her aesthetic approach. Mitchell enacted the first explicit utilization of African drumming, presaging the "world music" movement by Western pop musicians, in the composition "The Jungle Line" on *The Hissing of Summer Lawns*. Since she used a tape loop of Burundi drummers, Mitchell was arguably one of the first mainstream pop artists to begin obscuring the differences between "real" musicians and "sampled" music. While Mitchell stated that the Burundi drummers were "the greatest rock 'n' roll I ever heard," she also realized, given the adverse critical reception to the album (*Rolling Stone* magazine listed it as the worst album of the year), that "while [critics and fans] liked rock 'n' roll, they didn't really like it's [sic] roots."[38] This conflictual relationship between roots and branches obliged her to perform an unconventional positionality in which she sought to inhabit a racialized and transgendered alterity.

In describing her attraction to the Burundi drumming and its "Bo Diddley lick," Mitchell also confessed to providing "this black cultural poem under it. I thought I was black for about three years. I felt like there was a black poet trapped inside me, and that song was about Harlem—the primitive juxtaposed against the Frankenstein of modern industrialization; the wheels turning and the gears grinding and the beboppers with the junky spit running down their trumpets. All of that together with that Burundi tribal thing was perfect. But people just thought it was weird."[39]

The easy response is to attack her appropriation, especially given her admittedly retrogressive alignment of black primitivist freedom against (white) modernist industrialization and the evocation of heroin-addicted bebop trumpeters. While I do not mean to allow Mitchell to escape from this problematic predicament (she assuredly does not), I would like to continue to describe how she sees her attachment to non-Western, nonwhite cultures as the result of an early childhood alliance with marginality. As I have mentioned, Mitchell was unable to fit herself into neat categorizations or collective identifications. Her inability to cling to conventional classifications can be traced to her childhood. As a self-described loner, Mitchell never fit into the various groups that childhood and adolescence provide for socialization. Her childhood polio alienated her from other children yet provided an isolation that allowed her the time to develop her artistic interests and impulses. Later, as a teenager, even as she continued her creative work, she became a self-described party girl, as interested in rock 'n' roll dances as she was in poetry. Still, she admits remembering "a recurrent statement on my report card—'Joan does not relate well.' I knew that I was aloof."[40] When she completed high school, no longer content to split her free time between what she called "the sororities" and "juvenile delinquents [who were] suddenly [becoming adult] criminals," her interest in folk music and social protest was also a way of cultivating a different social scene.[41] Her subsequent experiences as a young folksinger on the "coffeehouse" circuit, which would determine the outlines of her music throughout her early career, were a result of these endeavors.

As I have noted, she described herself as a liminal subject, and with her recordings from *Court and Spark* through *Mingus* she attempted to balance her creative work in the interstices—the broken middles—between jazz, high art, mainstream tastes, and artistic ambitions. Her ability to negotiate the thresholds of these categories productively can be attributed in part to her sense of "unbelonging." The rendering of jazz as a universalizing trope, at least in one of its current guises, was undermined by the critical reception of Mitchell's work, strengthening her continued sense of artistic isolation during this period.

The mutable and othered positionalities that Mitchell articulated during this period were reified in her artwork for the cover of *Don Juan's Reckless Daughter*. Against a bare red and blue backdrop suggesting a desolate red landscape and an equally barren blue sky, Mitchell mounted a number of blue-toned black-and-white photographs, obviously cut-and-pasted from a number of different photography sessions. A series of doves float about, rather than fly across, the gatefold sleeves. Unfolding the double-gated album cover to view the picture in its entirety, one finds four human figures positioned among the doves: a young boy in profile, dressed in a formal tuxedo but wearing sneakers; Mitchell, "clothed in her own nakedness," wears a dress imprinted with her own nude torso and hips (her head and legs are obscured by doves), which are surrounded by Mickey Mouse-like balloons;[42] and, prominently in the foreground, a mustachioed black man, dressed rather gaily in a three-piece suit, a large hat, and sunglasses

(*Opposite*) Joni Mitchell's *Don Juan's Reckless Daughter* front cover (top) and back cover (bottom).

with a pendant and scarf hanging loosely down the front of his vest. The black man's right arm, bent at the elbow, allows his right hand, cigarette stub dangling precariously between two fingers, to display a large and rather gaudy ring. He also has a cartoon-style "dialogue balloon" with the album title in it. The fourth figure, alone on the left panel (or back cover section), is a young, white female child, dressed up in "play" Indian clothes, an "Indian-style" tom-tom drum and drumstick in her hands. This character also has a cartoon-style "dialogue balloon" containing the single word, "How."

The two "speaking" characters on the cover are both Joni Mitchell per-forming otherness. The album cover was not the first appearance of the black male alter ego she named Art Nouveau, however. According to her biogra-pher, Kate O'Brien, Mitchell was inspired by an African American man, who, walking past her one Halloween night, declared, "Lookin' good, sister!" On her way to a party thrown by the comedic team of Cheech and Chong, she stopped at a thrift store and transformed herself into the image of an urban stereotype associated, particularly in the blaxploitation-fixated 1970s, with the swaggering pimp, completed by an extroverted sartorial style. By nam-ing her alter(ity) ego, Art Nouveau, or "new art," Mitchell clues us in to her tackling of alterity by an "inhabiting" of alterity through art. The origi-nal art nouveau movement sought to aestheticize, in the sense of "making beautiful," everyday objects as a way to beautify an increasingly industrial-ized world. In the same way, Mitchell can be seen "making beautiful" the street hustler, the con, the pimp—a way of granting dignity, even gravitas, to otherwise disreputable subaltern lives and epistemes. The other "speak-ing" character, the young girl playacting her part as an Indian, appears to be a childhood picture of Mitchell.

As mentioned, these are the only characters who "speak" in this mon-tage. Art Nouveau, leaning back, sunglasses obscuring his eyes, is physically mimicking what one imagines was the bodily stance of Mitchell's Hallow-een admirer, slyly speaking the title, "Don Juan's Reckless Daughter," to us, unambiguously naming her audacity and hinting at his possible role in her adventures. The child, more innocent, has an earnest, concentrated counte-nance, looking past us at an imagined Indian life beyond her simple perfor-mance. The fact that these two figures "speak" is significant as other char-acters (Mitchell as "herself" and the young boy), both white, are mute. What can these figures, and their relationship to each other, as well as to viewers, reveal about Mitchell's conflictual stance with regard to self-expression and performances of alterity?

As Mitchell admits, First Nations cultures were her first involvement with "outsider" positionality. "The first dream I remember having was about Indians. The Indians in that part of Canada were mahogany faced and very serious, at least within the context of our culture. They were woodlands Indians, so they were covered in smoked leathers with elaborate floral beading and satin skirts and long braids. On our sports days they would put up aspen lean-tos and skin teepees, and they'd have their own dances at night. I remember sneaking over and listening to their chants at the fringes of town."[43]

Confessing that she was told "they were dirty and stank," Mitchell, nevertheless, "found their creativity fascinating," though frightening, as she was also warned that Indians kidnapped small children. This combination of forbidden desires, fearful admiration, and creative inspiration adhere to problematic issues of cultural appropriation, racialized alterity, and Euro- and North American condescension, typified as "love and theft" by Eric Lott in his trenchant study of blackface minstrelsy. Correspondingly, Carole Carpenter outlines a Canadian context in which "Anglo-Saxons freely exploited the Natives and their cultures while simultaneously romanticizing these indigenous people."[44]

Again, Mitchell's Canadian upbringing illuminates, at least partially, her willingness to push against the limits of embodiment. As Berland argues, "Rather than remaining invisible behind the veil of the raced body, the Canadian hides behind verisimilitude, 'passing' as the other while recognizing the other as not oneself. This vantage point is double-reflected through a one-way mirror in which 'America' does not see Canada at all. The nonknowing of the other is part of what the Canadian knows, and it shapes her scholarship and art."[45] Borrowing W. E. B. Du Bois's idea of double consciousness, in which blacks view themselves both from their own position and from a white perspective and experience the gap between the two, Berland's assertion about Canadians' double consciousness in relation to the United States speaks to Mitchell's "nervy" performativity here.

Like the sad clown in the Henry Miller tale, Mitchell's performative "minstrelsy" was an "inauthentic" means to make a point about authenticity. It not only spoke to Mitchell's increasing distance from mainstream pop songwriting practices and concerns but also demonstrated her efforts to develop as an artist whose aesthetic concerns were not necessarily circumscribed by gender or race but attempts to articulate the universal from within the subjective. Recognizing her subjectivity as merely one facet in a universal perspective that is performed publicly as an "incomplete truth," as she confessed to Bill Flanagan, indicated her awareness of the incompleteness of any performance of alterity, even self-representations by subalterns. I do not mean to negate the vexed histories othered subjects embody or face in representing their perspectives but seek to grapple with alterity and the limits of universality in Mitchell's representation and creative work.

By examining Mitchell's giving of the word *How* to the child, we can begin to tease out some sense of Mitchell's articulation of performative alterity. The word *how* is a popularization of a Native American term that comes down to us from Hollywood and probably derives from the Lakota Sioux greeting *Hau*. My concern here, though, is not whether it is an actual word that can be traced with certainty to a specific etymology. Rather, I find it significant in this context that *how* signifies a greeting to viewers familiar with genre conventions of the Hollywood western. *How*, in other words, invites the viewer into Mitchell's performative space, inviting us into this "not quite real" world of the imagined other. *How* also asks us to question the assumptions we make in understanding both alterity and authenticity: how do we gauge veracity in the performing arts? Isn't all performance representation? Moreover, are performances restricted to depictions of "reality"?

Mitchell's use of her childhood performance of indigenous North American culture on the cover of *Don Juan's Reckless Daughter* ably demonstrates how a First Nations articulation of universality inspired her rather than the rationalism of Enlightenment Europe, as she attested to Vic Garbarini in the pages of *Musician* magazine:

> In my search for a centering device, a unifying fetish, I came upon this North-South-East-West grid in Indian tradition, though I don't remember which tribe. Wisdom was north, heart was south, clarity was east and introspection was west. It was a chief's wheel, designed to develop the ability to speak a whole truth in a person who was to be a central figure in speaking to other people. The concept was that you were born with a predilection towards one of the four and the opposing arm would be your weak point. If you had wisdom, your weak point would be your heart. If you had clarity, which is overview—the flying eagle, right?—your weak point would be introspection. *And your life's work and goal would be the ability to speak from all points and eventually unify them in a central truth.* To be able to speak to all people regardless of their predilections.[46]

Carpenter describes a similar process at work in Anglo-Canadian appropriations of First Nations culture: "The amount of Anglified materials concerning Native traditions available in the culture has encouraged many Anglo Canadians to adopt bastardized Native materials as their own, or as

'Canadian' traditions. An excellent example of this tendency is the inclusion of Indian or pseudo-Indian legends, especially those referring to place names, within the traditions common to many western Anglo Canadians."[47] Further, Himani Bannerji, speaking to current political realities, asserts, "The issue of the First Nations—their land claims, languages and cultures— provides another dimension entirely, so violent and deep that the state of Canada dare not even name it in the placid language of multiculturalism."[48] Mitchell's use of First Nations traditions, then, is not only one instance of a longer history of white Canadian appropriation but might also serve as an example of the elision of the violence on which that longer history rests (note her forgetfulness as to the specific tribal tradition from which she is drawing). But, if she is using First Nations symbolism to articulate a point of view that, as she argues, is embedded within a cosmology that is itself meant to describe all humans—that is, a universalist position (there is little indication that the chief's wheel was meant to describe merely a single tribe's idea of ideal leadership)—does that desire mitigate *any* historical injustice?

As Berland notes:

Canada is "never homogeneous, never 'pure,' but constructed by First Nations peoples, Francophones, other European groups (from Russians to Italians), Asians (Chinese, Japanese and Indian), and yes, Africans (primarily African American and West Indian)." The ambiguity of this composite identity prevents the contributions of Second World countries from registering in First World postcolonial writing, with its fundamentally binary model of "the West and the Rest." . . . [The irony, then, is one in which] the Second World writer recognizes her complicity in colonialism's territorial appropriation of land, voice, and agency in the very act of voicing opposition to power.[49]

Mitchell, the "Second World writer," personifies the fraught position Berland draws for Canada writ large.

The Canadian ethnomusicologist James Robbins put it this way: "Latin American society shares with Canada what Sidney Mintz describes as 'American-ness.' We are 'people whose ways of being share the common quality of a foreign past,' and, we may add, the heritage of an exceptionally long period of direct colonial rule by Europeans or the descendents of Europeans. And most importantly, we share with Latin America and the Caribbean a relatively subordinate role to that country which has preempted the Hemispheric name America. We are Americans who are not Americans."[50] In 1988 *Musician* magazine ran a cover story featuring four "living legends" of

American music: Johnny Cash, Sonny Rollins, Stevie Wonder, and Mitchell. Mitchell's inclusion with U.S. musicians, in an article subtitled "Four Corners of American Music," indicates her recognition as an "American" rather than "Canadian" musician. Accordingly, Mitchell is in the vexed position of participating in a system that paradoxically also marginalizes and displaces her.

Mitchell's "unifying fetish," or organizing principle behind her performative alterity, can be traced to her desire to "speak to all people," then, and may not simply register as an appropriative gesture either to gain "real" authenticity (i.e., "street cred" or some sense of an affirmative relationship to Others) or to subsume her own lived experience and actual positionality in an attempt to gain an exoticized and marginal but aesthetically powerful authorial voice of the fugitive subaltern. She is, after all, an "American who is not American," whose desire, at once straightforward and disingenuous, is to be able to speak the universal from and through the singular—indeed, *despite* a singularity that has endured silencing by people of Mitchell's ethnic and racial background, as her admission to the prejudices she learned as a child demonstrate. Like McLaughlin, her contradictory stance and positioning do not free her from the legacies of painful racism, de facto segregation, and discrepant power relationships inherent in social and cultural structures, but it does reveal a deeply considered alternative to crude appropriation of ulterior cultural values or simple evasion of the ethical and moral complications raised by her performances of alterity. It also speaks to her use of inauthenticity as a creative methodology.

For example, as mentioned earlier, at her infamous 1970 Isle of Wight Festival performance, she was interrupted by an acquaintance of hers named Yogi Joe, who was subsequently taken off the stage by stagehands— an action that brought boos and other yells of disapproval from the audience. In her emotional response to the crowd, Mitchell explicitly disconnected ethnic or racial background from cultural authenticity in her appeal that the audience calm down and let her perform: "Last Sunday I went to a Hopi ceremonial dance in the desert and there were a lot of people there and there were tourists . . . and there were tourists who were getting into it like Indians and there were Indians getting into it like tourists, and I think that you're acting like tourists, man. Give us some respect."[51] Her distinguishing between "tourists" and "Indians" as "inauthentic" and "authentic" experiences drains those categories of conventional, even normative, essentialisms and transposes them in a similar way that her blackface persona, Art Nouveau, highlights the constructedness of blackness and masculinity.

Indeed, Mitchell's race- and gender-bending character was part of the reason Charles Mingus wanted to collaborate with her. She elaborated: "Two things [made him think I was nervy]: he thought I had a lot of nerve to be dressed up like a black dude on the cover of *Don Juan's Reckless Daughter*. He couldn't get over that. He was sort of thrilled by it."[52] In fact, when asked whether Mingus's "being black" had anything to do with her interest, she declaimed elsewhere, "No, my blackness was a part of it, actually, because I appeared on the cover of *Don Juan's Reckless Daughter* as a black man. Charles thought I had a lot of audacity to do that, and that was one of the reasons he sent for me."[53]

Musically, Mingus's work with extended forms, his careful manipulation of African American blues and gospel idioms, and his integration of straight-ahead and avant-garde jazz practices, considered alongside Mitchell's own musical experiments, makes the alignment of their aesthetic approaches into a compatible vision less surprising despite the seeming distance between their respective musical careers. For example, Mitchell's "Paprika Plains" is arguably one of her most experimental compositions. Similar to Miles Davis's work with Teo Macero, "Paprika Plains" was compiled from a number of recordings. Mitchell improvised four piano tracks, recorded at various times throughout the course of some months. She edited together the four improvisations, inserting a song into the edited version. During the course of these recordings the piano was tuned a number of times, so when she handed the piano pieces to an arranger for string parts, the orchestra ended up performing their parts against a shifting piano tuning. Mitchell recalls, "That really infuriated Charles. 'The orchestra's out of tune—they're in tune, they're out of tune!' Well, that drove him crazy [laughs]. So he thought I was a nervy broad."[54] Mitchell's aesthetic concern with individuality resonated with Mingus's arguments for self-expression, effectively linking their musical visions. As Mitchell admitted later, "So, all things transpired in a natural order. I did one album cover dressed up like a black man; Charles Mingus, who was dying, saw it and called me to write his epitaph. And who would refuse a thing like that?"[55]

Similar to other events in Charles Mingus's life, his final creative work has become a point of contention, even among participants. Sue Mingus, in *Tonight at Noon: A Love Story*, claims the original idea for Mingus and Joni Mitchell to collaborate on a musical setting of T. S. Eliot's *Four Quartets* came from the Italian film producer Daniele Senatore (Mitchell, in fact, thanks

Senatore for introducing her music to Mingus in her album liner notes). In *Myself When I Am Real: The Life and Music of Charles Mingus* the critic Gene Santoro accuses Mingus's interest in Mitchell was an ill-conceived attempt to generate income, ultimately backfiring on everyone involved. Additionally, the charge that Mitchell worked with Mingus in order to raise her own share of cultural capital by tethering herself to a jazz master is an accusation to which she is sensitive. Mitchell has spoken emphatically about the racialized dimension to cultural capital: "I find it offensive to see certain white artists praised and called geniuses, when the person they're emulating went to the grave poor and unrecognized. Look at Bird [the alto saxophonist Charles Parker]. You hear a lot of white saxophonists being called geniuses, and you say, 'No, man, they're not the one who started it.' I hurt for Bird. I hurt for all the great ones who were never fully appreciated."[56] She stated elsewhere that she understood why Mingus composed "If Charlie Parker Were a Gunslinger, There'd Be a Whole Lot of Dead Copycats," citing the lack of originality in most music—rock, jazz, or otherwise. She was also determined to pay homage to Mingus and, perhaps more broadly, to jazz musicians, who she believed were so often denied the respect they deserved.

The recording, in any case, did not sell well, alienating jazz and pop audiences alike. Mingus, dying of amyotrophic lateral sclerosis (better known as Lou Gehrig's disease or its initials, ALS) at the time of the recording, is a mute presence at the center of the music, unable to communicate at length about the music while it was being produced and succumbing to the disease shortly before it was completed and released. Mitchell's testimonial remains the sole audible witness in the public record of their collaboration, which became, in the end, the realization of Mitchell's own vision of Mingus, the man and his art.

She was initially reticent to collaborate on a musical project with Charles Mingus. Jazz music was, as she told Leonard Feather, her "private music . . . quite separate from my own music. I never thought of making that kind of music. I only thought of it as something sacred and unattainable."[57] Her subordinate sense of apprenticeship throughout the period she worked with Mingus assisted in setting a respectful, even solemn, tone for much of the album. Respect and admiration vied with her aesthetic vision and sense of craft, producing a recording marked by the continuous movement between her artistic desires and her obligation to produce music of which Mingus might approve. As she joked during the tour to promote the *Mingus* recording, "Well, just the notion of a folksinger flirting with jazz is seen as presumptuous rather than [as] someone enthusiastically exploring her potential."[58] Yet, elsewhere, she admitted, "My goals have been to constantly remain interested in music. I see myself as a music student. That's why this project with Charles [Mingus] was such a great opportunity. Here was a chance to learn, from a legitimately great artist, about a brand-new idiom that I had only been flirting with before."[59]

Her defensive ambivalence about *Mingus* stemmed from her recognition as a self-described "Joni come lately" to jazz but was tempered by her claims to artistic growth and aesthetic curiosity. Yet she recognized that any collaboration with Mingus was a situation "people thought . . . was too far-out to be true. They had all sorts of reasons for thinking it was an impossible or ridiculous combination. To me, it was fascinating. I was honored. I was curious."[60]

People did, in fact, have good reason to doubt that Mingus was trying to meet her. Mingus's well-known willingness to voice his frank observations of fellow musicians or to issue straightforward critiques of music he found unsatisfactory often intimidated fellow jazz musicians, and some incredulity on the part of Mitchell's acquaintances can be forgiven. When Mitchell finally contacted him, however, she found him "so *warm*, there was no barrier at all. And when I got to know him and read his book [*Beneath the Underdog*], I understood why. He's a romantic and very spiritual man—very eccentric with a big chip on his shoulder, which has kind of devoured him all his life. It's very bewildering, this combination, you know, but it's very beautiful."[61] Mingus's combination of romanticism and spirituality resonated with her own exploration throughout her oeuvre of the dialectical relationship between romantic entanglements and the requirements of a professional music career, and the chip on Mingus's shoulder paralleled Mitchell's frustration with Asylum's resistance to her widening musical palette, the label's patriarchal marketing schemes, and the resistance by critics and audiences to her continued artistic growth on her own terms.

Mingus's interest revealed his recognition of these shared sympathies. On one hand, Mitchell's cross-dressing blackface persona, Art Nouveau, serviced Mingus's agenda of challenging the racialized boundaries of creative work. Mingus once asserted, "American music, which is what we play, belongs with people who have a feeling of freedom and like to play together without discrimination."[62] His interest in working with her was undertaken in a similarly ecumenical spirit of musical association, as well as an appreciation for her boldness in posing on the cover of *Don Juan's Reckless Daughter* as a black man in full "pimp regalia." Eric Porter argues that Mingus's artful figuring of the pimp in *Beneath the Underdog* enabled Mingus to articulate the corrosive effects of a racialized hierarchy based on the dehumanization of black bodies while affirming masculine power.[63] Ironically, Mitchell's eventual domination of their collaborative work, while undoubtedly indicating Mingus's weakened physical capacity, might also indicate Mingus's move from a strongly masculinist stance to one that questioned normative gender relations.

In any case Mingus's struggles to manifest his universalist aesthetic agenda in the face of racial discrimination — as well as his own self-identification as a biracial person — resonated favorably with Mitchell's efforts to sound out a transcendent aesthetic while grappling with the gendered relations in her professional workplace. While Mingus announced an antiracist agenda predicated on a transcendent universalism, Mitchell articulated a gender politics that presaged third-wave feminist critiques of earlier mainstream feminism, as witnessed by her criticism of the regulation of women artists in separate but unequal spaces in the marketplace, the studio, and the bandstand by fellow musicians; by critics who grouped female artists together regardless of idiomatic and aesthetic differences; and by industry executives whose decisions, based on economic concerns rather than aesthetic ones, determined the terms of engagement between record label/boss and artist/worker.

Their collaboration was not without its trials and disagreements. The initial arrangement for the setting of T. S. Eliot's *Four Quartets* to music — regardless of who actually thought of the idea — was Mingus's own conception. His idea was to pair a symphony orchestra and a bass and guitar duo together, with each group performing different but related pieces simultaneously. As Santoro notes in *Myself When I Am Real*, Mingus — inspired by the Pentecostal Baptist Church's tradition of two readers reciting biblical texts, where one reader would read the Bible directly while the second reader rendered it colloquially — called for intermittent formal recitations of Eliot's work while, at the same time, Mitchell was to sing a rendition of the same text distilled into vernacular language.[64] Mitchell, admitting her own interest in musical textures and collage, was fascinated by the idea. However, after failed attempts to mold Eliot's text into vernacular language, she told Mingus, "It [would be] easier for me to condense the Bible."[65] At this point Mitchell abandoned the project, regretting the lost opportunity to work with Mingus.

Her failure motivated Mingus to rethink their collaboration, however, and he composed six new themes for which he wanted Mitchell to write lyrics and perform. When Mitchell first heard the themes, she was again intrigued. However, two of the themes she discarded almost immediately, citing her inability to "find any new way I could transcend them. I had to just lock into them and do them and I just couldn't get inspired" by them. A third theme also proved difficult. In order to find a way to work with this particular theme, Mingus pointed her to a passage in *Beneath the Underdog* in which he and the trumpeter Fats Navarro discuss God.[66] She admitted, "I couldn't just lift that literally and make it adhere to his melody. That threw me into my own confrontation with my own metaphors about God, and it boggled my mind; it just fried my brain. I somehow or other could not really figure that puzzle out."[67] These three themes never made it to the final release.[68]

As she worked on the remaining new themes, fleshing them out into full compositions, she asked Mingus what these untitled themes meant to him.[69] Partially paralyzed and confined to a wheelchair by this time, he replied, "The things I wish I'd done and the people I'm going to miss."[70] Mitchell claims she never meant *Mingus* as a commemorative album, yet his statement forced her to confront a whole new set of meanings for the term *deadline*, and her sense of urgency in completing the project was heightened by his increasingly ill health. In addition, working for another composer was a new experience for her, and while she wanted to please Mingus, she also needed to follow her own aesthetic program, her own muse. One senses the difficulty this often conflictual desire exerted on her work when she discussed how she felt she had to update his material, some of which she heard as "these phrases [that] are almost set up to be crooned, that's the kind of lyrics that were written for a lot of those old songs—moon, June, croonisms. Although there were some great old standards. But the problem is to take the knowledge of progressive pop writing and apply it to this old form."[71] Similar to the other fusion musicians profiled in this study, Mitchell saw jazz as needing the invigoration contemporary popular music could provide it, but she also recognized the added cultural value jazz provided to less-sacralized forms of popular music.

In her liner notes for *Mingus* she thanks a number of musicians who do not appear on the recording itself. The roll call of famous jazz musicians includes the baritone saxophonist Gerry Mulligan, alto saxophonist Phil Woods, drummer Tony Williams, guitarist John McLaughlin, and bassist Eddie Gomez, all of whom participated in early workshops for the recording. Mingus was present at some of these early sessions described later by Mitchell: "The groove was more there, it was closer to what Charles [Mingus] wanted, they swung more and Charles was a stickler for them to swing. So, in some ways, they were stronger in that area. . . . In some ways you could even say that I sang better because the time was so solid. But something happened, something was missing; to me, [these sessions] could have been cut twenty years ago; they didn't contain something that we know now."[72]

Mitchell, increasingly frustrated by her attempts to keep Mingus vital and alive through his music even while his physical decay became increasingly apparent, tried other musicians in different contexts. But Mitchell's decision to take a largely electric ensemble, although it ran counter to Mingus's own aesthetic program, was based on her desire to update Mingus's music and not merely her effort to override Mingus's preferences with her own predilections.

The musicians she eventually ended up using were Jaco Pastorius (bass), Don Alias (percussion), Peter Erskine (drums), Herbie Hancock (piano), Emil Richards (percussion), and another important musical partner for Mitchell, Wayne Shorter (saxophone). These musicians had performed together in various situations in the past, and she was apprehensive about dealing with a band of accomplished male jazz musicians. Mitchell's failure to handle Pastorius at an early Mingus session activated the power relations gender unleashed within the microcosm of a working band, interacting with and affecting the music itself.[73] She realized her musical illiteracy played into the gendered relationships within the band: "Owing to a sense of feminine inferiority that comes on me every once in a while when I'm in a position of leading men — every once in a while I get that, coupled with inferiority and illiteracy, you can understand that there can appear a complex from time to time. Especially when I'm looking for something that I can't articulate."[74]

Mitchell continued, describing how "the vocalist, while . . . a leader of sorts, is kind of apart from what's going on behind them."[75] Supporting Mitchell's description of this dynamic between vocalist (read female) cum leader and her band lies more than half a century of jazz discourse privileging a masculinist, homosocial perspective that effectively excluded women excepting the rare virtuosi who subsumed their gender and sexuality beneath an ability to perform "as well as a man," exemplified by an artist such as the pianist Mary Lou Williams.[76] Additionally, jazz musicians, whose experiences range from friendly blowing contests among friends to the more serious auditions, jam sessions, and gigs of a professional musician, privilege the ability to not only display their "chops" (technical skill) but engage in music practices represented as contestations of virility, endurance, and raw strength. As a performer whose dominant experience was as a solo act, Mitchell faced the challenge not only of integrating her voice into a band situation but also of leading a band of musicians whose collective experiences had been shaped by an immersion in the distinctly gendered world of the jazz musician.

Mitchell's eventual ease with the situation was enabled by Wayne Shorter's presence. His musical sympathies were apparent from the start, and she warmly recounts his value for her: "Shorter . . . plays so beautifully, not off of a high linear line, not just matching tones, but he plays so brilliantly off of lyrics because he has such a pictorial mind that he is talking. He's such a metaphorical player. I love the way he related to me. He especially made me feel like an integral band member. So we all seemed to be one organism on this music."[77] Elsewhere, Mitchell acknowledges her musical kinship with Shorter, citing the time he "played high heels clicking on stones for me. He takes to this kind of instruction like a champ, knows exactly what to do. And he plays off a lyric, in terms of onomatopoeic instrumentation. But very few players I've worked with can even conceive of that."[78]

Shorter's and Mitchell's mutual use of metaphor to instruct musicians in a particular performance has its roots in a shared sensibility of nonlinearity, a privileging of intuitive epistemes over intellectual ones, and the pursuit of an ever-elusive moment of awe, as Shorter describes it.[79] Her willingness to allow each musician to interpret her metaphorical instructions in his own fashion was a way of achieving some balance between competing artistic visions and capabilities. Mitchell, describing her working methodology during these sessions, recalled, "Wayne Shorter, Jaco Pastorius—I would give them metaphorical instruction and they would thrill me, whereas musicians that are still in numerical/alphabetical reference-points would not feel the way it swelled or they would play something too repetitive through a place where the music was not repetitive—they couldn't feel the expression of it."[80]

Only three of the themes Mingus gave to Mitchell made it to the final release, becoming "A Chair in the Sky," "Sweet Sucker Dance," and "The Dry Cleaner from Des Moines." Interestingly, Mitchell inserted snippets of tapes Sue Mingus gave her, opening the album with the first "rap," as Mitchell called them, of a birthday celebration for Mingus. The segment ends with Sue and Charles Mingus arguing about whether he is fifty-three or fifty-four, segueing into "God Must Be a Boogie Man," Mitchell's musical rendering of the opening pages of *Beneath the Underdog*. Mingus asserts his triune personality in the very first sentence—"In other words, I am three"—and Mitchell explores the outlines of Mingus's theme, simultaneously evoking the Christian idea of the Trinity while mocking the notion of a "divine plan," insisting that God must be a boogie man. Mingus, as his book and the argument about his age clearly indicate, was involved with a complex, sometimes contradictory, relationship with the different ways he experienced subjectivity, as well as the impact of the objective world on his "subjectivities," and Mitchell ably captures his deep ambivalence about his own identity.

"A Chair in the Sky" picks up the theme of regret and missed opportunities Mingus described to Mitchell. "Sweet Sucker Dance" tackles familiar Mitchell territory, mapping the vagaries of romantic entanglements as a dance of revolving partners, missteps, and missed cues, with only a handful of dancers fortunate enough to find compatible partners in the midst of a crowded but lonely dance floor. "The Dry Cleaner from Des Moines" is the most upbeat musically with its energetic horn charts and "up swing" feel, but the tale the narrator of the song tells is bittersweet. A gambler, steadily losing her money to slot machines, watches a "cat from Des Moines" hit nothing but jackpots. She keeps repeating the refrain, "It's just luck, nothing to it!" fully aware she is destined to lose all her money while the nonchalant winner from Des Moines blithely adds to his winnings.

"The Wolf That Lives in Lindsey" ranks among Mitchell's most experimental works, with its tape loops of wolves howling and crying, their vocalizations echoing the wind—a nonhuman ostinato to the more standard music on the track. Even her guitar performance is unconventional. She attacks the strings of her guitar, intermittently strumming roughly, allowing the distortion of the strings hitting the soundboard to clearly articulate itself in contrast to her consonant fingerpicking. Don Alias's conga is the only other instrument, accenting and following her aggressive strumming, as well as the nuances of her vocals. Mitchell included this composition, even though she began writing it before she met Mingus, because "the wolves constituted his musical concept about cacophony. Someone found me an actual tape to use, of wolves singing away, and it's beyond dissonance—it transcends dissonance."[81] Cacophony and dissonance frame the otherwise consonant music, echoing Mingus's own works, such as "Fables of Faubus," where sections of free improvisation are framed by through-composed sections, musically demonstrating how human will deludes itself into thinking it has structured order from the seeming chaos in which it finds itself, in contrast to the greater order of "chaos" that swirls just beyond human comprehension. Death, life's greatest mystery, haunts this composition, and like the dissonance constraining the more consonant music on the track, defines the limits of life—an idea, in the context of Mingus's own situation at the time of this work, which resonates forcefully and unambiguously.

It is her version of "Goodbye Porkpie Hat," however, that illustrates the rich texture of their collaboration, in equal measure stating Mitchell's respect for Mingus and linking him to both his past work in jazz and the future of black music.[82] Mitchell's lyrics illustrate how one of Mitchell's ongoing themes—the various tensions between individual desires and collective belonging—manifests itself in relation to race. She describes the process of writing the lyrics in an interview with Vic Garbarini, from which I quote at length:

> He gave me this melody and I didn't know what kind of a theme to lay on it. He kept saying, "This guy was the sweeeeeetest guy," and he kept saying that over and over about Lester Young, who was gone, and it was given to me to write by a man who was about to go. And somehow or other, I felt that in the lyric—the lyric should contain both of them. So, the first verse was easy. But how to get out of this was a mystery, and the last verse wouldn't come. So one night, we're going uptown, my boyfriend and I, and we decided to get off the subway a block early. And we came out near a manhole with steam rising all around us, and about two blocks ahead of us was a group of black guys—pimps, by the look of the hats—circled around, kind of leaning over into a circle. It was this little bar with a canopy that went out to the curb. In the center of them are two boys, maybe nine years old or younger, doing this robot-like dance, a modern dance, and one guy in the ring slaps his knees and says, "Aaaah, that looks like the end of tap dancing, for sure!" So we look up ahead, and in red script on the next bar down, in bright neon, it says "Charlie's." All of a sudden I get this vision, I look at that red script, I look at these two kids, and I think, "The generations . . ." Here's two more kids coming up in the street—talented, drawing probably one of their first crowds, and it's . . . to me, it's like Charlie and Lester. That's enough magic for me, but the capper was when we looked up on the marquee that it was all taking place under. In big capital letters, it said "Pork Pie Hat Bar." All I had to do was rhyme it and you had the last verse.[83]

Neil Tesser, in his *Down Beat* review of the recording, noted how Mitchell's delivery evoked Billie Holiday and Annie Ross, and he described her version of "Goodbye Porkpie Hat" as a "masterpiece." He asserted, "Joni's lyrics, quite frankly, are profound: in the first five words, she manages to weave the song's original subject (Lester Young) and its composer into an epic framework of great emotional power."[84] Additionally, the first verse traces the racial barriers faced by black musicians during the swing era, marking their "underdog" positionality, while linking Mingus to his mentor, Lester Young:

> When Charlie speaks of Lester
> You know someone great has gone
> The sweetest swinging music man
> Had a Porkie Pig hat on
> A bright star
> In a dark age
> When the bandstands had a thousand ways
> Of refusing a black man admission
> Black musician
> In those days they put him in an underdog position
> Cellars and chittlins'

The second verse links the violence brought to bear on Lester Young and his white wife, Mitchell touching on the dynamic relationship between bandstand and bedroom, discursively disconnected but materially linked as the lines reveal:

> When Lester took him a wife
> Arm and arm went black and white
> And some saw red
> And drove them from their hotel bed
> Love is never easy
> It's short of the hope we have for happiness
> Bright and sweet
> Love is never easy street!

The latter part of the verse also registers the miscegenational nature of her merging of jazz and pop music and the historical currents revolving around transcultural fusions, noting the dangers, as well as the pleasures. Her use of *unlikely* attests to the prevailing legacy of antimiscegenation laws and the physical danger continually lurking for those whose embrace crosses the color line:

Now we are black and white
Embracing out in the lunatic New York night
It's very unlikely we'll be driven out of town
Or be hung in a tree
That's unlikely!

She continues in the third verse:

For you and me
The sidewalk is a history book
And a circus
Dangerous clowns
Balancing dreadful and wonderful perceptions
They have been handed
Day by day
Generations on down

The links between the street and the music, as well as her rendering of the pimps as "dangerous clowns" who "balance dreadful and wonderful perceptions" shaped by a legacy "they have been handed" from previous generations, situate the history of racial oppression as continuing into the present while she notes the active agency of these black bodies to counteract, or counterbalance, those forces.

In the final verse Mitchell describes the scene she related to Garbarini, linking the personal histories of Mingus, Young, and herself with the ongoing collective history of race relations by setting her scenes within discrepantly accessible public spaces—the sidewalk, the bar, the hotel bed— "dangerous and wonderful" in equal measure:

We came up from the subway
On the music midnight makes
To Charlie's bass and Lester's saxophone
. . . .
So the sidewalk leads us with music
To two little dancers
Dancing outside a black bar
There's a sign up on the awning
It says "Pork Pie Hat Bar"
And there's black babies dancing . . .
Tonight!

Private actions are echoed in public performances, and, similar to the two young dancers in front of the Pork Pie Hat Bar, individuals move within the spaces and histories provided for them, but, equally important, they are not limited to these legacies. The "black babies dancing" indicate how the present embodies the legacies of the past as well as the promises of the future ("that's the end of tap dancing for sure"), linking Mingus to his apprenticeship with Young and his mentorship, even if distantly, to the young dancers.

Mitchell's rendering of "Goodbye Pork Pie Hat" emphasizes the relationships between various binaries (public/private, individual/collective), exploding them through a placement in history and dynamically framing the movement between these terms through material bodies. Moreover, using "Goodbye Pork Pie Hat" as the final track on *Mingus* allows Mitchell to commemorate Mingus in a manner cognizant of Mingus's tribute to Young. In the end, despite the arguments about repertoire and ensembles, Mitchell found a way to honor Mingus's past, recognize his present contributions, and point toward his legacy in the future. "Joni's jazz," so to speak, is "real" jazz, then, in the way that "jazz" itself defies rigid categorization while retaining the ability to claim a history, or, more accurately, histories, actively pushing the present into the future. The back album cover—a painting by Mitchell of Mingus, his back to the viewer, a large yellow sombrero obscuring his head, a bright space among an otherwise muted palette—registers the passing of Mingus, a mute but larger-than-life presence.

Mitchell, reminiscing about her time with Mingus, noted that she had "met him when he was paralyzed and couldn't really do the violence he was capable of. But he was a very open person and very vulnerable. He cried easily and got angry easily and couldn't stand bullshit. If he thought a guy was faking his notes, playing jive, showing off, he was liable to come swinging at the guy right on the bandstand. He was very true in a certain way and kind of crazy because of it. That's my take on him, anyway. I may have romanticized it some because I was so fond of him."[85]

As her version of "Goodbye Pork Pie Hat" makes evident, her fondness for Mingus rested on their mutual antipathy for "playing jive," a shared recognition of each other's verity in creative focus and how they were both considered "kind of crazy because of it." Charles Mingus died at the age of fifty-six in Mexico, where he had been seeking a cure. His body was cremated, and Sue Mingus, according to his request, scattered his ashes in India, at the source of the Ganges River. Mitchell states in the liner notes that the same day Mingus was cremated, "fifty-six sperm whales beached themselves on

AAD

E2 505

Joni Mitchell's *Mingus* back cover.

the Mexican coastline and were removed by fire," an event providing a poetic closure to the recording. Mitchell, in her attempt to fuse jazz to her own expanded vision of popular music aesthetics, and Mingus, in his desire to collaborate across racial, gender, and genre lines, together created a space for jazz to both anchor itself to its own tangled histories and reach out toward an unknown future.

Mitchell's public name, "Joni Mitchell," is a combination of her youthful pretensions and her first, brief marriage. "Joan" Anderson became "Joni" at the age of thirteen because she "admired the way [her art teacher, Henry Bonli's] last name . . . looked in his painting signatures."[86] Her marriage to an older folksinger, Chuck Mitchell, lasted less than two years, yet she has used the last name, Mitchell, publicly for almost four decades. Her complex nominative self-identity mirrors her engagements with inauthenticity and performative alterity, reflecting her lifelong interest in identity play.

It is fitting, then, that she would find a musical mentor in Charles Mingus, who also held an ambiguous relationship with identity. Mitchell repeats Mingus's fragmented sense of identity—"He is three"—as the first, as well as the last, line of "God Must Be a Boogie Man," emphasizing his multiple self-description. Moreover, because they both encompassed a wide spectrum of music, their shrewd mobilization of shifting identities allowed both Mingus and Mitchell to inhabit widely discrepant aesthetic spaces simultaneously, if not always successfully or coherently.

Mitchell, whose fusion is an unwieldy merging of pop and jazz music, iterated through discrepantly positioned performative identities, can point, like Mingus, to a varied, contradictory, and contentious engagement of an itinerant aesthetic vision that negotiated the broken middle between generic incommensurabilities, hierarchical valuations, and racialized and gendered positionalities. Perhaps her own liner notes to *The Hissing of Summer Lawns* articulate her fusion music best: "The whole [recorded work] unfolded like a mystery. It is not my intention to unravel that mystery for anyone." And with her challenge, as well as through her own problematic example, she encouraged her listeners to manifest a similarly independent perspective, to look at received ideas and conventional wisdom regarding art, music, and belonging from both sides, now.

seven   Chameleon / *Herbie Hancock*

I've used this analogy before: one can accumulate a wardrobe of clothes of different styles. One day, you might want to wear a suit, the next day something more casual and the next day something sporty. You might want to wear sporty things for a couple of weeks. Nobody pays that much attention to a person changing his clothes like that. I don't think they should pay that much attention to a person who maybe has a wardrobe of musical styles within himself and wants to play one style one day and another style the next. I just want the freedom to do any of it I want to whenever I want to. — **Herbie Hancock**

The New York critics always hated electronic jazz. One guy claimed Herbie had ruined his career with it, promise unfulfilled. — **Patrick Gleeson**

A chameleon is able to transform its epidermal hue, adapting to its surroundings for protection, to attract mates, or to claim or protect territory. In the United States, such a protean ability can be seen as inconsistency, and the support for Herbie Hancock's claims to a broad range of "home territories" or links to popular constituencies helped (re)define the *popular* in "popular music" in the 1970s. Hancock composed "Chameleon" at a time when economic interests vied with his formation of a fusion aesthetic. His decision to pursue commercial and aesthetic goals simultaneously raised critical skepticism regarding his motives and the nature of his "real" aesthetic fealties. Similar to the chameleon, Hancock emphasized musical colorations — instrumental texture and harmonic ambiguity — in the service of alternately providing camouflage or sharp visibility to the broken middle among genre, aesthetics, and commerce in his fusion efforts.

His involvement with technology, electronic musical gear, and computers contributed not only to the design of new instruments, or ways of sounding, but also new ways of listening. Hancock's perspective throughout the 1970s was filtered through Nichiren Shoshu Buddhism (he continues to be motivated by his Buddhist beliefs), a modest black nationalist sentiment, and a desire to achieve popular appeal. His view was further complicated by his conception of "the popular" and exactly what "popular appeal" might mean if sundered from charges of debasing artistic integrity. Hancock's fusion works were produced with an understanding that commercial interests and aesthetic concerns need not be incompatible, and they challenged the easy division between art and commerce.

During this period Hancock combined funk, avant-garde experiments, and jazz, realizing his version of a proto-Afrofuturism. *Afrofuturism* is a term that Mark Dery coined in his 1995 essay "Black to the Future" to describe an aesthetic he traced through works by black American writers, musicians, and artists. A blend of science fiction, African iconography, technology, and fantasy, Afrofuturism allowed a place for blacks both in history, not merely myth, and in a "high tech" future in which they were largely absent. Afrofuturists freed blacks from a past that was either unknowable or tragic while envisioning a future that could hold promise rather than peril.

As I noted in my introduction, Hancock's cover of the *Head Hunters* album neatly captures the Afrofuturist encounter of technology and blackness. Hancock, seated at an electronic keyboard, wears an African-styled mask with a VU meter as its mouth and red potentiometers for eyes. His next album, *Thrust* (Columbia 1974), pictures Hancock in the lower left corner, seated in front of another electronic keyboard but functioning as a spaceship's control panel. A moon dominates the sky above a landscape that recalls Machu Picchu and the Andes Mountains. Hancock looks back at us with a wary boredom, archly gauging our response to his entrance from a bank of purple clouds. Hancock's connection to both the future (the spaceship) and the past (the Machu Picchu ruins) illustrates the "pushing [of] the conceptual boundaries of blackness beyond the historic confinements of place, period, and identity" that Herman Gray affirms for Afrofuturist cultural production.[1]

The cover to *Sextant* (Columbia 1972) is the most overtly Afrofuturist, depicting African tribal dancers performing under a large moon on a barren, alien landscape. Mythical animal forms cast long shadows in front of a Latin American–styled ziggurat. The painting extends to the back panel, connected by the robes of another African tribesman who points upward to the moon on the front panel. Behind him, a large Buddha with glowing red eyes stands grimly, a halolike sun rising behind him. Lotus flowers and Buddhist rosary beads float through the back panel, connecting the tribesman

Herbie Hancock's *Thrust* front cover.

Herbie Hancock's *Sextant* gatefold cover.

and the Buddha. This semiotic interconnectivity between Asian, African, and Latin American signs, configured in a faintly psychedelic, outer-space modality, embodies the various tropes Afrofuturists utilize in their reimagining of black identities and representations. Hancock continually used these figurations to renegotiate his relationships to "blackness," "Africa," and "technology" in creative and provocative ways.

His professional music career was given an initial boost when his roommate at the time, Donald Byrd, asked him to join his group in 1961. Hancock's career soon "took off," as his debut Blue Note recording, Takin' Off (1963), declared, thanks to a song titled "Watermelon Man." Its success set the tone for Hancock's subsequent relationship to critical discourse and his own grapplings with artistic pretense and popular success. While the blues-based hard bop tune appeared on Takin' Off, it was Ramon "Mongo" Santamaria's version that became a best-selling single in 1963, and its route to hit status reveals the contours of Hancock's relationship to the music industry, as well as critical discourse.

His journey began when he was hired as the substitute pianist for Santamaria's band one evening. A nearly empty club provided an unusual opportunity for Hancock, Byrd, and Santamaria to spend time between sets discussing the links between Afro-Cuban music and jazz. While they were certain there were connections, they were unable to trace them satisfactorily. As Hancock recalled,

> Mongo said he had been looking for some time for the link. Then Don [Byrd] said, "Hey, Herbie, play 'Watermelon Man' for Mongo." I had been writing the tune at the time, but it wasn't quite right yet. I didn't see what Don was getting at, but I played it, and Mongo jumped up saying, "Keep playing! Keep playing," and he started playing and the tune fell right into place, it was just the right setting. We had found a link. Then Mongo recorded it and it became a hit. He said it was like a tune the Cubans sing up in the mountains, a folk tune.[2]

"Watermelon Man" became Hancock's entrée into the popular realm, not only granting him a certain amount of economic success as the composer of a hit song but also placing his music within a broader set of Afro-diasporic music practices linked through what he termed, in a 1965 Down Beat interview, his own "personal American Negro background." Although he lacked the personal experiences he believed necessary to produce work songs, Hancock recalled the watermelon seller of his childhood Chicago neighborhood, imagining the call-and-response between the seller and a prospective buyer, rhythmically and melodically duplicating his imagined dialogue.

It is not the details of Hancock's transcription that concern me here but, rather, the way in which Hancock drew on personal experience as an authenticating gesture, a strategy he continued to utilize to defend his aesthetic choices in the face of critical disparagement. His admission that he was a fan of classical music as a child and that, as a teenager, his musical tastes were rhythm-and-blues groups such as the Ravens indicate his long-standing personal involvement with a wide range of nonjazz music as musician and listener. Hancock confessed, "I started listening to R&B before jazz. When I was in grammar school I started off listening to classical music and R&B. Around the time I was 14, I started listening to jazz. I was overtaken by it. I didn't become interested in R&B again until I heard James Brown's 'Papa's Got a Brand New Bag' [released in 1970]."[3]

Significantly, with the success of "Watermelon Man" Hancock began his ambivalent relationship with critics. His own ambivalence toward the music industry was leavened by his self-acknowledged dependency on its large-scale systems of production and distribution. Determined to forge a "new idiom," Hancock tested the limits of the music industry, his audiences, and other musicians' capacities for change, exchange, and interchange.

But Hancock's identification with "Watermelon Man" became troublesome for a number of reasons as the decade progressed, especially as he increasingly integrated his interest in avant-garde and experimental electronic music with jazz. As he noted when he left Miles Davis's group to resume his solo career:

> I like ["Watermelon Man"] and it was fun to write it; but it represented only a very small part of what I am. People say, "Why don't you do some more things like that? You could make a fortune." Maybe I could, but it isn't what I want to do. I want to contribute something that is true to my personality. I'm looking for universal symbols within me that are also part of everybody else.
>
> The record buying public of today isn't as narrow-minded as some of the businessmen seem to think. Anything with a strong beat can get across to them; they can accept 7/4; and they're willing nowadays to listen not just to notes, but to sound.[4]

Three items stand out in Hancock's decision to pursue his vision to merge artistic and commercial goals. One was his strong contestation of what he perceived as a cynical view by music industry personnel of a benighted listening and buying audience for his music. Second, he recognized the importance of a "strong beat" in creating music that had wide appeal. Third, and most important, was his assertion that there were "universal symbols within me." Similar to Mitchell, Hancock was interested in touching the universal from within the subjective and, like other fusion musicians, nurtured a strong populist desire to connect with listeners on a variety of levels. He pointed to "Watermelon Man" as a realization of how he might serve these divergent purposes: "The first [reason I wrote "Watermelon Man"] was to help sell the album, but I didn't want to prostitute myself to do that. I also wanted to write something that was actually authentic, something that I knew something about."[5] Hancock would be challenged in the 1970s about linking economic concerns with his own sensibilities regarding "authentic knowledge."

Throughout the 1960s Hancock maintained both a high-profile sideman's post as pianist in Miles Davis's famous "second quintet," as well as a solo recording career with Blue Note records. His own recordings as a leader during this period — My Point of View (1963), Empyrean Isles (1964), Maiden Voyage (1965), and Speak like a Child (1968) — cataloged an eclectic program of introspective ballads, blues-inflected compositions, and impressionistic arrangements, while Inventions and Dimensions (1963) showcased Hancock's interest in Latin jazz.

Hancock's wide range of musical interests was evidenced by his unique use of unconventional lineups. For instance, on Speak like a Child Hancock reconfigured the standard front line of trumpet and alto and/or tenor saxophone by hiring Thad Jones on flugelhorn, Peter Phillips on bass trombone, and Jerry Dodgion on alto flute, focusing on the lineup's softer hued sonic palette. More provocatively, Hancock used the "front line" only as accompaniment, taking all the solos himself. This unique arrangement exhibited Hancock's growing interest in timbre and his belief that audiences responded to coloristic components, as well as rhythmic or melodic elements. It was also his response to critics and music industry executives who constantly asked him why he didn't record a solo piano or piano trio album. While he admitted that he had little interest in a solo piano or piano trio format, his response was to arrange the tracks on *Speak like a Child* that could be heard as emphasizing either his piano skills or the small-group interaction.

Hancock's interest in nonjazz popular music was already evident in these early solo recordings. Though three years elapsed between *Maiden Voyage* and *Speak like a Child*, Hancock linked the two recordings by exploring "the concept that there is a type of music in between jazz and rock." He elaborated: "It has elements of both but retains and builds on its own identity. Its jazz elements include improvisation and it's like rock in that it emphasizes particular kinds of rhythmic patterns to work off of."[6] His interest in finding this "in between" music was motivated by a combination of factors.

Hancock's work in the Miles Davis group, in which a "time, no changes/ free bop" aesthetic slowly evolved, was one element. As I have mentioned, Davis was listening to rock and funk bands owing to the influence of Betty Mabry and Tony Williams, both of whom were younger than he and fans of popular musical groups. Hancock also admitted to being introduced to rock and soul musical acts by Williams. But it was Miles who introduced Hancock to the Fender Rhodes electric piano for the *Miles in the Sky* sessions in 1968. Hancock, recalling this initial encounter with the electric piano, stated,

> I walked into the studio, and I looked for the acoustic piano, and I didn't see one in this big studio at Columbia Records. So, I looked and there was this piano—it said "Fender Rhodes piano." I said [to Miles Davis], "You want me to play this?" He said, "Yeah." So, I touched it and the sound that came out was much bigger than I really expected to hear. It was much, much fuller and it had a blending quality that the acoustic piano doesn't have. The Fender Rhodes piano blends so well with other instruments. And I could hear myself much, much better. Plus the vibrato effect—I liked that right away.[7]

As Hancock attests, the development of the Fender Rhodes enabled pianists to be heard in the increasingly amplified world of popular music. Prior to the invention of the electric piano, pianists often had difficulty hearing themselves even in all-acoustic jazz groups, especially in small, noisy clubs where they were often at the mercy of out-of-tune pianos. The Fender Rhodes displaced all of these hindrances for a pianist's full participation by not only providing volume but also somewhat more reliable tuning. The important element, though, was the increased volume; thus, as Hancock reveals above, the superior "blending" quality of the Fender Rhodes touched on Hancock's interest with orchestration and harmonic coloration. Sparked by his apprenticeship to the noted large ensemble arrangers Oliver Nelson and Thad Jones, and an appreciation of Gil Evans's work, Hancock's preference for showcasing unconventional front lines in a unique interplay with his piano was enhanced by the Fender Rhodes's smooth, round tone, which was joined to a keyboard that was touch sensitive—the harder you banged down on the keys, the brighter the tone would get, with the sharp little attack of a hammer hitting a metal tine (rather than the wire string of an acoustic piano) thrown in for expressive good measure.

There were other reasons Hancock, and other pianists, began to employ Fender Rhodes electric pianos. The electronic circuitry not only allowed for factory preset manipulations such as vibrato but also encouraged customization. Hancock connected a wah-wah pedal and other sound-processing units to achieve, among other things, a pitch-bending ability. The vibrato and pitch-bending ability allowed keyboardists to "bend" notes in a way similar to that in which string instrumentalists manipulated the expressive quality of a musical line by exerting pressure on a string to vary its pitch. The "bent blue notes" of guitarists or the sliding glissandos of a saxophonist were now something keyboardists could emulate, expanding their expressive palette. The increasing complexity and power of keyboard synthesizers and computers, coupled with Hancock's interest in orchestration and arrangement, would continue to motivate his work with technology.

Hancock also composed tunes for television commercials, including "Maiden Voyage," which was originally scored for a Yardley's Men's Cologne advertisement. He scored films, including a critically acclaimed score for Michelangelo Antonioni's *Blow Up*, as well as television shows such as Bill Cosby's animated series, *Hey, Hey, Hey, It's Fat Albert*. Again, his interest in producing music for explicitly commercial endeavors complicated his position for jazz critics who were advocating jazz as art music. Hancock insisted that there was little, if any, distance between "tunes" marked as "commercial" and "compositions" demarcated as "art." When he recorded "Maiden Voyage" on the album of the same title, he was clearly not attempting to sell more cologne for his one-time client but felt the composition worthy of inclusion among his more valorized creative work.

In creating compositions that openly straddled economic and aesthetic concerns, Hancock forced the confrontation between "high art" and "commerce" within jazz discourse. As an African American, Hancock was well aware of the social and economic inequities of American life. He held a double major in electrical engineering and music while enrolled at Grinnell College because of his concern for earning a living. Except for rare instances, musicians—particularly jazz musicians—do not labor within a framework of steady employment, health benefits, or retirement plans, and Hancock cannot be faulted for seeking those employment opportunities that ensured greater access to a standard of living enjoyed by other workers. In 1960, however, when he was twenty, the chance to work in Donald Byrd's group alleviated any qualms he had about the life of a professional musician, and he was soon recording and working for Byrd, Oliver Nelson, and others. By 1963 his own debut album and the success of "Watermelon Man" assured his occupation as a professional musician.

Hancock's concerns about financial security were not completely erased, however, in spite of his successes as a session musician for Creed Taylor and others. In 1969 he released *Fat Albert Rotunda* (Warner Bros.), a recording that reflected his interest in the soul music of the time. Jazz critics, however, accused him of "selling out," and while hard bop successes such as "Watermelon Man" might not entail the type of high cultural capital he also desired as a creative artist, Hancock was not insensitive to their criticisms. While I will return to Hancock's own defense of *Fat Albert Rotunda* and his subsequent recordings, I want to juxtapose *Fat Albert Rotunda* with another album he released in 1969, *The Prisoner* (Blue Note).

The Prisoner is unique among Hancock's recordings as a bandleader because of its explicitly political associations. The opening composition, "I Have a Dream," is an overt homage to Dr. Martin Luther King Jr. and the civil rights movement. The title track is next, and "the prisoners" to whom Hancock refers are African Americans constrained by the U.S. apartheid sociopolitical landscape. Yet, as Hancock asserts in the liner notes, he wanted to connect with as large an audience as possible by "trying to write hummable tunes with a kind of rhythmic element people can be infected with."[8] Hancock, coupling an interest in cultivating a broad appeal with a politicized subtext—the political struggles of African Americans for an equitable society—detailed the troubled relationship between an interest in economic success and progressive political goals. This is a theme he would continually address throughout the 1970s (and it is one that continues to feed his creative and commercial concerns to the present day).

The composition "He Who Lives in Fear" succinctly displays the conflictual forces at play in his work at this time. Originally composed for a Silva Thins cigarette commercial, Hancock retitled the song when the advertising agency would not grant him permission to record it. In retitling the tune, as well as reharmonizing it, Hancock also reconceptualized its purpose. Instead of selling cigarettes, Hancock retooled the composition to highlight "the fact that [Dr. Martin Luther] King had to live in an atmosphere charged with intimidation."[9] Paralleling his lack of access to his own creative work by an advertising agency, Hancock recognized how King's political struggles were a contestation of the physical, legal, and social intimidations blacks in America faced daily. The ironic rendering of a commercial song resonates against older African American strategies of resistance including such practices as work slowdowns and "pan toting."[10] Jazz musicians had long contested ownership of their music by reharmonizing popular songs or by performing different melodies on top of the harmonic progressions of popular songs in order to avoid copyright and licensing fees for their recordings. Hancock's "trickster" performance of a song with a title that recognized the forces set against him also attempted to show how producing "hummable tunes" might generate resistive feelings in his listeners.

Fat Albert Rotunda, as the soundtrack to the first African American–produced cartoon series on network television, was a critical failure. Though Hancock performed on the Fender Rhodes electric piano on various Miles Davis dates, he had used it very sparingly on his own solo recordings. Fat Albert Rotunda, however, signaled Hancock's full-fledged entry into his engagements with the popular music world. In a 1970 Melody Maker interview he was explicit about his switch from a jazz-based label, Blue Note, to a larger, major label, Warner Bros.: "Doing Fat Albert on [Blue Note] would have been almost impossible, and a waste. They don't have the facilities nor the desire nor the belief in me as an artist exposing my material to another element. They can't think that way." More important, Hancock asserted, "I want to sell albums—but people will misinterpret that. I want to reach people. At this point there are too many people who haven't been exposed to my music, and too many who can't relate to it at this point. That's too few as compared to, say, the Beatles or Iron Butterfly. My best album sold maybe 30,000 copies. People say how great such-and-such a tune is, so how come the record only sold 30,000? I'm tired of those little numbers—I'm looking for some other stuff now."[11]

Hancock's interest in reaching out to a popular audience militated against his desire to hold onto his jazz audience. He acknowledged in the same interview that his goals might not have been served by his desire to reach out beyond his core jazz following:

The funny thing is that in my haste, and the record company's haste, to get it exposed firstly to the R&B market and secondly to the underground

Chameleon   193

rock market, we neglected the people to whom it would probably appeal most: those who buy albums by the Fifth Dimension, Blood Sweat and Tears, and maybe Miles.

It's not a real rock album—it doesn't have that strong rock beat, or a heavy jazz top to it either. I hate to use the term "middle of the road" because that sounds like watered-down bullshit, but I was just trying to make something that I really felt.[12]

Hancock continued, arguing for his open sense of multiple interests and motivations: "A lot of people were disappointed because they compared it to my previous records. Now how are you going to do that? You just can't compare them. Jazz records only show a certain part of me, and *Fat Albert* shows another part. I'm still a black man, and *Fat Albert* is probably more basic than the Blue Note things like *The Prisoner*. *Fat Albert* is [sic] to do with my roots, and people forgot that. *And understand, I don't like the idea of having to be stuck within the mainstream of jazz.*"[13] An audience who listened to the Fifth Dimension or "maybe Miles" in 1970 could be described as a mainstream popular music audience. Hancock recognized the risk in pursuing a "middle of the road" audience, and his articulation of that danger—critical dismissal—was only leavened by his hope for increased audience approval and thus "bigger numbers" (i.e., larger sales).

Hancock voiced his bifurcated desires as early as 1965, when he announced that his next album "for Blue Note is going to be a rhythm 'n' blues album."[14] He was aware of the provocative nature of his plans, as this excerpt from the article demonstrates: "With a smile, Hancock explained that it would not be a jazz version of rhythm 'n' blues, but a real rhythm 'n' blues album ('straight down the line'). 'I want to see,' he went on, 'if I can do it, if I can produce authentic rhythm 'n' blues with that particular essence that makes it good.'"[15]

In the same interview Hancock also cited his interest in Karlheinz Stockhausen, Igor Stravinsky, Lili Boulanger, Robert Farnon, Béla Bartók, and Ali Akbar Khan. Similar to other fusion musicians, his musical influences were wide, and he accessed various traditions at will. However, his recognition of his embodied position as a black American authenticated, in his view, his performances of jazz, rhythm and blues, and, later, funk, disco, and soul music. Hancock, by emphasizing his familiarity with jazz, rhythm and blues, and European concert music traditions, sought to level their placement within a racialized hierarchy. But he was not initially interested in the type of confrontational music his former band mate Tony Williams initiated with Lifetime. He elaborated on the qualities he embraced in Hentoff's liner notes to *Speak like a Child*, explaining that the title

> came from Frank Wolff, and it's a result of a picture that a friend of mine, David Bythewood, took. I dug it so much I brought it to Frank for use as the cover for this album. Frank said it was so evocative a photograph because of the innocence and naiveté in it. And so I started thinking about the quality of innocence while writing this song. Clearly the music doesn't sound too much like what's going on today—war, riots, the stock market getting busted up. And the reason it doesn't, I realized, is that I'm optimistic. I believe in hope and peace and love. It's not that I'm blind to what's going on, but I feel this music is a forward look into what could be a bright future. The philosophy represented in this number, and to a large extent in the album as a whole, is child-like. But not childish. By that I mean there are certain elements of childhood we lose and wish we could have back—purity, spontaneity. When they do return to us, we're at our best. So what I'm telling the world is: "Speak like a child. Think and feel in terms of hope and the possibilities of making ourselves less impure."[16]

Distinguishing between *childlike* and *childish*, Hancock transformed "innocence" into a type of wisdom, a knowingness that he linked to purity. A loss of innocence, then, becomes a type of unknowingness, a lack of wisdom, as well as an indication of impurity. This linkage—knowingness-wisdom-purity, as well as its complement, unknowingness-ignorance-impurity—is given a further twist by innocence's affiliation with spontaneity or improvisation. Without pushing this series of analogies too far, Hancock's music argues that to "speak like a child" is to be willing to open up, to act spontaneously and thus authentically. Like McLaughlin, Hancock is not proclaiming his music for changing listeners a *fait accompli* but, instead, rallies his music to sound out a hoped-for future within a realm of open-ended potentialities. Why else lead with a track titled "Riot," a heady and bracing showcase for the fluid capabilities of the piano trio at the heart of this recording?

Despite Hancock's assertions that he was going to produce a "straight rhythm 'n' blues" recording throughout the late 1960s, his forays into popular music remained tentative and exploratory. For example, contrary to Hancock's declamations in the liner notes to *Speak like a Child* of the recording's rock and jazz mergings, the recording's fusion, if it can be called such, sounds tenuous in retrospect, and the rock elements, as he had admitted, tended to the middle of the road rather than its earthier shoulders. The acoustic instrumentation and the approach of the musicians on the recording was distant from any music that listeners might have called "rock" in 1968.

Even *Fat Albert Rotunda*, for all its dismissal at the time of its release owing to its nods to funk and rhythm and blues, sounds more like mainstream jazz than Tony Williams's Lifetime's *Emergency!* or Mahavishnu Orchestra's *Inner Mounting Flame*. His former bandleader, Miles Davis, also fomented more *Sturm und Drang* in *Bitches Brew* than the younger Hancock managed on *Fat Albert Rotunda*. Still, it is difficult to resist the funky drive of "Wiggle-Waggle," and "Jessica" remains one of the more poignant ballad recordings of the era.

Hancock produced another sort of fusion, merging a lighter, melodic approach with a deepening appreciation throughout the decade for establishing a "groove." His early hits "Watermelon Man" and "Cantaloupe Island" were compelling owing to that ill-defined popular musician's term, *groove*, as well as the "hummable" themes for which Hancock was noted throughout the 1960s. Unsurprisingly, advertising agencies and record labels became interested in his work, but it was his success in the 1970s that cast a shadow with issues that his earlier successes with "Watermelon Man" and "Cantaloupe Island" never raised.

The "groove" is, like "swing," an elusive musical element, and in order to properly focus on the temporal and participatory emphases of either term, it is more appropriate to discuss "to groove" and "to swing." Charles Keil and Steven Feld, in *Music Grooves*, elucidate a number of ways in which the title of their book resonates; however, I want to focus on their idea of the participatory nature of the groove, as well as the repetitive yet nonidentical nature of "grooving," reminding the reader, as do Keil and Feld, of Amiri Baraka's elucidation of the "changing same." Baraka's notion succinctly captures the mode of participatory engagement that listeners and musicians share within the phenomenal, emotional, and intellectual registers of black music comprehension, consumption, and production by highlighting the emergence of those comprehensive registers through redundant structures that incorporate minute variances through time. In fact, temporal displacement allows grooving to occur, dispelling the "grooves" of the static object of commodified music production (i.e., the vinyl LP), as well as the frozen "grooves" of notational text.

Hancock's use of a groove-oriented aesthetic rather than a purely irruptive or confrontational music reflected his popular music preferences, as well as the terms of social engagement with which he was comfortable. Whereas his former band mate Tony Williams aimed to foreground his preference for hard rock and its more confrontational gestures, Hancock preferred the music of Sly Stone, whose band membership, as I pointed out earlier, reflected an interracial, cross-gender political and social stance. Hancock, in "speaking like a child," was more interested in collaborative solidarity across racial lines than confrontation. In 1965 Hancock was asked about the relationship between the avant-garde jazz scene and the radical black politics of the time. He replied, "I don't feel that I hate white people. It's like the shoe being put on the other foot—you change the label from white people hating black people to the other way around. Since I don't feel the hate-white thing, I don't identify with it. I understand what those who do are talking about, and to a certain extent I can see a partial validity to what they say, but that extremist thing I can't go for. I can't hate the people who feel that way, but I'm just sorry that they believe in that sort of thing."[17] His position of hopeful engagement—his desire to "speak like a child"—remained his dominant perspective through the late 1960s and was reflected in his desire to produce "middle of the road" recordings. As the late 1960s gave way to the early 1970s, however, his centrist position, both politically and aesthetically, began to move toward a more activist and radicalized space.

Fat Albert Rotunda was Hancock's entrée into a "kind of rock/R&B bag," as he described to Richard Williams, but after its cool critical reception Hancock and executives at Warner Bros. Records changed strategies to transform him into a crossover "star" along the lines of Miles Davis at Columbia. As I mentioned previously, the term crossover speaks to the racialized genre definitions that lurk behind classifications such as "rock," "rhythm and blues," and "jazz." When nonwhite recording artists "cross over" the color lines implicit in generic demarcations, they enter the listening habitus of "the (white) mainstream audience." "Crossing over" might offer significant material rewards, but artists risk a loss of authenticity and symbolic as well as material connections to their "home" communities. Within this context Hancock hoped to mitigate such losses by reiterating his artistic agenda of creating and performing music that, in its transcendence of generic categories, also spoke to the transformation of the links between musical soundings, its representations, and, in turn, its role in audience identification. He detailed his thoughts in a 1970 interview with Dan Strongin:

DAN. What I'm getting at is there are some black jazz musicians who live under the illusion that they can woo the young, white rock 'n' roll audience.

HERBIE. Isn't that right?

DAN. In other words, you wouldn't live under that illusion, you're trying to speak for yourself—you're not trying to woo the great masses of the rock 'n' roll people.

HERBIE. No. That's not true. I would like to; I would really like to woo as many of the masses as I can, if there's a chance that I can woo them. I mean, I realize that part of the reason that these rock groups are making it, forgetting the fact that they get all the promotion and so forth, is the fact that the white audience can identify with them, because they both have long hair that they can shake, and they both have white skin and hair on their chest and all these things; I realize that this is, as far as getting to the audience is concerned, a real advantage. If you're trying to get a white audience, it's an advantage just being white; *even if the audience isn't prejudiced, isn't overtly prejudiced, it's just the underlying subconscious thing that almost forces the audience to identify with the performers of their own race.*[18]

Hancock's recognition of the value of whiteness in promoting a musical artist or group was explicit. In a 1985 interview with Wynton Marsalis, Marsalis reminded Hancock of his strategic displacement of his own black body from one of the first videos by a black artist to air on MTV. Marsalis quoted Hancock, stating, "He said, 'I hear that people from MTV were racist oriented and I didn't want to take any chances, so when I did my video I made sure they didn't focus on me and that some of the robots' faces were white.'"[19] Hancock deftly elided Marsalis's accusatory revelation by countering that he had no interest in being in his own videos or on the covers of his albums. As is evident from the interview fifteen years previous, however, Hancock had an awareness of the racial dynamics in the promotion of musicians, and his lack of interest in displaying his own blackness visually—if, in fact, Hancock was uninterested—was inversely proportional to the blackness, however configured, that was exhibited in his music.

To return to the economic pressures in place in 1970, Hancock recognized the situation for his new venture:

Well, financially, jazz is in a very rough position right now. I think it's going to get better, but it hasn't been too good for the past couple of years, because, as we said before, clubs have been closing. And the jazz performers are not in contact as much with the people that are promoting concerts and colleges as rock groups, you know. And we've never even bothered with it, because the club scene was always ours and now that the clubs are closing, we don't have the contacts; but now we're starting to get them. . . . I feel that I would like my music, hopefully, to appeal to more people. Consequently, I've changed my record label: from Blue Note Records, which is specifically a jazz label, to Warner Brothers, which has no specific tag attached to it at all. Hopefully, it'll allow me to write not [only] jazz as "mainstream Afro-jazz" but a whole spectrum of musical thought, *anything that I want to get into. I've had experience with different things.*[20]

Hancock described his professional direction at this point: "[The producer David Rubinson] was suggested to me by the people at Warners. They thought he could influence me to do a better version of *Fat Albert Rotunda* because he had an attachment to the major corporate record companies; he wasn't involved with indie jazz labels [such as Blue Note]. They were looking for hit records."[21] Hancock believed that a mainstream audience would embrace avant-garde experiments in an otherwise conventional popular music setting (e.g., a funk "backbeat" rhythm or a "hummable" theme). His optimism concerning a mass audience acceptance of his unique fusion of experimental, jazz, rock, and funk music partially motivated his interest in accepting the responsibilities and the hardships of leading a band of unknown musicians engaged in unconventional music.

In 1970 Warner Bros. released *Mwandishi*, an album title that was also Hancock's African name. Hancock took the African name *Mwandishi*, meaning "composer" or "author," a nominative designation that emphasized his creativity was rooted in a connection to Africa. The rest of his sextet also took African names: Mganga Eddie Henderson on trumpet and flugelhorn; Mwile Benny Maupin on bass clarinet and alto flute; Pepo Mtoto Julian Priester on trombone; Jabali Billy Hart on drums; and Mchezaji Buster Williams on bass, the sole member of the sextet who remained from the group who recorded *Fat Albert Rotunda*.[22] Hancock, however, and the others in his band, continued to use their better-known names in their promotional interviews and materials. The only journalist to address Hancock during this period as "Mwandishi" was a *Down Beat* writer whose byline simply read "Jagajivan."[23] The musicians' continued use of their English names was driven by economic concerns; that is, their "name recognition" in the marketplace superseded their attempts to connect to Africa, even nominally.

The best-known band member was Julian Priester, who had recorded with Sun Ra in 1956 and Max Roach on Roach's *We Insist: Freedom Now Suite* (Candid 1960). Just as significantly, Buster Williams, a practicing Nichiren Shoshu Buddhist, introduced Hancock to his beliefs and practices, and they began incorporating Buddhist rituals into their working lives, including chanting the *gongyo* before rehearsals and live performances. Hancock's religious practices indicated "the deep spiritual connection that held the band together" and influenced the working aesthetic for the band.[24]

Continuing his pursuit of timbre as a central element, Hancock described his lineup to *Down Beat*'s Brooks Johnson:

> In using this instrumentation, I've got the same flexibility a small group has and yet I have a vehicle for getting orchestral colors the way a large group might. I've got three horns—that's almost like a lower limit for making what we call harmony. You can do it with two instruments, but three is the least *comfortable* number of instruments for getting harmonic colors. . . . This way, I get a chance to really use different kinds of colors, not just because of the harmony I can use, but because of the instruments that I have.[25]

Though the group's official name was simply the Herbie Hancock Sextet, the group that came to be known as Mwandishi was Hancock's first working unit, and he was clearly stimulated by the opportunity to "play my music and, as a group . . . to evolve the music."[26] Hancock was interested in a collaborative approach to music, hoping to emphasize the participatory element in improvisation, explaining, "Well, this isn't much of a problem with this band [but] a bandleader could run into the problem of not allowing enough of the personality of the individual players to be present in the music. They have to all feel that they are responsible for doing the best they can. If they don't feel that responsibility, if they don't feel that they're really contributing, then they may feel that they're sort of dead weight in the band—just holding an instrument and not serving a real function. So their personality has to be present in the music."[27]

Hancock's interest in merging avant-garde elements with jazz and other popular music was based on presenting "the whole, total picture of music." The audience's participation and acceptance of the more experimental elements would be facilitated by the band's use of rock and funk elements. He insisted that audiences could be drawn to this "total picture of music" because the band, as "a vehicle that the music comes through," needed the audience to complete the full musical circuit. Hancock noted, however, that though Mwandishi performed a merging of avant-garde and popular music, the idiomatic jazz elements that the band continued to utilize—improvisation involving "changes"—were transformed but not abandoned: "there usually is a chordal basis that underlies whatever direction that we go in."[28]

Hancock, perhaps realizing the demands he was placing on audiences—particularly salient since he was seeking larger, mainstream audiences—encouraged audience members to "hear like a child": "Actually, the person shouldn't listen for anything. The person should just go in there and listen to whatever is going on and then make his decision. He should try not to walk in with criteria in his arms, but just walk in empty-handed and listen to whatever's going on. If it feels good he digs it—doesn't deny it—but if it doesn't feel good, familiar or unfamiliar, nobody should object if he is not able to accept it."[29]

Though they had not performed as a unit for very long when they made their first recording, as they embarked on a long series of tours, the band members began to coalesce around Hancock's aesthetic, which began to manifest itself in the increasingly coherent yet open-ended music onstage. The band's first tour went through Europe, and bootleg recordings reveal a growing affinity among the players with one another's performance styles, coupled with a willingness to explore spontaneous modifications to compositional form, as well as content. Similar to Miles Davis's groups of the period, Mwandishi segued from composition to composition, exploring the tunes in novel ways. Jazz audiences were accustomed to jazz musicians' conventional practice of stating the theme, followed by a series of solos, and ending with a recapitulation of the theme. Mwandishi, however, shaped by Hancock's time in Davis's "second quintet," often had only a thematic line written out without any harmonic indication, and band mates engaged in group improvisations akin to free jazz practice. As indicated above, however, Mwandishi did not completely abandon functional harmony, but the musicians were liberated from strictly adhering to set routines of harmonies during the statement of the theme as well as during improvisatory sections.

Significantly, the second Mwandishi recording was titled *Crossings* (Warner Bros. 1971). The synthesist Pat Gleeson had been introduced to Hancock by Hancock's producer-turned-manager, David Rubinson. Gleeson was an early adopter of the new synthesizers that were becoming available to keyboardists at the time. Prior to the 1970s, access to synthesizers was exclusively available to university-funded music departments such as the Columbia-Princeton Electronic Music Center. Western art music composers such as Vladimir Ussachevsky and Otto Luening composed early computer and synthesizer music in the 1950s and 1960s at the jointly operated music laboratory, and the rationalization of music was pursued in tandem with other like-minded efforts at institutions such as the Institut de Recherche et Coordination Acoustique/Musique (IRCAM), in Paris. These synthesizers, moreover, were room-sized instruments that were used in conjunction with tape-recording mechanisms, making it impractical, if not impossible, to reproduce the music in nonlocalized situations. Even if they had been available to musicians, they were prohibitively expensive because of the amount of engineering hardware, the cost of recording media, and the impracticality of transporting the instrument.[30] Moreover, the music that early synthesizer composers were producing was reflected in the lab coats worn by composers such as Ussachevsky and Luening, whose computers and synthesizers were utilized to create orderly, rationalized compositions.

It took an engineer turned instrument maker, Robert Moog, through his efforts to produce an affordable synthesizer, to bridge the gap between experimental electronic music and popular music. Moog was soon joined by other electronic instrument makers, and the "personal" synthesizer revolutionized not only musicians' practice but also listeners' willingness to hear electronic soundings as music—not simply white noise, static, or incoherent beeps and blips but as functional elements in modern music—in the same way tonal harmony had become a fundamental way of hearing musical development and adjudicating compositional integrity. Ironically, the recording that popularized synthesizer music was Walter Carlos's *Switched-On Bach* (CBS 1968), which featured his performances of well-known Bach compositions on the Moog synthesizer.[31]

Gleeson, however, used the synthesizer in ways that recalled computer music's experimental beginnings, foregrounding the types of sounds that contemporary synthesizers eventually abandoned (becoming, instead, machines that emulate acoustic instruments rather than being utilized to explore sounds not attainable on acoustic instruments, as had been envisioned by early computer and synthesizer musicians). The synthesizer became a textural instrument in Gleeson's hands, adding an electronic element to Hancock's timbral palette. A self-confessed "non musician," Gleeson was a former California State University, San Francisco (now San Francisco State University), English professor who became interested in multimedia art and synthesizers in the mid-1960s.

Gleeson's "audition" consisted of adding synthesizer parts to a single master track for the upcoming release, *Crossings*. Hancock liked the results and sent the rest of the recording to Gleeson for further additions to the already recorded master tracks. Hancock admitted that Gleeson's contributions "just killed me. It just blew me away. Right after [hearing Gleeson's synthesizer additions] I hired him. It was so funny because the synthesizer was still such a new instrument. It was only used on recordings; there was no precedent for him to follow."[32] Gleeson, somewhat surprised at Hancock's eager endorsement, confessed that while Hancock admitted having never heard anything like Gleeson's synthesizer work, Gleeson had never heard anything like it, either, as he was "just making it up, you know."[33]

Similar to Miles Davis's postproduction work on his fusion recordings, Hancock ignored the jazz imperative that regarded capturing live, in-the-moment spontaneity as the only authentic recording methodology. In his effort to move away from symptomatic and idiomatic jazz gestures, Hancock gave *Crossings* to Warner Bros. without apologies, fully embracing the experimental aspects of the recording. Bennie Maupin, Mwandishi's woodwind player, indicated the expressive contours that Hancock talked about in relation to his focus on timbre and texture when he commented on Gleeson's involvement:

> When Pat came into the band that was a different element, because that was totally revolutionary. Nobody had ever done that before, not in a band like this. He had his instrument that he came into the Sextet with, the ARP 2600, and at the time that was the synthesizer of choice—everybody wanted one. And it brought an incredible array of unique things that contributed to the whole raw sound. I would say Pat's involvement definitely opened the music much more, because we started to get more and more away from the note, and into sounds and colours and textures. That gave us a much broader range of choices. Sometimes there was noise, which was great. It gave us an opportunity to go in a whole different direction.[34]

Hancock, his interest in electronics revitalized by his introduction to Gleeson and his bank of Moog and ARP synthesizers, noted Gleeson's activities and constantly asked questions about the equipment. At this time synthesizers were not programmable and synthesists often relied on handwritten schematic notes in order to reprogram various sounds and textures. The exact location of each patch cord had to be diagrammed in addition to the exact position of each knob and/or slider. Synthesizers did not come with a set of factory "presets" (preset sounds), and each synthesist was notably proud and somewhat secretive about his or her sound. Combinations of equipment also impacted the individuality of a keyboardist's particular sound, and *Contemporary Keyboard* magazine, a publication devoted to promoting and otherwise engaging this emerging world, listed famous keyboardists' equipment inventories while increasingly affordable keyboards of the early 1970s filled bedrooms and basements. Pointedly, interviews with electronic keyboardists focused almost exclusively on the instrumentation and sound equipment arsenals of famous interviewees along with "secret" patches and other synthesizer esoterica.

Aware of his own musical limitations, Gleeson was also aware of the other members' "reps, and their chops [musical skills], and they were so hip and black, and here was this white schoolteacher. And from their point of view, they were exactly the same: they were hip guys who'd paid their dues, and here was this idiot with his telephone apparatus."[35] Gleeson was also constrained by early synthesizer technology. As noted above, modular synthesizers had to be reconfigured for each distinctive sound—a process that could take hours. Live performance, especially the interactive music in which Mwandishi participated, dictated a much quicker response to an extremely dynamic sound environment.[36] The limitations of then-current synthesizer technology were soon apparent in live ensemble situations. Hancock recalled:

> When I hired Pat Gleeson to travel with us and play synth, I didn't know that synths weren't programmable back then. So you had to do everything by hand, live patching. It was kind of impractical. The problem was going from one sound to another. In the studio you could take the time to program the synth, but on stage you can't do that. So the sounds he made on the road were a lot less interesting. He was playing an ARP 2600, using white noise and filters, a wah-wah pedal, but there wasn't a lot he could do to get that variety. So I had to limit him, make him do some live editing. It started to get in the way a bit because that's all he had available.[37]

While Hancock was beginning to move beyond virtuosity for its own sake, ideas about high musical value continued to be linked to the virtuoso, even as the term had been expanded to include the unconventional instrumental techniques of artists such as Thelonious Monk (at least in jazz). Yet, as contractual leader, Hancock voiced concern for the economic well-being of his band mates:

> Well, I'm responsible for paying the guys and making sure that they work so I can keep a band. That's one rough thing, because I have to worry not only about my family, I have to worry about six families—I have to be aware that they're there, and if I'm going to keep a band, *I have to make*

sure that we're working so that they can feed their families as well as I feed mine. Secondly, I guess the leader, depending on the guys in the group, can run into problems with personalities, and I guess it's up to the leader to really keep the situation open enough so that personality conflicts don't erupt, keep some kind of harmony in the band. It's kind of rough.[38]

In truth, the sextet was touring more like a beginning rock band than an experienced jazz band. They toured together in a van, sharing the space with their equipment, and acting as their own road and stage crews, setting up and breaking down their equipment. Hancock would not have had even the limited opportunities he was offered without the support of his manager. Although Rubinson was brought in by Warner Bros. to mold Hancock into a "crossover star," Hancock explained, Rubinson "believed in what we were doing, it reached him in a deep place [so] when we won him over, he felt like it was his job to convince [Warners] to promote what we were doing."[39] Even with Rubinson supporting his efforts at the record label, however, Hancock would still bear the responsibility for feeding his band mates' families.

Hancock's journey from highly paid and fully accommodated pianist in a successful quintet, both economically and critically, to a struggling road musician underlined his commitment to fuse experimental electronic, free jazz, funk, and rock music. In 1973 Hancock articulated his aesthetic to Jagajivan in the pages of *Down Beat*:

When the music is at its best, the player is not the one that's initiating the action. It's coming through him rather than coming from him. So he's as much a victim of the situation as the audience is. Although he is the physical mechanism and can't perceive what's happening in the same sense that the audience does, he is as much surprised at the outcome. We're talking about the musicians being the medium of the message and the audience being the receivers in a sense, but it doesn't stop there. The audience doesn't play a physical part in what goes on the same way the musician does, but there is a feedback that the audience gives in vibes. The audience puts energy into the air. I'm not talking about applause, really. *The true measure of the accuracy of a musical performance is the energy in the air that's produced by the vibes of the listeners and the players.* It's the magic in the atmosphere of this performing situation. . . . [Applause] is a direct way for people to give a boost to what's happening. When I'm listening—as long as the music is sincere, even if it's really not that good—I'll applaud. Even if nothing is really happening, my applause might help something to happen the next time. Sometimes the music can have a sublime character that can seem to the listener to make applause trite, but if it's sincere, applause has nothing to do with a spectating or entertainment situation. I like applause, myself.[40]

By stressing the interactive, participatory feedback loop between musicians and audiences, Hancock preserved music's ritualistic elements and fetishistic power—indeed, music's seductive sirenlike qualities were foregrounded, particularly with the addition of Gleeson's synthesizer work. Hancock admitted, "After we recorded *Crossings*, David Rubinson was still looking for a way to make that far out music as palatable as possible without interfering with the direction."[41] Similar to his fusion peers, Hancock's concerns about merging electronic experimentalism with funk and jazz in a way that facilitated audience involvement rather than creating an esoteric, or elitist, idiom resonated with larger discussions regarding the role of popular culture. He tried to wrest experimental soundings from the conservatories of the concert music tradition and liberate (musical) technology from elite institutions and their commitments to continued ideological, rhetorical, and material debasement of non-elite music.

Mwandishi recordings did not sell well, however, nor were their concerts as successful, financially or aesthetically, as Hancock had hoped. Fortunately, Rubinson became aware of Warner Bros.' intention to drop the Herbie Hancock Sextet from its roster and talked Hancock into signing with Clive Davis and Columbia Records, home of Miles Davis, Mahavishnu Orchestra, Santana, Sly and the Family Stone, and fellow ex-Warner Bros. employees Earth, Wind, and Fire. The first Columbia album, *Sextant*, extended the Mwandishi aesthetic, continuing the group's merging of Afrofuturist consciousness and electronic experimentalism coalescing within a heady brew of jazz, funk, and rock music.

In the end, however, *Sextant*, like the other Mwandishi recordings, failed to connect with album buyers. Concert audiences, especially the mainstream audiences that Hancock and his manager, Rubinson, were attempting to attract, thought even less of the group's music despite the band members' recollections that the group's exploratory improvisations were highlights in their careers. But while Eddie Henderson and Bennie Maupin have both spoken publicly about the energy of the live performances and the growing affiliation between their expanding college-age crowds and the band's "far out" musical explorations, Hancock saw the "special audience" that Maupin celebrated as overly insular and, perhaps most compellingly, as economically marginal and nonsupportive for the "larger numbers" he had been seeking for the more than three years since he had spoken with Richard Williams. Hancock protested: "We weren't trying to make records for ourselves, I can tell you that. I was trying to not just create a music that only the diehards and the crazies would respond to, I was trying to figure out a way to make people who were unaccustomed to music like that want to listen to it—commercialize it, but not in a negative sense. The whole of *Sextant* was an evolution of our approach to getting some level of commonality with people who otherwise would have no idea what we were doing."[42]

The opening bass riff to "Chameleon" may be one of the most recognized riffs to emerge from the fusion movement of the 1970s. It is so well known that Hancock once used it as the opening soundtrack to his official website. The riff also signaled a creative turn for Hancock, and the beginning of an economically successful run of fusion albums. Joining Columbia under Clive Davis, whose agenda to move Columbia from its stodgier "middle of the road" image to a younger, hipper one, as reflected in his signing of Carlos Santana and Sly and the Family Stone, as well as in his encouraging Miles Davis's entry into fusion, meant Hancock would receive support for his own fusion project. Hancock recorded what would be the last Mwandishi recording, *Sextant*, for Columbia. As I have mentioned, *Sextant* continued the experimental nature of the band's approach to fusion, and record sales were small. Hoping to build an audience the "old-fashioned way," Mwandishi toured incessantly. The sextet, however, remained financially insolvent. Finally, Hancock called a band meeting and opened the accounting books for each band member to inspect. Bennie Maupin recalled:

> It was a sad feeling when we broke up because I think it was getting to a point where it was really beginning to open up. But Herbie's accountant had told him that the band was not paying for itself. Herbie was paying out of his pocket to keep the band alive. There were a lot of jobs that we played where Herbie didn't make a note. He paid the band to keep the band together because he believed in what we were doing. So we met; he opened up the books and he showed us what we'd been spending and what we were actually earning, and the earnings were in many cases not enough to cover the salaries.[43]

Hancock was able to survive on commercial work, producing jingles for Pillsbury and others, as well as the continuous stream of royalty checks for "Watermelon Man," as more than 250 cover versions kept the song popular around the globe. But there was another component to Hancock's decision, as he explains in the liner notes to the compact disc reissue of his second Columbia album, *Head Hunters* (1973):

> By the end of 1972, my feeling was that the sextet had reached a peak [and] we lost the connection somehow. I suspected that my own energy needed something else. It was more spiritual, and it had more to do with me as a human being. I began to feel that I had been spending so much time exploring the upper atmosphere of music and the more ethereal kind of far-out, spacey stuff. Now there was this need to take some more of the earth and to feel a little more tethered; a connection to the earth. People were evolving. We began to hear jazz artist's interests, including paying attention to Rock-and-Roll, [and] including that into whatever they were doing.[44]

He stated elsewhere that "the group was a losing proposition but I believed in what we were doing. For me, it was an investment in my soul. But that got further and further out and I got tired of playing that direction. It stayed too heavy for too many years for me. It got to the point where I wasn't looking forward to the next gig. . . . I thought that band had gone as far as it could. It wasn't fun anymore. I felt weighed down. So I broke the band up."[45]

Hancock's choice to break up the ensemble was also an aesthetic decision. In the liner notes to the reissue compact disc of *Head Hunters* Hancock explained his motivation for moving into fusion:

> I began to feel that we [the Hancock sextet] were playing this heavy kind of music, and I was tired of everything being heavy. I wanted to play something lighter. . . . It happened one day. I was chanting. I knew I didn't want to play the music I had been playing, but I didn't know what music I wanted to play. . . .
>
> The more I chanted, the more my mind opened up, relaxed and began to wander. I started thinking about Sly Stone and how much I loved his music and how funky "Thank You (Falettinme Be Mice Elf Agin)" is. . . . Then I had this mental image of me playing in Sly's band playing something funky like that. . . . My unconscious reaction was, "No, I don't want to do that."

What I saw in this reaction was seeing in myself the same things I hated about many other jazz musicians that put jazz on a pedestal, and at the same time putting Funk and Rock on a secondary level. I don't like that about anything. There's room for everything. But I noticed my gut reaction was the same kind of hierarchical look of putting jazz on a pedestal. I said to myself, "Whoa! What are you doing?" I knew I had to take the idea seriously. Would I like to have a funky band that played the kind of music Sly or someone like that was playing? My response was, "Actually, yes."[46]

As Hancock explicitly details, his new direction came as a result of his spiritual practice, a motivation he shared with fellow "fusioneers" John McLaughlin and Chick Corea.[47] Religion or spirituality could, indeed, pay. Further, the desire to "lighten" the music in order to "make it more palatable" explicitly registered Hancock's desire to reach listeners. Hancock's singling out of Sly Stone was an indication of his new musical direction. Stone, an African American keyboardist and vocalist, formed a band celebrated for its integrated lineup, featuring a female trumpeter, Cynthia Robinson; white saxophonist, Jerry Martini; and Stone's own sister, Rosie Stone, on piano. Hancock also recalled a song from Sly's oeuvre that is explicit regarding the nonrestrictive nature of fusion music — is it simply coincidence that Hancock did not begin to hum "Luv N' Haight"?[48]

His "conversion" to actively engage the public occurred when the sextet opened for the popular soul group the Pointer Sisters at the Troubadour in Los Angeles. The Pointer Sisters showed him "how they *immediately* communicated with the audience, I knew that we weren't prepared in the same way to do that. I was trying to learn from them just what things would have to be done in order to help people get into our music a little easier. You see, it was more than just the music. They had a presentation and we really didn't have one."[49]

Hancock continued to learn from nonjazz musicians about performing "authentic inauthenticity" similar to the manner Joni Mitchell accessed her own performance personas. In his efforts to play "authentic" funk Hancock learned a valuable lesson from the guitarist Johnny "Wah Wah" Watson:

When I first hired him to play in the band, we played this one tune each night that he would solo on. He would play the same solo every night because that was the way he was taught. His training was to perfect one way of doing something.

He didn't have a lot of things to draw on, either. What amazed me was that, every night, he'd play the same solo the same way, but every night, it sounded like it was the first time he ever played it. It was fresh every time. And I didn't know how to do that, because jazz doesn't teach you that. I said, "I've got to learn that."

He would just play two or three things and the audience would immediately remember and respond to that. I could play rings around this guy, play all over the place and that little statement that he would make would get incredible acknowledgment every night. I wasn't playing rings around him. I was just playing a lot of notes around him. It really taught me a lesson about what music is about and the value of the direction I was going in at the time.[50]

Hancock, in acknowledging the craft of funk musicianship, redrew the hierarchical map that privileged jazz over rhythm and blues, disco, and soul music. As he admits, when he decided to pursue a more explicitly rhythm and blues–based fusion, he hesitated because of "pure jazz snobbism," continuing, "[rhythm and blues] was a kind of music I really dug, but I felt it wasn't 'good enough' to be included in my own repertoire. I was really disappointed in myself for that narrow-mindedness."[51] Hancock was an active and conscious participant in fusion music's contestation of genre categories and the musical evaluations attached to them. "Jazz snobbery" was undoubtedly the cause of the Headhunters being booed off the stage at the 1974 Berlin Jazz Festival for using "smoke bombs and flares and theatrics a la Earth, Wind and Fire and the Ohio Players."[52] Hancock admitted to Bert Primack, "Something that's opening up for me is a concept of entertainment. I never had a great respect for entertainment because my vision was shallow. I always loved the movies and watching actors and entertainers. I enjoy Frank Sinatra and all these people and yet in the '60s if anybody had asked me about entertainment, I might have said it was bullshit. Now, I think my scope is a little wider and I can see entertainment as being a vital and valuable cultural function."[53]

Hancock's increasingly active engagement of rhythm and blues and funk music was much more explicit than his tentative explorations in the 1960s. While his soul jazz hit "Watermelon Man" drew from the blues, it was still deeply interwoven within jazz practices. As he confessed in 1985 to Bill Flanagan, "When I did Headhunters [sic] I was trying to make a funk album, not a jazz album. Not anything having to do with jazz. But as it developed it became what it was. So I let it be what it was. I didn't make a real funk album 'til *Feets Don't Fail Me Now* [Columbia 1978]. That was the first one that I could say was not a jazz album in any way, shape or form."[54]

Hancock's woodwind player, Bennie Maupin, was the only member of the so-called Mwandishi group to join the Headhunters. Pat Gleeson departed as Hancock familiarized himself with synthesizer technology, assisted by the fact that synthesizers were becoming easier for end users to manipulate. Hancock, however, like many synthesists, customized his keyboards and tried various combinations of keyboards, sound systems, and other electronic equipment in order to develop a unique sound. This is an important goal for musicians using "machines" considered by many to lack the qualities that give traditional acoustic instruments their "warmth," allowing musicians to express their innermost thoughts and feelings without apparent mediation—an argument that ignores the manufactured origins of the violin or piano. In any event it was on *Head Hunters* that Hancock became a synthesizer player, a relatively new kind of pop musician at the time.

Hancock originally intended *Head Hunters* to be a "straight up" funk record, and he found his new group of musicians from outside the jazz world, forming the band, the Headhunters. The drummer Harvey Mason was recommended to Hancock by the jazz drummer Billy Hart while the rest of the rhythm section—Paul Jackson (bass) and Bill Summers (percussion)—were San Francisco Bay Area funk musicians recommended by Rubinson. The transformation in the types of musicians, instrumentation, and repertoire Hancock initiated on *Head Hunters* was a challenge to jazz orthodoxy, and his subsequent career has been marked by the overwhelming success of this recording.

Head Hunters was the first jazz recording to earn platinum record status (sales of one million copies) and was, until relatively recently, the biggest-selling jazz recording. The opening track, "Chameleon," is readily identifiable by nonjazz fans and became a best-selling single; the album topped the Billboard jazz charts and reached number thirteen on the pop charts, a certified top-twenty success. Subsequently, within a year Hancock had three albums on *Billboard*'s pop LP charts.[55] His fortunes continued to rise throughout the next two decades, when hit singles were buttressed by a successful movie scoring career and his intermittent acoustic "straight-ahead" jazz work continued to solidify his jazz credentials among jazz critics. But situating Hancock within a bifurcated musical career would take the next decade to fully develop, and jazz critics did not initially regard his popularity as a positive development (and this critical rapprochement with the full catalog of his works is still not universally shared, particularly by jazz critics, as indicated by Gleeson's quote at the beginning of the chapter).

By 1973 the fusion landscape had changed significantly from the late 1960s as carnivalesque juxtapositions of acid rock, free jazz, and experimental "new music" were abandoned in favor of increasingly mannerist performances of jazz-rock fusion. By the end of the year the original Mahavishnu Orchestra would disband, Weather Report was beginning to perform more tightly composed tunes on their records rather than the free-form experimentalism of their first recording, Lifetime seemed unsure of its direction, and Miles Davis, increasingly inactive following an accident in 1972, would withdraw from public music in 1975 for five years. However, Return to Forever released *Hymn to the Seventh Galaxy* in 1973, an album that marked the group's transformation from a Latin-tinged jazz band into an electric jazz-rock unit. The success of *Head Hunters*, *Hymn to the Seventh Galaxy*, and Weather Report's *Sweetnighter* and *Mysterious Traveller* (both released in 1973) signaled a shift from the early fusion experiments that sought to combine avant-garde "new music" with rock and funk and jazz toward the tightly structured compositions of Mahavishnu Orchestra. It also indicated the increasing influence of progressive rock on fusion musicians. Rock musicians, going through their own "growing pains" and reaching toward the same marriage of high cultural capital and raw, visceral energy that jazz musicians had enacted since at least the bebop era, began to look to jazz music as one way to engage music that did not forsake the pleasures of the body in its efforts to engage the intellect.

When Hancock decided, for artistic as well as economic reasons, to embrace funk music, he was merely one of the more visible of jazz musicians to head in this direction. Others included the vibraphonist Roy Ayers, drummer Norman Connors, trumpeter Donald Byrd, guitarist George Benson, and the hard-bop-turned-fusion group the (Jazz) Crusaders (the band dropped "Jazz" from its name when its turn to fusion was complete at the release of the 1971 recording 1 [Blue Thumb], a title that indicated its new direction). The CTI/Kudu record label became known for its large roster of funk- and soul-inflected fusion recordings with the flutist Hubert Laws, multi-instrumentalist Joe Farrell, and pianist Bob James, among others. In fact, Hancock was a seminal figure for the funk-soul-rhythm and blues–influenced type of fusion both as session pianist for CTI and as leader of the

Headhunters, paving the way for the "smooth jazz" style of later fusion that would prove most successful commercially.

The importance of *Head Hunters* cannot be understated, for it not only set the stage for subsequent fusions of funk, rhythm and blues, and jazz but also resonated broadly with a mainstream audience—one of the explicit desires for early fusion musicians such as Miles Davis, John McLaughlin, and Tony Williams. While the other musicians were unwilling or unable to abandon the more experimental aspects of their fusion music, Hancock not only consciously turned away from the experimental elements in his Mwandishi recordings but also began incorporating the acoustic piano into his fusion efforts. On the live double album *Flood* (Columbia 1975), originally a Japan-only release, Hancock devoted the first side to extended acoustic piano renderings of "Maiden Voyage" and "Actual Proof," setting his acoustic piano within the Headhunters' electric funk rhythm section.

The commercial success of *Head Hunters* was surprising, however, even for Hancock, and he explained that for "a long while, I've wanted to know more about other aspects of black music apart from jazz. I love funky music, y'see, but I've never really had a vehicle for playing it." [56] Hancock echoed his fellow fusion keyboardist Mike Nock, who asserted that while jazz musicians often denigrated rhythm and blues and funk players, they were often unable to perform rhythm and blues or funk well. Hancock agreed: "There's a lot more to playing funky than I thought, too. *It's a whole different set of criteria, too, based as much on what you don't play as what you do.*" [57]

While the magnitude of the recording's commercial success may have been surprising, the nature of its aesthetic appeal was a decisive move by Hancock to reengage "the earth," a space he described in opposition to the "ethereal kind of far-out, spacey stuff" Mwandishi had created. The funky remake of "Watermelon Man" on *Head Hunters* exposes the contingencies and contradictions in Hancock's move to "give back the funk" to jazz. Recording artists had already covered "Watermelon Man" literally hundreds of times across a wide spectrum of genres and idioms. As I noted above, Mongo Santamaria's version explicitly cited the Afrodiasporic movement that Hancock unconsciously accessed in his composition. Hancock was certainly aware of the racialized connotations watermelons held for audiences in the United States. The blues-inflected, groove-oriented composition, like many hard bop tunes, drew on images of southern black life, and, in combination with his title, Hancock's artfully casual composition was a sober reflection on race and class.

Hancock explained the rationale behind recording another version of "Watermelon Man": "[The drummer] Harvey Mason thought we should do a new version of 'Watermelon Man.' The conception was basically his. Except the beginning of the tune, that was [percussionist] Bill Summers's idea. The intro was actually from Pygmy music with Bill blowing in a beer bottle and making a melodic, rhythmic thing."[58]

As Steven Feld notes, however, while Bill Summers is credited with performing the *hindewhu* on the recording's liner notes, the term is actually a BaBenzélé Pygmy word for the sound of the human voice in alternation with the sound of a single-pitch papaya stem whistle. As noted in my introduction, Summers modeled his arrangement on a commercial Nonesuch release of an ethnomusicological field recording. Feld noted the irony of an African American group, sonically demonstrating primitivism through an explicit evocation of BaBenzélé music, who did not, however, elect to credit the source of the soundings, the central African Pygmies themselves. When Feld discussed this situation with Hancock, asking whether Hancock "felt any legal or moral concern surrounding the *hindewhu* copy on *Head Hunters*," Hancock "was quite cordial, and quick with his comeback":

> "You see," he answered, "you've got to understand, this is a brothers kind of thing, you know, a thing for brothers to work out. I mean, I don't actually need to go over there and talk to them, I could do it but I know that it's OK 'cause it's just a brothers kind of thing." I then asked if musicians could sidestep the music industry and copyright conventions to directly remunerate the sources of their inspiration. "Look," he replied, "we're the people who've lost the most, who've had the most stolen from us. We know what it means to come up with, you know, a sound or a tune, then to have it copped and turned into a big hit or something like that. We've been through all of that. But this isn't like that. This is a different thing, you see, brothers, we're all making African music, that's what I'm talking about."[59]

While Feld deliberately lays aside the fraught polemics regarding appropriation in order to tease out the complexities of Hancock's subject position with regard to music industry practice and what he terms "the musical-political-industrial habitus," I want to think about how Hancock positioned himself in relation to Pygmy music within a framework not of a global music industry but within an Afrodiasporic oral tradition of recycling with a difference, or, in Amiri Baraka's construction, the "changing same," within an intracultural understanding that it's a "brother's kind of thing."

Still, Hancock's and Summers's access to that oral tradition was enabled by a commercial record label, Nonesuch, which was carving a market out of music that had been considered "noncommercial" because of Western audiences' unfamiliarity with the cultures, languages, musical aesthetics, and instrumentation of non-Western music. As part of a burgeoning interest by Western audiences in what would eventually be called "world music," Hancock's and Summers's dependence on the circuits of the music industry in putting them in touch with their Pygmy brothers is noted with some irony.

Feld rightly notes how Hancock's relationship with a major record label, Columbia, changes this dynamic relationship between artist and artistic tradition(s). Oral traditions are in continual transformation, and often what one considers "traditional" is a trick of history (for the record, I agree with Feld, who does not hold to the idea of an unbroken tradition, in a "never-ending same"; I am referring here to both popular beliefs about "traditional" music and the vestigial ethnomusicological models still used by some listeners).[60] "Traditions" have been largely set in the period of "first contact" as anthropologists and ethnomusicologists began to take notes, produce recordings, and set about codifying aesthetic and cultural practices for the West. As I have been arguing throughout this work, not only does the act of recording affect cultural practices—note how recordings have affected the way we listen to and hear music or any sounding—but the interchange between cultural practitioners, while perhaps accelerated due to technological advances, is not a new or, more important, necessarily destructive practice unless one hopes to freeze a particular set of cultural practices into a rigid code.

However, the polemics concerning the ownership of cultural practices pits hard-line "authentic culturalists" against equally hardnosed "postmodern appropriators," paying little attention to the vast and discrepant territory between them. The division disappears in light of Hancock's argument about the fluid nature of cultural practices as "a brother's kind of thing." When is one not a brother or sister? Hancock's cultural boundaries, for example, extend to Karlheinz Stockhausen, as well as the BaBenzélé Pygmies. As Hancock stated to Len Lyons in *Contemporary Keyboard*, "The music we call jazz, R&B, or rock comes from [the United States] and it comes from black people. That doesn't mean other people can't play it, and play it as if it came from their own heritage. All the standards in jazz aren't black, anyhow."[61]

Hancock's acknowledgment of the permeable borders between cultural practices and cultural practitioners recognized how the standard repertoire in jazz—the "standards"—was largely the creation of jazz musicians' appropriation of mainstream popular music of the early twentieth century. While their appropriative practice speaks to the fluid borders between sets of musical practices and practitioners, Hancock's reminder regarding the intimate relationship between black musicians and white music suggests the hybrid positioning of popular music writ large.

Yet as Feld warns, if by "invoking hybridity as one's own identity position, one then becomes licensed to claim the full spatiotemporal terrain of that identity as an artistic palette," Hancock's easy assumption of fraternal affiliation with BaBenzélé Pygmy culture can be questioned.[62] On the one hand, Feld's primary concern is the inequitable leeching of profits from, in this instance, the BaBenzélé Pygmies, who receive nothing in return for inspiring mimetic renderings of the primitive Other in a global (post)modern circulation of licensed, royalty-bearing, copyright-holding recordings. On the other hand, Hancock's appropriation of BaBenzélé Pygmy music was similar to his "appropriation" of funk, a practice consistent with his view of an Afrodiasporic tradition of reiteration, reinvention, and recirculation of cultural practices. The fact that his band's version of BaBenzélé music was not identical but imitative assists Hancock's argument. Yet Bill Summers's acknowledged ethnomusicological expertise problematizes the easy out afforded by Hancock's rationale that such appropriation is "a brother's kind of thing," a mimetic gesture effortlessly purchased by blood ties.

The trumpeter Lester Bowie criticized such easy fraternizing in a 1979 *Down Beat* "Blindfold Test," after listening to Hancock's hit single of the time, "You Bet Your Love." His scathing indictment of Hancock's lack of funk credentials, abilities to groove, and what Bowie viewed as bald economic reasons for turning to funk music was unequivocal:

> [Hancock and his band] don't know if they're going to be jazz or fusion or funk or disco. They're just tryin' to make some money, you can hear that. The reason I don't dig this is because I played this music seriously, for a living, up and down the highways for years, so I don't need to hear any more of that bullshit music. I won't participate in that again, lower myself and say, "Well, I'm doing this to communicate with the people." The people he's communicating with I don't even want to deal with. . . . They never been on the highway. Do thirty or forty of them one nighters with Albert King, then you'll learn how that shit goes. Play one song for two hours, vamping that mother 'til you learn how to make that form feel. These cats ain't got no funk at all. . . . I don't know what these cats are doing. Gettin' paid, that's all.[63]

Hancock's response, when questioned about this by Jon Balleras, was similar to his argument for a broader definition of jazz. Hancock countered, "There isn't just one kind of funk, either. In my estimation, there are different levels or degrees of it. It's not something that's limited to one small, specific area."[64] He continued: "However, when [Bowie] says that 'They're just tryin' to make some money, you can hear that'—I'm sorry to say that his ears must be deceiving him. Because I'm not just trying to make money. . . . I'm doing this kind of music because I like it. *It's part of my musical development.* And in order for me to be really honest with myself, I don't want to ignore these urges. Because if I didn't do it, then it would be really bullshit."[65]

Hancock was constantly asked about his "real" feelings about his music throughout the 1970s as jazz critics, in particular, seemed unwilling to believe he actually enjoyed nonjazz popular music enough to seriously engage with it by composing and performing it. The evidence made audible in both his original version and his fusion remake of "Watermelon Man" bears testimony to his continuous engagement with popular music. Ironically, while Hancock defended his fusion music by insisting it was his choice to perform and compose fusion rather than his record company's pressure to commercialize his music, his "return" to acoustic jazz in the early 1980s was due to George Butler, the head of A&R (the music industry acronym for "artists and repertoire," a talent scout) at Columbia Records at the time. Butler is also credited with assisting in the promotion of Wynton Marsalis. At this point, Marsalis was a young trumpeter, and his biggest jazz break was as a frontline musician in Art Blakey's Jazz Messengers.

In 1977 Hancock, Wayne Shorter, Ron Carter, and Tony Williams—essentially, Miles Davis's famous "second quintet" sans Davis—had recorded as the VSOP quintet, with Freddie Hubbard filling Davis's chair. Butler's suggestion to produce Marsalis's first album led to Marsalis substituting for Hubbard in a later tour of the VSOP quintet (Hubbard was featured in the first 1977 VSOP concert tour). Critics were quick to applaud Hancock's "return" to "real jazz," but his next record, *Feets Don't Fail Me Now*, was an unabashed fusion recording (it was also the very record that contained the track "You Bet Your Love," which Lester Bowie lambasted in his "Blindfold Test"). Yet when asked if he felt any obligations to his "old [jazz] fans," Hancock responded in an uncharacteristically terse way: "I'm not a chauffeur. *Nobody* would have bought any of my records if I were. I'd have had nothing to say. I'm supposed to be *presenting* things to the public, not accepting requests. I call the shots. They don't have to like it. I really wanted to develop my career in such a way that I have the freedom to do what I want to do, and not have that considered bizarre. . . . That's what I've wanted all this time."[66]

As the 1970s drew to a close, Hancock's recordings kept abreast of current popular music trends along with intermittent acoustic jazz recordings (and in the 1980s, his single "Rockit" not only introduced him to the "MTV generation," but the associated video had a significant impact on music videography at the time). As I have mentioned, Hancock and Wynton Marsalis held a joint interview for *Musician* magazine in 1985. By this time Marsalis had established himself as the head of the pride of Young Lions, as the jazz press dubbed a group of young, up-and-coming jazz musicians who enacted a "return" to jazz's acoustic roots. Marsalis had not only made a name for himself as a "double threat," a jazz trumpet player whose classical technique was unquestioned as witnessed by Grammy wins in both categories. He was also becoming a spokesman for a so-called neoconservative movement within jazz.

The interview was subtitled "The Purist and the Crossbreeder Duke It Out," a title that spoke to the racialized positioning of both of these jazz musicians, as well as evoking Duke Ellington, who famously declared, "There are only two kinds of music—good and bad." The title also pointed to the miscegenational nature of fusion music while positioning Marsalis and Hancock on opposite sides in a yet-contentious debate about the definition of jazz nearly two decades after Gary Burton's *Duster* recording.

Marsalis, the "purist," began by arguing that jazz was superior to popular music by maintaining a set of higher ideals and standards of musicianship; at one point Marsalis claimed, "Pop music is something you don't really have to know too much to know about." In turn Hancock was asked, "We all agreed apparently at one point that jazz was more meaningful, in some sense, than pop music. Since you work in the two idioms, what do you feel is different?" Hancock responded, "Wait a minute. I *don't* agree. Let me address myself to that. When we have life, we have music. Music can be manifest in many different forms, and as long as they all have purpose they shouldn't be pitted against each other as one being more important than the other. That's stupid. That's like apples and oranges."[67]

Hancock's argument—music is an ever-mutable set of practices—recalls Ellington's pronouncement that music is, on very deep levels, a set of practices serving a variety of purposes. Marsalis, on the other hand, argued for a hierarchical understanding of those practices, noting how popular music often served puerile aims targeting teenaged listeners. Hancock countered that covering "pop music" under one broad umbrella overdetermined Marsalis's critique of pop music and mentioned pop musicians who did not merely compose lascivious fare for teenage consumption. Pointedly, toward the end of their joint interview, Marsalis revealed, "Remember what you told me before? 'Yeah man, my record just went gold man. I need to get me some more records like that.' We had long conversations about that. We shouldn't be arguing about this in the press, man. We have to be cool."[68]

Hancock deflated Marsalis's accusation by pointing out that no one recorded an album without also hoping for large sales. But as Hancock testified in another interview, "A lot of people think that the reason I'm playing [fusion] music is because the record company is forcing me to play it. It ain't the record company."[69] The salient point here is that Hancock was continually compelled to respond to accusations of economic considerations overriding aesthetic concerns. The so-called neoconservative movement in jazz occurred during the Reagan administration and a general conservative turn in American civic life; neoconservative musicians and critics polemicized aesthetic debates in dogmatic and puritanical terms, recasting difference as rigid, impermeable, and static. Fusion music, then, sounded out its challenge even as it was itself being diluted by corporate music industry interest in marketing fusion as "smooth jazz" for "yuppie" consumption as the 1980s progressed.

However, Hancock's fusion of various Afrodiasporic musics, coupled with his engagements with experimental avant-garde music and his ongoing interest in electronics and computer technologies, positioned him as diametrically opposed to the neoconservative movement in jazz. His creative work stands as an exemplary refutation of the imposition of rigid idiomatic boundaries and of racialized conceptions regarding the ownership of genres or exactly who might skillfully utilize technology. Hancock's multiple subject positions—fusion musician, acoustic jazz pianist, synthesizer designer, computer programmer, "hit song" writer, and social critic—reveal, like the chameleon, his ability to make each distinct context a part of himself, blending into or standing out from the contextual background as necessary.

Hancock's own catholic tastes and understanding of the broken middle between idioms and generic categories can be traced throughout his career, from the finger-snapping soul jazz of "Watermelon Man" to the experiments of Mwandishi to the funky fusion of the Headhunters. His works sound out the flexibility of categories, the fluidity of genres, and the falsity of rigid classifications. His admonition to "speak like a child" echoes in his fusion release Future2Future (Transparent 2001), in which he has a young girl, Elenni Davis-Knight, recite on the song "Wisdom" the following words from his Buddhist mentor, Daisaku Ikeda:

Simply put, knowledge corresponds to the past
It is technology
Wisdom is the future
It is philosophy
It is peoples' hearts which move the age

While knowledge may provide a useful point of reference, it cannot become a force with which to guide the future:

By contrast, wisdom captivates peoples' hearts
And has the power to open a new age
Wisdom is the key to understanding the age, creating the times

Hancock, equally at home in funk, disco, and jazz, draws his aesthetics and musical practices from a number of cultural positions. His continuing inspiration from African music, evidenced in releases such as Village Life (Sony 1985), with the African kora master Foday Musa Suso, and Dis Is Da Drum (Polygram 1994), trace his chameleon-like ability to work within a number of seemingly disparate contexts. In addition, recordings such as Future Shock (Columbia 1983) not only updated his engagements with a constantly evolving technological landscape but reiterated his continually reworked version of Afrofuturist aesthetic practice. Invoking Afrofuturism through a cybernetic landscape on the recording's cover, as well as in the representation of virtuality and robotics in the groundbreaking video for the hit single "Rockit," Hancock's song title puns on rocket, as well as on the evocation of the phrase calling on one "to rock it." The first, a vehicle, however vulnerable and artificial as a material object, enables human travel free of terrestrial constraints and functions metonymically for technology writ large, while the second is a summoning of embodied pleasure, disciplined by gravity and the limits of physicality.

In this light Hancock's idea that music "is a reflection of the truth, a method of communicating the truth without many of the limitations or the connotations of words," is also a statement about truth. Hancock's skeptical view of words to convey truth lends his musicking, his sounding out of truth, special weight: "People sometimes use words to express what they think their feelings are or should be, but music expresses the inner truth. . . .

The real, inner truth comes through the music. It's the inner man that links us all—that is all."[70] Hancock's belief in music's ability to sound out a "real, inner truth" energized his pursuit of the broken middles between disparate music traditions, blending musical codes into new shapes and sounding out the broken middle in all its complementary and contradictory colors.

conclusion

There was a time when you could say that there was a direction in jazz, and the people who didn't follow that direction usually stood alone, you know. . . . Not so much today. I think there are many directions happening in jazz, and you can't pin it down to one. — **Herbie Hancock**

I remember the *New York Times* jazz critic saying about 12 years ago, "Thank god, this pestilence known as fusion is dead." What? Get a life! — **John McLaughlin**

With the release of *River: The Joni Letters* (Verve 2007) Herbie Hancock navigated down one of jazz's "many directions," placing Duke Ellington and Wayne Shorter compositions within a program otherwise dedicated to Joni Mitchell. Mitchell provided lead vocals on "Tea Leaf Prophecy," and her voice, its aged huskiness offset by a continuing fragility and wistfulness, was matched by the sensitive accompaniment of Hancock and his guitarist, Lionel Loueke, and by Shorter's lithe soprano saxophone obbligati. Mitchell's youthful vision of domesticity as compromise and containment was replaced with a knowing "this is your happy home." And though her lyrics admonish "don't have kids when you get grown," she also spelled out the domestic trivialities that bind people to place and others, while acknowledging a continued ambivalence regarding those connections — "she says I'm leavin' here but she don't go."[1] Norah Jones, Tina Turner, and Luciana Souza, among others, sang various Mitchell compositions on *River*, reaffirming Mitchell's poetic musicality while exposing her musical oeuvre's complexities.

But it is Hancock's instrumental version of "Both Sides, Now" that best marks the broken middle that fusion musicians sound out. Mitchell's early hit is transformed by his solo piano introduction into a profoundly austere statement of ambivalence, suggesting there are an infinite number of "sides," or perspectives and affiliations, to contemplate, and showcases his sensitivity to and familiarity with Mitchell's vocal sensibilities. As the recording track continues, with Shorter's saxophone providing wry commentary on Hancock's piano excursions, the tensions build slowly, percolating to a simmering heat. Loueke's guitar is integral but atmospheric, and the bassist Dave Holland and drummer Vinnie Colaiuta provide subdued but emotional propulsion.

Mitchell's jazz period, marked by commercial failure and critical dismissal in the 1970s, has undergone reappraisal. In 1994 Alice Echols wrote in the Los Angeles Weekly: "The critical and commercial black hole she entered in the late '70s, when she moved from pop into what she calls the 'forest of jazz,' is behind her. Even if she now prefers painting to music, as she claims, the buzz won't let her put down her guitar. After years of bad press, the musician whose mid- to late-'70s experiments with jazz and world music anticipated those of Sting, Peter Gabriel and Paul Simon, is finally beginning to get her due."[2] In 2007 a collection of Mitchell covers, A Tribute to Joni Mitchell (Nonesuch), by a range of popular artists, including Bjork, Annie Lennox, Prince, Caetano Veloso, Emmylou Harris, and Elvis Costello, revealed simultaneously the compositional elasticity and the structural integrity of Mitchell's work. Veloso's imaginative reinvention of "Dreamland" revealed the "already impure" mélange of cultures that marks his own multihued Brazilian musical background while boldly announcing his kinship with Mitchell's music.

Indeed, musicians' journeys back and forth between acoustic and electric instrumentation or their explicit mixing of genres can no longer be considered anything but matter-of-fact, ordinary, even banal. The contemporary fusion band Jazz Is Dead, whose name is a playful jab at the continuing debates surrounding the state of jazz, also puns on the source material for its early sessions, the repertoire of the psychedelic rock band the Grateful Dead. The piano trio the Bad Plus covered Black Sabbath's "Iron Man," claiming not performative irony but sincere homage, and Brad Mehldau's exploration of Radiohead's "Exit Music (for a Film)" was motivated by his enthusiastic interest in the group's music and not a bid for "street cred" or increased market share. Alex Skolnick, a founding member of the heavy metal band Testament, hung up his leathers and distortion boxes for jazz, transforming hard rock standards such as Kiss's "Detroit Rock City," Judas Priest's "Electric Eye," and Rush's "Tom Sawyer" into jazz vehicles that to ears unfamiliar with the original versions might be fooled into thinking that Skolnick had unearthed unknown jazz compositions from an earlier era.

Similar to Hancock's "double career" as both fusion keyboardist and jazz pianist, Skolnick continues to work in the heavy metal area.

In 2007 John McLaughlin was busily reestablishing his jazz-rock credentials on tour with the 4th Dimension band. Pat Metheny, Allan Holdsworth, CAB, Vital Information, and a host of other musicians and bands continue to create fusion music of compelling interest though with little mainstream critical attention (with the notable exception of Metheny). The pianist Robert Glasper's engagement of hip-hop and rock in jazz is no longer singular, as the trumpeter Roy Hargrove's progressive funk band, RH Factor; bassist Christian McBride's eclectic forays into electronica, old-school fusion, and funk; pianist Hiromi Uehara's engagement of stride piano, funk, bebop, and progressive rock; and tenor saxophonist Joshua Redman's fusion band, the Elastic Band, can audibly attest.

As the short list above suggests, listeners no longer need search for new blendings of musical traditions, cultures, or genres in "underground" music scenes or within a specific subgenre. The quotidian quality of blending endlessly mutable and multiple genres, idioms, and traditions is evidenced in mainstream offerings such as Missy Elliott's 2001 bhangra-influenced dance hit "Get Ur Freak On." Explicit, acknowledged blendings of genres have become so commonplace that some mixtures are ironically posited for arch consumption by knowing audiences and are typified by rock auteur Beck's genre-bending recordings or Danger Mouse's *Grey Album* "mashup" of hip-hop artist Jay-Z's *Black Album* recording with the Beatles' "White" album. Consumers no longer desire "authentic authenticity" but are satisfied with anachronistic fantasies or audio simulacra. Listeners readily acknowledge the "already impure" status of most musical genres, and arguments over authenticity, if they appear at all, might hinge on the veracity of a musician's expression rather than her or his adherence to or membership in a specific tradition.

Musical fusions, then, have become widely recognized by critical and popular discourse as more fundamental to musical production than previously acknowledged. Fusion *as a genre*, however, has long ceased to matter in the big-stakes imaginarium of the music industry, and its failure to realize itself as a genre speaks to both its commercial irrelevance as well as its aesthetic ubiquity. Its success may in fact be registered in the central position aesthetic mixture now maintains in popular and art music practice. Paradoxically, giving explicit voice to the ambivalent, the ambiguous, the in-between, and the out-of-bounds—the broken middles—may have hastened fusion's own commercial irrelevance as its liberatory liminal aesthetic began to resonate throughout mainstream culture. Indeed, fusion's effects continue to be heard, rippling just beneath the surface of the blurred gaps between high and low culture and between the broken middles among genres, idioms, and traditions exhibited by current popular music trends. For instance, the Yoshida Brothers, a pair of Japanese siblings who perform rock songs on their *shamisen*, are examples of the willingness of musicians who might previously have been confined to traditional works to engage in nonstandard repertoires. Moreover, fusion musicians' attempts to delink diversity from essentialized, "authentic" difference appear whenever recognizing the intersection between the global and the local—the "glocal"—in contemporary musical life.

To return to *River*: how do Hancock's reworkings of Mitchell compositions matter in terms of fusion music? Does it matter that the instrumentation is largely acoustic? Or, to put it another way, does fusion *require* electronic instrumentation? For perspective consider that the discussions regarding fusion's electronic instrumentation remained largely a matter within critical jazz discourse. Fundamentally, the debates about whether fusion was a type of jazz music rested partly on issues such as the use of electronic and acoustic instruments in genre formation and recognition. Defining characteristics between fusion and jazz was meant to inhibit critical legitimacy and authorization for fusion as a jazz subgenre. But as the group Oregon proved in the late 1970s, fusion music does not require electronic instrumentation, nor need it remain linked to jazz. Rather, fusion is a set of musical practices fundamentally concerned with merging distinct musical genres, idioms, or traditions and, in doing so, to sound out—articulate, represent, perform—the spaces in-between, the broken middles.

Hancock's acoustic piano introduction to his reading of Mitchell's "Both Sides, Now" is a poignant reminder of his melodic sensitivity and inventiveness. His gestures toward the blues at an improvisational peak in the track signal the importance of the blues in jazz while linking Mitchell to both musical traditions' signifying practices. While Mitchell's hit version of the song articulated experiential knowledge as a source of critique in 1968, nearly forty years later Hancock performs her composition as an expression of ambiguity and restrained restiveness. One may see both (and many more) sides, now, but Hancock's merging of Mitchell's pop folk song to postbop jazz aesthetics articulates a marked ambivalence at the heart of the broken middle. Importantly, Mitchell's original melody is obscured by Hancock's inventive interpretation, underscoring the manner through which fusion musicians drew from a variety of musical traditions while simultaneously reinventing them. In fact, Hancock's *River* charts Mitchell's aqueous journey through the forest of jazz, detailing the ways in which their shared aesthetic sensibilities draw from already-mingled waters. While artistically realizing the fragmentary nature of postmodern sensibilities and aesthetics in their recordings and performances, fusion musicians such as Hancock, Mitchell, McLaughlin, and Williams positioned their music as an articulation of the broken middle(s) between genres and identities by emphasizing ethics rather than ethnicities and contradiction over cohesion. The failure of fusion as a genre is indicative of their struggles to bear the tensions multiple loyalties exerted.

As Williams, McLaughlin, Mitchell, and Hancock reveal, part of fusion music's strength stems from its inability to be articulated by dominant discourse or to be pinned down to a particular set of musical characteristics. Its very failure to instantiate itself as a "legitimate" genre, then, speaks not only to the frustrations of its practitioners for recognition and authority but also to the nature of the broken middle as lack: the absence of straightforward precedents, strict adherence to regulatory or discursive borders, or allegiance to rigid affiliations and associations. Fusion music, as an expression of the broken middle, privileges flexibility, eclecticism, and idiosyncrasies over intransigence, purity, and orthodoxy. The resistance fusion musicians met in carrying out this process of self-definition revealed the constraints their sense of agency confronted from both hegemonic interests and countercultural ideologies that regarded sets of musical practices, that is, genres, as fixed—even if only "strategically"—along national, ethnic, and/or cultural lines.

In this way fusion musicians sounded out the possibilities of creating music from materials "partially coalesced" and radically transforming those elements into new musical formations through idiosyncratic practices and aesthetics. Their approach attenuated—though, certainly, did not eradicate—some of the historical determinants as well as the racialized and gendered legacies inhered within musical traditions and genres. This enabled them to both (re)focus and refract those legacies while initiating a standpoint of multiplicity that, as I have noted, continues to echo in contemporary popular and art music culture.

The very existence of genre mixing is tethered to notions of fixed identities and cultures—there is no mixing where there are no lines. However, a world without difference is both impractical and unimaginable. There *are* differences in the different music genres and traditions, and it is *between* those real distinctions that fusion music was realized. As Shakti's example shows, the nature of fusion music liberates musicians from the either/or implications of transcultural mixture by creating a space where musicians and listeners can use their imaginations and predilections to engage musical genres and traditions, no matter the positioning of the music they encounter. While not entirely free of institutional strictures, cultural affinities, or personal prejudices, fusion musicians' attempts to reconfigure musical traditions and genres is a way to mitigate those influences in order to push toward new musical formations. The significance of their music was in its ability to manifest liminality—maintaining a lack of coalescence without succumbing to appeals to prior "purities" for legitimacy. In other words, fusion musicians created music with an ambiguous core linked to a multitude of potential associations, and in doing so they articulated the broken middle, a space whose residents remain nonplussed with contradiction or ambiguity. It is not a matter of schizophrenia or duplicity, then, but of an interest in maintaining the discrepancies between authenticity and idiosyncrasy, tradition and innovation, and the struggles between collective and individual interests in creative tension.

Revolution rather than resolution was on Tony Williams's agenda when he recorded *Turn It Over*, and while he may have been exceptionally attracted to the subversive qualities of blending jazz and rock, fusion musicians of the time were keenly aware of the tensions their music brought to bear on the discursive landscape of contemporary music. Fusion musicians' music outlined the ways in which musical categories and traditions of critical thought obscure the racialized and gendered codings intrinsic to the formation of those categories and traditions. Indeed, by highlighting the ways in which musical genres and traditions are encoded by race and gender, fusion musicians performatively linked musical categories to identity. Fusing musical traditions, however, did not create a completely new musical idiom but reconceptualized older categories, along with their ideological assumptions, through unstable yet powerful transcultural musical practices.

As the world's population increasingly reflects or recognizes the blurriness of categorical borders, the *sounding out* in fusion music of the broken middle—*articulating* the racialized and gendered assumptions behind genre, music traditions, and histories, as well as those supporting the high/low cultural divide; *representing* identity as unfixed and negotiated; and *performing* liminality through the mixing of genres and traditions—is important for the increasing number of individuals whose multipositioned identities are lived within the broken middles between belonging and nonbelonging. Most significant, fusion's sounding out of the broken middle empowers individuals who do not fit neatly into given categories — or, more accurately, whose disheveled fit between categories allows them to challenge the displacements, misrecognitions, and histories that seek to silence them.

Introduction

1. "Rock Too Much for Newport," *Rolling Stone*, Aug. 9, 1969, 10.
2. Morgenstern, "Rock, Jazz, and Newport," 22 (emphasis added).
3. Wein, *Myself among Others*, 286; Morgenstern and Gitler, "Newport '69," 45.
4. Beyond the riots cited here, the Newport Jazz Festival was the site of a notorious 1960 riot of young jazz fans. See Saul, *Freedom Is, Freedom Ain't*, esp. chap. 3, "Riot on a Summer's Day: White Youth and the Rise of the Jazz Festival."
5. Morgenstern, "Oscar, Cannonball, Mahavishnu," 16.
6. For Hammer see Stix, "Jan Hammer"; for Laird see Berle, "Rick Laird."
7. For a broad discussion of musical change see Nettl, *The Study of Ethnomusicology*, esp. chap. 20, "The Continuity of Change." For more focused discussions of the impact of technology on music production and distribution see Katz, *Capturing Sound*; Sterne, *The Audible Past*; Timothy Taylor, *Strange Sounds*; Kenney, *Recorded Music in American Life*; and Théberge, *Any Sound You Can Imagine*.
8. Shank, "From Rice to Ice," 263.
9. Gracyk, *Rhythm and Noise*, 7.
10. Holt, *Genre in Popular Music*, 3 (emphasis added).
11. Armstrong, *The Radical Aesthetic*, 17 (emphasis added).
12. Ibid., 76.
13. Quoted in Flanagan, "Secret Places," 79 (emphasis added).
14. Quoted in Henderson, "Meterology and Me," 8.
15. Pond, "Head Hunters," 32.
16. Floyd, *The Power of Black Music*, 24.
17. See DeVeaux, "Constructing the Jazz Tradition." I will be addressing DeVeaux's work directly at various points in the book.
18. Quoted in Valentine, "Exclusive Joni Mitchell Interview," 48, 49.

one Bitches Brew / *considering genre*

1. Holt, *Genre in Popular Music*, 23, 19 (emphasis added). In addition to Holt see Negus, *Music Genres and Corporate Cultures*; Frith, *Performing Rites*; Small, *Musicking*; and Walser, *Running with the Devil*. Though differing in methodology and analytical tools, each of these works argues convincingly that critics, audiences, and musicians all contribute to the formation of a genre, scene, or tradition.

   I use the term *listener* rather than *musician, fan,* or *critic* because I do not want to necessarily differentiate the specialized listening habits of a professional critic and the gushings of a fan—both are important to genre formation, meaning, and usage. Additionally, many nonprofessional listeners have discerning ears. I will use the term *critic* in specific cases where it is the ideas of the "professional listening" class (or member of that class) that I mean to describe.

2. Pond, "Head Hunters," ix.

3. Brackett, *The Pop, Rock, and Soul Reader*, xvi. Beyond Holt's book-length study, for lengthier discussions of genre and the implications of genre categories on critical and popular discourse see Frith, *Performing Rites*, esp. the chapter "Genre Rules"; Coyle and Dolan, "Modeling Authenticity, Authenticating Commercial Models"; Negus, *Music Genres and Corporate Cultures*; and, particularly germane to this study, Washburne, "Does Kenny G Play Bad Jazz?"

4. Holt, *Genre in Popular Music*, 3.

5. Holt also points out that the term *jazz-rock fusion* was used by jazz writers as early as 1968 but that *fusion* became common from 1975. While he is correct about the terms' usage in the *New York Times* and various jazz magazines, I am reluctant to follow journalistic conventions. Magazines such as *Rolling Stone*, *Jazz & Pop*, and *Black Music and Jazz Review* were more inclined to use the term *fusion*, though much of their coverage of fusion was after 1971, the year that the fusion band Mahavishnu Orchestra released its chart-scaling debut LP.

6. Holt, *Genre in Popular Music*, 100, 91. While I agree with Holt, I understand fusion musicians as tapping other musical traditions beyond popular music genres.

7. Negus, *Music Genres and Corporate Cultures*, 28.

8. There is a sizable amount of scholarship linking identity and culture. See, e.g., Negus, *Popular Music in Theory*, esp. chap. 4, "Identities"; Bhabha, *The Location of Culture*; Blacking, *How Musical Is Man?*; Bohlman, *World Music*; Gilroy, *The Black Atlantic*; Goldberg, *Multiculturalism*; Guilbault, *Zouk*; Hall, "On Postmodernism and Articulation"; Nettl, *The Study of Ethnomusicology*; Radano, *Lying Up a Nation*; Small, *Music of the Common Tongue*; Stokes, *Ethnicity, Identity, and Music*; and Timothy Taylor, *Global Pop*.

9. There is a body of work focused on the ways in which nonprofessional musicians and listeners use and make meaning of the music they enjoy. See, e.g., Crafts, Cavicchi, and Keil, *My Music*; Frith, "Music and Identity"; DeNora, *Music in Every-*

day Life; and North, Hargreaves, and Hargreaves, "Uses of Music in Everyday Life." Beyond scholarly work dealing with individual uses of music, one may also point to the growing nonacademic literature devoted to using music to heighten work productivity or a child's cognitive abilities.

10. Miles Davis, *The Autobiography*, 310.

11. Frith, *Performing Rites*, 75.

12. Nicholson's *Jazz Rock* is an important book in its depth of coverage and historical reach. It will doubtless be a benchmark for future fusion histories. That said, while I am not pursuing the type of historical questions on which Nicholson focused, I am interested in tackling some of the assumptions he brings to his study. Another perspective is provided by Julie Coryell (former wife of the fusion guitarist Larry Coryell), who coproduced with the photographer Laura Friedman a book titled *Jazz-Rock Fusion*. Originally published in 1978, it arrived in the wake of fusion's "first wave" and offers an encyclopedic gathering of fusion artists' interviews.

13. Nicholson, *Jazz Rock*, xiii.

14. Nicholson implicitly recognizes this fact, as well, when he details the activities of bands such as Cream and Soft Machine.

15. See Gridley, *Jazz Styles*, 307.

16. Covach, "Jazz-Rock? Rock-Jazz?" 107. Progressive, or more often simply "prog," rock incorporated European concert music elements, borrowed mainly from the baroque and romantic eras though some also borrowed from contemporaneous experimental avant-garde practices. Notable prog rock bands included Emerson, Lake and Palmer; Yes; King Crimson; and Soft Machine.

17. West, "Jazz Workshop."

18. Negus, *Music Genres and Corporate Cultures*, 27.

19. Bourdieu, *Distinction*, 92.

20. I use high-cultural valuation to make my point about the confluence of capitalist interest in the arts and how its privileged status affects cultural value. I could, however, have used a "low" cultural form, such as hip-hop, to argue how the music industry is able to use its "street cred" to sell to mass youth audiences, instantiating as wide an institutional framework as Wagnerian opera though in vastly divergent locations.

21. Lopes, *The Rise of a Jazz Art World*, 9.

22. A large amount of scholarly material has investigated this move by jazz from vernacular expression to art music. Iain Anderson's "'This Is Our Music'" investigates the ways that free jazz artists looked increasingly to governmental and other bureaucratic agencies for sponsorship as their falling position in the marketplace dictated a change in survival tactics, reflecting the change in the type of audience their music attracted. Bernard Gendron, in *Between Montmartre and the Mudd Club*, notes how jazz increased its cultural capital as bebop domi-

nated critical discourse in the late 1940s and 1950s yet did not manage to keep jazz popular with mainstream audiences. Gendron's essay "'Moldy Figs' and Modernists" traces the internecine jazz battles over legitimacy and authenticity during the early bebop period. See also DeVeaux, *The Birth of Bebop*, as well as his essay "Constructing the Jazz Tradition."

23. For more on the underground FM phenomenon of the 1970s see Neer, FM.

24. Holt, *Genre in Popular Music*, 19.

25. Radano and Bohlman, *Music and the Racial Imagination*, 37.

26. Quoted in Feld, "From Schizophonia to Schismogenesis," 258.

27. Richard Cullen Rath begins his cogent study *How Early America Sounded* by describing the largely natural (e.g., birdsong, thunder) sound world of a time before sound recording. As Rath makes abundantly clear, our world of iPods, karaoke bars, and Muzak-filled public spaces is conspicuously clamorous in comparison.

28. See Ake, *Jazz Cultures*, esp. chap. 5, "Jazz 'Traning: John Coltrane and the Conservatory," which investigates contemporary methods of jazz training methodologies and their underlying pedagogical assumptions that have much to do with ideas of oral transmission vis-à-vis written notation; see also Berliner, *Thinking in Jazz*. For a cogent criticism of the understanding that an oral tradition and a written tradition are fundamentally different see Prouty, "Orality, Literacy, and Mediating Musical Experience." As Steven Feld argues in "Orality and Consciousness," labeling a set of practices as an oral culture "[dismisses] rather than [addresses] the meanings, uses and creative intentions that characterize music in societies of oral tradition" (25).

29. Scanlan, "The Impeccable Mr. Wilson," 39 (emphasis added).

30. Wonder's *Innervisions* (Tamla-Motown 1973) and *Fullingness' First Finale* (Tamla-Motown 1974) featured Wonder on most, if not all, of the instrumental tracks. He provided the bulk of the vocals, as well. Later artists such as Prince and Beck also took advantage of multitracking to produce recordings in which they were the sole performer on a multitude of instruments. Multitrack pioneer and guitarist Les Paul had a number of hits in the 1950s with his then-wife, Mary Ford, that utilized overdubbing to produce hit recordings such as "How High the Moon" in 1951, in which their two voices were expanded into a backing chorus; overdubbing allowed Paul to record multiple instrumental tracks.

31. See Rasula, "The Media of Memory."

32. For more detailed explorations of recording developments see Brooks and Spottswood, *Lost Sounds*; and Sterne, *The Audible Past*.

33. The original recording was for the UNESCO *Anthology of African Music* (Barenreiter Musicaphon, 1966), a series of eighteen recordings of noncommercial African music, of which "Ba-Benzélé Pygmies" was volume 3. For a more detailed discussion of this issue see Feld, "Pygmy POP." Footnote 3 traces the various recordings of the BaBenzélé Pygmies.

34. DeVeaux, "Constructing the Jazz Tradition," 528.

35. Here *square* is not a slang word used to oppose a term such as *hip* but is a term used to indicate a fundamental reliance on a "four on the floor" feel that is achieved by emphasizing all four beats of standard meter relatively equally, with the first beat, or downbeat, being privileged slightly in order to indicate the pulse or tempo of a composition. Compare this with Western concert music's heavier stresses on the first and third beats or funk's heavy reliance "on the one" or the first beat of each measure. Jazz, however, has gone through various rhythmic styles, from New Orleans jazz with its heavy discolike insistence on all four beats to free jazz's loosening of the pulse, tempo, and any rhythmic privileging of a specific beat.

36. See the Dec. 25, 1969, issue of *Down Beat*.

37. For a contemporaneous overview of some of the "big band" rock bands of the early 1970s see Bourne, "Big Band Rock and Other Brassy Beasties." Beyond Blood, Sweat & Tears and Chicago, Bourne provides thumbnail sketches of such forgotten bands as Illustration and Ten Wheel Drive. The Brecker brothers, Michael (saxophone) and Randy (trumpet), co-led another fusion band, Dreams, before forming their self-named band.

38. It should be noted that the fundamental "rudiment" of Pastorius's performance style is an extension of the "slap" style of funk bass first introduced by Larry Graham of Sly and the Family Stone. Graham's style, revolutionary in its day, has become a ubiquitous bass style in fusion, rhythm and blues, and "urban contemporary" music, and has been sampled in numerous hip-hop, techno, and house compositions. It has even become a part of the language in a somewhat modified form of many straight-ahead jazz bassists.

39. See Feld, "The Poetics and Politics of Pygmy Pop."

40. James has recorded classical albums in attempts to overcome this image — a move that indicates his attentiveness to the critical dismissal of being labeled a "fusion keyboardist." The albums, however, received little attention and did not alter the widespread view of his musical talents. Contrastingly, an early recording, a self-produced effort released on ESP records in 1965, was a free jazz affair. His free jazz piano trio of the time included the bassist Barre Williams and percussionist Robert Pozar and was augmented on the recording by the experimental musicians Bob Ashley and Gordon Mumma, who contribute electronic tape manipulations.

41. Smith, interview with author, Sept. 12, 2002.

42. Washburne, "Does Kenny G Play Bad Jazz?" 143.

43. There have been earlier popular music mergings with non-Western music although with highly problematic orientalist leanings. Musicians such as Martin Denny and his cohort in what is now known as "exotica" or "tiki lounge" recordings often (mis)represented non-Western musical cultures and functioned in

the public imaginary as soundings from exotic, faraway places. However, many artists of color used this phenomenon to launch and sustain their musical careers, including Carmen Miranda, Alfred Apaka, and Yma Sumac.

44. Washburne, "Does Kenny G Play Bad Jazz?" 143, 137.

45. For instance, Miles Davis opened for the Grateful Dead on April 12, 1970, at the Fillmore West in San Francisco, and the Mahavishnu Orchestra opened for Emerson, Lake and Palmer on March 24 and 25, 1972, at Winterland in San Francisco.

two Where Have I Known You Before? / *fusion's foundations*

1. In terms of black American music, ragtime was an earlier example of this cultural move, in which claims for its high cultural status were based on ragtime's congruence with the Western concert music tradition. Arguably, ragtime laid the foundation for jazz's eventual triumph as "America's classical music."

2. Sargeant, *Jazz, Hot and Hybrid*, 265.

3. On the manner in which the abolitionists' focus on aesthetic appreciation of black music divorced black sounds from black meanings, foreshadowing the critical discourse in jazz, see Cruz, *Culture on the Margins*.

4. Quoted in Porter, *What Is This Thing Called Jazz?* 17.

5. See Finkelstein, *Jazz, a People's Music*.

6. Ellington, "We, Too, Sing 'America,'" 147.

7. Stearns, *The Story of Jazz*, 305.

8. Ibid., 296. The Hudtwalker quote is taken from a chapter appropriately titled "The Conquest of Jazz." Significantly, Stearns, who was not allowed to hold formal jazz courses while he was an English professor at Hunter College, established the Institute of Jazz Studies at his Greenwich Village residence in 1952. The institute later moved to its present location, Rutgers University.

9. Ibid., 305.

10. Ibid.

11. Ibid., 306–7.

12. Williams, *Where's the Melody?* ix.

13. Ibid., x. During the cold war the U.S. State Department called on jazz musicians such as Dizzy Gillespie and Louis Armstrong as part of its cultural diplomacy efforts. While these artists were often conflicted about their role in representing U.S. democracy as nonracist, they were also able to bring African American culture to otherwise inaccessible parts of the world. For an insightful study of this particular history see Von Eschen, *Satchmo Blows Up the World*.

14. See Spellman, *Four Lives in the Bebop Business*; and Baraka, *Blues People*.

15. Baraka, *Black Music*, 14.

16. Baraka, *Blues People*, 188 (emphasis added).

17. Monson, "The Problem with White Hipness," 398.
18. Baraka, *Black Music*, 12.
19. Baraka, *Blues People*, 235.
20. Ibid., 185–86.
21. Porter, *What Is This Thing Called Jazz?* 86. Porter is quoting from Bernard Gendron's *Between Montmartre and the Mudd Club*.
22. Ibid., 87.
23. See Feather, *The Passion for Jazz*, a compilation of articles written in the 1970s for the *Los Angeles Times*; Hentoff, *The Jazz Life*; Finkelstein, *Jazz, a People's Music*; Kofsky, *Black Nationalism and the Revolution in Music*; and Kofsky, *Black Music, White Business*. An expanded version of Kofsky's *Black Nationalism* was published under the title *John Coltrane and the Jazz Revolution of the 1960s*.
24. Kofsky, *John Coltrane and the Jazz Revolution of the 1960s*, 51.
25. Baraka, *Blues People*, 235.
26. Mingus, "Interview," 21.
27. Yet, as Lewis Porter notes in his insightful study of the tenor saxophonist, audiences were often less enthusiastic about Coltrane's half-hour modal and free excursions. Porter describes Coltrane's tour of England in 1961, in which he and his fellow band member Eric Dolphy performed increasingly experimental jazz music, as proving disastrous with British critics and audiences. See L. Porter, *John Coltrane*, 194.
28. Gioia, *The History of Jazz*, 335.
29. Ayler, " 'Free Music' . . . Discorded Chaos?"
30. In addition to Arthur Taylor's book see Wilmer, *As Serious as Your Life*; Such, *Avant-Garde Jazz Musicians*; and Kofsky, *John Coltrane and the Jazz Revolution of the 1960s*.
31. Anderson, "Jazz Outside the Marketplace," 139.
32. Quoted in Nicholson, *Jazz Rock*, 9.
33. Corea, "The Function of an Artist," 16.
34. Toner, "Chick Corea," 15.
35. Anderson, "Jazz Outside the Marketplace," 140.
36. Ibid., 139.
37. For a detailed investigation of hard bop's critical reception see Rosenthal, "Hard Bop and Its Critics"; and Rosenthal, *Hard Bop*.
38. Latin contributions to jazz have been marginalized in jazz discourse similar to fusion though, when mentioned, "Latin jazz" does not carry the same taint. There are even earlier examples than Bauza and Pozo in jazz, of course, including the trombonist Juan Tizol, who composed "Caravan" and "Perdido" while a member of Duke Ellington's big band ensemble.
39. Admittedly, some of Ellington's creative work was highly anachronistic and not based on studied research. His "Far East Suite," for example, was "Eastern" mostly in Ellington's imagination though, to be fair, he never claimed to be inte-

grating actual Asian music with his own but, rather, was setting to music his impressions of Asia.

40. Lopes, *The Rise of a Jazz Art World*, 9.

41. See Gendron, *Between Montmartre and the Mudd Club*; and Gracyk, *Rhythm and Noise*; see also Middleton, "Locating the People."

42. Gendron, *Between Montmartre and the Mudd Club*, 6.

43. Anderson's article, "Notes for the New Geology," is reprinted in Cateforis, *The Rock History Reader*, under the chapter title, "Rock and the Counterculture."

44. Paul Williams, "Along Comes Maybe," 21.

45. Peter Guralnick quotes Presley from an interview that the up-and-coming young singer did with Kays Gary for the *Charlotte Observer*'s June 27, 1956, issue. Presley admitted, "The colored folks been singing it and playing it just like I'm doin' now, man, for more years than I know. They played it like that in the shanties and jook joints, and nobody paid it no mind 'til I goosed it up. I got it from them" (Guralnick, *Last Train to Memphis*, 288–89).

46. Sun Records released "Rocket 88" as a Jackie Brenston and His Delta Kats recording although Peter Guralnick, among others, believes it was actually Ike Turner's session, with business considerations leading to the recording's release under Brenston's name.

47. Brackett, "(In Search of) Musical Meaning," 71–72.

48. See Shank, "From Rice to Ice."

49. For a concise yet multifaceted view of the technological, social, and musical conditions of possibility that led to, first, the formation of rhythm and blues and its subsequent transformation into rock 'n' roll see Garofalo, "Crossing Over."

50. It should come as no surprise to anyone that Presley's transformation from "Elvis the Pelvis" to "the king of rock 'n' roll" or, more simply, "the King," mirrored Benny Goodman's ascent as "the king of swing." Nor should the shortage of black "royalty" be a surprise—I am merely indicating another way in which critical and popular journalism help maintain racialized historiographical claims about U.S. popular music.

51. It is ironic that while Phillips recorded many of rock 'n' roll's early hit makers, including Elvis Presley, Chuck Berry, Carl Perkins, and Roy Orbison, as well as blues artists such as Rufus Thomas, James Cotton, and Junior Parker, he would sell his contract with Elvis Presley in 1955 to RCA (or, perhaps more accurately, to "Colonel" Tom Parker) for a mere $35,000.

52. See Berry in the film *Chuck Berry: Hail, Hail, Rock 'n' Roll* (directed by Taylor Hackford [Delilah 1987]), in which he discusses this strategy. For a similar example from jazz, one could cite Nat "King" Cole and his mainstream achievements.

53. Marcus, *Mystery Train*, 166.

54. Berry, "In His Own Words," 13.

55. Wicke, *Rock Music*, 39.

56. For a more detailed investigation of rock's aesthetic moves, particularly as it was articulated distinctly from "rock 'n' roll," see Gracyk, *Rhythm and Noise*.

57. See Adorno's and Horkheimer's seminal essay, "The Culture Industry," in which they argue that the "constant pressure to produce new effects (which must conform to the old pattern) serves merely as another rule to increase the power of the conventions when any single effect threatens to slip through the net. Every detail is so firmly stamped with sameness that nothing can appear which is not marked at birth, or does not meet with approval at first sight" (5).

58. Gleason, "Like a Rolling Stone," 65.

59. Quoted in Gioia, *The History of Jazz*, 36.

60. There is *The Funk Era and Beyond*, edited by Tony Bolden, with essays by Amy Nathan Wright and Scot Brown that deal directly with the music of the 1970s. Matthew Brown's article, "Funk Music as Genre" is a cogent study of funk music's aesthetics and provides a complementary perspective to this chapter by focusing on funk's development through the 1980s. It is interesting, however, that oft-cited texts on black music such as Paul Gilroy's *The Black Atlantic*, Christopher Small's *Music of the Common Tongue*, Samuel Floyd Jr.'s *The Power of Black Music*, Tricia Rose's *Black Noise*, Mark Anthony Neal's *What the Music Said*, Albert Murray's *Stomping the Blues*, Amiri Baraka's *Blues People*, as well as many other well-known examples, say little about funk music, either directly or indirectly.

   For more on *funk* as a musical term and its historical resonance with racialized and hypersexualized conceptions of black life see Vincent, *Funk*; Danielsen, *Presence and Pleasure*; and Sidran, *Black Talk*. Guthrie Ramsey's *Race Music* deals with James Brown in some depth, and Steven Pond places Hancock's *Head Hunters* recording within a larger funk world; see, in particular, chap. 3, "At the Crossroads of Genre: Funk in Action," in *Head Hunters*. Barbara Browning's *Infectious Rhythm* has much to say about the anxieties white imagination placed on Afrodiasporic music, and her analysis of rap and funk in this regard is cogent and provocative (see esp. 5–8). Finally, although Lawrence Levine's *Black Culture and Black Consciousness* does not discuss funk or soul music per se, it provides a rich contextual backdrop to the more explicit discussions found in the other texts.

61. Gray, *Cultural Moves*, 10.

62. See Matthew Brown, "Funk Music as Genre," 484.

63. Vincent, *Funk*, 4.

64. Dent, "Black Pleasure, Black Joy."

65. For a more detailed look at Brown's hit single "Say It Loud" see Ramsey, *Race Music*, 151–55. For another perspective see Vincent, *Funk*.

66. Vincent, *Funk*, 19.

67. See, in particular, Ward, *Just My Soul Responding*, 339–45. Also see Lipsitz, *The Possessive Investment in Whiteness* for a longer historical investigation of the ways

race has impacted the material conditions of groups racialized as "black" and "white" in the United States.

68. Quoted in Tate, *Flyboy in the Buttermilk*, 39.

69. Quoted in Wright, "A Philosophy of Funk," 36.

70. Many point to Mark Dery's essay "Black to the Future" as a formal beginning to the use of the term. See also Kodwo Eshun's *More Brilliant Than the Sun*, which cites Greg Tate as first articulating this idea of an Afrocentric reading of science fiction.

71. Matthew Brown, "Funk Music as Genre," 496.

72. See Monson, "The Problem with White Hipness," for a cogent analysis of the ways in which white bebop audiences participated in bebop's subcultural formation, heightening the correspondences between nonconformist social behavior and the music. For an example of the type of thinking Monson critiques see Norman Mailer's oft-referenced essay, "The White Negro."

73. There were other movements in jazz during the 1950s that represented its moves toward the symphony hall. Third stream, a blend of jazz and Western concert music traditions, led by Gunther Schuller and John Lewis, soon dissipated itself in mannerist preciosity. Cool, or West Coast, jazz is counterposed to hard bop, or East Coast jazz, in both musicological and racialized terms. West Coast players, predominantly but not exclusively white, were heard as performing an effete, diluted version of "real jazz," while East Coast musicians, again, predominantly but not exclusively African American, performed a masculine, "hard" jazz. For a detailed explication of the "West Coast vs. East Coast jazz wars" see Gioia, *West Coast Jazz*.

74. Rosenthal, *Hard Bop*, 27.

75. Quoted in ibid., 70–72.

76. Definitions for *hard bop* (or synonymous terms such as *soul jazz*) are, like the word *jazz*, hotly contested. Jazz performers whose careers blur distinctions between hard bop and bebop, such as Sonny Rollins or Miles Davis, illustrate the ways in which these designations often serve marketing departments more than historians or critics.

77. Porter, *What Is This Thing Called Jazz?* 69.

78. The reader should keep in mind the overlapping of styles both in terms of chronological time and in the different styles musicians participated in. For example, Miles Davis, while recording classic hard bop albums such as *Walkin'* (Prestige 1954) and *Cookin'* (Prestige 1956), was involved in a number of projects that later became known as cool jazz (1949–50)—styles often thought of as "oppositional" to one another by jazz listeners. Davis's collaborations with the arranger Gil Evans in the late 1950s and early 1960s are also associated with cool, though some critics cite these as precursors to modal jazz. Again, the messiness of jazz practice in terms of aesthetic choices in performance styles and compositional strategies continually troubles critical perspectives.

79. Williams, *The Art of Jazz*, 233.
80. Quoted in Rosenthal, *Hard Bop*, 73. While Rosenthal does not mention any details of *The Soul Brothers* recording, my best guess is the reference is to a Milt Jackson and Ray Charles recording of the same name released in 1957 (Atlantic 1279).
81. For more details about Betty Davis's checkered musical career see Ballon, "Liberated Sister."
82. Scot Brown, "A Land of Funk," 81.
83. Quoted in Lyons, "Herbie Hancock," 28.
84. Ibid., 26.
85. Bolden, "Theorizing the Funk," 21.
86. Similarly, in *Beyond Exoticism* Timothy Taylor traces this historical rendering of white and othered musical traditions as a result of the colonialist encounter with non-Western peoples and cultures.

three Vital Transformation / *fusion's discontents*

1. Beckett and Merton, "Stones/Comment," 116.
2. Sandford, *Keith Richards*, 48.
3. Miles Davis, *The Autobiography*, 324.
4. Ibid., 328 (emphasis added).
5. Quoted in Carr, *Miles Davis*, 285.
6. The anecdote begins Chris Albertson's 1971 *Saturday Review* article, "The Unmasking of Miles Davis."
7. Quoted in Carr, *Miles Davis*, 284.
8. Quoted in Szwed, *So What*, 275.
9. Miles Davis, *The Autobiography*, 329.
10. DeVeaux, "Constructing the Jazz Tradition," 528.
11. Quoted in Hohman and Mitchell, "*Down Beat* in Review," 15. Feather's remarks were originally published in 1971.
12. Carson, *Jeff Beck*, 143.
13. "Thelonious" appeared on *Blow by Blow*, and "Goodbye Pork Pie Hat" appeared on *Wired*. As an aside, Wonder's 1976 song "Sir Duke" was a tribute to Duke Ellington.
14. See Denisoff, *Solid Gold*.
15. There were anomalies, such as Weather Report's hit single "Birdland," from the *Heavy Weather* recording (Columbia 1977). However, "Birdland" is a big band ensemble arrangement reduced for fusion band, which helps explain its success. The vocal group Manhattan Transfer sang Jon Hendricks–penned lyrics and enjoyed an even bigger hit with the song in 1980, earning the group its first Grammy for Best Contemporary Jazz Performance, Vocal or Instrumental.
16. Nicholson, *Jazz Rock*, xiv.

17. Nicholson, "The Song of the Body Electric," 48.

18. Carroll, review of *The Story of Rock*, 40.

19. Nicholson, *Jazz Rock*, 181.

20. Henderson, "Meterology and Me," 8.

21. Francis Davis, "The Book on Miles," 205–6.

22. Mandel, "Sketches of Miles," 20.

23. Miles Davis, *The Autobiography*, 273 (emphasis added).

24. Brackett, *The Pop, Rock, and Soul Reader*, 291.

25. Miles Davis, *The Autobiography*, 329.

26. Zwerin, *Duster*, n.p. (emphasis added).

27. Zwerin, "Mona Lisa with Moustache," 17.

28. For example, Emerson's "Benny the Bouncer," from the Emerson, Lake and Palmer recording *Brain Salad Surgery* (Manticore 1973), is a hyperragtime, stride piano showcase that makes little concession to the rock practices of the time. The composition indicated the depth of Emerson's keyboard abilities, as well as the open-eared sensibilities of not only the band but its audience, as well. Bruford's recordings of the period such as *Feels Good to Me* (Editions EG 1978) with a lineup that included the British jazz trumpeter Kenny Wheeler, and *One of a Kind* (Polydor 1979), which featured the guitarist Allan Holdsworth, were clearly influenced by jazz and fusion.

29. Quoted in Nicholson, *Jazz Rock*, 33.

30. Zwerin, *Duster*, n.p. (emphasis added).

31. Ibid.

32. The Free Spirits' record *Out of Sight and Sound* (1967 ABC) is heard as more closely aligned with psychedelic rock than with fusion (jazz-rock) by many listeners, including this author. In fact, the band was signed to the ABC-Paramount record label by Bob Thiele as a rock band, according to George Hoefer in a 1967 *Down Beat* cover story on Coryell.

33. In their defense, jazz musicians, particularly black musicians, emulated the serious, almost solemn, performance styles of the symphony hall or concert recital as a way to diminish the racialized primitivism attached to them and their music.

34. Quoted in Nicholson, *Jazz Rock*, 33.

35. Paul Williams, "Along Comes Maybe," 21.

36. Quoted in Nicholson, *Jazz Rock*, 34–35 (emphasis added).

37. Quoted in ibid., 30.

38. See Miller, *Democracy Is in the Streets*; and Farber, *The Columbia Guide to America in the 1960s*.

39. Bromell, *Tomorrow Never Knows*, 10.

40. For a nonacademic but cogent description of the relationship between the drug counterculture and covert U.S. governmental agencies see Lee and Shlain, *Acid*

Dreams. Lee's and Shlain's text also bears some interest for contextualizing the ways in which the federal government infiltrated various political and social activist groups—even those as loosely defined as "the hippies"—and its role in manipulating counterhegemonic structures of feeling. Unfortunately, I cannot spend time detailing these activities but recognize the need to point toward these conjunctures.

41. Bromell, *Tomorrow Never Knows*, 68, 72.
42. Ibid., 93.
43. One can hear Hendrix referring to his music this way in a bootleg recording of a 1969 concert in Stockholm, Sweden.
44. Quoted in Nicholson, *Jazz Rock*, 42 (emphasis added).
45. Quoted in ibid., 44.
46. Feather, "Blindfold Test, pt. 1," 33.
47. Klee, "Dreams Come Through," 16.
48. Quoted in Nicholson, *Jazz Rock*, 29.
49. Smith, "Brian Torff," 36.
50. Quoted in Szantor, "Chase," 13. Chase had been a featured trumpet soloist in Woody Herman's Thundering Herd band in the early 1960s.
51. Ibid.
52. In addition to the reasons I cite in the text, the fact that many jazz artists were composing their own songs rather than "jazzing" popular songs of the day and rarely performed someone else's original composition meant that "standards"—songs a majority of musicians would know—necessarily decreased in number and importance.
53. Milkowski, "A Master's Perspective," 24.
54. The recording titles also reflect Montgomery's—or his management's—desire to "cross over" genres and demographic groups. "California Dreamin'" had been a major pop hit for the folk-rock group the Mamas and the Papas, and "A Day in the Life" was a song taken from the Beatles' *Sgt. Pepper's Lonely Hearts Club Band.*
55. Duke Ellington, *Hits of the Sixties: This Time by Ellington* (Reprise 1964); Count Basie, *Basie's Beatle Bag* (Verve 1966); Woody Herman, *Light My Fire* (Cadet 1969).
56. The Brill Building was the name of a building in which a number of early rock composers wrote songs for the leading recording acts of the day. Don Kirshner and his partner, Al Nevins, headed Aldon Music in the building where cubicles with upright pianos were filled with songwriters whose works were then peddled to popular singers and groups by Kirshner and Nevins. Carole King and her partner Gerry Goffin, Neil Sedaka, Neil Diamond, and Leiber and Stoller were employed as songwriters there. In rock history this is a moment when the producers, arrangers, and songwriters behind the recording stars rose in importance. Once the Beatles "invaded" with their own self-penned songs and Bob

Dylan popularized the singer-songwriter, rock music became the increasingly "authentic" expression of the recording musicians themselves.

The tensions between craft, authenticity, and the recording and music publishing industries impacted the discourse about fusion. Although there remained a large pool of professional songwriters hidden behind the popular recording artists who performed their songs, the rise of the self-contained band in the 1960s relegated the songs produced in this older production scheme largely to nonrock popular music such as that found in "middle-of-the-road" and Broadway artists such as Barbra Streisand, Andy Williams, and Robert Goulet.

57. Quoted in Nicholson, *Jazz Rock*, 35.

58. For more on rock aesthetics and its relationship to electronic technology see Waksman, *Instruments of Desire*; and Gracyk, *Rhythm and Noise*.

59. For more on the progressive rock movement see Macan, *Rocking the Classics*; and Stump, *The Music's All That Matters*. For a provocative investigation of the links between jazz and progressive rock see Holm-Hudson, "Apocalyptic Other-ness."

60. See, e.g., Auslander, *Performing Glam Rock*, which focuses on a highly theatrical, gender-bending substyle of rock that was contemporaneous with fusion.

61. Worby, "Cacophony," 150.

62. Ibid.

63. Waksman, *Instruments of Desire*, 7.

64. Olly Wilson's idea of a heterogeneous sound ideal for black music aesthetics resonates with Waksman's assertions about the uses of distortion and other timbral possibilities electric amplification gave black blues guitarists. Briefly, Wilson argues that black musical aesthetics privileges a wider sound palette than that allowed within European high culture musical traditions, including sounds that are simply dismissed as "noise." See Wilson, "The Heterogeneous Sound Ideal in African-American Music."

65. Waksman, *Instruments of Desire*, 177.

66. Davis, in his autobiography, recalled, "The music I was really listening to in 1968 was James Brown, the great guitar player Jimi Hendrix, and a new group . . . Sly and the Family Stone, led by Sly Stewart, from San Francisco. . . . So, that's the way my head was as far as music was going" (292–93).

67. Waksman, *Instruments of Desire*, 184.

68. Moorefield, *The Producer as Composer*, xiii.

69. Bromell, *Tomorrow Never Knows*, 96.

70. Burton quoted in Suber, "Gary Burton's Back-Home Bag," 12.

71. Gracyk, *Rhythm and Noise*, 105.

72. Morgenstern, "Oscar, Cannonball, Mahavishnu," 16.

73. Gracyk, *Rhythm and Noise*, 106.

74. Waksman, *Instruments of Desire*, 7.

75. Berendt, *The Jazz Book*, 53.

76. Martin Williams, *The Jazz Tradition*, 212.

77. Rusch, "Hodgepodge and Shorties," 12. I have kept the original capitalization as it appears in *Cadence*.

78. Quoted in Nicholson, *Jazz Rock*, 34 (emphasis added).

79. For a cogent argument for the place of the street and the road as important spaces for countering black cultural devaluation see Gray, "Jazz Tradition, Institutional Formation, and Cultural Practice."

80. See Paul DiMaggio, "Cultural Entrepreneurship in Nineteenth-Century Boston: The Creation of an Organizational Base for High Culture in America."

81. Brett, "Masculinity, Essentialism, and the Closet," 12.

four Emergency! / *Tony Williams*

1. Ephland, "Tony Williams," 22.

2. The organist Larry Young's post-Lifetime recordings enjoyed neither critical nor mass appeal when they were finally issued, and his 1970s band, Fuel, is little mentioned today. His earlier Jimmy Smith–influenced Blue Note organ trio recordings received little notice during the 1990s revival of 1960s soul jazz artists by acid jazz DJs, to say nothing of his jam session with Jimi Hendrix titled "Young/Hendrix," preserved on Hendrix's posthumous release, *Nine to the Universe* (Reprise 1980). Young had also been a member of an organ quartet called Love Cry Want, with a guitarist credited simply as Nicholas, the multi-instrumentalist Joe Gallivan, and the drummer Jimmy Molneiri. In 1997 Love Cry Want's debut recording appeared twenty-five years after they recorded it. The continued obscurity of the recording is an ironic rebuff to the liner notes' claim that the music was created to "levitate the [Nixon] White House." The idea may seem laughably of its time today, but Love Cry Want was hoping, we can be sure, to achieve something more than cult status. Young's last Blue Note recording, *Mother Ship*, was released in 1980, although, like *Nine to the Universe*, it was recorded in 1969. Poignantly, by the time of *Mother Ship*'s release, the thirty-seven-year-old "heart of Lifetime" (Williams's phrase for Young) had been dead for two years as a result of complications from undiagnosed pneumonia.

3. Cox, "Tony Williams," 14.

4. Feather, *The Pleasures of Jazz*, 29. For a more recent reiteration of jazz musicians' and fans' abilities to attenuate the color line through the mutual appreciation of jazz music see Lees, *Cats of Any Color*.

5. Quoted in McDermott, *Spectrum*, n.p.

6. Woods, "Tony Williams Interview," 18.

7. Ibid. (emphasis added).

8. Ibid.

9. Ibid.

10. The McLean group was hired for a play titled *The Connection*; see Underwood, "Tony Williams," 21. Williams was the drummer on Eric Dolphy's recording *Out to Lunch* (Blue Note 1964). Cecil Taylor appears on a duet track, "Morgan's Motion," on Williams's *Joy of Flying* (Columbia 1979).

11. Miles Davis, *The Autobiography*, 274.

12. Point, "Tony Williams," 24.

13. Milkowski, "A Master's Perspective," 24 (emphasis added).

14. In his interview with Bill Milkowski, Williams, in describing the difference between his playing with Miles Davis and in Lifetime, stated unequivocally that when "I decided to leave Miles in 1968 . . . I thought, 'Gee, that would be a nice way to do it — organ, guitar and drums — *but do it real aggressively, with a lot of rock 'n' roll kind of feeling, energy, power . . . BAM!*" (Milkowski, "A Master's Perspective," 70 [emphasis added]).

15. See Hodeir, *Jazz*; and Baraka, *Blues People*. Two important writers, Albert Murray and Stanley Crouch, also had much to say about the state of jazz at this time. Though Murray did not single out rock music as having a directly deleterious effect on jazz, Crouch has been an outspoken critic of fusion. I would like to thank one of my anonymous readers for pointing out that though these writers were forming their ideas during the 1970s, their influence would become prominent in the decades after the first fusion artists came on the scene and, thus, does not represent an ideological position against which fusion musicians of this period engaged. However, the disparagement of rock by jazz critics and musicians at the time held grave implications for the critical reception of fusion.

16. Heineman and Morgenstern, "Rock, Jazz, and Newport." While Hodeir and Baraka reference swing as a "strategically essentialist" mode of rhythmic acculturation, the exchange in *Down Beat* underscored the dichotomy drawn between "jazz as art" and rock as music for the "kindergarten." To be fair, Morgenstern did not dismiss the entirety of rock music, and, as I have stated, he had opened up the editorial perspective of *Down Beat* to include rock.

17. See Garofalo, "Crossing Over." Also, Shank, in "From Rice to Ice," quotes from Charles Hamm's essay, "The Fourth Audience" (*Popular Music* 1 [1981]: 123–41), where Hamm notes that "the rise of rock 'n' roll in the 1950s marked the first and the last time that a single recording could top all three of the music industry's culturally (that is racially) distinguished charts" (Shank, "From Rice to Ice," 265). Notably, it was exclusively white rock-and-roll performers who accomplished this feat: Elvis Presley, the Everly Brothers, Johnny Horton, and Jerry Lee Lewis. The three charts are Country and Western (white), R&B (black), and Popular (white). For an interesting study of the relationship between "crossover" and "cover version" see Coyle, "Hijacked Hits and Antic Authenticity."

18. See Gendron, *Between Montmartre and the Mudd Club*.

19. See, e.g., Sales, *Jazz*. For writings of the era see Martin Williams's *The Jazz Tradi-*

tion, particularly his discussion of Duke Ellington. By the late 1960s, jazz musicians had begun to speak publicly of jazz as an art music in interviews. This stance can be seen in a number of the interviewees in Arthur Taylor's *Notes and Tones* and in Bill Dixon's *Down Beat* column during this period.

20. Besides Garofalo's "Crossing Over," see chap. 4 in Negus, *Popular Music in Theory* ("Identities"); and Mahon, *Right to Rock*. Mahon's contention that black rock musicians in the 1990s were ignored by the music industry because of entrenched ideas concerning black musicians and their generic "place" resonates here.

21. See Steven Pond's *"Head Hunters"* for a careful consideration of the effects of race on Herbie Hancock's fusion music of the 1970s. Pond's investigation of the dynamics of public relations, advertising, and other music industry practices on the reception and dissemination of Hancock's *Head Hunters* recording ably dissects the too often mystified role of commercial considerations on musical productions. I am primarily interested in the discursive moves of Tony Williams in a limited time period, but I would like the reader to keep in mind the relationship between music industry practices and "commonsense" ideas about genre categories.

22. A suggestive example is this quote from Jim Szantor regarding a midnight jam session of the Newport Jazz Festival: "Tony Williams was a revelation and a joy as he took utmost care of business with some very in-context drumming— *stepping out of his usual style to accommodate* the setting and the sidemen" (Morgenstern and Szantor, "Newport in New York," 14 [emphasis added]).

23. See Mahon, *Right to Rock*, for an ethnographic study of the Black Rock Coalition of the 1990s, a coalition formed by black rock musicians to combat the music industry's deafness to their efforts.

24. Travis Jackson, "'Always New and Centuries Old,'" 369.

25. Woods, "Tony Williams Interview," 19.

26. Richard Williams, "Williams and His Electric Rhythms," 12.

27. Gibbs, "Tony Williams," 17 (emphasis added).

28. For a careful investigation into the contradictions between free jazz rhetoric and the efforts of free jazz artists to gain institutional support see Iain Anderson, "This Is Our Music." John Gennari's recent *Blowin' Hot and Cool* focuses on the way in which jazz critics participated in various historical shifts in jazz's perception by listeners and the broader general public. See esp. chap. 5, "Swinging in a High-Class Groove," which investigates the strategies for raising jazz music's cultural status before the appearance of fusion.

29. DeVeaux, *The Birth of Bebop*, 27.

30. For a cogent discussion of the shifts in journalists' perspectives on jazz (touched on briefly here) see Lewis Porter, *Jazz*. Also see Lopes, *The Rise of a Jazz Art World*, for an incisive discussion of the critical discourse weighing the merits of jazz as art and as commodity throughout the 1950s and 1960s.

31. McDermott, *Spectrum*, n.p.
32. Arthur Taylor, *Notes and Tones*, 161 (emphasis added).
33. Keightley, "Reconsidering Rock," 109–10 (emphasis added).
34. For a detailed investigation of changes in the aesthetics of rock, particularly as rock was articulated to be distinct from "rock 'n' roll," see Gracyk, *Rhythm and Noise*. Waksman's *Instruments of Desire* is a noteworthy account of the ways in which race, technology, and aesthetics articulated rock music as a politics of pleasure, as well as the ways in which some of its adherents' aesthetic and political agendas helped construct an intellectual basis for the rise in critical appreciation during the late 1960s.
35. Ephland, "Tony Williams," 22.
36. Milkowski, "A Master's Perspective," 69–70.
37. Sonny Sharrock was born on August 27, 1940. Tony Williams was born on December 12, 1945.
38. Quoted in Arthur Taylor, *Notes and Tones*, 58.
39. See, e.g., Woods, "Tony Williams Interview."
40. Ephland, "Tony Williams," 22.
41. Winwood was a fifteen-year-old rock prodigy and virtuoso when he joined the Spencer Davis Group, cowriting and singing on their hits "Gimme Some Loving" and "I'm a Man." With his abilities on keyboards, guitar, and assorted wind instruments, in addition to his dramatic vocal range, Winwood later provided Traffic with its own brand of generic mixing, combining rock, jazz, rhythm and blues, and experimental music. Flutist Anderson suggested recording Rahsaan Roland Kirk's "Serenade to a Cuckoo" on the debut recording of Jethro Tull.
42. See Hall, "New Ethnicities." Briefly, Hall's use of *ethnicity* emphasizes the construction of identity rather than, for example, the use of "race," as a biologically determined category that fixes identity, thereby opening up the possibilities for as-yet-unrealized hybrid identities, or "new ethnicities."
43. Morgenstern, "Rock, Jazz, and Newport," 45. Additionally, the adverse reactions by some jazz critics following the 1969 Newport Jazz Festival were focused mostly on rock fans, who rioted and destroyed much of the festival's main grounds, rather than directed at rock musicians themselves. My point remains, however: jazz critics maintained jazz was a more complex musical idiom and deserved to be valued above rock.
44. Here I am indebted to Pierre Bourdieu's idea of cultural capital, particularly in the sense of material value increasing as a corollary to elevations in the symbolic value of a given cultural product or process. See Bourdieu, *Distinction*. Gennari traces jazz critics' concerns about jazz in the 1960s in "The Shock of the New," chap. 6 in Gennari, *Blowin' Hot and Cool*. Gennari explores at length the polemics surrounding free jazz. Also see Saul, *Freedom Is, Freedom Ain't*, for a detailed study of jazz musicians' own participation in the efforts to give jazz music greater

cultural prestige. Notably, fusion is not discussed at any length in either book. This is not to detract from the value of either book but, rather, to point out the continuing absence of fusion from discussions within jazz studies. For more on this subject see Christopher Washburne's insightful essay "Does Kenny G Play Bad Jazz?"

45. Morgenstern, "A Message to Our Readers," 13 (emphasis added).

46. Morgenstern, "Rock, Jazz, and Newport," 23. Also see Hodeir, *Jazz*, esp. chap. 15, "The Essence." For a contrasting view see Baraka, *Black Music*.

47. See the comments made by Julian "Cannonball" Adderley, Dave Brubeck, John "Dizzy" Gillespie, Ralph J. Gleason, Stan Kenton, Charles Mingus, Gerry Mulligan, George Russell, and Gunther Schuller in a roundtable discussion organized by *Playboy* magazine for its February 1964 issue, reprinted as "A Jazz Summit Meeting" in Walser, *Keeping Time*. Almost every author who has turned to jazz has written about the complexity of the race issue in jazz during the 1960s, and the range of attitudes about the relationship of racialized thinking to jazz has reflected this widespread attention.

48. See DeVeaux, *The Birth of Bebop*, esp. 17–29, for a trenchant review of the ways in which jazz's position as an art music obscured the racial terms under which its musicians, critics, and listeners produced, critiqued, and listened to the music.

49. Gracyk, *Rhythm and Noise*, 147.

50. Cox, "Tony Williams," 14 (emphasis added).

51. Underwood, "Tony Williams," 54.

52. It is important to recall how the U.S. State Department used jazz musicians, and, pointedly, African American jazz musicians, as "ambassadors of goodwill" during this cold war period. State Department–sponsored tours of the former USSR and various Eastern Bloc countries were touted as representing the democratic practices of the United States. The irony was not lost on jazz musicians, however, and even Louis Armstrong, who toured under the auspices of the U.S. State Department, gave statements unapologetically critical about the continued institutional racism in the United States.

53. McDermott, *Spectrum*, n.p. (emphasis added).

54. Arthur Taylor, *Notes and Tones*, 163.

55. Ibid.

56. McLaughlin was so little known to the jazz world in 1969 that Alan Heineman misspelled his name as "McGlocklin" in an October 16, 1969, *Down Beat* review of a Lifetime show at the Jazz Workshop in Boston.

57. Gibbs, "Tony Williams," 17.

58. Cox, "Tony Williams," 33.

59. Arthur Taylor, *Notes and Tones*, 163.

60. Underwood, "Tony Williams," 54.

61. Richard Williams, "Williams and His Electric Rhythms," 12.

62. Cox, "Tony Williams," 14.

63. In an interview with Vernon Gibbs, Williams is asked about Bruce's possible role in breaking up Lifetime. Williams responded, "No musical differences, it was just business that came into it. His people naturally wanted to have control over [the band, but] that would have meant me canceling my people. Even though [my management] weren't equipped and we were having problems because of them, I didn't think it was the right thing to do" (17). Williams also mentions this situation in the 1992 interview with Bill Milkowski (see Milkowski, "A Master's Perspective").

64. McDermott, *Spectrum*, n.p.

65. Milkowski, "A Master's Perspective," 74.

66. Towns, "John McLaughlin Interview with Mark Towns," n.p.

67. Woods, "Tony Williams Interview," 12.

68. Lake, "Wah-Wah Jazz and All That Rock!" 28.

69. McDermott, *Spectrum*, n.p.

70. Angela Davis, *Blues Legacies and Black Feminism*, xv.

five Meeting of the Spirits / John McLaughlin

1. Schaffer, "Mahavishnu Apocalypse," 34 (emphasis added).

2. Henderson, "The One Truth and the Absolute Truth," 11–12 (emphasis added).

3. Ibid., 11.

4. For more on white privilege see McIntosh, "White Privilege and Male Privilege"; and Lipsitz, *The Possessive Investment in Whiteness*. Briefly, they argue that whiteness grants unearned privileges that are either unavailable or circumscribed for people of color, demonstrated, for example, in the ways housing or educational opportunities are apportioned in ways that favor white individuals.

5. Hurwitz, "John McLaughlin's Immaculate Conception," 26.

6. Lipsitz, *Dangerous Crossroads*, 63.

7. Besides Ellwood's *The Sixties Spiritual Awakening*, see Flowers, *Religion in Strange Times*.

8. For more on Dizzy Gillespie's involvement with the Baha'i faith see his autobiography, *To Be or Not to Bop*. For information about Albert Ayler see Wilmer, *As Serious as Your Life*, esp. chap. 6, "Spiritual Unity."

   John Coltrane's experiments with non-Western musical values can be traced back to his 1961 recording *Africa/Brass* (Impulse). For a more detailed investigation of Coltrane's cross-cultural musical explorations, as well as the spiritual component to these explorations, see Nisenson, *Ascension*. For a lucid account of how African and South Asian spiritual practices and traditions impacted Coltrane's music see Cole, *John Coltrane*. Frank Kofsky's *John Coltrane and the Jazz Revolution of the 1960s* remains a worthy examination of how leftist and black nationalist politics influenced, and were influenced by, Coltrane. Dismissed in many critical circles, Kofsky was one of the few writers on jazz whose commitment to a Marxist analytics shaped a powerful critique of jazz practice, as well as conventional jazz analysis. An excellent investigation of Coltrane's work is Lewis Porter, *John Coltrane*.

There is also an intriguing essay by Hafez Modirzadeh linking John Coltrane and Chinese music theory, "Aural Archetypes and Cyclic Perspectives in the Work of John Coltrane and Ancient Chinese Music Theory." While Modirzadeh admits to a tenuous link, the article is provocative and indicates the similarities, if not direct connections, between Coltrane's musical expression of spiritual values and ideas with the spiritual underpinnings of ancient Chinese music theory.

For more on Alice and John Coltrane, and the links they forged between music and spirituality, see Berkman, "Appropriating Universality." I want to thank the anonymous reviewer who pointed me toward Berkman's work.

9. Shipton, *A New History of Jazz*, 834. Shipton delineates a historiography of non-U.S. jazz, as well as cross-cultural collaborative efforts, such as between Mayer and Harriott; see esp. the chapter titled "Jazz as World Music."

10. Schaffer, "Mahavishnu Apocalypse," 15.

11. Ibid.

12. Snyder-Scumpy and DeLigio, "Two Sides to Every Satori," 48.

13. Ibid. While McLaughlin chooses to sound somewhat casual about his drug use, Jack Bruce recalled, "John was really playing great [during 1966–67] but he was getting very stoned, which was really saying something in those days. He actually fell off the stage at one gig in Coventry and played this death chord as he landed; kkkkrrruuuuggggg!" (Stump, *Go Ahead John*, 22). In fact, according to McLaughlin's biographer, Paul Stump, a nameless friend of McLaughlin's during this period "admitted that of all the people he knew who he would have expected to have killed themselves with narcotics, McLaughlin had been top of the list" (22).

14. Henderson, "The One Truth and the Absolute Truth," 12 (emphasis added).

15. By 1969 Tony Oxley was already a presence on the British avant–free jazz scene, working with guitarist Derek Bailey and bassist Gavin Byars. John Surman became one of ECM's most prolific and interesting artists. An album under his leadership, with John McLaughlin supporting him, *Where Fortune Smiles* (Deram 1971), is often mistakenly listed under McLaughlin's leadership. The error is understandable in light of the fact that McLaughlin's presence on it is somewhat overwhelming, which is ironic given Surman's own dominance on *Extrapolation*. During the late 1980s and early 1990s Surman participated with the pianist Cecil Taylor and the bassist William Parker in the Feel Trio. He also founded one of Europe's leading avant–free jazz labels, Incus Records. Brian Odges, a last-

minute replacement for McLaughlin's regular bassist, Dave Holland (who left England to join Miles Davis's band in New York City), was a blues session bassist, according to Howard Mandel in his liner notes to the compact disc release of *Extrapolation*.

16. The phrases in parentheses following song titles are taken from McLaughlin's liner notes.

17. Some writers have speculated that Chick Corea is the unnamed pianist, but he has not sought credit for the recording, nor have any of the other performers named him. There are also conflicting stories about whether it was actually Holland or DeJohnette who gave Williams the fateful recording. In an interview with Chuck Berg, McLaughlin states that DeJohnette recorded the session and gave the tape to Williams (see Berg, "John McLaughlin," 16).

18. Nicholson, *Jazz Rock*, 136.

19. Korall, "Extending beyond Mahavishnu," 46.

20. Feather, "Blindfold Test," 35.

21. Besides appearing on Davis's *In a Silent Way* (1969) and *Bitches Brew* (1969), McLaughlin is also featured on *Tribute to Jack Johnson* (1970), *On the Corner* (1972), *Big Fun* (1974), and *Live/Evil* (1970).

22. Berg, "John McLaughlin," 16.

23. Ibid.

24. Berg, "John McLaughlin," 16.

25. Nicholson, *Jazz Rock*, 147.

26. The *Inner Mounting Flame* reached number eighty-nine on the Billboard charts, and the following recording, *Birds of Fire* (CBS 1973), reached number fifteen, an incredible feat for a jazz — or instrumental — album.

27. Milkowski, *Jaco*, 98.

28. Trigger, "Mahavishnu John McLaughlin," 14, 31.

29. Belden, *The Inner Mounting Flame*, liner notes, 7.

30. Berg, "John McLaughlin," 15.

31. Quoted on McLaughlin's website, www.johnmclaughlin.com (click on "Influences," then "25–26") (accessed Oct. 29, 2010).

32. Snyder-Scumpy and DeLigio, "Two Sides to Every Satori," 48.

33. Chinmoy, *The Source of Music*, 4.

34. Woodward, "John McLaughlin's Life in the Emerald Beyond," 38.

35. Bourne, "The Magic of Mahavishnu," 16.

36. Baraka, *Black Music*, 198. Besides jazz artists such as the trumpeter Wadada Leo Smith, tenor saxophonist Francis Wong, and pianist Randy Weston, who explicitly cite Coltrane's influence in their twinning of spiritual and musical values, rock musicians also name Coltrane as an inspiration that reaches beyond musical practices. For example, the drummer Christian Vander, leader of the French progressive "postrock" band Magma, whose works delineate a complete and

esoteric cosmology similar in fashion to Sun Ra, claims Coltrane's death in 1967 was the catalyst for his composition "Kobaïa" ("eternal"), a reaction to "the musical chaos and the misunderstanding of mankind" (quoted in Holm-Hudson, "Apocalyptic Otherness," 484).

Coltrane explained his motivations for linking his musical and spiritual interests: "I've already been looking into those approaches to music—as in India—in which particular sounds and scales are intended to produce specific emotional meanings. . . . I would like to bring to people something like happiness. . . . *The true powers of music are still unknown. To be able to control them must be, I believe, the goal of every musician.* I'm passionate about understanding these forces" (quoted in Lewis Porter, *John Coltrane,* 211 [emphasis added]. The chapter entitled, "So Much More to Do," from which this quote is taken, deals at length with Coltrane's interconnected interest in spirituality and music).

Later, in another interview, Coltrane elaborated:

> I think the best thing I can do at this time is to try to get myself in shape and know myself. . . . That's what I'm sure of, man, I'm really sure of this thing. As I say, there are things which, as far as spirituality is concerned—which is very important to me at this time—I've got to grow through certain phases of this to other understanding and more consciousness and awareness of just what it is that I'm supposed to understand about it; and I'm sure others will be part of the music. To me, you know, I feel I *want to be a force for good.* (Kofsky, *John Coltrane and the Jazz Revolution of the 1960s,* 450–51 [added emphasis])

37. Berg, "John McLaughlin," 16.
38. McLaughlin discusses this book in his interview with Chuck Berg (see Berg, "John McLaughlin").
39. Quoted in Korall, "Extending beyond Mahavishnu," 18.
40. For instance, the *Rolling Stone* writer Stephen Davis wrote about a benefit concert McLaughlin and his wife at the time, Eve Mahalakshmi, held in the Memorial Church in Harvard Yard, as well as numerous Sri Chinmoy community centers across the United States, in the March 30, 1972, issue (see Stephen Davis, "Mahavishnu's Inner Flame Mounts").
41. Ibid., 26.
42. Korall, "Extending beyond Mahavishnu," 18.
43. Keil and Feld, *Music Grooves,* 319.
44. Schaffer, "Mahavishnu Apocalypse," 15.
45. Ibid.
46. For more on black musicians and their relationship to rock music discourse see Mahon, *Right to Rock.*
47. Stephen Davis, "Mahavishnu's Inner Flame Mounts," 26.

48. Mahavishnu Orchestra, later reduced to simply, Mahavishnu, in the 1980s, went through several incarnations involving different musicians. McLaughlin was the sole member to remain through each of the various lineups. Jonas Hellborg, a virtuoso bassist and member of Mahavishnu in the early 1980s, pursued his own engagement with Indian music and, like McLaughlin, formed groups with Indian musicians. Hellborg also speaks about a spiritual connection with regard to his music.

49. Snyder-Scumpy and DeLigio, "Two Sides to Every Satori," 53.

50. Quoted in Nicholson, *Jazz Rock*, 149.

51. Snyder-Scumpy and DeLigio, "Two Sides to Every Satori," 52.

52. Ibid.

53. Ibid.

54. Ibid.

55. Quoted on McLaughlin's website, www.johnmclaughlin.com (click on "Past," then "1971–86") (accessed Oct. 29, 2010).

56. Berg, "John McLaughlin," 48.

57. McLaughlin's departure from active engagement with Chinmoy's teachings is also indicated visually by a change of hairstyle on the cover of Shakti's debut album. During his days as a Chinmoy acolyte, McLaughlin kept his hair very short and close cropped. The cover of Shakti displays McLaughlin with a noticeably longer coiffure. Santana, in a joint interview with McLaughlin, admitted, "My hair is short because it's Guru's [Sri Chinmoy's] will" (Rensin, "Cruisin' with the Guru," 29), suggesting that McLaughlin's hairstyle was also a reflection of Chinmoy's will.

58. Berendt, *The Jazz Book*, 135.

59. Stephen, "The Cultural Improvisation of John McLaughlin," n.p.

60. Ibid.

61. Underwood, "Profile: L. Shankar," 42–43 (emphasis added).

62. Rozek, "Caught . . . McLaughlin's Shakti and Weather Report," 36.

63. Quoted on the Innerviews website: www.innerviews.org/inner/shakti.html.

64. Quoted on McLaughlin's website, www.johnmclaughlin.com (click on "Past," then "1975–78") (accessed Oct. 29, 2010).

65. Prasad, "Remembering Shakti," 166.

66. Levy, "True Believer," n.p.

67. Stephen, "The Cultural Improvisation of John McLaughlin," n.p.

68. Underwood, ""Profile: L. Shankar," 43.

69. Henderson, "The One Truth and the Absolute Truth," 12 (emphasis added).

70. Berg, "John McLaughlin," 48.

71. Milkowski, "Past, Present, and Future," 91.

72. Schaffer, "Mahavishnu Apocalypse," 14.

73. Stephen, "The Cultural Improvisation of John McLaughlin," n.p.

six Don Juan's Reckless Daughter / Joni Mitchell

1. This was Mitchell's response, recorded on *Miles of Aisles* (Asylum 1974), to audience members who yelled song requests to her while she retuned her guitar between songs. She later used, as an album cover for 1994's *Turbulent Indigo*, an ironic repainting of Van Gogh's "Self-Portrait with Bandaged Ear" (1889) in which she replaced Van Gogh's face with her own. The title of the album is also an ironic reminder of her earlier recording, *Blue*, arguably her most self-confessional recording.

2. These chart positions are taken from O'Brien, *Shadows and Light*.

3. *Court and Spark* was Mitchell's "breakthrough" album, a music industry term describing how a particular recording's sales reflect a significant increase in market share, achieving increased critical attention and public recognition for the artist.

4. The following example may serve as a conventional representation of women's contributions to fusion. Howard Mandel, in a short piece on Gayle Moran in the July 14, 1977, issue of *Down Beat*, began his article: "Gayle Moran may look like a wisp of a woman in her long dress, singing from the second keyboard spot in Chick Corea's Return to Forever, but she's a determined trouper" ("Gayle Moran," 20). Moran also muses on the possibilities of a family and raising children in the article—issues that do not enter into the interviews with the male members of Return to Forever, whose conversations remained strictly focused on music.

5. McLuhan, "Canada as Counter-Environment," 85.

6. Valentine, "Exclusive Joni Mitchell Interview," 48–49.

7. Frye, "Conclusion to the *Literary History of Canada*," 117.

8. Mookerjea, Sourayan, Szeman, and Faurschou, eds. *Canadian Cultural Studies*, 15 (emphasis added).

9. Dickie, "No Borders Here," n.p.

10. Crowe, "Joni Mitchell," 381.

11. Echols, "Thirty Years with a Portable Lover," 28.

12. Prince has spoken publicly about his admiration for Mitchell's *Hissing of Summer Lawns*, claiming that it was the last recording he enjoyed from beginning to end. In addition to Prince an eclectic group of fellow musicians have publicly acknowledged Mitchell's influence: Speech (né Tony Thomas) of the hip-hop group Arrested Development; Jimmy Page and Robert Plant of the hard rock group Led Zeppelin; the rhythm-and-blues diva Janet Jackson, who sampled Mitchell's "Big Yellow Taxi" (1970) for her own hit single "Got 'Til It's Gone" (1997); the postmodern rock artist Beck (né Beck David Campbell, but he adopted his mother's maiden name, Hansen, as a teenager); and Sting (né Gordon Sumner). Other artists who have spoken publicly of Mitchell's inspira-

tion for their music include Seal (né Sealhenry Samuel), Morrissey (né Stephen Patrick Morrissey), Tori Amos, Alanis Morissette, and Suzanne Vega. Additionally, the recording A Tribute to Joni Mitchell (Nonesuch 2007) features a who's who of contemporary popular music from Caetano Veloso, Bjork, Emmylou Harris, Annie Lennox, Elvis Costello, and k.d. lang to jazz artists such as Cassandra Wilson and Brad Mehldau, illustrating her wide appeal and influence.

The rap artist Speech, in describing Mitchell's influence on his own work in an idiom not normally associated with Mitchell, links her aesthetics and hip-hop's strategic connections between lyrical and musical elements: "[Joni Mitchell] is definitely one of my greatest influences. . . . I'd say get Ladies of the Canyon. You can't help but come away from that with a definite appreciation for her vocal arrangements and her vocal and lyrical ability" (quoted in O'Brien, Shadows and Light, 123). The connection Speech recognizes between "vocal arrangements" and "lyrical ability" indicates the delicate balance Mitchell achieves in her creative work.

Additionally, the wide range of artists who list Mitchell's work as influential in Reder and Baxter's Listen to This! includes both obvious artists, as well as some surprises: Bruce Hornsby, Ani DiFranco, Roseanne Cash, Daniel Lanois, Bobby McFerrin, Branford Marsalis, Louie Perez (Los Lobos), Mark Eitzel (American Music Club), Pete Seeger, Lucinda Williams, and Victoria Williams.

13. Campbell, "Joni Chic."

14. Since I began this project, there has been an increased scholarly attention on Mitchell. See, e.g., Lloyd Whitesell, The Music of Joni Mitchell, a cogent study of her work as a composer. With regard to the music under consideration here, Whitesell focuses on Hejira and Don Juan's Reckless Daughter for his penultimate chapter, "Collections and Cycles," though references to her work from this period appear throughout the book.

15. Her album just previous to Court and Spark, For the Roses, also employed jazz artists such as Wilton Felder and Tom Scott. However, it is a transitional album between her earlier folk-pop recordings and the bulk of her 1970s output, as credits on For the Roses include a "Rock 'n' Roll Band," consisting primarily of Stephen Stills, and appearances by other rock musicians, including Graham Nash and James Burton.

16. Guerin was Mitchell's paramour at the time of Court and Spark. However, there is little indication that this was a major reason her music began to include sophisticated jazz melodies and harmonic progressions. Tangentially, I have avoided, for reasons that I hope become clear in the text, listing Mitchell's romantic liaisons during various recordings because much has been speculated about those relationships with the sometimes not-so-hidden agenda of displacing Mitchell's own artistic agency for that of a male musician. The significance of various relationships will be noted, but they will be mentioned in their importance as peers

or working partners. Sensitive to the strategy involving the normative occlusion of female artists' own creativity and production in favor of promoting the "man behind her scene," as if Mitchell or any other well-known female artist would have been less artistically engaged without a man in her life, I will provide ample evidence for Mitchell's independent authority.

17. She spoke about this incident to Mary Dickie (see Dickie, "No Borders Here").

18. Doerschuk, "Embrace the Tiger," 34.

19. She began her tenure with the jazz group the L.A. Express, producing the hit single, "Turn Me On (I'm a Radio)," from For the Roses (Asylum 1972), followed by the even higher-selling singles from Court and Spark: "Help Me," "Free Man in Paris," and "Raised on Robbery." The live double-album follow-up to Court and Spark, Miles of Aisles (Asylum 1974) was a stopgap collection of her hit songs and familiar favorites, some transformed by their performance by an entire band rather than her recorded versions as a solo artist. The next studio recording, The Hissing of Summer Lawns (Asylum 1975) will be considered in more detail in the body of the text, but it is important to recognize that the critical denigration of this album was fairly unanimous and unequivocal. As noted in the text, Rolling Stone magazine voted Hissing of Summer Lawns the worst album of the year.

20. Doerschuk, "Embrace the Tiger," 40.

21. Ibid.

22. Feather, "Joni Mitchell Makes Mingus Sing," 17.

23. Flanagan, "Joni Mitchell Loses Her Cool," 67–68.

24. For an in-depth study of jazz musicians' improvisational and compositional strategies and methodologies see Berliner, Thinking in Jazz.

25. Poignantly, Mingus composed a performance piece titled "The Clown" in 1957. Scott Saul describes it as

> a dark and absurd allegory about the musical clown, a figure of self-destructive pathos who is trapped within the culture of kitsch. While Mingus elsewhere labeled crowd-pleasing entertainers as Uncle Toms and traitors to the black community, he took their dilemma seriously enough to endow it with sympathetic psychological depth. In a narration set to straight waltz time, the protagonist in "The Clown" discovers that his audience has no appetite for his emotional complexities—"all these greens and all these yellows and all these oranges bubbling around inside him." His act elicits a lukewarm response until he makes an unintentional pratfall on a stage in Dubuque—at which point the crowd roars with laughter, and the performer is as hooked as any junkie. Soon he is descending to the most self-brutalizing physical comedy in order to please his audience. The final twist, worthy of O. Henry, occurs when the performer suffers a fatal accident onstage, which the audience happily, unthinkingly, applauds. (Saul, Freedom Is, Freedom Ain't, 153)

The clear parallels between Mitchell's clown story and Mingus's own piece are striking; however, I will simply point to a common aspect of both stories in the context of Mitchell's "inauthenticity." Both stories indicate a hidden self-knowledge the performer keeps for himself, presenting a "false self" to the audience in exchange for applause and acceptance. The self-awareness of the artifice involved in the performer's appeal to the audience, however, is never adequate to the task of saving the performer. In both stories the clowns suffer for their art(ifice) while audiences are free to accept the stagecraft at various valences, from complete absorption and suspension of disbelief to dismissive rejection. In other words, performers are shown as bound to their audiences—their agenda, their applause, their acceptance—while audiences can freely accept or reject any performance rather than passively partaking of an artist's creative output.

The "truth" or "falsity" of any given performer, then, is less meaningful in terms of the impact and reactions of an audience to that performer. Mitchell and Mingus, in telling these narratives, also indicate how audiences are often misled into responding to "false" performances. The deaths of the performers in both of these stories indicate the ultimate price paid by performers for misleading their audiences.

26. Quoted in Flanagan, "Secret Places," 79, original emphasis.
27. Feather, "Joni Mitchell Makes Mingus Sing," 17.
28. Garbarini, "Joni Mitchell Is a Nervy Broad," 44.
29. Fawcett, California Rock, California Sound, 52.
30. Quoted in the film, Joni Mitchell: Woman of Heart and Mind.
31. Ephland, "Alternate Tunings," 24.
32. Fawcett, California Rock, California Sound, 57–58.
33. Swartley, "The Babe in Bopperland and the Great Jazz Composer," 55.
34. Moon, "Joni Mitchell Interview for Canadian Broadcast Company 'Magazine,'" n.p. (emphasis added).
35. The nonjazz cover song is the hit by Frankie Lymon and the Teenagers, "Why Do Fools Fall in Love." The song, an early rock/doo-wop hit, though, is decidedly not a "folk" song and points to the distance between Mitchell's image as a folksinger and her decision to redirect listeners toward her other musical interests.
36. Carpenter, "The Ethnicity Factor in Anglo-Canadian Folkloristics," 125.
37. See Berland, North of Empire, 41.
38. Ehrlich, "Joni Mitchell," n.p. At the time of this interview Mitchell also demurred, "Now [world music of various kinds has] been assimilated." For reasons cited in the text, I find this assertion problematic.
39. Garbarini, "Joni Mitchell Is a Nervy Broad," 52.
40. O'Brien, Shadows and Light, 34.
41. Crowe, "Joni Mitchell," 381.

42. Because Disney refused to grant permission for the use of Mickey Mouse, Mitchell chose to include a similar but not identical image. Here, again, Mitchell worked against the constraints of industrial-corporate desires, challenging its power over her art, as well as revealing its often petty and arbitrary guidelines.

43. Garbarini, "Joni Mitchell Is a Nervy Broad," 52.

44. Carpenter, "The Ethnicity Factor in Anglo-Canadian Folkloristics," 127.

45. Berland, *North of Empire*, 3.

46. Garbarini, "Joni Mitchell Is a Nervy Broad," 52 (emphasis added).

47. Carpenter, "The Ethnicity Factor in Anglo-Canadian Folkloristics," 127.

48. Bannerji, "On the Dark Side of the Nation," 328.

49. Berland, *North of Empire*, 41–42 (Berland draws here from Slemon, "Unsettling the Empire").

50. Robbins, "What Can We Learn When They Sing, Eh?" 193.

51. Quoted in the film *Message to Love: The Isle of Wight Festival 1970* (directed and produced by Murray Lerner [Castle Music Pictures 1997]), as well as on the sound recording of the same name (Columbia/Legacy C2K 65058).

52. Garbarini, "Joni Mitchell Is a Nervy Broad," 46.

53. Sutcliffe, "Joni Mitchell," 148.

54. Garbarini, "Joni Mitchell Is a Nervy Broad," 46.

55. Flanagan, "Joni Mitchell Loses Her Cool," 69.

56. Quoted in O'Brien, *Shadows and Light*, 224.

57. Feather, "Joni Mitchell Makes Mingus Sing," 17.

58. C. Hall, "The New Joni Mitchell."

59. Crowe, "Joni Mitchell," 379.

60. Ibid.

61. Fawcett, *California Rock, California Sound*, 56.

62. Morgenstern, "Rotating with Satchmo and Miles," 20.

63. See Eric Porter, *What Is This Thing Called Jazz?* esp. 142–45.

64. Santoro, *Myself When I Am Real*, 375.

65. Fawcett, *California Rock, California Sound*, 56.

66. Mitchell does not specify the passage, but it is almost certainly the scene in pages 315–20.

67. Feather, "Joni Mitchell Makes Mingus Sing," 52. She also admitted later in the interview, "[Those] three melodies somebody else should write words to, because they're beautiful."

68. Eventually, they decided she would record six songs: four of the new compositions (eventually only recording three of them) and two older Mingus compositions (the recording only yielded a single older piece). Searching through his recorded works together, they decided immediately on "Goodbye Porkpie Hat." At another point in their listening session Mingus warned Mitchell that the record he was going to play had five melodies going on at once. She immediately said,

"'Yeah, I bet you want me to write five different sets of words for each one of the melodies, right?' And he grinned and said, 'Right.' He put on the record, and it was the fastest, smokingest thing you ever heard, with all these melodies going on together" (Crowe, "Joni Mitchell," 379). Mingus's genial teasing extended to the nickname he gave her, Hillbilly, and their work together is marked by strands of respect and warmth.

69. Her curiosity stemmed not only from her own need to anchor the musical themes to a textual one but paralleled Mingus's view on the importance of titling compositions appropriately. Mitchell remembers Mingus's first question about any of the themes was, "What's the title of the song?"

70. Fawcett, *California Rock, California Sound*, 56.

71. Ibid.

72. Feather, "Joni Mitchell Makes Mingus Sing," 52.

73. She admitted later that Pastorius was "such an absolutely dominant male that I couldn't control him" (Flanagan, "Joni Mitchell Loses Her Cool," 68), even though he told her to take more control of her sessions. She also confessed that people assumed that the two of them were involved romantically, as his bass was so prominent in the final mix of the recording. She denies this but does admit that his forceful personality, coupled with her more retiring character, allowed him to assume control of the mixing sessions. In a later session with McLaughlin she realized Pastorius was ignoring her leadership by performing for McLaughlin, instead of concentrating on the recording as a whole, ruining the session. As she recalls, "It was a duet as far as Jaco was concerned" (Flanagan, "Joni Mitchell Loses Her Cool," 68). Failing to rein him in that evening, Mitchell ended up discarding these sessions, as well. Pastorius, in spite of his volatile personality, was one of Mitchell's primary musical partners during this period, as witnessed by their work together on *Mingus, Hejira,* and *Shadows and Light.* Besides performing on bass for the *Mingus* recording, Pastorius also contributed the horn arrangement for the song, "The Dry Cleaner from Des Moines."

74. Feather, "Joni Mitchell Makes Mingus Sing," 52.

75. Ibid.

76. Mary Lou Williams is explicit about how gender shapes audience perception, as well as a female artist's own self-conception: "You've got to play, that's all. They don't think of you as a woman if you can really play. I think some girls have an inferiority complex about it and this may hold them back. If they have talent, the men will be glad to help them along. [And] working with men, you get to think like a man when you play. You automatically become strong, though this doesn't mean you're not feminine" (quoted in Dahl, *Stormy Weather,* 67). For a detailed account of the way gender operates within jazz discourse, and its impact on the construction of female jazz artists as either hyperfeminized subjects or disembodied virtuosi, see Tucker, *Swing Shift.*

77. Feather, "Joni Mitchell Makes Mingus Sing," 52. Shorter and Mitchell also found a mutual interest in painting, further solidifying their relationship.

78. Joe Jackson, "Witness of Life," n.p.

79. Shorter wrote about this moment in an article titled "Creativity and Change" for *Down Beat* in 1968: "At this point in my life, when I see people who are famous and great, I don't want to ever lose the memory of the awe I had when I was younger. I don't want to become so sophisticated and confident that I can say, 'We're all in this together'—a sort of smug 'thing'" (quoted in Koransky, "Lighting the Future," 38). In August 2003 Shorter expanded on this idea: "Of course, the awe is not about music. It's about the mystery of life, of human beings. Have you ever been somewhere and you start thinking, then you go blank? You're not thinking about anything. Then this feeling comes over you, that the whole thing about life, the answer, if there is such a thing, is creeping up, creeping up, creeping up. It's almost there—and it cuts off. There's always a cut-off. It's not words, it's a convergence" (ibid.).

80. Fawcett, *California Rock, California Sound*, 57. An anecdote from Danilo Perez, the pianist in Shorter's current touring and recording group, describing a session for Shorter's recording *Alegría* (Verve 2003), serves as an example of the similar working processes in which Shorter and Mitchell engaged: "There was a part in a piece—I think it was 'Vendiendo Alegría'—on which he said, 'Danilo, put some water on those chords.' I played some other chords. He said, 'No, no. Put some *water* on them.' I went to my room that night, and I wrote ten chords that I thought were water. The next day I came in, played these chords. He said, 'Yeah, now we're talking. But the water has to be clear.' Finally, I played another chord, and he said, 'That's what I'm talking about!'" (Koransky, "Lighting the Future," 40). Their shared sensibilities with regard to working methodologies and other aesthetic considerations illustrate the real compatibilities between Mitchell, the hippie folksinger, and Shorter, the "real" jazz musician.

81. Feather, "Joni Mitchell Has Her Mojo Working."

82. This composition, picked immediately by Mitchell as a candidate for inclusion on the recording, is also one of Mingus's most well-covered songs with versions from John McLaughlin, Jeff Beck, Alex de Grassi, and Jay Beckenstein, among many others.

83. Garbarini, "Joni Mitchell Is a Nervy Broad," 45–46.

84. Tesser, review of *Mingus*, 26.

85. Flanagan, "Joni Mitchell Loses Her Cool," 68.

86. O'Brien, *Shadows and Light*, 30.

seven Chameleon / *Herbie Hancock*

1. Gray, *Cultural Moves*, 153.
2. Strongin, "Herbie Hancock," 33.
3. Balleras, "Herbie Hancock's Current Choice," 16.
4. Feather, "Herbie's Set to Clear the Last Hurdle," 8.
5. Heckman, "Herbie Hancock," 132.
6. Quoted in Hentoff, *Speak like a Child*, n.p. (emphasis added).
7. This quote is taken from a recording Hancock produced when he was the spokesman for Fender Rhodes electric pianos. The recording was part of a multipage advertisement entitled "Herbie Hancock Demonstrates the Rhodes Sound" that included a plastic flexidisc insert. Readers of the November 8, 1973, issue of *Down Beat* could find the ad and disc on pages 25–28, which, coincidentally, featured a cover announcing "Jazz Rock."
8. Wong, *The Prisoner*, n.p.
9. Ibid.
10. The term *pan toting* is used to describe African American domestic workers' practice of taking leftover food from employers' kitchens to their own homes. See Kelley, *Race Rebels*, esp. 18–20.
11. Richard Williams, "Herbie," 24.
12. Ibid.
13. Ibid. (emphasis added).
14. Heckman, "Herbie Hancock," 133.
15. Ibid.
16. Hentoff, *Speak like a Child*, n.p.
17. Heckman, "Herbie Hancock," 133.
18. Strongin, "Herbie Hancock," 32 (emphasis added).
19. Zabor and Garbarini, "Wynton vs. Herbie," 58.
20. Strongin, "Herbie Hancock," 31 (emphasis added).
21. Herrington, "Tomorrow People," 34.
22. Hancock's sextet for *Fat Albert Rotunda* included the tenor saxophonist Joe Henderson, who doubled on alto flute; Johnny Coles on trumpet and flugelhorn; Garnett Brown on trombone; Buster Williams on acoustic and electric bass; and Albert "Tootie" Heath on drums. Following his aesthetic interests, Hancock was still engaged with producing music that emphasized, as he stated in the liner notes to *Speak like a Child*, "sounds [timbres] rather than definite chordal patterns."
23. At this point I have been unable to uncover any other information about this journalist.
24. Herrington, "Tomorrow People," 34.
25. Johnson, "Herbie Hancock," 14.

26. Ibid. Buster Williams is quoted in Tony Herrington's article "Tomorrow People" as declaring, "The Mwandishi band? It was called that only after it was over. Back then we were The Herbie Hancock Sextet" (32).
27. Johnson, "Herbie Hancock," 14.
28. All quotes in this paragraph from Johnson, "Herbie Hancock," 15.
29. Ibid., 34.
30. For more comprehensive discussions of synthesizer history see Timothy Taylor, *Strange Sounds*; Holmes, *Electronic and Experimental Music*; Kettlewell, *Electronic Music Pioneers*; and Shapiro and Lee, *Modulations*.
31. Walter Carlos is now known as Wendy Carlos and remains one of the first publicly "out" transgender performance artists. Wendy Carlos remains involved with electronic music and has moved steadily toward works more experimental than her series of *Switched-On* recordings might have suggested to critics and listeners. She received a master's in composition while studying with Vladimir Ussachevsky and Otto Luening at the Columbia-Princeton Electronic Music Center.
    In 1972, she introduced the vocoder to the general public in her score for Stanley Kubrick's *A Clockwork Orange*, a device that uses the pitches of vocal sounds as a formant signal and combines it with a carrier signal that is triggered from an alternate source, usually a keyboard. Hancock used the vocoder extensively throughout the late 1970s and 1980s.
32. Coryell and Friedman, *Jazz-Rock Fusion*, 205.
33. Pond, "Herbie Hancock's 'Head Hunters,'" 153.
34. Quoted in Herrington, "Tomorrow People," 35.
35. Ibid., 36. Interestingly, though Gleeson was hired as a member of the band, performed on recordings and onstage with the band, group members, including Hancock, continued to call the group a "sextet."
36. This was true for rock music, as well, and hindered the introduction of synthesizers in live settings for a period.
37. Quoted in Herrington, "Tomorrow People," 36.
38. Johnson, "Herbie Hancock," 14 (emphasis added).
39. Herrington, "Tomorrow People," 35.
40. Jagajivan, "Musing with Mwandishi," 14 (emphasis added).
41. Herrington, "Tomorrow People," 36.
42. Ibid., 38.
43. Ibid.
44. Hancock, *Head Hunters*, n.p.
45. Herrington, "Tomorrow People," 38.
46. Hancock, *Head Hunters*, n.p.
47. In the case of Hancock the religion is Nichiren Shoshu Buddhism, as I have mentioned. In Corea's case, whatever one thinks of Scientology and L. Ron Hub-

bard, the practice of scientology's believers can arguably be described as "religious." As we have seen, John McLaughlin was a devout follower of Sri Chinmoy throughout the 1970s, when he led Mahavishnu Orchestra. It is interesting to note that none of these musicians engaged in a conventional Western religious practice.

48. "Luv N' Haight" is the first track on the Sly and the Family Stone album *There's a Riot Goin' On* (Epic-Columbia [now Sony] 1971).

49. Townley, "Hancock Plugs In," 14.

50. Woodward, "Herbie & Quincy," 20.

51. Lyons, "Herbie Hancock," 28.

52. Lake, "Soul Food," 18.

53. Primack, "Herbie Hancock," 42.

54. Flanagan, "Herbie Hancock," 60.

55. According to *Billboard*, Hancock's next Headhunters album, *Thrust* (Columbia 1974), also reached number one on the jazz chart, number two on the "black" chart, and number thirteen on the pop chart. I use scare quotes around *black* to indicate that this term applied to a number of differently named charts throughout the 1960s and 1970s, including "urban contemporary," "rhythm and blues," "soul," "funk," "dance," and "disco."

   Subsequent U.S. releases such as *Man-Child* (Columbia) and *Secrets* (Columbia), released in January and June 1976, respectively, continued Hancock's chart successes, with each album reaching number one on the *Billboard* jazz charts. Hancock's grip on the pop and black charts, however, would weaken throughout the decade. His success with *Future Shock* (Columbia 1983) and the hit single "Rockit" would reverse his downward commercial spin in the 1980s.

56. Lake, "Herbie Rides Again," 31.

57. Ibid. (emphasis added).

58. Thompson, *Head Hunters*, n.p.

59. Feld, "The Poetics and Politics of Pygmy Pop," 257–58.

60. See Feld, "Orality and Consciousness."

61. Lyons, "Herbie Hancock," 20.

62. Feld, "Schizophonia to Schismogenesis," 269.

63. Balleras, "Herbie Hancock's Current Choice," 16.

64. Ibid., 15.

65. Ibid., 16 (emphasis added).

66. Flanagan, "Herbie Hancock," 90.

67. Zabor and Garbarini, "Wynton vs. Herbie," 57.

68. Ibid., 64. While I do not take up this topic, it is interesting to note Marsalis's rhetorical double move here. In raising a private discussion in a public forum— while simultaneously advocating that the private discussion remain private— Marsalis has his cake and makes Hancock eat it, too. By this I mean, Marsalis

accuses Hancock that his sole, or primary, motivation for his fusion music is an economic one and then effectively forecloses Hancock's defense by averring, "We shouldn't be arguing about this in the press, man. We should be cool." Marsalis's casual "insider" status is also displayed by his use of *man* and *cool* rather than more formal terms of address. Finally, in revealing this private conversation, Marsalis indicates the distant, or at least oblique, nature of the relationship between jazz musicians and jazz writers. Tellingly, there isn't any mention of Wynton Marsalis's early recorded work on the Fuse One label—a CTI subsidiary that specialized in fusion—in this or any other interview or article, nor is it mentioned in his online discography.

69. Primack, "Herbie Hancock," 13.
70. Jagajivan, "Musing with Mwandishi," 14.

Conclusion

1. All lyrics in quotation marks from "Tea Leaf Prophecy," by Joni Mitchell.
2. Echols, "Thirty Years with a Portable Lover," 24.

bibliography

Adorno, Theodor, and Max Horkheimer. "The Culture Industry: Enlightenment as Mass Deception." In *Dialectic of Enlightenment*. New York: Continuum, 1993. Originally published as *Philosophische Fragmente* (New York: Institute of Social Research, 1944).

Ake, David. *Jazz Cultures*. Berkeley: University of California Press, 2002.

Albertson, Chris. "The Unmasking of Miles Davis." *Saturday Review*, Nov. 27, 1971.

Anderson, Chester. "Rock and the Counterculture." In Cateforis, *The Rock History Reader*, 99–102.

Anderson, Iain. "Jazz Outside the Marketplace: Free Improvisation and Nonprofit Sponsorship of the Arts, 1965–1980." *American Music* 20, no. 2 (summer 2002): 131–67.

———. "'This Is Our Music': Free Jazz, Cultural Hierarchy, and the Sixties." PhD diss., Indiana University, 2000. Ann Arbor: UMI, 2000 (9981054).

Armstrong, Isobel. *The Radical Aesthetic*. Oxford: Blackwell, 2000.

Auslander, Philip. *Performing Glam Rock: Gender and Theatricality in Popular Music*. Ann Arbor: University of Michigan Press, 2006.

Ayler, Albert. "'Free Music' . . . Discorded Chaos?" *Cleveland Call & Post*, Feb. 9, 1963.

Bailey, Beth, and David Farber, eds. *America in the Seventies*. Lawrence: University Press of Kansas, 2004.

Balleras, Jon. "Herbie Hancock's Current Choice." *Down Beat*, Sept. 1982.

Ballon, John. "Liberated Sister: Siren Betty Davis Found Funk as a Platform for Empowerment." *Wax Poetics*, April-May 2007.

Bannerji, Himani. "On the Dark Side of the Nation: Politics of Multiculturalism and the State of 'Canada.'" In Mookerjea, Szeman, and Faurschou, *Canadian Cultural Studies*, 327–43.

Baraka, Amiri (LeRoi Jones). *Black Music*. New York: Apollo-William Morrow, 1968.

———. *Blues People: Negro Music in White America*. New York: William Morrow, 1963.

Barker, Hugh, and Yuval Taylor. *Faking It: The Quest for Authenticity in Popular Music*. New York: W. W. Norton, 2007.

Beckett, Alan, and Richard Merton. "Stones/Comment." In Eisen, *The Age of Rock*, 109–17.

Beebe, Roger, Denise Fulbrook, and Ben Saunders, eds. *Rock over the Edge: Transformations in Popular Music Culture.* Durham: Duke University Press, 2002.

Belden, Bob. Liner notes. *The Inner Mounting Flame.* Sony, 1998. CD. Originally released by Columbia Records in 1971.

Berendt, Joachim. *The Jazz Book: From Ragtime to Fusion and Beyond.* Translated by H. Bredigkeit and B. Bredigkeit, with Dan Morgenstern and Tim Nevill. New York: Lawrence Hill, 1992.

Berg, Chuck. "John McLaughlin: Evolution of a Master." *Down Beat,* June 15, 1978.

Berkman, Franya. "Appropriating Universality: The Coltranes and Sixties Spirituality." *American Studies* 48, no. 1 (spring 2007): 41–62.

Berkowitz, Edward D. *Something Happened: A Political and Cultural Overview of the Seventies.* New York: Columbia University Press, 2006.

Berland, Jody. *North of Empire: Essays on the Cultural Technologies of Space.* Durham: Duke University Press, 2009.

Berle, Arnie. "Rick Laird: Jazz Bassist with Richie Cole, Buddy Rich, and the Mahavishnu Orchestra." *Guitar Player,* July 1980.

Berliner, Paul F. *Thinking in Jazz: The Infinite Art of Improvisation.* Chicago: University of Chicago Press, 1994.

Berry, Chuck. "In His Own Words." In Cateforis, *The Rock History Reader,* 3–13. Originally published in *Chuck Berry: The Autobiography* (New York: Harmony, 1987).

Bhabha, Homi. *The Location of Culture.* London: Routledge, 1998.

Blacking, John. *How Musical Is Man?* 1973. Seattle: University of Washington Press, 1995.

Bloom, Steve. "Second Generation of Fusion: The Melding of Musical Worlds with Spyro Gyra, Seawind, Auracle, Caldera." *Down Beat,* Aug. 9, 1979.

Bohlman, Philip. *World Music: A Very Short Introduction.* Oxford: Oxford University Press, 2002.

Bolden, Tony, ed. *The Funk Era and Beyond: New Perspectives on Black Popular Culture.* New York: Palgrave Macmillan, 2008.

———. "Theorizing the Funk: An Introduction." In Bolden, *The Funk Era and Beyond,* 13–29.

Bourdieu, Pierre. *Distinction: A Social Critique of the Judgement of Taste.* Translated by Richard Nice. Cambridge: Harvard University Press, 1984.

Bourne, Mike. "Big Band Rock and Other Brassy Beasties." *Down Beat,* Feb. 4, 1971.

———. "The Magic of Mahavishnu." *Down Beat,* June 8, 1972.

Brackett, David. "(In Search of) Musical Meaning: Genres, Categories and Crossover." In *Popular Music Studies,* edited by David Hesmondhalgh and Keith Negus, 65–83. London: Arnold-Oxford University Press, 2002.

———, comp. *The Pop, Rock, and Soul Reader.* New York: Oxford University Press, 2005.

Brett, Philip. "Musicality, Essentialism, and the Closet." In Brett, Wood, and Thomas, *Queering the Pitch,* 9–26.

Brett, Philip, Elizabeth Wood, and Gary C. Thomas, eds. *Queering the Pitch: The New Gay and Lesbian Musicology.* New York: Routledge, 1994.

Bromell, Nick. *Tomorrow Never Knows: Rock and Psychedelics in the 1960s.* Chicago: University of Chicago Press, 2000.

Brooks, Tim, and Richard Keith Spottswood. *Lost Sounds: Blacks and the Birth of the Recording Industry.* Champaign: University of Illinois Press, 2004.

Brown, Matthew. "Funk Music as Genre: Black Aesthetics, Apocalyptic Thinking and Urban Protest in Post-1965 African-American Pop." *Cultural Studies* 8, no. 3 (1994): 434–508.

Brown, Scot. "A Land of Funk: Dayton, Ohio." In Bolden, *The Funk Era and Beyond*, 73–88.

Browning, Barbara. *Infectious Rhythm: Metaphors of Contagion and the Spread of African Culture.* New York: Routledge, 1998.

Burns, Ken, dir. *Jazz: A Film by Ken Burns.* Florentine, 2000. DVD.

Burton, Gary. Interview. *Village Voice*, July 6, 1967.

Campbell, Laura. "Joni Chic." *Sunday Telegraph* (London), Feb. 8, 1998.

Carpenter, Carole H. "The Ethnicity Factor in Anglo-Canadian Folkloristics." In Diamond and Witmer, *Canadian Music*, 123–37.

Carr, Ian. *Miles Davis: The Definitive Biography.* New York: Thunder's Mouth, 1998.

Carroll, Jon. Review of *The Story of Rock*, by Carl Belz. *Rolling Stone*, Dec. 13, 1969.

Carroll, Peter N. *It Seemed Like Nothing Happened: The Tragedy and Promise of America in the 1970s.* New York: Holt, Rinehart, and Winston, 1982.

Carson, Annette. *Jeff Beck: Crazy Fingers.* New York: Backbeat Books, 2001.

Cateforis, Theo, ed. *The Rock History Reader.* New York: Routledge, 2007.

Chinmoy, Sri. *The Source of Music: Music and Mantra for Self-Realisation.* New York: Aum, 1995.

Cleveland, Barry. "Parallel Lines: A Conversation with Fusion Giants John McLaughlin and Allan Holdsworth." *Guitar Player*, Oct. 1, 2005.

Clifford, James. "Taking Identity Politics Seriously: 'The Contradictory, Stony Ground . . .'" In *Without Guarantees: In Honour of Stuart Hall*, edited by Paul Gilroy, Lawrence Grossberg, and Angela McRobbie, 94–112. London: Verso, 2000.

Cole, Bill. *John Coltrane.* New York: Da Capo, 2001.

Corea, Chick. "The Function of an Artist." *Down Beat*, Oct. 28, 1971.

———. "The Function of an Artist, Part II." *Down Beat*, May 10, 1973.

Coryell, Julie, and Laura Friedman. *Jazz-Rock Fusion: The People, the Music.* Milwaukee: Hal Leonard, 2000.

Covach, John. "Jazz-Rock? Rock-Jazz? Stylistic Crossover in Late-1970s American Progressive Rock." In *Expression in Pop-Rock Music: A Collection of Critical and Analytical Essays*, edited by Walter Everett, 113–34. New York: Garland, 2000.

Cox, Pat. "Tony Williams: An Interview Scenario." *Down Beat*, May 28, 1970.

Coyle, Michael. "Hijacked Hits and Antic Authenticity: Cover Songs, Race, and Post-war Marketing." In Beebe, Fulbrook, and Saunders, *Rock over the Edge*, 133–57.

Coyle, Michael, and Jon Dolan. "Modeling Authenticity, Authenticating Commercial Models." In *Reading Rock and Roll: Authenticity, Appropriation, Aesthetics*, edited by Kevin J. H. Dettmar and William Richey, 17–35. New York: Columbia University Press, 1999.

Crafts, Susan D., Daniel Cavicchi, and Charles Keil, eds. *My Music: Explorations of Music in Daily Life*. Middletown, Conn.: Wesleyan University Press, 1993.

Crowe, Cameron. "Joni Mitchell." In *The "Rolling Stone" Interviews, 1967–1980: Talking with the Legends of Rock & Roll*, edited by Peter Herbst, 376–91. New York: St. Martin's, 1981.

Cruz, Jon. *Culture on the Margins: The Black Spiritual and the Rise of American Cultural Interpretation*. Princeton: Princeton University Press, 1999.

Dahl, Linda. *Stormy Weather: The Music and Lives of a Century of Jazzwomen*. New York: Pantheon, 1984.

Dame, Joke. "Unveiled Voices: Sexual Difference and the Castrato." In Brett, Wood, and Thomas, *Queering the Pitch*, 139–53.

Danielsen, Anne. *Presence and Pleasure: The Funk Grooves of James Brown and Parliament*. Middletown, Conn.: Wesleyan University Press, 2006.

Davis, Angela. "Art on the Frontline." In *The Angela Davis Reader*, edited by Joy James, 235–47. Malden, Mass.: Blackwell, 1998.

———. *Blues Legacies and Black Feminism: Gertrude "Ma" Rainey, Bessie Smith, and Billie Holiday*. New York: Vintage-Random, 1998.

Davis, Francis. "The Book on Miles." *Atlantic Monthly*, Jan. 1990.

Davis, Miles, with Quincy Troupe. *The Autobiography*. New York: Simon and Schuster, 1989.

Davis, Stephen. "Mahavishnu's Inner Flame Mounts." *Rolling Stone*, March 30, 1972.

Degiorgio, Kirk. "Journeys into Space." *Wax Poetics*, spring 2008.

Demicheal, Don. "Miles Davis: The Rolling Stone Interview." *Rolling Stone*, Dec. 13, 1969.

Denisoff, R. Serge. *Solid Gold: The Popular Music Industry*. New Brunswick, N.J.: Transaction, 1982.

DeNora, Tia. *Music in Everyday Life*. Cambridge: Cambridge University Press, 2000.

Dent, Gina. "Black Pleasure, Black Joy: An Introduction." In *Black Popular Culture*, edited by Gina Dent, 1–19. Seattle: Bay Press, 1992.

Dery, Mark. "Black to the Future: Interviews with Samuel R. Delany, Greg Tate, and Tricia Rose." In *Flame Wars: The Discourse of Cyberculture*, edited by Mark Dery, 179–222. Durham: Duke University Press, 1994.

Dettmar, Kevin J. H., and William Richey, eds. *Reading Rock and Roll: Authenticity, Appropriation, Aesthetics*. New York: Columbia University Press, 1999.

DeVeaux, Scott. *The Birth of Bebop: A Social and Musical History*. Berkeley: University of California Press, 1997.

———. "Constructing the Jazz Tradition." *Black Music Research Journal* 25, no. 3 (1991): 525–60.

Diamond, Beverley, and Robert Witmer, eds. *Canadian Music: Issues of Hegemony and Identity*. Toronto: Canadian Scholars' Press, 1994.

Dickie, Mary. "No Borders Here." *Impact*, Dec. 1994.

DiMaggio, Paul. "Cultural Entrepreneurship in Nineteenth-Century Boston: The Creation of an Organizational Base for High Culture in America." In *Rethinking Popular Culture: Contemporary Perspectives in Cultural Studies*, edited by Chandra Mukerji and Michael Schudson, 374–97. Berkeley: University of California Press, 1991.

Doerschuk, Robert L. "Embrace the Tiger: Joni Mitchell Interview." *Musician*, Dec. 1998.

Echols, Alice. "Thirty Years with a Portable Lover." *Los Angeles Weekly*, Nov. 25, 1994.

Ehrlich, Dimitri. "Joni Mitchell." *Interview*, April 1991.

Eisen, Jonathan, ed. *The Age of Rock: Sounds of the American Cultural Revolution*. New York: Vintage-Random House, 1969.

Ellington, Edward Kennedy. *Music Is My Mistress*. New York: Da Capo, 1973.

———. "We, Too, Sing 'America.'" In *The Duke Ellington Reader*, edited by Mark Tucker, 146–48. New York: Oxford University Press, 1993.

Ellwood, Robert S. *Religious and Spiritual Groups in Modern America*. Englewood Cliffs, N.J.: Prentice-Hall, 1973.

———. *The Sixties Spiritual Awakening: American Religion Moving from Modern to Postmodern*. New Brunswick: Rutgers University Press, 1994.

Ephland, John. "Alternate Tunings." *Down Beat*, Dec. 1996.

———. "Tony Williams: Still, the Rhythm Magician." *Down Beat*, May 1989.

Eshun, Kodwo. *More Brilliant Than the Sun: Adventures in Sonic Fiction*. London: Quartet, 1998.

Everett, Walter, ed. *Expression in Pop-Rock Music: A Collection of Critical and Analytical Essays*. New York: Garland, 2000.

Farber, David. *The Columbia Guide to America in the 1960s*. New York: Columbia University Press, 2003.

Fawcett, Anthony. *California Rock, California Sound*. Los Angeles: Reed, 1978.

Feather, Leonard. "Blindfold Test: Larry Coryell." *Down Beat*, July 18, 1974.

———. "Blindfold Test, pt. 1: Gary Burton—Larry Coryell." *Down Beat*, March 7, 1968.

———. "Herbie's Set to Clear the Last Hurdle." *Melody Maker*, Aug. 16, 1969.

———. "Joni Mitchell Has Her Mojo Working." *Los Angeles Times*, June 10, 1979.

———. "Joni Mitchell Makes Mingus Sing." *Down Beat*, Sept. 6, 1979.

———. *The Passion for Jazz*. New York: Horizon, 1980.

————. *The Pleasures of Jazz*. New York: Horizon, 1976.

Feld, Steven. "From Schizophonia to Schismogenesis: On the Discourses and Commodification Practices of 'World Music' and 'World Beat.'" In Keil and Feld, *Music Grooves*, 257–89.

————. "Orality and Consciousness." In *The Oral and the Literate in Music*, edited by Tokumaru Yoshiihiko and Yamaguto Osamu, 18–28. Tokyo: Academia Music, 1986.

————. "The Poetics and Politics of Pygmy Pop." In *Western Music and Its Others: Difference, Representation, and Appropriation in Music*, edited by Georgina Born and David Hesmondhalgh, 254–79. Berkeley: University of California Press, 2000.

————. "Pygmy POP: A Genealogy of Schizophonic Mimesis." *Yearbook for Traditional Music* 28 (1996): 1–35.

Finkelstein, Sidney. *Jazz, a People's Music*. 1948. New York: International Publishers, 1988.

Flanagan, Bill. "Herbie Hancock: A Man for All Seasons." *Musician*, Jan. 1985.

————. "Joni Mitchell Loses Her Cool." *Musician*, Dec. 1985.

————. "Secret Places: Joni Mitchell Builds Shelter from the Rainstorm." *Musician*, May 1998.

Flowers, Ronald B. *Religion in Strange Times: The 1960s and 1970s*. Macon: Mercer University Press, 1984.

Floyd, Samuel A. *The Power of Black Music: Interpreting Its History from Africa to the United States*. New York: Oxford University Press, 1995.

Frith, Simon. "Music and Identity." In *Questions of Cultural Identity*, edited by Stuart Hall and Paul du Gay, 108–27. London: Sage, 1998.

————. *Performing Rites: On the Value of Popular Music*. Cambridge: Harvard University Press, 1996.

————. "Toward an Aesthetic of Popular Music." In *Music and Society: The Politics of Composition, Performance, and Reception*, edited by Richard Leppert and Susan McClary. Cambridge: Cambridge University Press, 1987.

Frith, Simon, Will Straw, and John Street, eds. *The Cambridge Companion to Pop and Rock*. Cambridge: Cambridge University Press, 2001.

Frye, Northrop. "Conclusion to the *Literary History of Canada*." In Mookerjea, Szeman, and Faurschou, *Canadian Cultural Studies*, 111–28.

Gabbard, Krin, ed. *Jazz among the Discourses*. Durham: Duke University Press, 1995.

————, ed. *Representing Jazz*. Durham: Duke University Press, 1995.

Gallagher, Bob. "Hancock's Half Hour." *Melody Maker*, Nov. 18, 1978.

Garbarini, Vic. "Joni Mitchell Is a Nervy Broad." *Musician*, Jan. 1983.

Garofalo, Reebee. "Black Popular Music: Crossing over or Going Under?" In *Rock and Popular Music: Politics, Policies, Institutions*, edited by Tony Bennett et al., 231–48. London: Routledge, 1995.

————. "Crossing Over: From Black Rhythm & Blues to White Rock 'n' Roll." In *R&B,*

Rhythm and Business: The Political Economy of Black Music, edited by Norman Kelley, 112–37. New York: Akashic, 2002.

Gendron, Bernard. *Between Montmartre and the Mudd Club: Popular Music and the Avant-Garde*. Chicago: University of Chicago Press, 2002.

———. "'Moldy Figs' and Modernists: Jazz at War (1942–1946)." In Gabbard, *Jazz among the Discourses*, 31–56.

Gennari, John. *Blowin' Hot and Cool: Jazz and Its Critics*. Chicago: University of Chicago Press, 2006.

Gibbs, Vernon. "Tony Williams: Report on a Musical Lifetime." *Down Beat*, Jan. 29, 1976.

Gillespie, John Birks "Dizzy," with Al Fraser. *To Be or Not to Bop: Memoirs*. New York: Doubleday, 1979.

Gilroy, Paul. *The Black Atlantic: Modernity and Double Consciousness*. Cambridge: Harvard University Press, 1999.

Gioia, Ted. *The History of Jazz*. New York: Oxford University Press, 1997.

———. *West Coast Jazz: Modern Jazz in California, 1945–1960*. Berkeley: University of California Press, 1998.

Gitlin, Todd. *The Sixties: Years of Hope, Days of Rage*. Toronto: Bantam, 1987.

Glasser, Brian. *In a Silent Way: A Portrait of Joe Zawinul*. London: Sanctuary, 2001.

Gleason, Ralph J. "Like a Rolling Stone." In Eisen, *The Age of Rock*, 61–76.

———. Liner notes. *The Complete "Bitches Brew" Sessions*. Sony, 1998. CD.

———. Liner notes. *Emergency!* Verve-Polygram, 1997, CD. Originally released by Polydor-Polygram in 1969.

Goldberg, David Theo, ed. *Multiculturalism: A Critical Reader*. Oxford: Blackwell, 1994.

Gosse, Van, and Richard Moser. *The World the Sixties Made: Politics and Culture in Recent America*. Philadelphia: Temple University Press, 2003.

Gottlieb, Robert, ed. *Reading Jazz: A Gathering at Autobiography, Reportage, and Criticism from 1919 to Now*. New York: Pantheon, 1996.

Gracyk, Theodore. *Rhythm and Noise: An Aesthetics of Rock*. Durham: Duke University Press, 1996.

Gray, Herman. *Cultural Moves: African Americans and the Politics of Representation*. Berkeley: University of California Press, 2005.

———. "Jazz Tradition, Institutional Formation, and Cultural Practice: The Canon and the Street as Frameworks for Oppositional Black Cultural Politics." In *Sociology to Cultural Studies: New Perspectives*, edited by Elizabeth Long, 351–73. Malden, Mass.: Blackwell, 1997.

Gridley, Mark. *Jazz Styles: History and Analysis*. 9th ed. Upper Saddle River, N.J.: Prentice-Hall, 2006.

Guilbault, Jocelyne. *Zouk: World Music in the West Indies*. Chicago: University of Chicago Press, 1993.

Guralnick, Peter. *Last Train to Memphis: The Rise of Elvis Presley*. Boston: Little, Brown, 1994.

Hale, Jeff A. "The White Panthers' 'Total Assault on the Culture.'" In *Imagine Nation: The American Counterculture of the 1960s and '70s*, edited by Peter Braunstein and Michael William Doyle, 125–56. New York: Routledge, 2002.

Haley, Alex. "Miles Davis: September 1962." In *The "Playboy" Interviews*, edited by Murray Fisher, 3–12. New York: Ballantine, 1993.

Hall, Carla. "The New Joni Mitchell: The Songbird of Woodstock Soars into Jazz." *Washington Post*, Aug. 25, 1979.

Hall, Gregg. "Teo . . . the Man behind the Scene." *Down Beat*, July 16, 1974.

Hall, Stuart. "New Ethnicities." In *"Race," Culture and Difference*, edited by James Donald and Ali Rattansi, 252–59. London: Sage, 1992.

———. "On Postmodernism and Articulation: An Interview with Stuart Hall." In *Stuart Hall: Critical Dialogues in Cultural Studies*, edited by David Morley and Kuan-Hsing Chen, 131–50. London: Routledge, 1997.

Hancock, Herbie. "Herbie Hancock Demonstrates the Rhodes Sound." Fender Rhodes, 1973. Flexi-disc. The recording was distributed as part of a 1973 Fender Rhodes electric piano advertising campaign.

———. Liner notes. *Head Hunters*. Sony, 1997. CD. Originally released by Columbia Records in 1973.

Heckman, Don. "Herbie Hancock: Watermelon Man." *Down Beat*, Oct. 21, 1965. Repr. in *Down Beat: 60 Years of Jazz*, edited by Frank Alkyer, 131–33. Milwaukee: Hal Leonard, 1995. Page citations refer to the reprint.

Heineman, Alan. Review of *Right On*. *Down Beat*, Dec. 11, 1969.

Heineman, Alan, and Dan Morgenstern. "Rock, Jazz, and Newport: An Exchange." *Down Beat*, Dec. 25, 1969.

Henderson, Bill. "Meterology and Me: The Joe Zawinul Interview." *Black Music & Jazz Review*, Dec. 1978.

———. "The One Truth and the Absolute Truth." *Black Music & Jazz Review*, Dec. 1978.

Henderson, Stuart. "'All Pink and Clean and Full of Wonder?' Gendering 'Joni Mitchell,' 1966–74." *Left History* 10, no. 2 (fall 2005): 83–109.

Hentoff, Nat. *The Jazz Life*. 1961. New York: Da Capo, 1975.

———. Liner notes. *Speak like a Child*. Blue Note, 1968. LP.

Herrington, Tony. "Tomorrow People." *The Wire*, Aug. 1998.

Hirshey, Gerri. "Women Who Rocked the World." *Rolling Stone*, Nov. 13, 1997.

Hodeir, André. *Jazz: Its Evolution and Essence*. Translated by David Noakes. New York: Grove, 1956.

Hoefer, George. "Larry Coryell: Now!" *Down Beat*, June 29, 1967.

Hohman, Marv, and Charles Mitchell, eds. "*Down Beat* in Review: A Collection of Lunacy, Prophecy, Controversy, and Commentary from 42 Years of the Contemporary Music Magazine." *Down Beat*, July 15, 1976.

Holmes, Thom. *Electronic and Experimental Music: Technology, Music, and Culture.* New York: Routledge, 2008.

Holm-Hudson, Kevin. "Apocalyptic Otherness: Black Music and Extraterrestrial Identity in the Music of Magma." *Popular Music and Society*, Dec. 2003.

Holt, Fabian. *Genre in Popular Music.* Chicago: University of Chicago Press, 2007.

Hoskyns, Barney. "Our Lady of the Sorrows." *Mojo*, Dec. 1994.

Hurwitz, Robert. "John McLaughlin's Immaculate Conception." *Creem*, June 1972.

Isaacs, James. Liner notes. *Tony Williams: Once in a Lifetime.* Verve, 1982. LP.

Jackson, Joe. "Witness of Life." *Irish Times*, Feb. 6, 1999.

Jackson, Travis A. " 'Always New and Centuries Old': Jazz, Poetry, and Tradition as Creative Adaptation." In *Uptown Conversation: The New Jazz Studies*, edited by Robert G. O'Meally, Brent Hayes Edwards, and Farah Jasmine Griffin, 357–73. New York: Columbia University Press, 2004.

Jagajivan. "Musing with Mwandishi." *Down Beat*, May 24, 1973.

Johnson, Brooks. "Herbie Hancock: Into His Own Thing." *Down Beat*, Jan. 21, 1971.

Joni Mitchell: Woman of Heart and Mind. Directed by Susan Lacy. Eagle Vision, 2003. DVD.

Katz, Mark. *Capturing Sound: How Technology Has Changed Music.* Berkeley: University of California Press, 2004.

Kauffman, Linda S., ed. *American Feminist Thought at Century's End: A Reader.* Cambridge, Mass.: Blackwell, 1993.

Keightley, Keir. "Reconsidering Rock." In Frith, Straw, and Street, *The Cambridge Companion to Pop and Rock*, 109–42.

Keil, Charles, and Steven Feld. *Music Grooves.* Chicago: University of Chicago Press, 1994.

Kelley, Norman, ed. *Rhythm and Business: The Political Economy of Black Music.* New York: Akashic, 2002.

Kelley, Robin D. G. *Race Rebels: Culture, Politics, and the Black Working Class.* New York: Free Press, 1996.

Kenney, William Howland. "Historical Context and the Definition of Jazz: Putting More of the History in 'Jazz History.' " In Gabbard, *Jazz among the Discourses*, 100–116.

———. *Recorded Music in American Life: The Phonograph and Popular Memory, 1890–1945.* New York: Oxford University Press, 1999.

Kettlewell, Ben. *Electronic Music Pioneers.* Vallejo, Calif.: artistpro.com, 2001.

Klee, Joe H. "Dreams Come Through." *Down Beat*, Nov. 12, 1970.

Kofsky, Frank. *Black Music, White Business: Illuminating the History and Political Economy of Jazz.* New York: Pathfinder, 1998.

———. *Black Nationalism and the Revolution in Music.* New York: Pathfinder, 1970.

———. *John Coltrane and the Jazz Revolution of the 1960s.* New York: Pathfinder, 1998.

Korall, Burt. "Extending beyond Mahavishnu." *Down Beat*, June 7, 1973.

Koransky, Jason. "Lighting the Future." *Down Beat*, Aug. 2003.

Lake, Steve. "Herbie Rides Again." *Melody Maker*, Aug. 10, 1974.

———. "Soul Food: Headhunter's Conversion." *Melody Maker*, July 24, 1976.

———. "Wah-Wah Jazz and All That Rock!" *Melody Maker*, Aug. 17, 1974.

Lee, Martin A., and Bruce Shlain. *Acid Dreams: The Complete Social History of LSD: The CIA, the Sixties, and Beyond*. Rev. ed. New York: Grove, 1986.

Lees, Gene. *Cats of Any Color: Jazz, Black and White*. Oxford: Oxford University Press, 1995.

Leonard, Neil. *Jazz and the White Americans: The Acceptance of a New Art Form*. 3rd ed. Chicago: University of Chicago Press, 1972.

Levine, Lawrence. *Black Culture and Black Consciousness: Afro-American Folk Thought from Slavery to Freedom*. Oxford: Oxford University Press, 1977.

Levy, Adam. "True Believer: John McLaughlin Reaffirms His Faith in Improvisation." *WBTG Articles: True Believer*, Aug. 10, 2003. www.italway.it/morrone/jml-TrueBeliever.htm.

Lewis, George E. "Purposive Patterning: Jeff Donaldson, Muhal Richard Abrams, and the Multidominance of Consciousness." *Lenox Avenue: A Journal of Interarts Inquiry* 5 (1999): 63–69.

Lipsitz, George. *Dangerous Crossroads: Popular Music, Postmodernism and the Poetics of Place*. London: Verso, 1994.

———. *The Possessive Investment in Whiteness: How White People Profit from Identity Politics*. Philadelphia: Temple University Press, 1998.

Lopes, Paul. *The Rise of a Jazz Art World*. Cambridge: Cambridge University Press, 2002.

Lott, Eric. *Love & Theft: Blackface Minstrelsy and the American Working Class*. New York: Oxford University Press, 1993.

Lott, Tommy Lee. "The 1960s Avant-Garde Movement in Jazz." *Social Identities* 7, no. 2 (2001): 1–11.

Luftig, Stacy, ed. *The Joni Mitchell Companion: Four Decades of Commentary*. New York: Schirmer, 2000.

Lyons, Len. "Herbie Hancock: Keyboard Wizard." *Contemporary Keyboard*, Nov.-Dec. 1975.

Macan, Edward. *Rocking the Classics: English Progressive Rock and the Counterculture*. New York: Oxford University Press, 1997.

Mahon, Maureen. *Right to Rock: The Black Rock Coalition and the Cultural Politics of Race*. Durham: Duke University Press, 2004.

Mailer, Norman. "The White Negro: Superficial Reflections on the Hipster." In *Advertisements for Myself*, 337–58. New York: Putnam, 1959. Originally published in *Dissent* (1957).

Mandel, Howard. "Gayle Moran." *Down Beat*, July 14, 1977.

———. Liner notes. *Extrapolation*. Polygram, 1991. CD.

———. "Sketches of Miles." *Down Beat*, Dec. 1991.

Marcus, Greil. *Mystery Train: Images of America in Rock 'n' Roll*. London: Omnibus, 1977.

McClary, Susan. *Feminine Endings: Music, Gender, and Sexuality*. Minneapolis: University of Minnesota Press, 1991.

McDermott, John. Liner notes. *Spectrum: The Anthology*. Verve, 1997. CD.

McDonald, Marci. "Joni Mitchell Emerges from Her Retreat." *Toronto Star*, Feb. 9, 1974.

McIntosh, Peggy. "White Privilege and Male Privilege: A Personal Account of Coming to See Correspondences through Work in Women's Studies." Working Paper no. 189. Wellesley College Center for Research on Women, 1988.

McLuhan, Marshall. "Canada as Counter-Environment." In Mookerjea, Szeman, and Faurschou, *Canadian Cultural Studies*, 71–86.

Meltzer, Richard. *The Aesthetics of Rock*. 1970. New York: Da Capo, 1987.

Middleton, Richard. "Locating the People: Music and the Popular." In *The Cultural Study of Music: A Critical Introduction*, edited by Martin Clayton, Trevor Herbert, and Richard Middleton, 251–62. New York: Routledge, 2003.

Milkowski, Bill. *Jaco: The Extraordinary and Tragic Life of Jaco Pastorius*. San Francisco: Miller Freeman, 1995.

———. "A Master's Perspective." *Modern Drummer*, July 1992.

———. "Past, Present, and Future." *JazzTimes*, July-Aug. 1992.

Miller, James. *Democracy Is in the Streets: From Port Huron to the Siege of Chicago*. Cambridge: Harvard University Press, 1994.

Mingus, Charles. *Beneath the Underdog: His World as Composed by Mingus*. 1971. New York: Vintage-Random, 1991.

———. "Interview." *Down Beat*, May 26, 1960.

Mingus, Sue Graham. *Tonight at Noon: A Love Story*. New York: Da Capo, 2002.

Modirzadeh, Hafez. "Aural Archetypes and Cyclic Perspectives in the Work of John Coltrane and Ancient Chinese Musical Theory." *Black Music Research Journal* 21, no. 1 (spring 2001): 75–105.

Monson, Ingrid. "The Problem with White Hipness: Race, Gender, and Cultural Conceptions in Jazz Historical Discourse." *Journal of the American Musicological Society* 48 (fall 1995): 396–422.

———. *Saying Something: Jazz Improvisation and Interaction*. Chicago: University of Chicago Press, 1996.

Mookerjea, Sourayan, Imre Szeman, and Gail Faurschou, eds. *Canadian Cultural Studies: A Reader*. Durham: Duke University Press, 2009.

Moon, Lindsay, transcriber. "Joni Mitchell Interview for Canadian Broadcast Company 'Magazine.'"

———, transcriber. "Words and Music: Joni Mitchell and Morrissey."

Moorefield, Virgil. *The Producer as Composer: Shaping the Sounds of Popular Music*. Cambridge: MIT Press, 2005.

Moraga, Cherríe L., and Gloria E. Anzaldúa, eds. *This Bridge Called My Back: Writings by Radical Women of Color*. Berkeley: Third Woman, 2002.

Morgenstern, Dan. "A Message to Our Readers." *Down Beat*, June 29, 1967.

———. "Miles in Motion." *Down Beat*, Sept. 3, 1970.

———. "Oscar, Cannonball, Mahavishnu." *Down Beat*, Sept. 14, 1972.

———. "Rotating with Satchmo and Miles." *Metronome*, June 1961.

Morgenstern, Dan, and Ira Gitler. "Newport '69: Bad Trip." *Down Beat*, Aug. 21, 1969.

Morgenstern, Dan, and Jim Szantor. "Newport in New York." *Down Beat*, Sep. 14, 1972.

Neer, Richard. FM: *The Rise and Fall of Rock Radio*. New York: Random House, 2001.

Negus, Keith. *Music Genres and Corporate Cultures*. London: Routledge, 1999.

———. *Popular Music in Theory: An Introduction*. Hanover, N.H.: Wesleyan University Press, 1996.

———. *Producing Pop: Culture and Conflict in the Popular Music Industry*. London: Arnold, 2001.

Ness, Bob. "Have You Dug . . . Larry Coryell." *Down Beat*, May 9, 1974.

Nettl, Bruno. *The Study of Ethnomusicology: Thirty-One Issues and Concepts*. Urbana: University of Illinois Press, 2005.

Nicholson, Stuart. *Jazz Rock: A History*. New York: Schirmer, 1998.

———. "The Song of the Body Electric." In Yuval Taylor, *The Future of Jazz*, 43–63.

Nisenson, Eric. *Ascension: John Coltrane and His Quest*. New York: Da Capo, 1995.

North, Adrian, David J. Hargreaves, and Jon J. Hargreaves. "Uses of Music in Everyday Life." *Music Perception* 22, no. 1 (fall 2004): 41–77.

O'Brien, Karen. *Shadows and Light: Joni Mitchell, the Definitive Biography*. London: Virgin, 2002.

Palmer, Bob. "Jazz/Rock '74: The Plain Funky Truth." *Rolling Stone*, Aug. 1, 1974.

Panassié, Hugues. *Hot Jazz; The Guide to Swing Music*. Translated by Lyle Dowling and Eleanor Dowling. 1936. New York: Greenwood, 1970. Originally published as *Le jazz hot* (Paris: Éditions R.-A. Corrêa, 1934).

Point, Michael. "Tony Williams: The Final Interview." *Down Beat*, April 1997.

Pond, Steven F. *"Head Hunters": The Making of Jazz's First Platinum Recording*. Ann Arbor: University of Michigan Press, 2006.

———. "Herbie Hancock's 'Head Hunters': Troubling the Waters of Jazz." PhD diss., University of California, Berkeley, 2000. Ann Arbor: UMI, 2001 (9981127).

Porter, Eric. "Affirming and Disaffirming Actions: Remaking Race in the 1970s." In *America in the Seventies*, edited by Beth Bailey and David Farber, 50–74. Lawrence: University Press of Kansas, 2004.

———. *What Is This Thing Called Jazz? African American Musicians as Artists, Critics, and Activists*. Berkeley: University of California Press, 2002.

Porter, Lewis. *Jazz: A Century of Change*. New York: Schirmer, 1997.

————. *John Coltrane: His Life and Music*. Ann Arbor: University of Michigan Press, 1999.

Prasad, Anil. *Innerviews, Music without Borders: Extraordinary Conversations with Extraordinary Musicians*. Cary, N.C.: Abstract Logix, 2010.

————. "Remembering Shakti." In *Innerviews, Music without Borders*, 155–68.

————. "Remember Shakti: Four People as One." Innerviews: Music without Borders. www.innerviews.org/inner/shakti.html.

Priestley, Brian. *Mingus: A Critical Biography*. New York: Da Capo, 1982.

Primack, Bert. "Herbie Hancock: Chameleon in His Disco Phase." *Down Beat*, May 17, 1979.

————. "Remembering Miles." *JazzTimes*, Feb. 1992.

Prouty, Kenneth E. "Orality, Literacy, and Mediating Musical Experience: Rethinking Oral Tradition in the Learning of Jazz Improvisation." *Popular Music and Society* 29, no. 3 (July 2006): 317–34.

Radano, Ronald M. *Lying Up a Nation: Race and Black Music*. Chicago: University of Chicago Press, 2003.

Radano, Ronald M., and Philip V. Bohlman, eds. *Music and the Racial Imagination*. Chicago: University of Chicago Press, 2000.

Ramsey, Guthrie P., Jr. *Race Music: Black Cultures from Bebop to Hip-Hop*. Berkeley: University of California Press, 2003.

Rasula, Jed. "The Media of Memory: The Seductive Menace of Records in Jazz History." In Gabbard, *Jazz among the Discourses*, 134–62.

Rath, Richard Cullen. *How Early America Sounded*. Ithaca: Cornell University Press, 2003.

Reder, Alan, and John Baxter. *Listen to This! Leading Musicians Recommend Their Favorite Artists and Recordings*. New York: Hyperion, 1999.

Rensin, David. "Cruisin' with the Guru: The Backseat Revelations of Carlos Santana and Mahavishnu John McLaughlin." *Creem*, March 1974.

Rideout, Ernie. "Master Class: Herbie Hancock." *Keyboard*, Feb. 2002.

Robbins, James. "What Can We Learn When They Sing, Eh? Ethnomusicology in the American State of Canada." In Diamond and Witmer, *Canadian Music*, 193–202.

Roberts, John Storm. *Latin Jazz: The First of the Fusions, 1880s to Today*. New York: Schirmer, 1999.

"Rock Too Much For Newport." *Rolling Stone*, Aug. 9, 1969.

Rohter, Larry. "Jeff Beck: The Progression of a True Progressive." *Down Beat*, June 16, 1977.

Rosenthal, David H. *Hard Bop: Jazz & Black Music, 1955–1965*. New York: Oxford University Press, 1992.

————. "Hard Bop and Its Critics." *Black Perspective in Music* 16, no. 1 (spring 1988): 21–29.

Roszak, Theodore. *The Making of a Counter Culture: Reflections on the Technocratic Society and Its Youthful Opposition.* 1968. Berkeley: University of California Press, 1995.

Rowland, Mark, et al. "Sketches of Miles." *Musician*, Dec. 1991.

Rozek, Michael. "Caught . . . McLaughlin's Shakti and Weather Report: Some Defused Fusions." *Down Beat*, June 17, 1976.

Rusch, Bob. "Hodgepodge and Shorties." *Cadence*, March 1976.

Sales, Grover. *Jazz: America's Classical Music.* New York: Prentice Hall, 1984.

Sandford, Christopher. *Keith Richards: Satisfaction.* New York: Da Capo, 2004.

Santoro, Gene. *Myself When I Am Real: The Life and Music of Charles Mingus.* New York: Oxford University Press, 2000.

Sargeant, Winthrop. "Is Jazz Music?" *American Mercury* 57, no. 238 (Oct. 1943): 403–9. Repr. in *The Duke Ellington Reader*, edited by Mark Tucker, 207–8. New York: Oxford University Press, 1993.

———. *Jazz, Hot and Hybrid.* 3rd ed., enlarged. New York: Da Capo-Plenum, 1976.

Saul, Scott. *Freedom Is, Freedom Ain't: Jazz and the Making of the Sixties.* Cambridge: Harvard University Press, 2003.

Scanlan, Tom. "The Impeccable Mr. Wilson." *Down Beat*, Sept. 2009. Originally published in *Down Beat*, Jan. 22, 1959.

Schaffer, Jim. "An Innermost Vision." *Down Beat*, April 26, 1973.

———. "Mahavishnu Apocalypse." *Down Beat*, June 6, 1974.

Schulman, Bruce J. *The Seventies: The Great Shift in American Culture, Society, and Politics.* New York: Da Capo, 2001.

Shank, Barry. "From Rice to Ice: The Face of Race in Rock and Pop." In Frith, Straw, and Street, *The Cambridge Companion to Pop and Rock*, 256–71.

Shapiro, Peter. "Interview: Teo Macero." In *Modulations: A History of Electronic Music: Throbbing Words on Sound*, edited by Peter Shapiro and Iara Lee, 54–55. New York: Caipirinha, 2000.

Shipton, Alyn. *A New History of Jazz.* London: Continuum, 2001.

Sidran, Ben. *Black Talk.* New York: Da Capo, 1981.

Slemon, Stephen. "Unsettling the Empire: Resistance Theory for the Second World." *Journal of Postcolonial Writing* 30, no. 2 (1990): 30–41.

Small, Christopher. *Musicking: The Meanings of Performing and Listening.* Hanover, N.H.: Wesleyan University Press, 1998.

———. *Music of the Common Tongue: Survival and Celebration in African American Music.* Hanover, N.H.: Wesleyan University Press, 1998.

Smith, Arnold Jay. "Brian Torff." *Down Beat*, June 17, 1976.

Snyder-Scumpy, Patrick, and Frank DeLigio. "Two Sides to Every Satori." *Crawdaddy!*, Nov. 1973.

Spellman, A. B. *Black Music: Four Lives.* New York: Schocken, 1970.

———. *Four Lives in the Bebop Business.* New York: Pantheon, 1985.

Stearns, Marshall W. *The Story of Jazz.* New York: Oxford University Press, 1956.

Stephen, Bill. "The Cultural Improvisation of John McLaughlin." *Int'l. Musician and Recording World*, March 1979. www.italway.it/morrone/JmL-Cultural.htm.

Sterne, Jonathan. *The Audible Past: The Cultural Origins of Sound Reproduction*. Durham: Duke University Press, 2002.

Stewart, Zan. "Herbie's Search for New Standards." *Down Beat*, April 1996.

Stix, John. "Jan Hammer: McLaughlin, Beck, and Beyond . . ." *Contemporary Keyboard*, Aug. 1976.

Stokes, Martin, ed. *Ethnicity, Identity, and Music: The Musical Construction of Place*. Oxford: Berg, 1997.

Strongin, Dan. "Herbie Hancock." *Jazz & Pop*, Oct. 1970.

Stump, Paul. *Go Ahead John: The Music of John McLaughlin*. London: SAF, 1999.

————. *The Music's All That Matters: A History of Progressive Rock*. London: Quartet, 1998.

Suber, Charles. "Gary Burton's Back-Home Bag." *Down Beat*, Feb. 17, 1972.

Such, David G. *Avant-Garde Jazz Musicians: Performing "Out There."* Iowa City: University of Iowa Press, 1993.

Sutcliffe, Phil. "Joni Mitchell." In Luftig, *The Joni Mitchell Companion*, 139–52.

Swartley, Ariel. "The Babe in Bopperland and the Great Jazz Composer." *Rolling Stone*, Sept. 6, 1979.

Sylvan, Robin. *Traces of the Spirit: The Religious Dimensions of Popular Music*. New York: New York University Press, 2002.

Szantor, Jim. "Chase: Brass Roots Jazz Rock." *Down Beat*, Feb. 4, 1971.

Szwed, John. *So What: The Life of Miles Davis*. New York: Simon and Schuster, 2002.

Tate, Greg. "Black and Blond." *Vibe*, Dec. 1998 / Jan. 1999.

————. *Flyboy in the Buttermilk: Essays on Contemporary America*. New York: Simon and Schuster, 1992.

————. "The Long Run." *Vibe*, Feb. 1997.

Taylor, Arthur. *Notes and Tones: Musician-to-Musician Interviews*. Exp. ed. New York: Da Capo, 1993.

Taylor, Billy. "America's Classical Music." In Walser, *Keeping Time*, 327–32.

Taylor, Clyde R. *The Mask of Art: Breaking the Aesthetic Contract — Film and Literature*. Bloomington: Indiana University Press, 1998.

Taylor, Timothy D. *Beyond Exoticism: Western Music and the World*. Durham: Duke University Press, 2007.

————. *Global Pop: World Music, World Markets*. New York: Routledge, 1997.

————. *Strange Sounds: Music, Technology and Culture*. London: Routledge, 2001.

Taylor, Yuval, ed. *The Future of Jazz*. Chicago: A Cappella, 2002.

Tesser, Neil. Review of *Mingus*, by Joni Mitchell. *Down Beat*, Aug. 9, 1979.

Théberge, Paul. *Any Sound You Can Imagine: Making Music / Consuming Technology*. Hanover, N.H.: Wesleyan University Press, 1997.

Thompson, Scott H. Liner notes. *Head Hunters*. Sony, 1997. CD. Originally released by Columbia Records in 1973.

Toner, John. "Chick Corea." *Down Beat*, March 28, 1974.

Townley, Ray. "Hancock Plugs In." *Down Beat*, Oct. 24, 1974.

Towns, Mark. "John McLaughlin Interview with Mark Towns." *Jazz Houston*, Sept. 21, 2003.

Townsend, Peter. "Free Jazz: Musical Style and Liberationist Ethic, 1956–1965." In Ward, *Media, Culture, and the Modern African American Freedom Struggle*, 145–60.

Trigger, Vic. "Mahavishnu John McLaughlin." *Guitar Player*, Dec. 19, 1972.

Tucker, Mark, ed. *The Duke Ellington Reader*. New York: Oxford University Press, 1993.

Tucker, Sherrie. *Swing Shift: "All-Girl" Bands of the 1940s*. Durham: Duke University Press, 2000.

Underwood, Lee. "Profile: L. Shankar." *Down Beat*, Nov. 2, 1978.

———. "Tony Williams: Aspiring to a Lifetime of Leadership." *Down Beat*, June 21, 1979.

Valentine, Penny. "Exclusive Joni Mitchell Interview." In Luftig, *The Joni Mitchell Companion*, 45–55.

Vincent, Rickey. *Funk: The Music, the People, and the Rhythm of The One*. New York: St. Martin's Griffin, 1996.

Von Eschen, Penny. *Satchmo Blows Up the World: Jazz Ambassadors Play the Cold War*. Cambridge: Harvard University Press, 2004.

Waksman, Steve. *Instruments of Desire: The Electric Guitar and the Shaping of Musical Experience*. Cambridge: Harvard University Press, 1999.

Walser, Robert, ed. *Keeping Time: Readings in Jazz History*. New York: Oxford University Press, 1999.

———. *Running with the Devil: Power, Gender, and Madness in Heavy Metal Music*. Hanover, N.H.: University Press of New England, 1993.

Ward, Brian. "Jazz and Soul, Race and Class, Cultural Nationalists and Black Panthers: A Black Power Debate Revisited." In Ward, *Media, Culture, and the Modern African American Freedom Struggle*, 161–96.

———. *Just My Soul Responding: Rhythm and Blues, Black Consciousness, and Race Relations*. Berkeley: University of California Press, 1998.

———, ed. *Media, Culture, and the Modern African American Freedom Struggle*. Gainesville: University Press of Florida, 2001.

Washburne, Christopher. "Does Kenny G Play Bad Jazz? A Case Study." In *Bad Music: The Music We Love to Hate*, edited by Christopher Washburne and Maiken Derno, 123–47. New York: Routledge, 2004.

Wattstax. Directed by Mel Stuart. Columbia Pictures, 1973.

Wein, George, with Nate Chinen. *Myself among Others: A Life in Music*. New York: Da Capo, 2004.

West, Michael J. "Jazz Workshop: In Defense of Fusion, Part 2 — On the Rock Side." *Blogcritics*. http://blogcritics.org/archives/2007/06/25/090515.php.

Whitesell, Lloyd. *The Music of Joni Mitchell*. Oxford: Oxford University Press, 2008.

Wicke, Peter. *Rock Music: Culture, Aesthetics and Sociology.* Cambridge: Cambridge University Press, 1990.

Williams, Martin. *The Art of Jazz.* New York: Oxford University Press, 1959.

———. *The Jazz Tradition.* New York: Oxford University Press, 1983.

———. *Where's the Melody? A Listener's Introduction to Jazz.* New York: Pantheon, 1966.

Williams, Paul. "Along Comes Maybe." *Crawdaddy!*, Aug. 1966.

Williams, Richard. "Herbie: Jazz, Jingles and Rock." *Melody Maker*, Aug. 29, 1970.

———. "Williams and His Electric Rhythms." *Melody Maker*, Aug. 29, 1970.

Wilmer, Valerie. *As Serious as Your Life: John Coltrane and Beyond.* London: Serpent's Tail, 1992.

Wilson, Olly. "The Heterogeneous Sound Ideal in African-American Music." In *New Perspectives on Music: Essays in Honor of Eileen Southern*, edited by Josephine Wright and Samuel A. Floyd Jr., 327–38. Warren, Mich.: Harmonie Park, 1992.

Wong, Herb. Liner notes. *The Prisoner.* Blue Note, 1969. LP.

Woods, Stu. "Tony Williams Interview." *Jazz and Pop*, Jan. 1970.

Woodward, Josef. "Herbie & Quincy: Talkin' 'bout the Music of These Times." *Down Beat*, Jan. 1990.

———. "John McLaughlin's Life in the Emerald Beyond." *Musician*, March 1987.

Worby, Robert. "Cacophony." In *Music, Electronic Media and Culture*, edited by Simon Emmerson, 138–63. Aldershot, U.K.: Ashgate, 2000.

Wright, Amy Nathan. "A Philosophy of Funk: The Politics and Pleasure of a Parliafunkadelicment Thang!" In Bolden, *The Funk Era and Beyond*, 33–50.

Zabor, Rafi, and Vic Garbarini. "Wynton vs. Herbie: The Purist and the Crossbreeder Duke It Out." *Musician*, March 1985.

Zwerin, Michael. Liner notes. *Duster.* RCA, 1967. LP.

———. "Mona Lisa with Moustache." *Village Voice*, July 6, 1967.

Both/And (club), 32
"Both Sides, Now" (Hancock), 222–23
"Both Sides, Now" (Mitchell), 148, 150
Both Sides, Now (Mitchell), 160
Boulanger, Lili, 194
Bourdieu, Pierre, 20, 246n44
Bowie, Lester, 216–17
Brackett, David, 16, 48
Brain Salad Surgery (Emerson, Lake and
    Palmer), 240n28
Brand X (group), 19, 29
Brecht, Bertolt, 50
Brecker, Michael, 28, 153
Brecker Brothers (group), 27
Brenston, Jackie, 47
Brett, Philip, 89
broken middles, 8–9, 11, 17, 68, 118, 137,
    224
Bromell, Nick, 52, 78–79, 85
Brown, James, 55–57, 64, 67, 88–89, 121,
    188, 242n64
Brown, Matthew, 55–56, 58
Brown, Sam, 80
Brown, Scot, 62
Brubeck, Dave, 2
Bruce, Jack, 108, 115, 118, 137, 248n63
Bruford, Bill, 74, 149, 240n28
Bruford (group), 19
Buchla, Don, 83
Buddhism, 184, 187, 200, 220, 261n47
Buffalo, Norton, 31
Bull, Sandy, 50
Burns, Ken, 41
Burton, Gary, 31, 67, 74–77, 80, 86–87,
    131, 150, 218
Butler, George, 217
Byrd, Donald, 187, 192, 212
Byrd, Robert "Professor Longhair," 47
The Byrds, 104
Byrne, David, 124

Cage, John, 34
California Dreamin' (Montgomery), 82

Cameo (group), 57
Campbell, Laura, 152
Canada, 149–50, 160, 164–67
"Cantaloop" (Us3), 30
"Cantaloupe Island" (Hancock), 30,
    196
Capaldi, Jim, 29
Carlos, Walter, 202, 261n31
Carpenter, Carole, 160, 165–66
Carroll, Jon, 71, 117
Carter, Ron, 106–7, 111, 217
Cash, Johnny, 48–49, 168
Castillo, Emilio, 59
Catalyst (group), 11
"Centerpiece" (Mandel and Hendricks),
    160
"A Chair in the Sky" (Mitchell), 175–76
"Chameleon" (Hancock), 183, 207
Charlie Haden's Liberation Orchestra,
    115
Chase (group), 27, 81–82
"Chelsea Morning" (Mitchell), 157
Chicago (group), 27
Christgau, Robert, 104
Christian, Charlie, 116
"The Circle Game" (Mitchell), 148
Civil Rights Act of 1964, 53, 56, 115
Clark, Dick, 93
Clarke, Stanley, 28
class, 15, 20, 30, 37, 39–40, 43–44, 47,
    62, 80. *See also* genre; race
classical music, 8, 93, 95
Clifford, James, 160
Clinton, George, 55, 57–58
Club 47, 94
Coasters (group), 93
Cobham, Billy, 92, 129, 133, 138–40
Colaiuta, Vinnie, 223
Cold Blood (group), 30
Coleman, Ornette, 30, 40, 95
Collins, Bootsy, 55
Collins, Judy, 150
Colosseum (group), 29

free jazz (subgenre), 21, 30, 35, 40–49, 71, 76–77, 87, 93–95, 114, 201, 212, 231n22
"Free Man in Paris" (Mitchell), 151
Free Spirits (group), 76, 78
Frith, Simon, 18
Frye, Northrop, 150
"The Function of an Artist" (Corea), 43
funk (genre): afrofuturism and, 58–59; as anti-intellectual, 4, 33; class and, 62–63; definitions of, 3–6, 13, 16, 54, 56, 59, 63–64, 237n60; electronic instrumentation and, 28–29; "funky" definitions and, 54; groups, 30; Hancock and, 210, 212, 216–17; history of, 12, 33; race and, 29, 34, 54–57, 62, 237n60; rhythms of, 26, 28–29, 57–58, 88–89
Funk Brothers (group), 59
"Funky Butt" (Bolden), 54
"The Funky-Hard Bop Regression" (M. Williams), 62
A Funky Space Reincarnation (Gaye), 58
fusion: commercial appeal of, 3, 13, 68–69, 75, 77, 82–83, 104, 118, 211–12; contemporary incarnations of, 224; cultural hierarchies and, 29, 95, 104, 108, 122; definitions of, 16–17, 19, 230n5; drugs and, 78–79; electronic instrumentation and, 28, 110, 225, 232n30; emergence of, 65, 68–69, 75, 77, 79–82; gender and, 122; hybridity of, 3, 5, 7–8, 13, 34, 115, 118, 130; instrumentation of, 69–70, 79; jazz criticism's inability to understand, 244n15–244n16; as "jazz rock," 18, 82; nondialectical nature of, 7, 15, 17, 19; "official" history of, 12; performance spaces of, 31–32; political ideologies of, 54, 115; problematic nature of, for critics and musicians, 5–6, 91, 96, 113, 140; race and, 21, 34, 42, 52, 90; relative legiti-

macy of, 115; reliance of, on jazz, 9, 18, 26, 41–42, 60, 66, 68, 71, 74–75; resistance of, to generic labels, 26, 66–67, 81, 88–90; rhythmic characteristics of, 88; rock criticism and, 104–5, 109; spirituality and, 43, 123–45; transcultural movements of, 138–45, 178–79, 225–26; volume and, 86, 100, 111; width of, as generic term, 19, 27–29, 31. *See also specific artists and groups*
Future2Future (Hancock), 220
"The F Word" (article), 5

Gabriel, Peter, 223
Garbarini, Vic, 166, 177, 179
Garofolo, Reebee, 97
Gaslight Au Go Go (club), 131
Gateway (group), 28
Gaye, Marvin, 58
Gaylor, Hal, 80
gender: countercultural views of, 52–53; genre and, 15, 22, 122; Mitchell and, 151–52, 160, 169, 172, 174, 182, 253n4, 254n16, 258n73
Gendron, Bernard, 46
"General Mojo's Well Laid Plan" (song), 76
generation gap, 65, 67, 72–74, 81, 89
genre: class and, 15, 20; construction of, 4–6, 21; culture and, 15; definitions of, 7, 12–13, 15–16, 18–19; distinctions among, 28, 80–81; fluidity of, 3–4, 7–9, 17, 20, 30–32, 96–97, 115, 118, 122, 145, 180, 219, 224, 226; gender and, 22, 122; Joni Mitchell and, 149, 151, 155–57, 159–60, 166; as limitation, 26; naturalization of, 21–22; race and, 6, 13, 20–21, 33–34, 48–49, 59, 92, 97, 109–10, 113, 116, 120, 136, 197–98, 215–16; recording studio norms and, 23–24. *See also* race; *specific genres, artists, and groups*

rhythm and blues (genre), 44, 51, 61
Ribot, Marc, 30
Rich, Buddy, 3, 129, 143
Richards, Emil, 174
Richards, Keith, 66
"Right On" (Williams), 99, 116
River (Hancock), 222, 225–26
Rivers, Sam, 94–95
Roach, Max, 39–40, 93, 200
Robbins, James, 167
Roberts, John Storm, 45
Robinson, Cynthia, 209
rockabilly (genre), 49
"Rocket 88" (Brenston), 47, 236n46
rock (genre): aesthetics of, 6, 28, 49–51,
    66, 71; as anti-intellectual, 3–4, 33,
    52, 108; audiences of, 1–3; class and,
    65; commercial success of, 53, 107;
    displacement of jazz in cultural hier-
    archies, 46–47, 52, 71, 81; generic
    boundaries of, 3–6, 13, 16; history
    of, 12, 33; influence of, in fusion,
    72, 74, 76–77, 87; intellectualiza-
    tion of, 106–9; jazz's reappropriation
    of, 44–45; listening practices and,
    93–94; musical roots of, 47; music
    criticism and, 47, 68, 77, 104; perfor-
    mance mores of, 84; racialization of,
    34, 49, 51–52, 84, 98–100, 236n45,
    236n50; recording norms and, 24,
    83, 85; role of, in fusion groups, 19;
    venues of, 32; virtuosity of, 81; vis-
    ceral nature of, 46; volume of, 47,
    78–79, 84, 87, 128
"Rockit" (Hancock), 218, 220
Rodgers, Jimmie, 47
Rogers, Joel, 36
Rogers, Shorty, 62
Rolling Stone: articles of, 1–2, 71, 137, 159;
    rock orientation of, 11, 71, 104, 136
Rolling Stones (group), 49, 53, 65–66,
    80, 100
Rollins, Sonny, 168

Rorem, Ned, 47
Rosenthal, David, 60
Ross, Annie, 153, 160, 177
Roy, Badal, 129
Rozek, Michael, 143
Rubin, Jerry, 74
Rubinson, David, 199, 205
Rusch, Bob, 88–89
Rush, Tom, 34, 150
Rushen, Patrice, 149

Sainte-Marie, Buffy, 150
Sample, Joe, 153, 161
Sandford, Christopher, 66
San Francisco Oracle (publication), 46
Santamaria, Ramon "Mongo," 187, 213
Santana, Carlos, 134, 136, 139, 207
Santoro, Gene, 170, 172
"Sapphire Bullets of Pure Love" (Maha-
    vishnu Orchestra), 86, 133
Sargeant, Winthrop, 35, 89
Sathe, Keshav, 125
The Sayings of Ramana Maharshi (book), 142
"Say It Loud (I'm Black and I'm Proud)"
    (Brown), 56
the Scene (club), 32
Schafer, Murray, 23
Schon, Neil, 149
Schultz, Ricky, 130
Scott, Tom, 153, 161
segregation, 47–48
Senatore, Daniele, 169–70
Sextant (Hancock), 184, 186, 206–7
S. F. Sorrow (The Pretty Things), 46
Sgt. Pepper's Lonely Hearts Club Band
    (Beatles), 46, 49, 76
Shadows and Light tour, 153
Shaft (film), 63
Shakti (group), 19, 124, 140–43, 145–46,
    227, 252n57
Shank, Barry, 6, 48
Shankar, Lakshminarayanan, 140–45
Shankar, Ravi, 34

Wechter, Abraham, 144

Weill, Kurt, 50

Wein, George, 1–3

"We Insist! Freedom Now!" (Roach), 39,
200

West, Michael J., 19

"What the World Needs Now is Love"
(Bacharach), 2

Wheeler, Kenny, 125, 240n28

"Where" (Lifetime), 116, 118–21

Where's the Melody? (Williams), 38

White Panthers (political group), 114

Whittemore, Jack, 67

The Who, 46, 76

Wicke, Peter, 51, 104

"Wiggle-Waggle" (Hancock), 196

Wildflower (Collins), 150

Williams, Hank, 47; collaborations of,
with Hancock, 217

Williams, Lenny, 59

Williams, Martin, 38, 88–89, 92

Williams, Marvin, 62

Williams, Mary Lou, 174, 258n76

Williams, Mchezaji Buster, 199–200

Williams, Paul, 47, 77

Williams, Richard, 100, 197, 207

Williams, Tillmon, 93

Williams, Tony: drumming technique
of, 105–7; generic labels and, 96–97,
150; Herbie Hancock and, 190; interviews with, 82, 91, 113–17, 136–37;
as jazz musician, 34–35, 73, 92–95;
as Lifetime leader, 91, 94–104; race
and, 13, 22, 91–92, 98–99, 146; re-
invigorating effect of, on jazz, 102;
rock's effect on, 4, 51, 57, 86–88, 91,

93, 99–100, 102, 107–8, 197; vocals
of, 117–19. See also Lifetime (group);
McLaughlin, John

Wilson, Brian, 24, 85

Wilson, Cassandra, 159

Wilson, Olly, 95, 242n64

Wilson, Teddy, 24

Winwood, Stevie, 29, 108, 246n41

Wired (Beck), 69

"Wisdom," 220

"The Wolf That Lives in Lindsey"
(Mitchell), 176

Wonder, Stevie, 24, 57, 69, 149, 168

Woods, Stu, 100

Woodstock (festival), 52

Worby, Robert, 84

"Work Song" (Adderley), 61

world music. *See* non-Western music

Wyatt, Robert, 149

Xenakis, Iannis, 83

Yasin, Khalid. *See* Young, Larry

Yes (group), 57

Yoshida Brothers (group), 225

"You Bet Your Love" (Hancock), 217

Young, Larry, 91, 105, 118–19, 122, 129,
134, 243n2

Young, Lester, 70, 154, 178–80

Youth International Party, 74

Zappa, Frank, 49, 149

Zawinul, Josef, 9, 28, 72

Zorn, John, 30

Zwerin, Michael, 75

Kevin Fellezs is an assistant professor of music at
the University of California, Merced.

Library of Congress Cataloging-in-Publication Data
Fellezs, Kevin.
Birds of fire: jazz, rock, funk, and the creation of fusion /
Kevin Fellezs.
p. cm. — (Refiguring American music)
Includes bibliographical references and index.
ISBN 978-0-8223-5030-9 (cloth: alk. paper)
ISBN 978-0-8223-5047-7 (pbk.: alk. paper)
1. Jazz-rock (Music) — United States — History and criticism.
I. Title. II. Series: Refiguring American music.
ML3506.F455 2011
781.640973 — dc22   2010049648